Yale Historical Publications
Miscellany 88
Published under the direction of the
Department of History

THE MIRROR OF LANGUAGE:
A Study in the Medieval Theory of Knowledge

by Marcia L. Colish

New Haven and London, Yale University Press, 1968

To my Mother and Father

Preface

Videmus nunc per speculum in aenigmate, tunc autem facie ad faciem.

—I Cor. 13:12

People who read books on the medieval mind are familiar with the dictum usually found on page one of any book on this subject: "Medieval man thought in terms of symbols." People who write books on the medieval mind acknowledge the symbolic mentality of the period with impartial and relentless frequency. Whether cited to attest to the clairvoyance or obscurantism, the subtlety or primitivism, the uniqueness or the universality of the Middle Ages, the symbolic attributes of the medieval mind have by now acquired the unexcogitated and prescriptive status of an *idée reçue*. The assertion that medieval men thought in terms of symbols is usually treated as a canon of explanation. It has rarely been treated as susceptible of explanation itself. More rarely still have those who study the place of symbols in medieval epistemology avoided the tendency to interpret them in anachronistic or otherwise extraneous terms. The study which follows is a partial attempt to remedy this situation. My aim throughout has been twofold. I have tried to examine how medieval men actually thought that symbols worked in the acquisition and transmission of knowledge, and I have tried to understand the epistemology of several major medieval thinkers who formed theories of signification in the historical context of their specific interests, ways of thinking, and intellectual environments.

The thesis which this examination has yielded will be demonstrated throughout the book, but I would like also to state it briefly in these prefatory remarks. To begin with, many Western medieval thinkers from the patristic period until roughly the beginning of the fourteenth century were greatly influenced by a certain theory of signs. Formulated by St. Augustine, this theory rests on the view that signs are fundamentally verbal in nature. The attribution of a verbal character to signs is the result of a combination of Christian and classical ideas. Classical philosophy, especially the sign theory of Aristotle, provided Augustine and his medieval successors with the notion that sensory data, in this case words perceived aurally, could conduce the subject to an accurate knowledge of prior and non-sensible realities. It was assumed that these non-sensible realities were truly prior in the order of being although posterior in the order of knowledge; most of the classical philosophy influential in the Middle Ages had a strong metaphysical bias. Classical epistemologists were not particularly verbal in orientation. They tended to regard words as signs as one species within the broad genus of sensible signs in general. On the other hand, St. Augustine, and most medieval epistemologists, tended to see signification as a whole in primarily verbal terms.

While this approach entailed a shift in the emphasis of classical philosophy, classical culture still supplied the forms in which the medieval redefinition of signs as words was expressed. These forms were the verbal disciplines of the seven liberal arts, the trivium, consisting of grammar, rhetoric, and dialectic. The seven liberal arts were the basis of the medieval educational curriculum. Grammar, rhetoric, and dialectic not only taught medieval men how to read, write, and think in Latin in logical order. These disciplines also provided them with epistemological methods, linguistic forms, and criteria which they used in theorizing how words functioned as cognitive intermediaries between subject and object and between speaker and audience. The same basic verbal epistemology could be expressed through any of the three modes of the trivium. At various times during the Middle Ages it was expressed through each of them.

Christianity, no less than the classical tradition, was an important source of the medieval theory of verbal signs. Medieval epistemologists dealt primarily with religious knowledge. They thus faced problems of a type not generally dealt with by classical epistemologists. Nevertheless, Christianity supplied them with a number of doctrines that strongly supported the plausibility of a verbal theory of knowledge. The Aristotelian certainty that sensory data lead to a knowledge of prior and non-sensible realities was paralleled by the scriptural assertions that God can be known through His creation, which He is believed to resemble. Yet, the kind of knowledge of God which the Christian regarded as normative in this life was faith. Knowledge by faith was firm and certain, but partial. It could be acquired only by an infusion of God's grace in the mind of the subject, and it involved his moral conversion as well as his intellectual assent. This set of beliefs predisposed medieval Christians to the view that cognition should be mediated through signs. At the same time, it led them to expect the knowledge of God to be mediated through signs *per speculum in aenigmate*. Signs, they held, would always be limited in their cognitive function, both in the degree to which they could represent the transcendent God at all and in the degree to which they could convey the knowledge of God to the subject in the first instance. They always distinguished the reflection of God in the mirror of faith from God Himself. They never confused signification with an identity between sign and object. They always regarded signs as instrumental, not heuristic; no one, they held, could acquire the religious knowledge necessary for salvation without the assistance of God.

Christianity also supplied medieval thinkers with a strong motive for a sign theory conceived in expressly verbal terms. This motive was the doctrine of the Incarnation. Medieval Christians believed that Christ the Word was God's perfect expression of Himself to man. Having taken on a human nature and having expiated man's sin, Christ had restored man to God. Previously vitiated by sin, the human mind could now come to a knowledge of God in Christ; and the human faculty of speech could now participate in the Incarnation by helping to spread the Word to the world. Medieval thinkers thus stressed verbal signs as the primary media of religious knowledge because they saw in Christ the Word the mediator between God and man, Whose redemption enabled them to know God and to bear God to each other in human words, as well as because their habits of mind were derived from the verbal disciplines of the trivium.

I have studied four thinkers in this book: St. Augustine, St. Anselm, St. Thomas Aquinas, and Dante. I maintain that they all share the same verbal epistemology, an epistemology formulated first by St. Augustine in the West. Each of them expresses this epistemology through one of the modes of the trivium. Augustine displays it in the mode of rhetoric; Anselm in the mode of grammar; Aquinas in the mode of dialectic; and Dante in a poetics conceived in rhetorical terms. These differences stem from the varying historical circumstances in which the four men lived, the requirements of their respective professions, and their personal idiosyncracies. This study attempts to elucidate their similarities as well as their differences, and to show the role which the sign theory that they share plays in the thought of each of them.

In the first flush of scholarly enthusiasm, I intended not merely to isolate the theoretical substructure of medieval symbolism and to explain its genesis, but also to show how the theory actually functioned in medieval culture. The accomplishment of this assignment would have entailed the treatment of various kinds of symbolic practice—the visual arts, literature, sacramental theology, mysticism, and the symbolism of the natural world being the most obvious candidates for inclusion. Once the research was under way, however, the vastness of such an undertaking quickly tempered my initial ardor (but did not quench it) and I saw that the study had to be reoriented in a more manageable direction. I have therefore confined myself to the discussion of the theory itself. Except

x

for showing its application in theology and in literature, in the case of Dante, I have made no systematic effort to deal with other aspects of medieval culture. Despite the fact that they are equally relevant to the theory of signs, and it to them, they have been ruthlessly excised for reasons of space. Furthermore, since I lack a knowledge of Greek, I have been forced to omit a systematic analysis of symbolic epistemology in the Greek patristic period, and, with the exception of a brief comment on iconic theory in the introduction to this book, its subsequent applications in Byzantine culture.

In concentrating on the theory of medieval symbolism, which is the focus of this book, I have narrowed my perspective still more by choosing to stress the role of the trivium in the formation of medieval verbal epistemology and by illustrating this role in the work of four specific thinkers. My emphasis on the trivium and on Augustine, Anselm, Aquinas, and Dante is partly arbitrary and partly logical. I have chosen them because each represents the application of one branch of the trivium to the problem of knowledge. The choice is arbitrary in that it rules out the examination of other thinkers whose works might be equally good examples of this application. It is also arbitrary in that it may appear to suggest, willynilly, that there was only one way to apply a discipline of the trivium to the problem of knowledge in the Middle Ages, the way in which each of these thinkers does it. It is arbitrary, finally, in that the choice of these men is not necessarily based on the extent of their influence, either within the Middle Ages or afterwards; Augustine, for example, was much more influential than Anselm.

However, the emphasis is not totally arbitrary. Although the scope is narrow, it concentrates on four of the most important thinkers of the Middle Ages, each of whom does, in fact, exemplify the application of the trivium to the problem of knowledge in a magisterial manner. Each of these men, furthermore, lived at a crucial time in the history of medieval thought, when new approaches were emerging and when older views no longer seemed completely adequate. The historical circumstances in which each of them lived help to explain why each uses the particular discipline of the trivium which he happens to use; in turn, each of the four, in the formulation of his own answer to the problem of knowledge, illustrates and specifies the intellectual circumstances of his age, no less than his own personality and interests. In this sense, four very different men may be taken as representatives of a civilization marked by as many diversities as uniformities.

Given the fact that a fairly wide range of classical sources influenced medieval thought, the reader may also wonder why I have chosen to emphasize the influence of the trivium. This emphasis is quite deliberate, and it reflects what I hope is a new approach to the manner in which classical influences in medieval thought are to be treated. One of the most frequently encountered traditional approaches to the medieval mind has been to seek out the classical backgrounds of medieval Christian treatments of philosophical problems. One might focus, for example, on St. Ambrose's appropriation of Ciceronian ethics in his *De officiis ministrorum,* or on St. Augustine's appropriation of Neoplatonic metaphysics. This book deals with epistemology, but it does not adopt a strictly analogous method. Without losing oneself in the question of the subconscious versus conscious choices and intentions of thinkers—a question that is rarely soluble unless the historian is willing to forfeit his reliance on documentable facts for the insights and uncertainties of retroactive psychoanalysis—it can still be said that some influences are more inadvertent than others. Specifically, the rules of speech and thought which comprise the trivium, along with their epistemological implications, cannot be treated in exactly the same way as classical ethical or metaphysical ideas. Medieval men were not as free to accept or reject the trivium as they were to accept or reject other aspects of the classical tradition. Their education saw to it that the trivium was as much a part of their mental equipment as their Christian faith. In the few cases

xii

where the presuppositions of classical grammar, rhetoric, or dialectic came into conflict with the content of the Christian ideas which they were used to express, they were either reinterpreted or used inconsistently. As intellectual methods, however, the modes of the trivium emerged as real options only when medieval thought was on the verge of shifting its emphasis from one of them to another. My treatment of the trivium in this study will, I hope, illustrate this point.

I would also like to call the reader's attention to the methods I have used to construct the four major sections of this study. The reader will note that the organization of these sections is not invariably parallel. In the sections dealing with Augustine and Anselm, particular works of theirs are singled out for commentary or are made the *point d'appui* of the chapter. With Dante, the development of his ideas on signification has been studied chronologically. With Aquinas, I have attempted to select those ideas of his which are relevant to signification and to present them in a logical order. In all four cases, I have paid a good deal of attention to the historical circumstances and general epistemology of the thinker at issue. This manner of arranging the material, no less than the scope and emphasis, is deliberate. Many mistaken impressions of medieval thought have been fostered by the practice of abstracting ideas from their contexts in the works of their authors, to be compared with other ideas similarly abstracted from the works of other thinkers, as if thought existed in a historical vacuum. The four men whose ideas on signs I am concerned with exhibit tremendous differences in personality, in the range of their interests, in the amount and the kind of importance they accord to sign theory, and in the ways that they illustrate this theory in their works. It is necessary to come to grips with these personal and contextual considerations if one is to grasp the historical importance of their sign theory. I have therefore made a conscious effort to reconstruct, so far as I can, the texture and emphasis, as well as the content, of Augustinian, Anselmian, Thomistic, and Dantean epistemology. The organization of each chapter represents my attempt to achieve such a reconstruction.

In the case of Augustine, I have used the *Confessiones* as the organizing principle of his ideas on signification. The reasoning back of this choice is threefold: I claim, first of all, that Augustine distills his epistemology in the *Confessiones*. All of his ideas on the role of signs in religious knowledge are to be found in this work. The *Confessiones* thus serves as an axis around which may be ordered his elaboration of these ideas in other works, both earlier and later. Secondly, the whole tenor of Augustine's thought on knowledge is developmental and concrete. His own intellectual growth and the exigencies of his intellectual and moral life dominate his work and lend it an intense and personal vitality. As the story of his spiritual struggles and changing epistemological states, the *Confessiones* is thus better able to provide a construct displaying the inner pulse of Augustine's thought than would an abstractly logical arrangement of his ideas, which, in preserving the letter, would destroy the spirit. Finally, one consequence of my analysis of the *Confessiones* has been a new interpretation of it, an interpretation that shows the relationship of its post-conversion sections, including the problematic passages on time and memory, to the whole work.

In the case of Anselm, I have concentrated my attention on his proofs for the existence of God, since this is his most original and significant contribution to speculative theology. However, in order to grasp what Anselm actually thought he was doing in these proofs, it is first necessary to understand what he meant by such terms as truth, rectitude, necessary reasons, and *intellectus fidei*. Thus, I include an analysis of these key terms, which emerge from a variety of works within his theological *oeuvre*, before approaching his proofs in the *Monologion*, *Proslogion*, and *Contra Gaunilonem*. I have also attempted to give a brief sketch of the decline of rhetoric and the rise of grammar between the fifth and eleventh centuries, the particular species of grammar used by Anselm, and the rapid decline of the popularity enjoyed by the grammatical substructure of his thought in the period following his death, questions which help to shed light on the genesis of Anselm's proofs and their immediate medieval fortunes.

In contrast to Augustine and Anselm, Thomas Aquinas does not provide us with any systematic treatment of the function of signs in religious knowledge. This is clearly not a topic which he thinks it necessary to discuss *ex professo*. Also, Thomas' thought, unlike that of Augustine and Anselm, is marked by a concern with the knowledge of the natural world as well as of God and the soul, and his epistemology is constructed with these broad interests in mind. Since Thomas scatters his ideas on signs throughout his works, I have attempted to collect them and to set them forth in logical order. It is true that Thomas' thought undergoes a certain amount of change and development, at least on some topics. Sign theory, however, is not one of them; his views on this subject remain more or less constant throughout his career. Thus, his ideas on signs may be presented in logical rather than chronological or thematic order without doing violence to them. While organizing Aquinas' sign theory logically, I have nonetheless tried to underline carefully the contextual qualifications that must be made in discussing them. This method, I feel, is far better suited to the presentation of Thomas' thought than the abstract, systematizing efforts of the vast majority of his commentators. Since Thomas himself insists that the knowledge of God begins with the knowledge of the natural world, I have followed this pattern in organizing the third chapter, attempting at the same time to show the limiting conditions which Thomas imposes on signs as well as the logical and theological powers which he grants them.

The chapter on Dante is designed to illustrate the application of Augustinian sign theory to literature by analyzing Dante's poetic theory and the manner in which he expresses it in the *Divine Comedy*. This chapter subdivides itself naturally into three main sections. The first deals with the classical tradition of poetic theory inherited by the Middle Ages and elaborated by medieval literary theorists. The second treats the chronological development of Dante's theological poetics during the course of his career through his theoretical treatises and lyric poetry, charting his changing relationship to the medieval poetic tradition. The last part is an analysis of the *Divine Comedy,* which aims at discovering the extent to which Dante uses his theory in practice. Since Dante connects both his poetry and his literary theory to the linguistic, political, ecclesiastical, and moral reform of the Europe of his own day, I have discussed these questions as they appear in his works in an effort to indicate the nature of this connection.

It is to be hoped that these methodological observations will clarify the procedure I have used in this study.

At this point I would like to insert a word of caution regarding my use of certain terms. The reader will frequently encounter such words as "sign," "symbol," "dialectic," "intuition," "allegory," as well as a number like them which have been used with specific technical meanings by various branches of recent or contemporary philosophy and literary criticism. If the reader comes to this book with a mind trained in contemporary epistemology, whether philosophical or literary, he should proceed with care. I have expressly avoided using philosophical and literary terms with the technical meanings and connotations that contemporary thought attributes to them. The meanings I give to such terms derive from the definitions given to them by the classical and medieval thinkers under consideration. Where no such definitions appear, the reader should understand epistemological terms in a general, not a technical, sense. This procedure admittedly lacks the verbal finesse that is characteristic of much contemporary logical and literary analysis. I have chosen it deliberately because I think that the application of anachronistic terminology or criteria of definition to medieval thought has at times had a disastrous tendency to distort the meanings and intentions of medieval thinkers. To impose a modern style of verbal precision on thinkers who may not have been particu-

xvi

larly prone to it is generally as nugatory in its results as asking a past philosopher for answers to questions into which, for one reason or another, it never occurred to him to inquire. All of this is fully self-evident to the historian, who is less interested in assessing the tenability of past theories in modern terms than in understanding what past theories meant to past ages. However, it may be to the point to mention it for the sake of philosophers or literary critics who may conceivably be interested in reading this book. The sole exception to my anti-anachronism rule is the term "epistemology" and its variants, which, the reader will note, I have already used several times in this preface and which I continue to use frequently throughout the book. I am aware of the fact that I am violating my own canons in using this term. My justification is simply that its suppression would entail the repeated use of wordy synonymous circumlocutions. To avoid this I have retained "epistemology," but the reader should understand the term simply as a way of describing speculation on knowledge, not necessarily as a separate, technical branch of philosophy in the modern sense.

Finally, I would like to comment on the bibliographical orientation of the book. In several chapters, particularly those dealing with Aquinas, Anselm, and Dante, I devote considerable attention in both text and notes to the literature on particular points under discussion. The chapter on Augustine is not characterized by such extensive bibliographical analysis, largely because I did not find myself embroiled in as many intensely controversial issues as was the case in the rest of the book. On those occasions where I do wish to outline controversies or to take a stand on debated points in the Augustine chapter, I confine myself to the notes.

I am grateful to several publishers for permitting me to quote from works on which they hold copyrights. These include Charles Scribner's Sons, for Richard McKeon's edition and translation of St. Anselm's *De veritate* in his *Selections from Medieval Philosophers;* the Clarendon Press, for William Walrond Jackson's translation of Dante's *Convivio*; J.

M. Dent & Sons Ltd., for A. G. Ferrers Howell's translation of Dante's *De vulgari eloquentia* in *The Latin Works,* translated by Ferrers Howell and Philip H. Wicksteed; the Open Court Publishing Company of La Salle, Illinois, for S. N. Deane's translation of St. Anselm's *Basic Works;* and E. P. Dutton & Co. Inc. and J. M. Dent & Sons Ltd., for the translation of Dante's *Divine Comedy* in the Temple Classics Edition by J. A. Carlyle, Thomas Okey, and P. H. Wicksteed, which I have quoted with a few changes. I thank all these publishers for their cooperation.

In concluding this preface, it is my welcome duty to thank a number of institutions and individuals, whose generous contributions, both financial and personal, have helped make this book possible. The Samuel S. Fels Foundation provided me with a fellowship during the academic year 1961–62, which permitted me to do most of the basic research for the first three chapters. A research grant from Oberlin College during the summer of 1965 enabled me to complete the research for the fourth chapter. I owe a large debt of gratitude to Professor Roland H. Bainton and Professor Jaroslav J. Pelikan, under whose skillful guidance the first three chapters of this book were undertaken and submitted, in a somewhat different form, as a doctoral dissertation for the department of history at Yale University. My colleague at Oberlin, Professor Andrew Bongiorno, read the entire manuscript with painstaking care, removing many egregious errors and making many helpful suggestions. My conversations with John Geerken of Yale University helped to shape my approach to Dante and suggested the title of the fourth chapter. Robert Evans' eagle eye and scrupulous attention to detail lightened considerably the task of reading the proofs. Of course, I remain responsible for the views expressed in the book and for any errors that it may contain.

M. L. C.

Oberlin, Ohio
February 1968
    xviii

Table of Contents

Abbreviations

(See bibliography for complete references.)

AHDLMA	*Archives d'histoire doctrinale et littéraire du moyen âge*
Beiträge	*Beiträge zur Geschichte der Philosophie des Mittelalters*
CC	*Corpus Christianorum*
Comp. theol.	St. Thomas Aquinas, *Compendium theologiae*, in *Opuscula omnia*, ed. P. Mandonnet
Convivio	Dante Alighieri, *Convivio*, in *Opere*, ed. Fredi Chiapelli
CSEL	*Corpus Scriptorum Ecclesiasticorum Latinorum*
DDJ	*Deutsches Dante-Jahrbuch*
Deane	St. Anselm, *Basic Writings*, trans. S. N. Deane
De anima	St. Thomas Aquinas, *Quaestio disputata de anima*, in *Quaestiones disputatae*, ed. R. Spiazzi et al.
De mon.	Dante Alighieri, *De monarchia*, in *Opere*, ed. Fredi Chiapelli
De pot.	St. Thomas Aquinas, *Quaestiones disputatae de potentia*, in *Quaestiones disputatae*, ed. R. Spiazzi et al.
De ver.	St. Thomas Aquinas, *Quaestiones disputatae de veritate*, in *Quaestiones disputatae*, ed. R. Spiazzi et al.
De vulg. el.	Dante Alighieri, *De vulgari eloquentia*, in *Opere*, ed. Fredi Chiapelli
GD	*Giornale dantesco*
Howell	Dante Alighieri, *De vulgari eloquentia*, trans. A. G. Ferrers Howell, in *The Latin Works*, trans. Philip H. Wicksteed and A. G. Ferrers Howell

In Boeth. *de trin.*	St. Thomas Aquinas, *Expositio super librum Boethii de trinitate,* ed. B. Decker
Inf.	Dante Alighieri, *Inferno,* in *Opere,* ed. Fredi Chiapelli
In Met.	St. Thomas Aquinas, *In duodecim libros Metaphysicorum Aristoteles expositio,* ed. M. R. Cathala
In Sent.	St. Thomas Aquinas, *Scriptum super libros Sententiarum magistri Petri Lombardi Episcopi Parisiensis,* ed. P. Mandonnet and M. F. Moos
Jackson	Dante Alighieri, *Convivio,* trans. W. W. Jackson
Jowett	*The Dialogues of Plato,* trans. B. Jowett
JP	*The Journal of Philosophy*
Loeb	Loeb Classical Library
MGH, QGM	*Monumenta Germaniae Historica, Quellen zur Geistesgeschichte des Mittelalters*
MRS	*Mediaeval and Renaissance Studies*
MS	*The Modern Schoolman*
NS	*The New Scholasticism*
Par.	Dante Alighieri, *Paradiso,* in *Opere,* ed. Fredi Chiapelli
PL	*Patrologia latina cursus completus,* ed. J. P. Migne
PR	*The Philosophical Review*
Purg.	Dante Alighieri, *Purgatorio,* in *Opere,* ed. Fredi Chiapelli
RM	*The Review of Metaphysics*
Ross	*The Works of Aristotle,* ed. W. D. Ross
RPL	*Revue philosophique de Louvain*
RSPT	*Revue des sciences philosophiques et théologiques*
RSR	*Recherches des sciences religieuses*
RT	*Revue thomiste*
SCG	St. Thomas Aquinas, *Summa contra gentiles,* in

	Opera omnia iussu impensaque Leonis XIII P.M. edita
Schneider	Dante Alighieri, *De monarchia,* trans. H. W. Schneider
Scholastik	*Scholastik: Vierteljahresschrift für Theologie und Philosophie*
ST	St. Thomas Aquinas, *Summa theologiae,* in *Opera omnia iussu impensaque Leonis XIII P.M. edita*
Toynbee	Dante Alighieri, *Epistolae,* ed. and trans. Paget Toynbee
Trésor	Brunetto Latini, *Li Livres dou Trésor,* ed. P. Chabaille
TS	*Theological Studies*

Introduction

From the patristic period roughly until the end of the thirteenth century, the period encompassed by this study, Western European thinkers produced a number of different yet re-
ciprocal expressions of one basic mental universe. This mental
universe embodied certain standard preconceptions about the
nature of reality, which in turn entailed standard preconceptions about the nature and methodology of knowledge. It will
be useful at the outset to enumerate these preconceptions. We
may thus orient our discussion of what is to follow by considering here the fundamental epistemological perspectives of
medieval thinkers during these centuries.

Most of the classical philosophers whom the Middle Ages
knew and regarded as authoritative held that there was an objective order of being prior to the subjective order of knowing.
Following their lead, medieval philosophers endorsed the idea
of an epistemology grounded in and controlled by its objects
of knowledge with equal assurance and vigor. And, notwithstanding the scholastic demand for a theory of cognition explaining man's knowledge of the world of nature, the object to
which medieval thinkers normally addressed themselves was
the world of spiritual reality, with preeminent attention to
God. The medieval theory of knowledge was a direct consequence of this radically ontological emphasis. Epistemology
was conceived as a function of metaphysics. The existence of
an objective order of being was the primary condition which
was held to make human thought possible at all. Furthermore,
medieval thinkers identified being par excellence with the God
of the Bible. Thus, they held, the Being of God Himself was
the guarantee, the criterion, and the *conditio sine qua non* of
whatever men might know about Him, or about anything
else.

1

The relationship between man as knower and God as object of knowledge depended not only on God's absolute and transcendent existence. It also depended on His decisive intervention into the mutable world of His creation. The belief that God had manifested His presence, inchoately in the history of Israel, consummately in the Incarnation of Christ, and continuously since Pentecost in His living extension in time and space, the Church, held for medieval thinkers specific epistemological consequences. On the one hand, God in His entirety remained unequivocally beyond the scope of the human mind. But, on the other hand, God had made such knowledge of Himself as He wished to communicate generally accessible to man. He had done this, however, solely on His own terms. The knowledge of God demanded from man the prior and unreserved acceptance of Him just as He had revealed Himself to be. Man might achieve the combined intellectual assent and loving personal adhesion which this acceptance required only on the basis of God's gracious gift of faith. Given through the Church, faith made possible to man his primary mental contact with God in the Person of Jesus Christ. Medieval men believed that Christ's redemptive action had been projected in time and that it was currently operative in the Church, His Mystical Body. Moreover, they believed that Christ had chosen to manifest Himself under the ecclesiastical dispensation, which would endure until the end of time, for the express purpose of enabling man to know and love God and other men through an integral union with Him in the life of the Church. Even as Christ on earth had joined the Transfiguration to the Incarnation in the economy of His redemption, so, in His Mystical Body, He continued to affiliate man to God, and thereby to transfigure the ordinary modes of human cognition and expression, while yet in time, into worthy vessels of His revelation.

The New Covenant of Christ, in which all major medieval thinkers believed themselves to participate, carried professional responsibilities as well as rewards. This was a condition duly recognized by the medieval commentators on the subject, most of whom had been ordained to preach and to teach the Word of God. They had been called, they believed, not only to attain a knowledge of God themselves, but also to convey the knowledge of God to the world. To this task they bent at once the resources of their Divine commission and the various techniques of thought and communication that human nature and their historical situation had imposed upon them and placed at their disposal. The acutely paradoxical implications of their mission did not fail to inspire in them mingled feelings of enthusiasm and unworthiness. God had commanded them to express the Inexpressible, in terms accessible to the speaker and the audience alike. These very terms, however, would remain permanently inadequate to the assignment. Neither their logical rigor nor their verbal precision or eloquence could compass the mystery of the Godhead. The hearer's intellectual entry into the life of the Trinity would be initiated and accomplished by God, through grace. This notion was a matter of faith. Yet, at the same time, this faith emphasized the possibility of active human cooperation with God's grace in the process of learning and teaching about Him. The tension between God's ineffability and the Divine mandate to preach the Word to all nations remained a permanent one in the minds of medieval thinkers concerned with religious knowledge. To the extent that they found a resolution of this tension, they found it in the doctrine of the Incarnation. The ineffable God had revealed Himself to man in Christ. Christ had taken on human nature and human faculties. By His life, death, and resurrection, He had renewed and restored these human faculties, re-enabling them to become Godlike. Medieval thinkers drew an important epistemological corollary from this doctrine. In the Christian dispensation, human modes of thought and expression, although still limited by the human condition, could now worthily take on the tasks assigned to them by God. Human language, reborn through the Incarnation, could now assist God in spreading the effects of the Incarnation to the world. The medieval con-

3

fidence that Babel had been redeemed in the gift of tongues was the immediate context in which men of this period judged, understood, and pressed into service the symbolic forms of human discourse.

Medieval thinkers combined their Christian heritage with a common educational tradition in their search for a theoretical explanation of the function of symbolism in the knowledge of God. In their formative years, these thinkers all learned the basic techniques of reading, speaking, and thinking clearly from the textbooks of grammar, rhetoric, and dialectic more or less standard throughout the Latin West. The permanent effects of this discipline were apparent in their general approach to the problem of religious knowledge. The medieval conception of symbolism was fundamentally linguistic. Crystallized in the categories of the trivium, the discussions of medieval epistemologists focused in the first instance on the role of language, literature, and logical statements in the cognition of Being. The high medieval extensions of their symbolic doctrine to nature, by the school of Chartres and the Franciscans, and to the visual arts, by the proponents of the Gothic aesthetic, were advanced and justified in the idiom of this essentially verbal mode of thought. The symbolic theory of knowledge developed in the Middle Ages was cast in terms of the relationship between words, on the one hand, and reality, on the other. It was the attempt of medieval men to reflect, in the mirror of the trivium, what they believed to be the one normative epistemological relationship between man and God.

The operation of language as a cognitive intermediary between the knower and the object of knowledge, and between the speaker and the listener, required full-scale analysis and description. Medieval thinkers conceded that a word might signify truly, if partially, a really existing thing. According to this theory, a real relation may obtain between the word and the thing, although significance and identity, meaning and being, are by no means to be confused. The accuracy of any

4

verbal formulation depends on its correspondence to the object it seeks to describe: *vox sequitur rem*. The object of knowledge always remains the yardstick against which any statement about it must be measured. Statements are thus held to be not heuristic, or productive of knowledge in the first instance, but expressive of a knowledge already existing in the mind of the knower. Axiomatic to this epistemology is the assurance of the subject's anterior knowledge of the object, a knowledge indispensable to his recognition of the truth of the words expressing it.

The second concern of the theory was the function of verbal signs in the mind of the knowing subject. If the subject has a prior knowledge of the object and can measure the accuracy of a verbal formulation by comparing it with the object to which it refers, then the function of language on the subjective level is either indicative or commemorative. The word of the speaker, although it cannot produce knowledge of the object, can point to it if it is not already in the mind of the subject. If the subject already knows the object, the word of the speaker can recall it to him, making it vividly present in his mind.

The subjective facet of this linguistic philosophy bears a certain resemblance both to the Platonic doctrine of reminiscence and to the epistemology of the icon developed in Eastern Christendom. It also differs from these theories in a number of important respects. In the *Meno*, Platonic dialectic is employed to bring to the forefront of the subject's mind a knowledge which has always been there.[1] In its medieval usage, on the other hand, the commemorative function of language recalls to the subject a knowledge of the object which had previously been introduced into his mind at some specific point by the object itself. This is the condition which enables the subject to judge whether or not the linguistic medium is truly significant.

The resemblance of this theory to Byzantine iconic epis-

1. Plato, *Meno*, 80e–87c, Jowett, *1*, 277–86.

5

temology is somewhat less superficial, although, in comparison with visual symbols, the cognitive functions of words are wider and more variegated. Icons share with verbal signs an acknowledged real relation to their objects, precluding identity with them. They are likewise designed to draw the believer into a deepened and reawakened mental relationship with the spiritual realities they represent.[2] The effect that icons produce in the subject, however, is strictly evocative. Intended primarily for the use of the faithful in a specifically devotional context, they do not generally lend themselves to the needs of extra-ecclesiastical polemic or apology. Words, on the other hand, play an indicative as well as a commemorative role in the theory of cognition posited by the medieval thinkers of the West. These Western thinkers were faced with two correlative questions. How could a word which they regarded as a *flatus vocis* with no objective referent be used by the nonbeliever as if it were a true *vox significans rem?* Conversely, how could a word which they regarded as a *vox significans rem* be, in the mouth of the nonbeliever or the heterodox, a hollow reverberation or a false note failing to harmonize with the reality as they believed it to be? In contrast to Byzantine iconic theory, the linguistic epistemology formulated by Western thinkers was simultaneously extensive and intensive. It extended beyond the realm of devotion because it had to account for the

2. The arguments of the iconodules at the Seventh Ecumenical Council at Nicea, 787, at which iconoclasm was formally condemned, sum up the theory of the icon, emphasizing the distinction between significance and identity, the commemorative function of icons, and their link with the doctrine of the Incarnation. See J. D. Mansi, ed., *Sacrorum conciliorum, nova, et amplissima collectio* (Florentiae, 1766), *12,* cols. 1069B, D; 1072A; 1080A–D. For an excellent discussion of these points, see Leonid Ouspensky and Vladimir Lossky, *The Meaning of Icons* (Olten, Switzerland, 1952), pp. 16, 24, 27–34, 37–38, 42–43; also Léonide Ouspensky, *L'Icone: Vision du monde spirituel. Quelques mots sur son sens dogmatique* (Paris, 1948), pp. 5–6, 12–15, 17–26; Gervase Mathew, *Byzantine Aesthetics* (New York, 1963), pp. 7, 38–47, 95–107, 124–25; Paul J. Alexander, *The Patriarch Nicephorus of Constantinople: Ecclesiastical Policy and Image Worship in the Byzantine Empire* (Oxford, 1958), pp. 23–53, 189–213, 217–24; Otto Demus, *Byzantine Mosaic Decoration: Aspects of Monumental Art in Byzantium* (London, 1948), pp. 5–6.

6

thinking of those outside the Church in their encounter with orthodox doctrine. It also turned inward in seeking to explain how words could inspire and sustain their own contemplative experience, and how they could communicate its fruits to their fellow Christians.

In the West, this central theory of religious knowledge was created in the early Middle Ages, and it remained normative until the epistemology of the later scholastics effected a decisive split between reality, thought, and language in the fourteenth century. Before this time, however, the *aenigma* of language was generally recognized as the key to the cognition and communication of objective reality. The verbal sign theory of the Middle Ages was translated into the three basic modes of the trivium, grammar, rhetoric, and dialectic, and, at the end of the period, into the mode of rhetorical poetics. From St. Augustine to Dante, its prime exponents worked in terms of verbal definitions, figures of speech, logical and analogical statements. In their choice of form, they took into account the vocabulary of the milieux in which they lived as well as their own intellectual solvency. The distinctive texture of medieval linguistic epistemology was hence a result of the period's corporate response to a uniform mental environment, mediated through the shifting configurations of individual temperament and concrete cultural situation. The concern of this study is to set several major medieval solutions to the problem of the knowledge of God in the historical framework of personality and circumstance which gave rise to them.

1 ST. AUGUSTINE:
The Expression of the Word

The thought of St. Augustine occupies a position of central importance in the development of linguistic epistemology in the medieval West. The most profound and prolific of the Latin Fathers of the Church, in the Middle Ages he became an authoritative source second only to the Bible. Standing as he does at the end of the classical age, he brought his habitual techniques of late antique thought and expression to the problems of Christian theology and pastoral concern. One of the products of this merging of classicism and Christianity was the formation of a verbal theory of the knowledge of God destined to become normative in European thought for almost a thousand years. At the same time, he succeeded in presenting, in theory and in practice, one of the basic modulations of that epistemology in the form of Christian rhetoric.

As a professional rhetorician thoroughly trained in the oratorical techniques of Cicero, Augustine already had a philosophy of verbal signification at his disposal before he became a Christian. Derived originally from Platonic and Aristotelian sources, this theory had been welded effectively to the art of exposition and persuasion by the tradition of Roman rhetoric. When he became a Christian, Augustine decided that his intellectual methods would have to be converted as well as his overall objectives. The manner in which he understood this intellectual conversion was thus of seminal importance to his later career as a pastor and a theologian. Augustine's conversion gave him the theoretical foundations for a positive theology. At the same time, it forced him to develop his views on the functions of language in the knowledge of God, and in the Christian life. Augustine's speculations on language bequeathed to his medieval successors a clearly outlined verbal epistemology, firmly grounded in both classical language study

8

and the theology of the Incarnation. His extensive writings contain many practical applications of this epistemology. Armed with the works of Augustine, his followers in the Middle Ages proceeded to absorb and to adapt his theory of language in the light of contemporary issues and their own interests. Augustine's contribution to this development was large and twofold. First, he constructed the basic medieval theory of linguistic symbolism; secondly, he expressed this epistemology in the mode of rhetoric. Concerned with establishing a theory of knowledge suitable for the work of the theologian and consistent with his own experience, Augustine focused his attention on the problem of the expression of the Word, a problem posed for him initially by his conversion to Christianity.

Although the theory of signs which Augustine eventually developed was his own creation, he by no means formulated it in a vacuum. In searching for an understanding of words as signs, he could draw upon the heritage of Greek philosophy as well as on his training in Roman rhetoric. The classical age, to be sure, was not lacking in highly penetrating analyses of language and signification. What was this tradition like? Here, as in so many other areas of philosophical discussion, the first major contribution was made by Plato, and an alternative conception was offered by Aristotle.

Plato's view of the function of language in the process of knowledge has both a positive and a negative side. Words certainly play an important cognitive role in his philosophy. Plato's antisophistic insistence that rhetoric should be joined to wisdom and virtue implies the idea that words can adumbrate truth, and that they can therefore serve as vehicles of instruction.[1] It is evident from Plato's incessant use of the dialogue form that he considers the spoken word the best method of teaching and of evoking truth. He also confirms this preference in the *Phaedrus*.[2] While, for Plato, words can

1. See references cited below, p. 27, note 45.
2. Plato, *Phaedrus,* 275d–77b, 278b, Jowett, *3,* 185–86, 188.

reflect realities, he nevertheless stresses that words are temporal entities perceived with the senses. Thus, they are epistemological underlings, which can be relegated to the category of probability and opinion.[3] Just as time, for Plato, is a moving shadow of eternity, so language is a moving shadow of reality. And, if the reality which a word happens to signify is itself transient and sensory, the word is the shadow of a shadow.

In Plato's philosophy, then, language is distinctly ambiguous. The *locus classicus* for his explanation of this ambiguity is the *Cratylus*. This dialogue includes three speakers: Cratylus and Hermagoras, who maintain opposed and mutually exclusive positions on the subject of language, and Socrates, who moderates between them. Cratylus consistently argues that words refer naturally and necessarily to realities. Names, he says, have by nature a truth. If they did not, it would be impossible to make true statements. Since true statements are in fact possible, names must logically indicate the nature of the things they represent.[4] Hermagoras, on the contrary, insists that the truth of names is by no means automatic. If words were necessarily true, he states, it would be impossible to make false statements; and false statements evidently can be made. The relationship between words and realities is not logical, he argues, but purely conventional and arbitrary.[5]

The controversy between these two speakers is settled, if settlement it may be called, by Socrates. With a bow in the direction of Cratylus, he observes that words do have a logical relationship to reality, as revealed by the study of etymology and verbal classification. All existing things, he says, have their correlative signs and names. The relationship between words and things is one of imitation; and this verbal mimesis would not be possible unless there really were a natural re-

3. Plato, *Timaeus*, 29b–c, Jowett, *3*, 716–17.
4. Plato, *Cratylus*, 391b ff., 428e, 435d–38d, Jowett, *3*, 50 ff., 92, 100–04.
5. Ibid., 429b ff., Jowett, *3*, 92 ff.

semblance between words and things.[6] However, he adds, with a nod to Hermagoras, there are some words and letters that are synonymous or homonymous, and in such a case, men may apply them to different things by convention, for the sake of clarity.[7]

Their logical or conventional characteristics notwithstanding, continues Socrates, all words have cognitive limitations. Since they are images, words are metaphysically one step removed from realities. Their mimetic capacities are qualitative, not quantitative. Thus, they cannot express their referents totally; if they could, they would be identical to them and would hence no longer be images of them. This limitation is even greater in the case of words that purport to imitate atemporal abstract ideas or ideal forms.[8] There is yet another problem. All realities, as Socrates has already observed, have their correlative signs and names. Words, however, are not similarly privileged. Not all of them have objective referents. In short, it is quite possible to utter gibberish. How can one tell whether or not a given word is truly expressive? Fortunately, Socrates notes, men already possess the transverbal criterion of truth. This observation suggests the principle that changeless realities may be known without benefit of verbal intermediaries. Clearly, the direct knowledge of real existence would be infinitely preferable to the partial and derivative information about it which language supplies. According to Plato, words are transient. But the knower, the human soul, and the supreme objects of knowledge, the ideal forms, are eternal. It would therefore be grossly imprudent for the man of intelligence to place any great confidence in the knowledge he can obtain through words, despite the fact that they may be accurate so far as they go. One who trusts in language, con-

6. Ibid., 392d ff., 423b ff., 427c–d, 428e, 434b, Jowett, *3*, 51 ff., 86 ff., 90–91, 92, 98.

7. Ibid., 434d–35b, Jowett, *3*, 99–100.

8. Ibid., 432b, 439c–40d, Jowett, *3*, 96, 105–06.

cludes Socrates, "condemns himself and other existences to an unhealthy state of unreality." [9]

For Plato, the sensuousness and ambiguity of verbal signs is understood in the context of an epistemology of two worlds, a world of ideal forms and a world of tangible realities, which mirror the ideal forms imperfectly at best. Aristotle also sees signs as sensory, and at times as ambiguous, but for entirely different reasons. The Stagirite is not faced with the problem of bridging the gap between two worlds. He finds one world quite sufficient. It is, moreover, a world which is thoroughly real in itself, and which can be known empirically. This being so, it is no surprise to find that Aristotle regards the signs of sensible realities as themselves sensible, an idea which he illustrates liberally in practice by sprinkling his discussion of signification with examples of empirically verifiable signs, drawn from his wide-ranging studies of natural history. On the whole, Aristotle shows great confidence in the ability of sensible signs to denote realities, and in his epistemology he therefore puts them to work as straightforward inferential tools. At the same time, he admits that signs may be ambiguous. This ambiguity, however, occurs simply because men have a tendency to misinterpret and to abuse signs, or because signs may refer to things which are themselves dubious; it does not indicate any inability on the part of signs to correspond satisfactorily to objective reality. [10]

The context in which Aristotle discusses signs is, in the first instance, logical rather than verbal. He nevertheless by no means divorces thought from language, language being for him the medium in which the logician operates. In order for a sign to be introduced as evidence in a proof, for Aristotle, it must be converted into a statement so that it may be discussed in relationship to other statements. This condition obtains

9. Ibid., 440c. See also 438e–39b, Jowett, *3,* 106, 104–05.

10. Aristotle, *De sophisticis elenchis,* I, 165a, 4–19, trans. Pickard-Cambridge, ed. Ross, *1; Rhetoric,* I, 1357a, 24–1357b, 21; III, 1404a, 20–23; 1405a, 9–12; 1410b, 10–21, Roberts, pp. 28–29, 166, 186–87.

equally whether the sign is natural or conventional. Hence Aristotle's definition of a sign: "A sign means a demonstrative proposition, necessary or generally approved: for anything such that when it is another thing is, or when it has come into being the other has come into being, before or after, is a sign of the other's being or having come into being." [11] Signs are used by Aristotle to demonstrate that propositions are necessarily true, and the logical form in which he does this is the syllogism: "The proper object of unqualified knowledge is something which cannot be other than it is. . . . By demonstration I mean a syllogism productive of scientific knowledge, a syllogism, that is, the grasp of which is *eo ipso* such knowledge." [12]

For Aristotle, the art of demonstrative proof, properly speaking, is the domain of logic. Rhetoric, on the other hand, is the art of persuasion. Rhetoric and dialectic alike are faculties for providing arguments, rhetorical persuasion being a subordinate branch of logical demonstration. Where dialectic employs the syllogism, rhetoric employs the enthymeme. Syllogisms and enthymemes differ in that syllogisms invariably deal with facts, which can be established with necessity. Enthymemes, however, generally deal with decisions about actions. They present us with alternative possibilities because of the contingent nature of actions, very few of which are determined necessarily. Although, Aristotle notes, the propositions on which enthymemes are based are sometimes necessarily true, most of the time they are only usually true. Enthymemes are thus constructed out of probabilities as well as signs. Probabilities, according to Aristotle, correspond to propositions that are generally true, if they can be classified as contingent or variable. The definition of sign which he uses in the *Rhetoric* echoes his definition of sign in the *Prior Analytics:* signs correspond to propositions that are necessarily true.

Signs, Aristotle continues, may be fallible or infallible. The

11. Aristotle, *Analytica priora,* II, 27, 70a, 7–9, trans. Jenkinson, ed. Ross, *1.*
12. Aristotle, *Analytica posteriora,* I, 2, 71b, 14–18, trans. Mure, ed. Ross, *1.*

infallible sign constitutes a complete proof. It has the same relationship to the statement it supports as the particular has to the universal. That is to say, it necessarily leads to one, and to only one, conclusion. Syllogisms proper may be based on this kind of proof; if the evidence adduced by the sign is empirically verifiable, it will terminate in a scientific and irrefutable demonstration. Conversely, the fallible sign has the same relationship to the statement it supports as the universal has to the particular. That is to say, it involves empirical evidence which may indicate more than one condition, and which thus may lead to more than one conclusion.[13] (While Aristotle does observe that words themselves may be signs,[14] he is basically interested in significant phenomena or events, as translated into propositional form, for the purposes of persuasion and demonstration.

It might be remarked parenthetically that the discussion of sign theory was continued in post-Aristotelian Greek philosophy, notably by the Stoics and Epicureans. The Stoics were rather original. They tended to reduce signs to conceptual entities, which they set in the context of a universe rigidly determined by logical necessity. The Epicureans, on the other hand, re-emphasized the sensuous aspect of signs and insisted that demonstrations involving their use be subject to empirical verification. The epistemological side of Stoic and Epicurean philosophy, however, seems to have escaped Augustine's notice. There is no evidence that he was aware of their debate on signs, of that he was in any way influenced by it.[15]

13. Aristotle, *Rhetoric,* I, 1355a, 4–10; 1356a, 32–34; 1357a, 24–1357b, 21, Roberts, pp. 22, 26, 28–29.

14. Aristotle, *De sophisticis elenchis,* I, 165a, 4–19, trans. Pickard-Cambridge, ed. Ross, *1; Rhetoric,* III, 1404a, 20–23; 1405a, 9–12, 1410b, 10–21, Roberts, pp. 166, 168–69, 186–87.

15. See Estelle Allen DeLacy, "Meaning and Methodology in Hellenistic Philosophy," *PR, 47* (1938), 390–409; Phillip H. DeLacy, "The Epicurean Analysis of Language," *American Journal of Philology, 60* (1939), 85–92; P. H. and E. A. DeLacy, *Philodemus: On Methods of Inference. A Study in Ancient Empiricism,* Philological Monographs published by the American Philological Association, *10* (Philadelphia, 1941); Alfons Nehring, "A Note on Functional Linguistics in the Middle Ages," *Traditio, 9* (1953), 430 ff.; R. A. Markus, "St.

As we mentioned earlier, Roman rhetoric, as well as Greek philosophy, dealt with the question of words as signs. The most authoritative source of Roman rhetorical ideas is Cicero. In turning from Plato and Aristotle to Cicero, we move from the realm of philosophical sign theory of the first magnitude to the realm of intellectual transmission. Cicero's ideas on signs are wholly derivative, and, in this case, it is largely Aristotle from whom he borrows. He does this, however, without sharing Aristotle's interest in the relationship of signification to the broader issues of epistemology. Cicero adopts Aristotle's definition of sign as well as the Stagirite's empirical emphasis. "A sign," says Cicero, "is something apprehended by one of the senses and indicating something that seems to follow logically as a result of it: the sign may have occurred before the event or in immediate connexion with, or have followed after it, and yet needs further evidence and corroboration." [16] Cicero retains Aristotle's general distinction between rhetoric and dialectic, the enthymeme and the syllogism, and repeats the further distinction between the probability, the fallible sign, and the infallible sign. For the most part, Cicero restricts his discussion to probabilities and fallible signs. Still, he retains the Aristotelian certainty that signs, including words, may be accurate tokens of the things they represent.[17]

By discussing signs in a primarily forensic context, however, Cicero makes a major departure from Aristotelian usage.[18] While Aristotle views rhetoric as a subordinate

Augustine on Signs," *Phronesis, 2* (1957), 60 ff. Markus is more concerned here with describing certain classical and patristic ideas on signification than with establishing Augustine's sources. Curiously, he omits Plato.

16. Cicero, *De inventione,* 1.30.48, Hubbell, p. 88. See also *Rhetorica ad Herennium,* 2.7.10–11, Caplan, p. 76.

17. Cicero, *Orator,* 32.14, Hubbell, pp. 388–90; *De inventione,* 1.30.48, Hubbell, pp. 86–88; *De divinatione,* passim, Falconer; *Rhetorica ad Herennium,* passim and especially 2.5.8, Caplan, pp. 70–72; *De partitione oratoria,* 2.5–7, Rackham, pp. 314–16; *Topica,* 8.35, Hubbell, p. 408.

18. For a particularly clear example of this tendency, found throughout Cicero's works, see *Rhetorica ad Herennium,* 2.4.6, Caplan, p. 66. This would seem to indicate that the early medieval tendency to conceive of logic in rhetorical terms, noted by Richard McKeon, "Rhetoric in the Middle Ages," *Speculum, 17* (1942), 7–10, begun as early as Cicero.

branch of dialectic, Cicero subordinates logic to rhetoric, making demonstration ancillary to persuasion. According to Cicero, the orator has three aims, "to prove, to please, to sway." [19] Of these three objectives, persuasion is the most important: "The supreme orator, then, is the one whose speech instructs, delights, and moves the minds of his audience. The orator is duty bound to instruct; giving pleasure is a free gift to the audience; to move them is indispensable." [20] This stress on persuasion seems to have outweighed any interest Cicero may have had in exploring the connections between epistemology and linguistic theory. His treatment of the ambiguity of language typifies this approach. Both Plato and Aristotle, as we have seen, assert that words or signs may be ambiguous, Plato on the grounds of their relative reality, and Aristotle on the grounds of logic and human fallibility. Cicero also observes that signs and words may be ambiguous, but he draws no epistemological conclusions from this insight. The ambiguity of language, for Cicero, is simply one of the operative conditions of rhetorical technique. The orator, he says, can and should take advantage of the multiple meanings of words in adapting his presentation to the ethos of his audience and in selecting the style, whether elevated, moderate, or plain, appropriate to the contents of his speech.[21] Indeed, were it not for the ambiguity of language, it would only be possible for the Ciceronian orator to give one kind of speech to one kind of audience.

Cicero's divorce of epistemology from linguistic theory is particularly evident in the *Academica,* where he shows his leanings toward mild skepticism. On the face of it, the primary implications of this view would seem to lie in the field of logic. Cicero, however, is not particularly interested in the effects of skepticism on induction, deduction, and inference. It is the moral consequences of skepticism which concern him. In

19. Cicero, *Orator,* 21.69, Hubbell, p. 356.
20. Cicero, *De optimo genere oratorum,* 1.3–4, Hubbell, p. 356.
21. Cicero, *De oratore,* 3.52.199, Sutton and Rackham, *2,* 158.

16

the *Academica,* Cicero concludes that uncertainty as to what is true forces the skeptic to withhold his assent to the validity of any given moral code. He wishes to prove, further, that this conclusion does not necessarily force the skeptic into a position of apathy or social irresponsibility. The attitude that Cicero recommends to the reader is one of *dégagé* adherence to conventional morality.[22] Throughout this discussion Cicero displays no interest in the effects that Academic skepticism might have in the realm of inference and persuasion. It may be just as well. If he had applied his skepticism consistently to rhetoric, the results would have been disastrous, both to his oratorical technique and to the ethical context in which he places it. His easy assurance that the facts of a case at issue can actually be determined would have been severely undermined, and his insistence on the possibility of uniting eloquence with wisdom and virtue would have been rendered farcical.

Notwithstanding this inconsistency, Cicero's thought was an important ingredient in the classical theories of language which Augustine inherited. Through Cicero, Aristotle's theory of signs could be acquired in the Latin language; and this theory, moreover, could now be appropriated within the framework of rhetoric. Outside of his importance as a transmitter of Greek philosophy, Cicero also presented to Augustine and to posterity the classic portrait of the Roman orator, a figure whom we shall meet again shortly, with some modifications, in Augustine's *De doctrina christiana.* Finally, Cicero made a valuable contribution to the discussion of linguistic symbolism in his analysis of figurative language. In the standard list of metaphors and rhetorical tropes which Cicero includes in the *De oratore,* we find the term *"aenigma."* He defines it as a species of metaphor: "Something resembling the real thing is taken, and the words that properly belong to it are then . . . applied metaphorically to the other thing. This is a valuable stylistic ornament; but care must be taken to

22. Cicero, *Academica,* 2.20.64–48.148, Rackham, pp. 548–658.

avoid obscurity—and in fact it is usually the way in which what are called riddles (*aenigmata*) are constructed." [23] This conception of aenigma as a kind of figure of speech, a usage also common in late Latin literature,[24] was to prove extremely influential in Augustine's theory of signification.

The heritage of classical sign theory was, as is evident, both rich and varied, and, as we shall see, Augustine incorporated a good deal of it in his own linguistic epistemology. Yet, for all their richness and profundity, the classical approaches to the question of how signs function in the process of knowledge could not handle the kinds of epistemological problems which beset Augustine after his conversion to Christianity. Augustine leaves no doubt in the reader's mind as to the exact nature of these problems. At the outset of one of his earliest works, the *Soliloquia*, he describes his epistemological aims. At the same time, he portrays the conditions which he thinks are appropriate to them. In Book I of the *Soliloquia*, Augustine depicts the troubled state of mind in which he had first broached the problem of knowledge. He alludes to his brooding and protracted quest of self, of the good he ought to seek, and of the evil he ought to avoid. At this juncture, the author's reason intervenes. Augustine's reason counsels him to begin by seeking God's aid. He takes his reason's advice. Prayer clarifies Augustine's thinking; having addressed himself to God, he then finds himself ready to answer his reason's request for a brief statement of purpose:

R.: What, then, do you want to know?
A.: The very things for which I have prayed.
R.: Summarize them concisely.
A.: I want to know God and the soul.

23. Cicero, *De oratore*, 3.41.166–42.167, Sutton and Rackham, *2*, 130.
24. Aegidius Forcellini, *Totius latinitatis lexicon* (Prati, 1858), *1*, s.v. "Aenigma"; *Thesaurus linguae latinae,* editus auctoritate et consilio Academiarum quinque Germanicarum Berolinensis Goetingensis Lipsiensis Monacensis Vindobonensis (Lipsiae, 1900), *1*, s.v. "Aenigma." Cf. C. DuCange, *Glossarium mediae et infimae latinitatis* (Graz, 1954), *1*, s.v. "Aenigma."

R.: Nothing else?

A.: Nothing else at all.[25]

Both the point in question and the way that Augustine arranges the inquiry in this brief excerpt from the *Soliloquia* neatly define his conception of the epistemological enterprise. The meditation in which he outlines his goal is a dialogue laced with prayer. Despite its title, the *Soliloquia* is not a monologue. Rather, it is an internal conversation, whose speakers are known in and through each other. The objects of knowledge are the participants themselves; their personal communication is both the end of knowledge and its means. Discourse helps to bring their relationship to consciousness, heightens that consciousness, and serves as the vehicle for its external expression.

A note sounded in one of his first works, the idea of cognition through speech became the underlying theme on which Augustine orchestrated the problem of knowledge during a long and diversified literary career. The circumstances prompting him to develop this idea were his conversion to Christianity and his consecration to the tasks of a priest and a bishop. He formulated it by renovating his intellectual heritage of classical eloquence and philosophy to suit the occasions of a new profession and to meet the demands of a new kind of epistemology. Augustine projected a redeemed rhetoric as the outcome of a revealed wisdom. On the basis of this theory, a twofold linguistic transformation was in order: the faculty of human speech was to be recast as a Pauline mirror, faithfully mediating God to man in the present life; and the agencies appointed for the translation of man's partial knowl-

25. St. Augustine, *Soliloquia*, I, ii, 7, *PL, 32*, 872. In connection with the structure of the *Soliloquia,* it is important to note the observation of John Burnaby, *Amor Dei: A Study of the Religion of St. Augustine* (London, 1938), p. 55: "It is never to be forgotten that the Augustinian 'intellect' is not the discursive reason but the mind at worship." This idea has also been developed with considerable insight by Roger Hazelton, "The Devotional Life," *A Companion to the Study of St. Augustine,* ed. Roy W. Battenhouse (New York, 1955), pp. 400–03.

19

edge by faith into his complete knowledge of God by direct vision were to be redefined as modes of verbal expression.

This new covenant between speech and knowledge was both the link and the point of demarcation between Augustine the pagan orator and Augustine the fluent Doctor of Grace. It is an idea running through his collected works, touching every facet of his theology. Augustine gives his linguistic epistemology express analysis in two of his works, the *De magistro* and the *De doctrina christiana*. An unparalleled illustration of this epistemology in action, however, can be found in his *Confessiones,* since his sign theory serves as the structural basis of the work. In the *Confessiones,* the spiritual autobiography in which he charts his journey from paganism to Christianity, Augustine links his changing states of self-awareness and his comprehension of the outside world with his growing ability to learn through language and to express himself verbally. The crisis leading up to his conversion, he says, was inspired by his rejection of a sterile rhetoric, which lacked cognitive content and moral relevance, in favor of a rhetoric put to the service of God and men. In the treatment of his conversion itself, Augustine illustrates the function of the spoken and written word as media of revealed wisdom, and he concludes the work with a schematic outline of the various uses of redeemed speech.[26]

When he wrote the *Confessiones,* Augustine had been active in ecclesiastical circles for almost ten years and had already set forth his rhetorical theology in some of his earlier works. In his later writings he continued to illustrate aspects of redeemed rhetoric which he had lightly sketched in the latter portions of the *Confessiones* with increasingly broader strokes. In the *Confessiones* Augustine stresses the importance of learning and teaching through speech and outlines the Divinely constituted sanctions and regulations of these processes with all the

26. Cf. Pierre Courcelle, *Recherches sur les Confessions de Saint Augustin* (Paris, 1950), pp. 20 ff., who states first that the *Confessions* is an *oeuvre de circonstance* devoid of plan, but who notes a few paragraphs later that its autobiographical structure is shot through with doctrinal passages of progressive difficulty.

20

immediacy of direct experience. Vivid and concrete, the work is also constructed with a degree of circumspection and doctrinal rigor which make it a paradigm of Augustine's idea of knowledge through speech. These same qualities also make it an index of the ways in which he relates his theological pursuits to his epistemology and to one another.

Since the *Confessiones* so aptly summarizes Augustine's philosophy of language, as well as illustrates his interpretation of his spiritual history, this work is particularly well suited to serve as a framework for our discussion of Augustine's theory of words as signs in the knowledge of God. Accordingly, we plan to use the *Confessiones* as the organizing principle of this chapter, gearing Augustine's other works to it at points where they supply a more fully developed treatment of the question at hand than the *Confessiones* does. This method has two advantages. It permits us to work from Augustine's own paradigmatic presentation of linguistic epistemology. Also, the analysis of the *Confessiones* from this point of view makes possible a new interpretation of the work, which permits an explanation of certain problematic parts of it.

From the very beginning of the *Confessiones*, Augustine makes perfectly clear the manner in which he plans to handle the problem of knowledge. He prefaces the story of his life with a long contemplative prayer. In the middle of this prayer, he interrupts himself and ruminates for a moment on the equivocal task of speaking about God: "And what do we say, my God, my life, my holy sweetness; what does anyone say when he speaks of You? Yet woe to him who is silent concerning You, of Whom the most eloquent man stands mute." [27] Set as it is in the midst of a long and fluent passage praising God, Augustine's statement about the poverty of language and his confession of his own literary ineptitude strike a para-

27. *Confessiones*, I, iv, 4, *CSEL, 33,* 4. See also XIII, x, 11, *CSEL, 33,* 352. The idea that the most man can do is to state that God is inexpressible is found in *Enarrationes in Psalmos* XXXV, 4; XCIX, 6, *CC, 38,* 324; *CC, 39,* 1396; *Epistola* CCXLII, *CSEL, 34,* pars 4, 563–67; *De doctrina christiana,* I, vi, 6, *CC, 32,* 9–10.

21

doxical note. While the fact that God is ineffable presents Augustine with inescapable difficulties, it does not prescind from the urgency of his mandate to express what he knows; nor, apparently, does it hinder him particularly from doing so. But, as Augustine takes pains to suggest even earlier in the *Confessiones,* the paradox he has presented here can be understood in terms of a still greater paradox. He directs the reader's attention to the aenigma which animates and sustains his attempts to express the Word: "I call upon You, Lord, by my faith," he says, "which You gave me when You inspired me by the humanity of Your Son, through the ministry of your preacher." [28] The crux of the matter is Augustine's faith, its content, and the way he received it. The doctrine of the Incarnation and the manner in which Augustine understands his conversion to it are thus essential to his conception of the redemption of language, which, he holds, makes theology possible. His deliberate juxtaposition of the ideas of Incarnation and expression at the beginning of the *Confessiones* is hence a directive. It instructs the reader to pay close attention to these ideas in Augustine's autobiography, and in his work as a whole.

Having proffered this advice, Augustine launches forthwith into a description of his period of unregeneracy. This includes his infancy, childhood, youth, and professional career up until his conversion at the age of thirty-three (354–87), a period during which he moves from his native Thagaste to study and then to teach in Carthage, Rome, and Milan. From the very beginning of the *Confessiones,* Augustine interprets his moral and intellectual failings in terms of the misuse of his linguistic faculties. The only exception to this rule concerns Augustine as a newborn baby. In this stage of development, he was incapable of perverting his verbal skills, a situation explained by the fact that as yet he did not have any. The infancy which ushered him into the "dying life and living death" [29] of his

28. *Conf.,* I, i, 1, *CSEL, 33,* 2.
29. Ibid., v, 7, *CSEL, 33,* 5.

unredeemed state, he observes, was marked by a lack of conscious life, a condition signified by his inability to speak. As a baby, he says, he could only grasp physically the presence or absence of physical well-being. His inner life seems to have been composed of a random agglomeration of sensations. He was devoid of any awareness of himself as a person who senses, acts, or is acted upon. Although Augustine seems otherwise afflicted with total recall, it is understandable that, for his treatment of this part of his childhood, he is forced to rely on his later observation of babies and the testimony of others about himself at the same age.[30]

As an older infant, Augustine notes, the range of his physical perceptions gradually widened; he sensed, little by little, where he was. At the same time he began to connect the care of his body with the presence of people outside of it and made his first attempts to communicate with them. His principal concern at this time was the gratification of his physical needs. The incoherent sounds and gestures he was now capable of producing, however, were an ineffectual means of bending his environment to his own will.[31] Referring to his endowments and strivings at the point when infancy was about to give way to childhood, Augustine states, "I existed then and I lived, and, already, at the end of my infancy, looked for signs with which to express my feelings to others."[32] Augustine now possessed being and life, but not consciousness; will and sensation, but no articulate means of expression. He therefore attributes his infant selfishness to original sin, since, in his isolation from the world of words, he lacked the means of conscious knowledge necessary for morally good or evil actions.[33]

Augustine gives a concise description of his passage into the age of reason: "For I was no longer a speechless infant; I was

30. Ibid., vi, 7–8, *CSEL, 33,* 6–7.
31. Ibid., 8, *CSEL, 33,* 7.
32. Ibid., vi, 10, *CSEL, 33,* 8.
33. Ibid., vii, 11–12, *CSEL, 33,* 9–11. For further discussion of the moral state of the infant in terms of speech and consciousness, see *Epistola* CLXXVII, vii, 24–viii, 26, *CSEL, 34,* pars 4, 101–04.

now a speaking child."[34] (As a boy, articulate and reasonable, Augustine found himself faced with new moral responsibilities, a challenge which he holds himself to have met without success. He learned to speak naturally, he observes, by listening to his elders, imitating them, and noting their habitual association of certain sounds with certain things. As Augustine analyzes it, learning how to speak and learning how to think go hand in hand. Both, he holds, occurred at the point in his own life when he realized that he existed in a social and religious context. The response he made to this state of affairs, from the vantage point of the *Confessiones*, was morally negative. He regarded his newly acquired powers of thought and language primarily as devices for getting his own way.[35] He resented the fact that he lived among adults who could legitimately prescribe his activities and who could make authoritative demands on him. When his parents sent him to grammar school, he disobeyed his teachers and shirked his lessons, preferring play to study.[36] This childhood peccadillo may seem harmless, but Augustine refuses to discount it, seeing in his boyhood misdeeds the same vices that motivate the serious defections of grown men.[37] His opposition to the will of his parents and teachers sprang less from idleness, he says, than from the pride of self-aggrandizement, the desire to surpass and manipulate his peers which induced him to steal and cheat in his games, and which he refused to admit when detected.[38] At the same time, he opposed his will to God by seeking to manipulate Him. In attempting to escape the punishment provoked by his disobedience, Augustine tried to form a vocal pact with God, by which the Almighty might be placed at his disposal: "In calling upon You, I broke the bonds of my tongue, and I asked You . . . that I might not be beaten in school."[39]

34. *Conf.*, I, viii, 13, *CSEL, 33,* 11.
35. Ibid.
36. Ibid., ix, 14, *CSEL, 33,* 12.
37. Ibid., x, 15; xix, 30, *CSEL, 33,* 14, 27–28.
38. Ibid., x, 16; xix, 30, *CSEL, 33,* 14–15, 27–28.
39. Ibid., ix, 14, *CSEL, 33,* 12.

24

This request, needless to say, received no answer. As Augustine sees it, he had distorted his faculty of speech on this occasion by praying selfishly. Instead of asking God to help him use his talents fitly, he had arrogantly sought a sanction for his willful failure to do so.[40]

The perversion of language is a defect that Augustine sees in his grammatical studies as well as in his personal life. He by no means regrets that he was taught to read, write, and speak correctly. Nor does he consider these disciplines useless or evil in themselves. Rather, he condemns the grammar schools for teaching such valuable arts through the study of pagan poetry. Augustine explains his rejection of the *auctores* here in terms of their abuse of language and the deleterious morality which he feels that this abuse encourages. The poets, he says, use words erroneously, since they use them to refer to things and ideas which are nonexistent or untrue. Furthermore, he adds, the poets depict ignorant and irresponsible actions in their fictitious characters, who operate in accordance with the unreal universe of the authors' creation. The beauty of this poetry is doubly dangerous, according to Augustine, since it is used to construct a world of shadows and to make the fantastic morality of that world attractive and convincing.[41]

Augustine takes issue with not only the materials used as teaching devices in the grammar schools but also with the grammarians' shallow and formalistic approach to learning.

40. Ibid., x, 15, *CSEL, 33,* 14.
41. Ibid., xiii, 20–xvi, 26, *CSEL, 33,* 18–24. Augustine states elsewhere that the use of words by pagan authors to signify things which have no existence is a falsification of speech; fictitous statements of this type denote nothing except insofar as they imitate the grammatical structure of true statements. He adds that it is important to know the intention of the author before judging his statements. Poems and tales which aim only to amuse are not false; they are false only when they aim to instruct. See *Soliloquia,* II, ix, 16; xv, 29, *PL, 32,* 892, 898–99. Augustine frequently uses the same kind of verbal argument in his attacks on heretics in order to support the contention that an orthodox confession of faith is necessary for truly moral actions. See, for example, *Tractatus in Ioannem,* CII, 1, *CC, 36,* 594–95.

He notes that his teachers devoted more attention to the laws of language than to the conduct of life. Although he was aware that he had moral obligations to others, his training thus led him to be more concerned with avoiding barbarisms than with barbarous behavior.[42]

Augustine's grammatical studies, unsatisfactory from the perspective of the *Confessiones,* lasted until he was sixteen years old. By that time, as he surveys his development, his personality had begun to crystallize. His self-consciousness had expanded to include a grasp of the unity of his senses and of his person. His tastes had also begun to form; he notes that he delighted in truth and friendship and that he detested deception, pain, baseness, and ignorance. His education up to this point, he says, had made him well spoken and retentive. But it had provided him with techniques rather than values. His grammar school days had increased his boyhood selfishness and had further deflected his budding talents and aspirations from moral ends. As he approached adolescence, Augustine concludes, his desires for sublimity, pleasure, and truth were to become increasingly directed away from God and toward His creatures, both himself and other men.[43]

At this point in the *Confessiones* Augustine takes up a new stage in the story of his life, encompassing the years from sixteen to twenty-eight. During this time he was preoccupied at Carthage with rhetoric, first as a student and then as a teacher. In his progression from grammar to rhetoric, his linguistic abilities were embellished and sophisticated. His ex post facto self-criticism in the *Confessiones* grows commensurately in range and intensity. Rhetoric, he states, was taught in as much of a moral vacuum as grammar. Detached from truth and goodness, the eloquence in which Augustine now rapidly excelled became the framework for his rich endowment of intellect and emotion, which he began to misdirect with all the freedom and power of adulthood. In general, Au-

42. *Conf.,* I, xviii, 29–xix, 30, *CSEL, 33,* 26–27.
43. Ibid., xx, 31, *CSEL, 33,* 28.

26

gustine interprets this period of his life as a movement away from Divine unity, toward a multiplicity of transient and self-centered goals.[44] He subdivides the period into two chronological sections. In the first one, which covers his student years from sixteen to nineteen, he portrays his behavior as a parody on human love and the love of God. In the second part, which includes his professional career up to the age of twenty-eight, he recasts his analysis, stressing the contrast between the temporal and corporeal, on the one hand, and the spiritual and eternal, on the other. In this latter section, too, he gives the first intimation in the *Confessiones* of his projected Incarnational reconciliation of love, time, and language.

Part one of this section, the years from sixteen to nineteen, shows Augustine studying a rhetoric clearly devoid of moral considerations.[45] He opens this part of the *Confessiones* with the famous affair of the green pears, the wanton theft which Augustine committed with a group of other boys during a year of enforced idleness at the age of sixteen. This crime is at first perplexing. Except for the fact that it enhanced Augustine's

44. Ibid., II, i, 1; IV, xvi, 31, *CSEL, 33,* 29, 87–88.

45. Ibid., II, ii, 4–iii, 5, *CSEL, 33,* 31–32. As Charles Sears Baldwin has pointed out in *Medieval Rhetoric and Poetic (to 1400) Interpreted from Representative Works* (New York, 1928), pp. viii, 6, 51, 54–55, 60, 71, Augustine is reacting away from the sophistic rhetoric current in his own day in the direction of an antisophistic rhetoric which would stress the union of wisdom, virtue, and eloquence. This antisophistic tradition has a long history in classical thought. It runs through the work of Plato; see in particular *Gorgias,* passim, and especially 456b–58b, 464c–65e, 523b–27e; *Phaedrus,* 275d–79b, Jowett, *2,* 544–46, 553–54, 622–27; *3,* 185–89. Cicero repeats the same idea frequently. See *De oratore,* 1.5.16–18, 1.6.20–22, 1.7.28, 1.14.60–16.70, 2.2.6, 3.5.20, 3.6.24, 4.14.54–20.77, Sutton and Rackham, *1,* 12–14, 16, 20, 44–50, 201; *2,* 16, 20, 44–62; *De inventione,* 1.1.1–3.5, Hubbell, pp. 2–10; *Orator,* 4.14, 22.72, Hubbell, pp. 315, 358. Cicero's antisophistic criticism is repeated by Quintilian, *Institutiones oratoriae,* 1.1.9–20, 12.1–2.1–10, Butler, *1,* 8–14; *4,* 352–86. Aristotle discusses rhetoric principally in relation to truth, touching on ethics only in the sense that the orator should be aware of his own ethos and that of his audience (*Rhetoric,* I, 1356a, 20–26, 32–34, Roberts, pp. 25–26). See also Charles Sears Baldwin, *Ancient Rhetoric and Poetic Interpreted from Representative Works* (New York, 1924), pp. 5, 9–12, 53–55, 247.

status among his peers, it does not seem to fit into his usual catalogue of sinful motives. After analyzing it, however, he concludes that this apparently inexplicable misdemeanor is a paradigm of the very mystery of sin. Augustine begins by eliminating the motives that he feels are irrelevant to the theft. He notes that he did not need or want the pears, and that he could not enjoy them since they were unripe; he did not steal out of a desire for power, out of an inordinate longing for attractive things, or out of the fear of losing them. Nor was the act a means to some other end.[46] The sin, he says, lay precisely in the fact that it was an end in itself, committed simply for the joy of a shared wantonness.[47] Augustine sees this love of sin for its own sake as an inverted reflection of the perfect love of God.[48] In both cases what is loved is the object itself, not its by-products. A travesty of the love of God, the theft was also a caricature of Christian charity. Sinfulness, like blessedness, observes Augustine, is not a solitary condition. Both are social in their nature and in their consequences. In this case, Augustine and his companions reinforced each other's downfall by their complicity in evil. Thus their behavior was the perversion of a perfect friendship, whose members reinforce their love of God and of each other through their mutual joy in the good. In its defiance of God's love, in its distortion of human love, the theft of the pears was thus a perfect parody of a perfectly virtuous act.

Having used the pear-stealing incident as an occasion to specify the nature of sin, Augustine goes on to analyze some of the other defections of his adolescence. These acts, he thinks, were characterized by disobedience, the misuse of his faculties, and the distortion of right relationships with other people. They all reflect a mistaken attitude toward God and man. Augustine identifies the motivation of these sins as his desire to please himself and to be pleasing in the eyes of oth-

46. *Conf.*, II, iv, 9–v, 11, *CSEL, 33,* 35–39.
47. Ibid., iv, 9; vi, 12; vii, 15, *CSEL, 33,* 35–36, 38, 40–41.
48. Ibid., vi, 13–vii, 15, *CSEL, 33,* 38–41.

28

ers.[49] He expressed these motives by rejoicing in his body, his emotions, and his mind as ends in themselves.

Two of Augustine's major temptations between the ages of sixteen and nineteen were women and the drama. In interpreting his sexual licentiousness and his fondness for the theater, Augustine finds that the same fault, the abuse of emotion, underlies both of them. Misdirected love also made both of them occasions for the abuse of friendship. His relations with women, Augustine confesses, were not inspired by reverence for their persons. He did not love his partners, but sought instead only the feelings of pleasure that they could produce in him. He quickly grasped that this cult of his own sensations would not yield happiness, for it at once mingled its insatiable sweetness with suspicion, jealousy, and pain.[50] Still, Augustine did not abandon or restrain his sexual exploits. The pain of love, he discovered, has its own subjective attractions; as Augustine loved to love, he also loved to grieve.

He sees his addiction to theatrical tragedies as rooted in the same kind of emotional introversion. Unlike sexuality, the stage produces its stimulus vicariously. According to Augustine, this very artificiality is the key to its perversity. The feeling of grief is sorry enough if one is forced to suffer it in one's own life, he states. If one's grief is aroused by the sufferings of others, the appropriate response is one of outgoing compassion. The theater, however, produces a solicitous relish for the fictionalized counterparts of grief and suffering, encouraging the viewer to turn inward and to revel irresponsibly in the illusion of his own compassion.[51] Thus, argues Augustine, his taste for the theater, like his licentiousness, distorted his personal morality by focusing upon himself emotions of pleasure and pain which should have signalized his obligations to others.

While Augustine interprets his sins of sense and feeling

49. Ibid., i, 1, *CSEL, 33,* 29.
50. Ibid., ii, 2, 4; III, i, 1, *CSEL, 33,* 29–30, 31, 43–44.
51. Ibid., III, ii, 2–4, *CSEL, 33,* 44–47.

29

mainly as an opportunity for the selfish indulgence of emotion—although he does note that his licentiousness was also encouraged by the admiration of his peers [52]—his desire for praise and preeminence, he notes, was achieved primarily through his intellectual life. Instead of overriding and manipulating his fellows outside of school, as he had done in childhood, he now fed his ambition by becoming the star pupil in rhetoric.[53] Also, at the age of nineteen, he read the *Hortensius,* attributed to Cicero. This work influenced him deeply, directing his attention to philosophy. Augustine's response to the *Hortensius* can be seen as a parody on his later conversion to Christianity. While the reading of the *Hortensius* inspired him to shift his emphasis from rhetorical form to philosophical content, it did not involve any basic change in his moral attitudes. Philosophy, like rhetoric, appealed to him at this point largely as a discipline in which he could expand his pride of intellect. As he puts it, he broadened the vanity which motivated his rhetorical strivings to include the equally vain desire for a personal immortality of wisdom.[54]

As if to specify the immediate outcome of such a misconception of wisdom, Augustine notes, he became a Manichee at this time. Manicheism seems apposite because, according to Augustine, this doctrine abuses both the form and the content of language. As he describes them in the *Confessiones,* the Manichees understand neither the function of language nor the nature of reality. In their mouths, the names of the Persons of the Trinity are *flatus vocis,* since they use these names to designate myths and materialistic falsehoods.[55] As a philosophy with claims to literal truth, Manicheism, he holds, is hence more misleading than the seductive fables of the poets. The latter, although incidentally didactic, are at least useful for constructive training in grammar.[56] Manicheism, on the

52. Ibid., II, iii, 7, *CSEL, 33,* 34.
53. *Conf.,* III, iii, 6, *CSEL, 33,* 47.
54. Ibid., iv, 7, *CSEL, 33,* 48–49.
55. Ibid., vi, 10, *CSEL, 33,* 50–52.
56. Ibid., 11, *CSEL, 33,* 52–53.

other hand, lacks the aesthetic and educational values of poetry. As with poetry, it perverts language as a means of communicating the truth and of conducing the hearer to the good, but it lacks the redeeming features of literature, since these distortions can never be excused as unintentional decorations. Thus, he concludes, the Manichees' false notion of God, like the falsehoods of the poets, leads to an unrealistic and distorted morality.[57]

This judgment is based on Augustine's view that an erroneous conception of reality can hinder a person from acting rightly; and, conversely, that a person's moral state affects his ability to know the truth, by either permitting or preventing him from recognizing the channels through which it can be known. At various points in this section of the *Confessiones* Augustine points out a number of these channels and admits that his moral obtuseness held him back as yet from hearing the voice of God through them. Characteristically, he thinks of God's communication to man in terms of speech. God speaks, as Augustine later observes in the events leading up to his conversion, through the precept and example of individual Christians, through Holy Scripture, and through the *magisterium* of the bishops of the Church. Augustine deals with precept and example first. He brings forward his mother, Monica, a chaste and devout Christian, who begs Augustine to give up his sexual incontinence, or at least to marry; "and what were these but Your words, singing in my ears through my mother, Your faithful servant?" he asks.[58] Augustine also interprets Monica's dream that her Manichean son would one day join her in the *regula* of Christianity as a message from God, confessing that he thought this piece of evidence foolish at the time.[59] In the first flush of his reading of the *Hortensius,* he picked up the Bible in his search for wisdom, but his literary sensibility made him shrink from the crude style of

57. Ibid., vii, 12–x, 18, *CSEL, 33,* 53–60.
58. Ibid., II, iii, 7, *CSEL, 33,* 33.
59. Ibid., III, xi, 19, *CSEL, 33,* 60.

the inspired writers.[60] Finally, the bishop whom Monica begged to exhort Augustine out of heresy perceived that the youth was too morally beclouded to be teachable and so declined to speak to him.[61] Thus, the frame of mind in which Augustine had begun his quest for wisdom had closed his ears to it.

Before developing the next section of the *Confessiones*, Augustine stops to summarize the caliber of his moral life at the beginning of the first nine years as a professional rhetorician. He notes that he still loved rhetoric because it brought him praise. Now, however, he intensified his misuse of the faculty of speech by becoming a teacher. He sold the art of persuasion out of cupidity, he says, despite his knowledge that it might well be used by his students for vain and unjust purposes. He also confined his sexual activities at this stage by installing a permanent mistress. Augustine interprets these sins as an expanded version of false friendship, widening the context of his analysis from personal to civic obligations. By failing to consider the values of the eloquence he taught and the uses to which his students might put it, and in shunning the duties of lawful wedlock, he was shirking his social responsibilities. He now sees his behavior as a parody on good citizenship, judging civic life by the same criteria which he thinks should guide personal morality.[62]

As the *Confessiones* reveal, Augustine is a man of naturally gregarious habits. He always sees himself as participating, whether morally or immorally, in a community. It is virtually impossible to conceive of him as a solitary and isolated individual. Throughout his life, and especially at its most crucial points, he shows himself surrounded by friends. Before his conversion, he observes, he usually misconstrued the nature of friendship, thus distorting the relationship in some way. In

60. Ibid., v, 9, *CSEL, 33,* 50.
61. Ibid., xii, 21, *CSEL, 33,* 62–63. Augustine also discusses the importance of moral states in the reception of knowledge in *De fide et symbolo,* IX, 19, *CSEL, 40,* 22–25; *De doctrina christiana,* II, vii, 11, *CC, 32,* 38.
62. *Conf.,* IV, i, 1–ii, 2, *CSEL, 33,* 63–65.

this section of the *Confessiones,* the problem of false friendship is as pervasive as ever, but Augustine treats it in a new light. The occasion for the change is the sudden death of a friend whom Augustine had loved inordinately. This loss left him utterly desolate. He responded first by selfishly nursing his grief, and then by plunging headlong into the society of his other friends, attaching himself to them with a love equally intense and excessive.[63] The pain of his first loss had evidently taught him nothing. Friendship, he stops to note, cannot be truly human unless its nexus is the love of God. When a friend is loved in God he can never be lost.[64] But, he says, he did not possess this insight at the time. Consequently, his inordinate love could only leave him wretched. "I was miserable," he says, "for every soul chained by friendship to mortal things is miserable, and is torn to pieces when it loses them, so that it even feels the misery before it has lost them." [65] The crux of his mistake, he observes, lay in his enslavement to transitory things, and in his search for an infinite consolation in pleasures which are good, but which are necessarily finite.

Augustine employs this same contrast between the transitory and the eternal to recast his interpretation of language. Up to this point in the *Confessiones* he generally regards his former attitude toward language as perverse, since he had oriented his eloquence to a variety of selfish goals and had detached it from the cognition of reality. But, he says, when language operates as God intended, it functions as a medium of truth. It should be used to deepen one's own knowledge of reality and also for the instruction of others.

But how is it possible for men to use language as God intended? Rightly ordered speech, according to Augustine, is a consequence of the Incarnation. The key to the linguistic epistemology which he posits is Christ, Whom he sees as the verbal and actual reconciliation of God and man. To begin

63. Ibid., iv, 7–ix, 14, *CSEL, 33,* 68–75.
64. Ibid., iv, 7; vii, 12; ix, 14, *CSEL, 33,* 68–69, 73, 75.
65. Ibid., vi, 11, *CSEL, 33,* 72.

33

with, he notes, speech is a man-made art, which is part of the created universe of time and corporeal nature. Words are transient auditory forms, whose sensuous reverberations are continually falling into nothingness in order to make way for each other.[66] As a means of adumbrating sustained and non-discursive realities, even on the purely human level, language is thus full of inadequacies. There always remains an opaque residuum of inexpressibility when a man tries to signify verbally his internal states of being.[67] In the face of the ineffable mystery of God, human language labors under crushing limitations. The possibility of intellectual contact with God through words would seem inadmissible. Yet, the role which God assigns to speech in the economy of His redemption demands a real and dynamic relationship between language and objective truth. This problem springs from the disparity between Divine and human nature. God overcomes it by uniting Divinity and humanity in the Word made flesh. In Christ, says Augustine, God speaks to man as man, "proclaiming aloud by words," through the sensible, temporal media of His life, deeds, death, descent, and ascension.[68] The Incarnation conveys the knowledge of God to the world by communicating God Himself. It also enables man to respond to God in human terms, by restoring man's words to God in Christ. Augustine explains this central idea most fully in a passage from his sermons on the Psalms:

> Before you perceived God, you believed that thought could express God. Now you are beginning to perceive Him, and you think that you cannot express what you perceive. But, having found that you cannot express what you perceive, will you be silent, will you not praise God? . . . Honor is due Him, reverence is due Him, great praise is due Him. . . . 'How,' you ask, 'shall I

66. Ibid., x, 15–xi, 17, *CSEL, 33,* 76–78.
67. *De catechizandis rudibus,* II, 3–4, *PL, 40,* 311–12.
68. *Conf.,* IV, xi, 19, *CSEL, 33,* 79. See also *De civitate dei,* XI, 2–3, *CC, 48,* 322–23.

praise Him?' I cannot now explain the small amount which I can perceive in part, through a glass darkly (*in aenigmate per speculum*) . . . All other things may be expressed in some way; He alone is ineffable, Who spoke, and all things were made. He spoke, and we were made; but we are unable to speak of Him. His Word, by Whom we were spoken, is His Son. He was made weak, so that He might be spoken by us, despite our weakness.[69]

For Augustine, then, God creates the world and man through His Word, and He takes on humanity in the Word made flesh so that human words may take on Divinity, thereby bringing man and the world back to God. In His redemptive plan, God has already solved for man the problem of His own ineffability. Once joined to God in Christ, human nature is restored in mind and body, and man's faculty of speech is empowered to carry on the work of Incarnation in expressing the Word to the world. For Augustine, redeemed speech becomes a mirror, through which men may know God in this life by faith. And Christian eloquence becomes, both literally and figuratively, a vessel of the Spirit, bearing the Word to mankind, incorporating men into the New Covenant of Christ, and preparing them through its mediation for the face-to-face knowledge of God in the beatific vision.[70]

The solution to man's verbal and moral problems that Augustine intimates at this point in the *Confessiones* and expands in his sermon on the Psalms is a retroactive one. It was not part of Augustine's mental equipment in his twenties. There are still several years of misguided activity that he

---

69. *Enarratio in Psalmum* XCIX, 6, *CC, 39,* 1396–97.

70. *Conf.,* IV, xi, 19, *CSEL, 33,* 78–80. On words as vehicles of God's Word, communicated to men through men, see also *De vera religione,* L, 99, *CC, 32,* 251; *De civitate dei,* X, 15, *CC, 47,* 288–89; *Enarrationes in Psalmos* XLVIII, 5; LXXVII, 5, *CC, 38,* 542; *CC, 39,* 1069–70; *Tractatus in Ioannem,* I, 4; XXIX, 4; LIV, 8, *CC, 36,* 2, 462–63, 485–86; *De fide et symbolo,* II, 3–III, 4, *CSEL, 40,* 6–8. Cf. Rudolph Berlinger, *Augustins dialogische Metaphysik,* (Frankfurt am Main, 1962), who treats the Incarnational aspect of Augustine's thought from a strictly metaphysical point of view.

wishes to relate and to interpret linguistically in the *Confessiones*. As he observes, his inordinate and by now habitual emphasis on himself and the created universe continued to motivate the burgeoning intellectual pursuits of his twenties. During this period Augustine wrote a treatise on aesthetics, no longer extant, *De pulchro et apto,* which he dedicated to a prominent orator whom his vanity urged him to imitate. The aesthetic theory expressed in this work was strictly sensuous, an offshoot of Manichean dualism, which encouraged Augustine to translate a material idea of God into a physical conception of beauty.[71] During these years, Augustine completed his formal education and became a teacher. Graduation, he says, found him mentally well equipped but poorly oriented morally. Philosophy, currently in the shape of Aristotle's *Categories,* continued to attract his interest, but it did not implement his quest for wisdom. He was able to understand Aristotle by himself, which only enriched his pride, while his attempts to understand God in terms of substance and predication, he feels, both demonstrated and encouraged his intellectual blindness.[72] On the whole, Augustine thinks that his ready mastery of the late classical curriculum refined his tendency to delight in his own excellence. Failing to perceive the source of his gifts or the value of his knowledge, he dissipated his accomplishments, neither profiting from them himself nor applying them to the needs of others less talented.[73]

We now move to the climactic portion of the *Confessiones,* the section of the work in which Augustine describes the ideas and events leading up to his conversion. Between the ages of twenty-nine and thirty-three, he indicates, his desire for a solution to his intellectual problems became more and more compelling. Under the constant pressure of philosophical criticism, his belief in Manicheism grew weaker, although he still

71. *Conf.,* IV, xiii, 20–xv, 27, *CSEL, 33,* 80–85.
72. Ibid., xvi, 28–29, *CSEL, 33,* 85–86.
73. Ibid., 30–31, *CSEL, 33,* 87–88.

hoped to resolve his doubts within the Manichean system. When Faustus, a prominent Manichean adept, appeared in Carthage for a series of public debates, Augustine listened to him enthusiastically and later interrogated him in detail. He left the debates feeling that his hopes had been betrayed. Although superficially brilliant, Faustus' eloquence, he discovered, was only a mask for the Manichee's ignorance and affectation.[74] Augustine was disappointed, but he was not disappointed enough to abandon Manicheism altogether. A move from Carthage to Rome for the sake of professional advantage at that time entangled him briefly in Academic skepticism. But, for the most part, he retained his association with the Manichees, largely out of habit, despite his increasing dissatisfaction with their interpretation of Scripture, creation, and goodness, and their general inability to explain adequately what he wanted to know.[75]

Just at the point when shallow eloquence, fantastic exegesis, and vacuous personal example were beginning to precipitate Augustine's defection from Manicheism, his appointment to the municipal chair of rhetoric at Milan put him in a position to experience these same occasions of knowledge in a Christian setting. He met Ambrose, the bishop of the city, and immediately noticed his warmth and cordiality, an impression that deepened in time into a profound respect for his exemplary life as a pastor and a teacher.[76] Still more impressive was Ambrose's example as a preacher. The bishop was a renowned orator. Augustine was first drawn to his sermons by his rhetorical technique rather than by his teachings. But an alarming change soon began to take place. Augustine was transformed from an observer into a hearer. He grasped the bishop's message, and also the fact that it was inseparable from its rhetorical form: "At the same time with the words, which I loved,

74. Ibid., V, iii, 3; vi, 10–vii, 13, *CSEL, 33,* 90–91, 96–100.
75. Ibid., x, 19–xi, 21, *CSEL, 33,* 106–08.
76. Ibid., xiii, 23; VI, iii, 3, *CSEL, 33,* 109–10, 116–17.

there came into my soul the very things that I wanted to refuse. Moreover, I could not separate the one from the other.
And, when I opened my heart to receive the eloquence of his
speech, little by little the truth of what he said also entered."
Particularly gripping for Augustine were Ambrose's expositions of knotty passages in the Bible: "I heard several passages in the Old Testament explained, often figuratively; and
when I understood them literally, I was undone." [77] The bishop
spoke, the words of revelation were made clear; the listener understood, and was spiritually slain. The importance of
this episode for the development of Augustine's philosophy of
language cannot be overestimated. This experience, his first
contact with redeemed eloquence, revolutionized his conception of rhetoric and religion alike. Shaken from his erstwhile
prejudiced rejection of Christianity, he resolved to give the
Church an equal hearing and enrolled himself as a cate-
chumen.[78]

Shortly afterward, an incident took place which substantiated Augustine's new awareness of the function of language
in the knowledge of God, and which gave that awareness an
added dimension. To his surprise, he discovered that his own
words could serve inadvertently as vehicles of Christian instruction. One day in his classroom, he illustrated the topic
under discussion with a satirical reference to the Circensian
races. The offhand comment struck to the heart of Alypius,
one of his students. The youth took the remark personally and
at once wrested himself from the brutalities of the arena, to
which he had formerly been addicted. No one was more star-
tled than Augustine in noting that "You made burning coals

77. Ibid., V, xiv, 24, *CSEL, 33,* 111. The integration of style and content is
another of Augustine's antisophistic Ciceronian ideas; see Baldwin, *Medieval
Rhetoric and Poetic,* p. 60.

78. *Conf.,* V, xiv, 25, *CSEL, 33,* 112. On the function of preaching, see *De
doctrina christiana,* prooemium, 5–6, 8; IV, passim and especially xvi, 33–xxvii,
59, *CC, 32,* 3–4, 5, 139–64; *De catechizandis rudibus,* IV, 8; V, 9; XV, 23, *PL,
40,* 315, 316, 328; *Tractatus in Ioannem,* I, 4; XVII, 2, *CC, 36,* 2, 170–71. On
episcopal instruction, see *Epistola* CCIX, *CSEL, 34,* pars 4, 356–71.

38

of my heart and tongue, with which You cauterized and healed this eager but diseased mind." [79] Without having intended it, he found that he had been a mouthpiece for God. He also could see that, while moral instruction had come through his words, its effectiveness derived from a source beyond himself.

In the two years immediately preceding his conversion, Augustine experienced a number of occasions—the Christian community at Milan, his companions, now beginning to act as true friends, moral example, the reading of philosophy and of Scripture, and his own meditation—through which God spoke to him. It will be remembered that he had unsuccessfully encountered many of the same occasions earlier and that he interpreted their function in a similarly linguistic fashion. But now, he says, he was capable of receiving instruction through these channels. He continued to attend Ambrose's sermons and assembled most of the central beliefs of Christianity through the bishop's magisterial eloquence.[80] At the same time he continued his philosophical inquiries and revised some of his views in the context of friendly debate. In a discussion with his companion Nebridius, the inconsistency of his spatial,

79. *Conf.*, VI, vii, 12, *CSEL, 33,* 126. On conversation, oral and written, see *Epistolae* CLXXXIX, CCXXXIII, *CSEL, 34,* pars 4, 131–37, 517–18.

80. *Conf.*, VI, iii, 4–v, 8; VII, vii, 11, *CSEL, 33,* 117–22, 152–53. Courcelle, *Recherches*, pp. 106–36, thinks that Ambrose was also Augustine's chief source of Platonism at this time. This view is repeated by Maurice Testard, *Saint Augustin et Cicéron: Cicéron dans la formation et dans l'oeuvre de Saint Augustin* (Paris, 1958), *1,* 81–82, 119 ff., who adds that Ambrose converted Augustine from sophistry to Ciceronianism. More recently, Courcelle, *Les Confessions de Saint Augustin dans la tradition littéraire: Antécédents et posterité* (Paris, 1963), pp. 29–30, has restated his view, citing supporters of it. While there is unquestionably a strand of Platonism in Ambrose's thought, it seems overly gallant to give him the major credit for having introduced Augustine to these ideas, particularly since Augustine was currently reading Platonic philosophy on his own. Courcelle himself notes, *Les Confessions,* p. 31, that there was a Christian Neoplatonic group in Milan, including Simplicianus, Theodorus, and others Augustine knew in addition to Ambrose. Cf. Johannes Hessen, *Augustins Metaphysik der Erkenntnis* (Berlin und Bonn, 1931), pp. 13–14.

quantitative idea of God was laid bare. Nebridius and another friend, Firmianus, were also able to demonstrate to his satisfaction the untenability of astronomical determinism, two positions which Augustine then predictably rejected as using words and ideas falsely.[81]

There remained a major philosophical question to which Augustine now directed his attention—the problem of evil. His discussion of the problem of evil indicates that at this point his Manicheism had already been tinctured considerably by Christian ideas. God, he held, is good; matter is evil. Yet, God creates and dwells immanently in the material universe.[82] The difficulty here arises from Augustine's conception of the relationship between God and creation. As immanent, God is in matter, he held. Yet matter is evil. Since God, as identified with the material creation, cannot act against His will, He must therefore will and participate in evil. This conclusion Augustine could not reconcile with his initial postulate of God's goodness. A possible alternative to this inconsistency seemed to be provided by Neoplatonism, with its doctrine of Divine transcendence over the transient world of material existence. Augustine began to study the works of the Platonists and was encouraged to note that their doctrine of emanation compared favorably at a number of points with the Christian beliefs he already possessed. In order to determine just how far the truth of Platonism went, to "spoil the Egyptians of their gold," [83] he withdrew to meditate on the Platonic concept of God and on its relationship to the problem of evil. In moments of intuition, he reached the certainty of God as absolute Being, immutable, unmixed with evil. With this realization came the certainty that the created universe, including himself, was radically different and separate from God, and

81. *Conf.,* VII, i, 1–ii, 3 ; vi, 8–10, *CSEL, 33,* 140–43, 148–52. On the function of argument and discussion, see *Soliloquia,* II, vii, 14, *PL, 32,* 891. For Augustine's rejection of Academic probablism on similar verbal grounds, see *Contra academicos,* II, xi, 26, *CSEL, 63,* 41–42.

82. *Conf.,* VII, iii, 4–v, 7, *CSEL, 33,* 143–48.

83. Ibid., ix, 13–15, *CSEL, 33,* 154–57.

that he was still capable of knowing a Being radically different from himself, even if briefly.[84] Augustine interprets this intuition, appropriated by spiritual empiricism, in verbal terms, as he interprets all forms of the temporal knowledge of God. He describes this kind of cognition as the voice of God speaking to him: "I heard, as it were, your voice from on high," he says.[85] The information which this intuition brought him enabled Augustine to solve the problem of evil while avoiding the difficulties of materialistic dualism. The solution he arrived at indicates that his Platonism, too, contained a certain amount of Christianity at this point. Since, he reasoned, it has being, order, and harmony, the material creation is good, although imperfect; and it may conduce man to God, since the world is derived from Him and reflects His sovereign glory. Evil is not a substance, he concluded, because being is good; rather, it is a perversion of the will—a distinctly biblical notion—whereby men love the created universe with improper reference to God.[86]

But, if Platonism helped Augustine to differentiate the world's goodness from God's goodness, it did not provide him with a way to attain to God in any sustained fashion while living in the world. The Platonists, he notes, lack the doctrine of the Incarnation, by which man may receive the power to share in the life of God in and through the conditions of temporal existence.[87] This is another passage in the *Confessiones* where Augustine proffers a retroactive insight. At the point

84. Ibid., x, 16; xi, 17; xiv, 20; xvii, 23; XII, x, 10–xi, 12, *CSEL, 33,* 157–58, 160, 162–63, 316–17. On intuition as a verbal medium of cognition, see *Epistolae* IV, CXLVII, i, 3; 5–ii, 7, *CSEL, 34,* pars 1, 9–11; pars 3, 276–77, 278–81; *De civitate dei,* XXII, 29, *CC, 48,* 857 ff. On the difference between Augustine's intuitive cognition of God and mystical experience, see Burnaby, *Amor Dei,* pp. 31–37.

85. *Conf.,* VII, x, 16, *CSEL, 33,* 157.

86. Ibid., ix, 13–xvii, 23, *CSEL, 33,* 154–63. On God speaking through the natural universe, an argument rarely used by Augustine, see *De civitate dei,* XI, 4, *CC, 48,* 323–24; *Tractatus in Ioannem,* I, 8–10, *CC, 36,* 4–6.

87. *Conf.,* VII, ix, 13–14; xviii, 24, *CSEL, 33,* 154–55, 163. Courcelle, *Les Confessions,* pp. 33–37.

when he was plagued by the problem of evil, he says, he did not have an accurate understanding of the doctrine of the Incarnation. He observes that his current idea of Christ was a rationalization. Thus, he thinks, his attempts to transcend the limitations of creation and human nature through Christ failed, because he had created Christ in the image of his own mind.[88] He had not yet realized that in the biblical Christ he would find a focal principle, capable of counterweighing his tendencies toward an immanental pantheism, with its identification of God and the material world on the one hand, and a Platonized idealism, abstracting God from the material world, on the other.

The final stage of Augustine's conversion, as he understands it, was dependent on his grasp of the Incarnation in the metaphysical and moral order. He achieved this insight when he grasped the meaning of the Incarnation for his own personal life. Two verbal media of God's Word, the Bible and the eloquence of moral example, played a determining role in sealing Augustine's conversion. Just as his metaphysical position dictated the conditions of his ethical philosophy, so his moral state affected his ability to learn about Christ.

Augustine shows himself beset by three moral problems at this time: intellectual pride, the desire for worldly fame, and sensuality. His pride, he says, was dealt with first. Taking up the study of Scripture, he read the Epistles of St. Paul. As soon as he acknowledged that the apostle's fulminations against pride applied to himself, he began to understand the doctrine of Christ which Paul sets forth.[89] Held back by his

---

88. *Conf.*, VII, xviii, 24–xx, 26, *CSEL, 33,* 163–66. Courcelle, *Les Confessions*, pp. 64–65.

89. *Conf.*, VII, xx, 26–VIII, i, 1, *CSEL, 33,* 165–69. On the Bible as a moral *speculum*, see *Enarrationes in Psalmos* XVI, 5; XXX, exp. II, serm. II, 1; XLVI, 1; CII, 4; CVI, 1, *CC, 38,* 92, 202, 529; *CC, 40,* 1453, 1570; *Tractatus in Ioannem*, x, 7; XXI, 2, *CC, 36,* 104–05, 213; *Epistolae* CLXXXIX, CCXXIX, *CSEL, 34,* pars 4, 131–37, 497–98. Ritamary Bradley, "Backgrounds of the Title *Speculum* in Mediaeval Literature," *Speculum, 29* (1954), 100–15, notes this usage of the Bible in Augustine, but confines the idea of *speculum* to it.

desire for fame, however, he still shrank from applying the directives of this doctrine to his own life completely. Appealing for aid to Simplicianus, a circumspect elder of the Milanese Christian community, he learned of the conversion of Victorinus, a famous Roman rhetorician and the translator of some of the Platonic volumes that Augustine had been reading. When Augustine heard that "the tongue of Victorinus, that great and sharp sword, with which he had slain many, . . . had been taken from him and purified, made fitting to Your honor and useful to the Lord for every good work," [90] he compared himself, "a vendor of the art of speaking," [91] to the courageous orator. Victorinus knew of the imperial decree forbidding Christians to teach rhetoric and the liberal arts, and, "in obedience to this law, preferred to abandon the wordy school rather than Your Word." [92] Augustine's own cupidity and desire for professional acclaim were put to shame, he says, and he was overcome by the desire to imitate Victorinus' example.

The third problem, sensuality, still remained. It was not unrelated to the other two. Augustine had already been persuaded by Alypius and by Monica, who had by this time joined him in Milan, to abandon his sexual indulgences. The alternatives to his mistress he saw as celibacy or marriage; he had decided on marriage out of habituation to sex and had chosen a fiancée who would bring financial support to his career.[93] The same alternatives, marriage and celibacy, now stood before him, but he realized that he could adopt neither of them within a Christian ethic if he acted out of selfish motives.[94] Just at this point, Pontitianus, a visiting compatriot, told Augustine the story of the monk Antony, who had undertaken a life of extreme asceticism in the Egyptian desert.

90. *Conf.*, VIII, iv, 9, *CSEL, 33,* 177.

91. Ibid., vi, 13, *CSEL, 33,* 180.

92. Ibid., v, 10, *CSEL, 33,* 178. On the eloquence of moral example, see also *Epistola* CVIII, *CSEL, 34,* pars 2, 612–34.

93. *Conf.*, VI, vi, 9; xi, 20–xiii, 23, *CSEL, 33,* 122–23, 134–37.

94. Ibid., VIII, v, 11–vi, 13, *CSEL, 33,* 178–81.

Pontitianus also related that a number of prominent young men, counseled by Scripture, had been inspired to follow Antony's example.[95] Contrasting himself to them, Augustine was struck by his own irresolution, his ties to wealth, fame, and sensual pleasure, and his unwillingness to take a moral stand on these matters that would conform to the dictates of his conscience.[96] In this state of internal division, he withdrew to the garden of his home with Alypius, where, self-condemned, he prayed for God's help. The famous cry, "Take up and read," turned his thoughts once again to Antony:

> For I had heard of Antony, who was admonished by reading the Gospel which he came upon by chance, as if what he read was being addressed to him personally: 'Go, sell all you have, give to the poor, and you will have treasure in heaven; and come, follow Me' [Matt. 19:21]; and this oracle converted him to You at once.

Augustine could procrastinate no longer. He took up St. Paul's Epistle to the Romans, and the book fell open to the text which specified the solution to his own particular moral dilemma: "Not in rioting and drunkenness, not in chambering and wantonness, not in strife and envying: but put on the Lord Jesus Christ, and make no provision for the flesh in its lusts" [Rom. 13:13–14]. At once he was suffused with the certainty that he could and should live in this way: "At the end of this sentence, a light, as of security, instantly irradiated my heart, and all the clouds of doubt dissolved."[97]

95. Ibid., vi, 14–15, *CSEL, 33,* 181–82.

96. Ibid., vii, 17; ix, 21; xi, 25–27, *CSEL, 33,* 184–85, 187–88, 191–93.

97. Ibid., xii, 29, *CSEL, 33,* 194–95. Professor Roland H. Bainton has brought to my attention that the child's cry, *"Tolle, lege,"* is another instance, like Augustine's chance remark to Alypius, in which a speaker expresses God's will involuntarily. See Courcelle, *Les Confessions,* pp. 133–63, for an illuminating discussion of the *tolle, lege* theme as a literary *topos* in classical and early Christian writings, a discussion which forms part of an extended analysis of the stylistic influence of the Platonists on the style of the *Confessions,* pp. 17–197.

Augustine's conversion to Christianity had been achieved.[98] In his decision to read these biblical words and to accept what they said as the foundation of his personal morality, he assented to the Incarnation as the criterion of his life and his metaphysical and moral speculation. The relevance of Christian ethics and Christian theology would have been unthinkable without the actuality of the Incarnation, and Augustine found that the doctrine and the task required the same humility of spirit. It is this humility, this reverence for the object of knowledge, as well as the alteration of his ideas, which is the keynote of the cognitive experience underlying Augustine's conversion, and his whole theology. And it is through speech —literally, the words of Scripture, and figuratively, the eloquence of moral example—that he grasped a distinctive methodology of knowledge, which he saw as a corollary of the distinctive doctrinal content and system of values of the Christian faith.

Many commentators on the *Confessiones* come to a halt at this point. After shepherding Augustine safely through his conversion, they seem to lose interest in him. But, from the point of view of Augustine's theory of words as signs in the knowledge of God, the last four books of the *Confessiones* are as important as the first part of the work, since it is here that he shows how words served to deepen his knowledge of God and to express it to others after he had received the gift of

98. Cf. Prosper Alfaric, *L'Evolution intellectuelle de Saint Augustin* (Paris, 1918), *1,* viii–ix and passim, who holds that Augustine was successively a Manichee and a Neoplatonist until the age of forty-six, when he finally became a Christian. Alfaric seems content to locate Manichean and Neoplatonic ideas in the writings of Augustine, without discussing the uses he made of them in their respective contexts. This latter approach is also found in Henri-Irénée Marrou, *Saint Augustin et la fin de la culture antique,* Bibliothèque des écoles françaises d'Athènes et de Rome, *145* (Paris, 1938), 242 ff., with respect to Augustine's style. Marrou thinks that Augustine's use of verbal arguments in his early works is a reflection of his classical education and indicates an incomplete grasp of Christian theology in the first few years after his conversion. This usage, however, is quite relevant to Augustine's theology, and is found in his later works also.

faith. Thus, in Books IX and X of the *Confessiones*, where Augustine presents himself as a neophyte Christian, he also begins to illustrate the functions of redeemed speech in the Christian life. The first function of words to and about God is theology, which Augustine describes as a confession of faith and an offering of praise and thanksgiving: "You have broken my bonds . . . I offer You the sacrifice of praise. My heart and my tongue praise You, and all my bones say, 'Lord, who is like You?' " [99] Augustine then depicts the new birth in faith which he experienced as a linguistic rejuvenation. He could now speak to God as unabashedly as a child: "I prattled to You," he says.[100] As a Christian, he no longer found it possible in good conscience to continue the profession of a *vendor verborum*,[101] although legally he might have done so until his baptism. He decided, therefore, to retire with some like-minded friends to a country house in Cassiciacum, outside Milan, so that they could prepare themselves for their reception into the Church.

In Books IX and X of the *Confessiones* Augustine centers his treatment of redeemed speech on its intensive functions, its role in deepening the believer's knowledge of God and of himself, and its uses in communicating the fruits of contemplation to other believers. The verbal media which Augustine stresses here are prayer, the reading of the Bible, Christian conversation, and the meditation of the believer. It will be noted that all of these channels of knowledge had been significant occasions of grace in the story of Augustine's conversion. He continues to view them as channels of Christian instruction within the Christian life. Or, put another way, for Augustine the Christian life is a continuous process of conversion.

Prayer, largely inspired by the reading of the Bible, and the

99. *Conf.*, IX, i, 1, *CSEL, 33,* 196. See also I, vii, 12; II, vii, 15; V, i, 1; IX, viii, 17; xiii, 36; XI, ii, 3; XII, ii, 2; xxiv, 33, *CSEL, 33,* 10, 40–41, 89, 210, 224, 281, 311, 334. This usage of the word *"confessio"* was first noted by Courcelle, *Recherches*, p. 14.

100. *Conf.*, IX, i, 1, *CSEL, 33,* 197.

101. Ibid., ii, 2; v, 13, *CSEL, 33,* 197, 206.

46

Scriptures themselves figure predominantly in Book IX of the *Confessiones* as types of religious dialogue which help Augustine to know God and himself.[102] Conversation with other Christians is still another verbal means of deepening these kinds of knowledge. Once established at Cassiciacum, Augustine wrote a series of five dialogues, which, he says, reproduce actual discussions that he held with the group, or with himself.[103] The *Contra academicos, De beata vita, De ordine, Soliloquia,* and *De immortalitate animae* were Augustine's first compositions as a Christian. Written in the dialogue form and involving the participation of his companions, they reflect his desire to reinforce his faith by philosophical debate, since they deal with a number of currently mooted ethical and epistemological questions which his recent conversion had solved for him on a religious basis. The five dialogues, read in chronological order, also reveal a progressive spiritual growth among the interlocutors themselves.[104]

Even more remarkable is Augustine's conversation with Monica, which takes place shortly after his baptism and a few days before her death. The passage deserves to be quoted at length:

> We were conversing together very sweetly. . . . Between ourselves we wondered . . . what the future eternal life of the saints would be like. . . . And when speech had brought us to the point where no sensuous delight and no corporeal light whatever could compare with the joy of that life, . . . lifting ourselves with a more ardent yearning to that life, we traveled gradually through corporeal things and through heaven itself. . . . And still we ascended, by inward thought, by speech, and by marveling at Your works. And we came to our own minds and transcended them, in order to arrive at

---

102. Ibid., iv, 8–12; xii, 32, *CSEL, 33,* 202–06, 221–22. See also XII, xiii, 16; xxiii, 32; xxvii, 37; XIII, xxix, 44, *CSEL, 33,* 320, 333, 337–38, 381.

103. Ibid., IX, iv, 7, *CSEL, 33,* 201–02.

104. Courcelle, *Recherches,* p. 36.

> the place . . . where life is that Wisdom by Whom all
> these things were made. . . . And while we were speak-
> ing and longing for it, we attained it, in some slight de-
> gree, with the undivided striving of the heart. . . . Then
> we returned to the noise of our mouth, where words both
> begin and end.[105]

During this discussion, Augustine and Monica receive a momentary intimation of the joyful state that transcends the created universe, the mind of man, and human language, all of
which come into being and pass away. Heaven, they speculate,
must be the state in which men can know and love God without the need for the modes of indirect discourse through which
He addresses them on earth:

> If, for any man, the tumult of the flesh were silent; if
> the images of the earth, the waters, and the air were si-
> lent; if the poles were silent; if the soul itself were silent,
> and transcended itself by not thinking about itself; if
> dreams and imaginary revelations were silent—for to
> him who listens, they all say, 'We did not make our-
> selves, but He Who abides in eternity made us'—if, hav-
> ing said this, they were silent and He spoke, raising our
> ears to Himself Who made them, not by the voices of
> angels, nor by the noise of the thundercloud, nor by the
> riddles of a simile (*per aenigma similitudinis*), but by
> Himself, Whom we love in these things; were we to hear
> Him without them, . . . and if it continued like this,
> . . . would it not be entering into the joy of the Lord? [106]

This passage has a strongly Neoplatonic cast, particularly
in its stress on the ascent beyond the temporal and material

105. *Conf.*, IX, x, 23–24, *CSEL, 33,* 216–17.
106. Ibid., 25, *CSEL, 33,* 217–18. Cf. Joseph A. Mazzeo, "St. Augustine's
Rhetoric of Silence," *Journal of the History of Ideas,* 23 (1962), 175–96, who
stresses the Platonic, while neglecting the biblical, sources of Augustine's doctrine
of the mimetic transience of language. Conversely, Burnaby, *Amor Dei,* pp.
78–79, stresses Augustine's biblical sources to the exclusion of all others.

modes of knowledge to the level of timeless, nondiscursive contemplation, through a series of graduated steps. The passage is also strongly Pauline, and it illustrates Augustine's tendency to view all channels of religious knowledge in verbal terms. For Augustine, created things of all kinds, various signs and symbols, are "spoken" media through which men may know God in this life. They provide the Christian striving to mature in Christ with a means of growth in the knowledge of God on a day-to-day basis. At the same time, the knowledge of God which they afford is necessarily limited, since earthly life is itself limited. Furthermore, it is conditioned by its propaedeutic role. The function of life on earth, according to Augustine, is to prepare the Christian for the vision of God in the life to come. Earthly ways of knowing are necessary, but they have a term. They reach the end of their usefulness in the life of the Christian when he leaves his earthly life and enters into life eternal. Augustine and Monica perceive the quality of this eternal life in their brief foretaste of heaven. In heaven, the things which serve on earth as cognitive channels between God and man fall silent, for their work is done. All languages, whether literally or figuratively verbal, will cease, for the heavenly communion is beyond language.

It is a deep and intimate conversation between Augustine and Monica which is the setting for their foretaste of heaven. From the point of view of Augustine's Incarnational theology, it is through words that we move from verbal to transverbal knowledge of God. As we have seen, a dynamic relationship between God and man is initiated and sustained, for Augustine, in and through the temporal, material conditions of human existence, by virtue of the Incarnation. This in no sense means that in moving from earth to heaven the Christian leaves the Incarnation behind him. In the knowledge of God, Christ is the beginning, the way, and the end. In his repeated encounters with the Christ Who acts in time, the Christian grows in the knowledge and love of God through verbal means, broadly conceived. In his eternal communion

49

with God in heaven, the Christian knows and loves the Christ Who is at once the timeless principle of creation and the resurrected Lord, through nothing other than Himself.

The conversation with Monica which suggests these thoughts, then, considerably enhances Augustine's understanding of the importance of life on earth for the Christian. He portrays his developing spirituality in describing his reaction to the death of Monica. Death cannot be made incidental, and Augustine mourns for Monica effusively. At the same time, he knows now that her death is her initiation into life everlasting, in which Monica, Augustine, and all the saved may be united.[107]

The believer's knowledge of God may be deepened by meditation as well as by conversation. This idea occupies most of Book X of the *Confessiones*. Augustine also takes this occasion to point out that meditation has a social function within the community of believers. The contemplative, he says, must serve others with his voice and pen; he must share his words with others so that all may share the same knowledge and joy.[108] The theology arising from meditation, he explains, helps others by presenting them with the example of the theologian's mind at work, as well as with the fruits of its labors. Since it is a way of knowing God, meditation is a form of verbal expression; Augustine defines thought as interior speech.[109] Underlining the contrast between the post-linguistic knowledge of God in eternity and the knowledge of God through speech on earth, he prefaces this meditative section of the *Confessiones* by restating St. Paul's maxim emphatically: "And truly we see now as in a glass darkly (*per speculum in aenigmate*), not yet face to face." [110]

Augustine's meditations in Book X are concerned with three

107. *Conf.*, IX, xii, 29–xiii, 37, *CSEL, 33,* 220–26. Note the parallel here to the death of Augustine's friend in Book IV.

108. Ibid., X, iii, 3–4, 6; IX, xiii, 37, *CSEL, 33,* 227–30, 225–26.

109. Ibid., X, ii, 2, *CSEL, 33,* 227. Cf. *De trinitate,* XV, x, 18, *PL, 42,* 1070–71.

110. *Conf.*, X, v, 7, *CSEL, 33,* 231.

50

questions: "What is God?," "How do we know God?," and "Why do we seek God?" He answers the first of these questions in a metaphorical dialogue. In order to establish that God is the creator of the universe, he addresses the earth, the heavens, the self, the whole created universe, asking them if they are God. When necessary, he personifies the respondents so that they can reply, "I am not He; He made me."[111] Next, Augustine takes up the question of how we know God. He solves this problem by turning the discussion back upon himself, centering his meditation on the nature of man, God's most wondrous and mysterious creature. The aspect of human nature on which this meditation comes to rest is the memory, since the knowledge of God can be found within it.[112]

Here follows Augustine's famous passage on memory, a section of the *Confessiones* so often interpreted as a rich, though irrelevant, digression. However, Augustine has good reason to discuss the memory, and to discuss it just at this point in the work. He is concerned here with the methodology of the knowledge of God. It is characteristic for him to advise the seeker to look within himself for this knowledge. But, once the searcher's gaze has been directed within, why should it fasten on the memory, rather than on some other faculty of the soul? At the end of the passage on memory Augustine suggests an answer to this question. The knowledge of God requires the use of memory, he states, because it is a knowledge learned as the truth at a particular point in time. Since the time when it was first learned, the knowledge of God, like the rest of man's knowledge, has been stored away in his memory. The memory also makes knowledge accessible, on call, to his present attention.[113] Augustine is attempting to distinguish here between his view, that the knowledge of God is learned in time and is accessible to the mind thereafter through the memory, and the Platonic view, that truth preexists in the mind from eter-

111. Ibid., vi, 8–10, *CSEL, 33*, 231–34.
112. Ibid., viii, 12 ff., *CSEL, 33*, 234 ff.
113. Ibid., xxiv, 35–xxvi, 37, *CSEL, 33*, 253–55.

nity and is made present to the mind through dialectically aroused reminiscence.[114]

Augustine's epistemology requires the active participation of the memory in any case. Since he holds that learning takes place through the transient, sensory medium of language, the memory is essential to the existence of sustained cognition of any kind. The memory creates a kind of artificial simultaneity. Words, phrases, and longer stretches of discourse represent, sensuously speaking, a series of sounds, which can neither be enunciated nor received aurally at the same time as each other. Through the memory, sounds which have already ceased to reverberate in time can still be retained in the present consciousness of the mind. Were it not for this function of memory, the receptive powers of the mind would be crippled. The mind would only be capable of perceiving the concrete single sound actually being spoken to it at any given moment. Man's ability to learn and to contemplate would thus be reduced to the intellectual appropriation and retention of things and ideas capable of being expressed in words of one syllable. Of all the faculties of the soul, therefore, the memory is supremely relevant to Augustine's discussion of the methodology of knowledge.

Augustine answers the third question, "Why seek God?," by developing the idea that the knowledge of God is equivalent to the happy life. Indeed, he defines beatitude as *gaudium de veritate,* joy in the truth. All men naturally seek a happiness that can never be lost, he states. If his definition of beatitude is accepted, he argues, it is easy enough to prove that they will find it perfectly in God alone.[115] Augustine's definition of beatitude bears some examination. Joy in the truth is an arresting idea, but from a logical point of view it is slightly out of order. Why should joy and truth be linked in this way? One tends to think of joy primarily in a moral context, as the concomitant of the possession of the good. On the other hand,

114. See above, p. 5; *De trinitate,* XII, xv, 24, *PL, 42,* 1011–12.
115. *Conf.,* X, xx, 29–xxiii, 33, *CSEL, 33,* 248–52.

one tends to think of truth primarily in an epistemological context, as the goal of knowledge. Augustine's combination of these two notions is not accidental. By interweaving truth and joy in his definition of beatitude, he is expressing in terminal form one of his favorite ideas, the interdependence of morality and cognition. Since he stresses this interdependence frequently, it is not surprising that he should conclude his discussion of meditation as a means to the knowledge of God by noting that a deepened consciousness of God will result in a deepened consciousness of the self in relation to God. The better a Christian knows himself, Augustine asserts, the more he realizes his sinfulness before God.[116] The struggle against sin is a permanent feature of his life on earth. Augustine adds a lengthy passage in which he catalogues the various temptations that the Christian must expect to face, organizing them under the Johannine headings of *concupiscentia carnis, concupiscentia oculorum,* and *ambitione saeculi.*[117] The present life, the time of faith, is also a time of trial. This situation, Augustine stresses, should inspire hope rather than despair. The Incarnation, which makes possible the redemption of language on which man's present knowledge and expression of God are based, also encompasses the Passion and the Resurrection, which enable man to die to sin and to live again in Christ.[118] The proximate and ultimate goal of Christian ethics and Christian epistemology, therefore, is newness of life, a life that is both goodness and truth.

Augustine has already outlined the social function of redeemed speech on the intensive level. It commemorates for the believer and his audience a prepossessed knowledge of God, and it raises that knowledge through words to the present awareness of the mind. After his ordination to the priesthood, Augustine notes, the scope of his theological activities widened to include the extensive use of speech, not only

116. Ibid., v, 7; xxviii, 39 ff., *CSEL, 33,* 231, 255 ff.
117. Ibid., xxx, 41 ff., *CSEL, 33,* 257 ff.
118. Ibid., xliii, 68–70, *CSEL, 33,* 278–80.

in preaching, but also in evangelizing men ignorant of God and in attempting to convince his doctrinal adversaries, both inside and outside the Church.[119] Augustine gives us a picture of himself as an apologist in those passages in the *Confessiones* where he censures the heterodox use of words about God as *flatus vocis*. We are given a glimpse of his budding zeal to correct the putative errors of others with the curious amalgam of solicitude and righteous indignation characteristic of the later Augustine in his polemical stance.[120] Faced with the problem of speaking about God with people who disagreed with him, Augustine was forced to conclude that, although redeemed speech may be truly expressive, it is not always completely efficacious in conveying the knowledge of God.[121] Words, he had to acknowledge, have both cognitive powers and cognitive limitations.

In becoming a catechist, an exegete, and a preacher, then, and in assuming the responsibility for training other men for these tasks, Augustine found it desirable to analyze at some length just how extensive these powers and limitations were. He does this most thoroughly in his *De magistro* and his *De doctrina christiana*, two treatises of central importance to his theory of knowledge. At this point it will be well to leave the *Confessiones* for the time being in order to discuss the *De magistro* and the *De doctrina christiana* as fully as their importance warrants, and to take up the question of the sources of the sign theory which Augustine elaborates in these works.

Augustine's first *ex professo* treatment of signification appears in the *De magistro*, a dialogue between Augustine and his son Adeodatus. Their discussion of the cognitive function of language is prefaced by a description of how words signify. Augustine quickly establishes that words are acoustic signs, which correspond accurately to the realities they represent. This correspondence, however, is partial, and it does not con-

119. Ibid., XI, ii, 1; xxx, 40; XII, xvii, 24–25; xxv, 34, *CSEL, 33,* 281, 309, 325–27, 334–35.

120. Ibid., IX, iv, 8, *CSEL, 33,* 202–03.

121. Ibid., X, iii, 3; vi, 10; XI, iii, 5; viii, 10; xi, 13, *CSEL, 33,* 227–28, 233, 283–84, 287, 290.

stitute identity with the things signified. Nevertheless, he says, signs are not inferior to their significata. Of all the various kinds of signs, states Augustine, words are the most universally useful and necessary. While other signs can only signify things, words can signify other words as well as things. They also adapt more readily than do other kinds of signs to the task of showing the nature of realities accurately, since they can be used to describe the limitations inherent in any given instance of signification, thus helping the reader to correct for error. The real significance of words is so thoroughgoing that a person may even speak the truth without knowing it. It is also possible to make false statements, Augustine notes. But the responsibility for this lies entirely with men. It occurs when they speak lies, thus deliberately perverting the true significance of words, or when a speaker is so inept as to define his terms too poorly for them to express what he means to say.[122]

Having described the nature of words as signs, Augustine moves on to discuss their function in knowledge. Speech, he says, serves the hearer either by commemorating or by indicating a knowledge that God provides. In neither case is language cognitive in the first instance:

> The import of words . . . consists in this: they serve merely to suggest that we look for realities. These they do not exhibit to us for our knowledge. . . . It is indeed purest logic and most truly said that when words are uttered we either know what they signify, or we do not know. If we know, we recall rather than learn; but if we do not know, we do not even recall, though perhaps we receive the impulse to inquire.[123]

122. *De magistro,* II, 3–IV, 10; VII, 19–20; IX, 28–X, 30; XIII, 41, *CSEL, 77,* 6–16, 26–29, 37–40, 50. See also *Epistolae* VII, CXLVII, xvii, 43, *CSEL, 34,* pars 1, 13–18; pars 3, 317–18; *Enarrationes in Psalmos* III, 5; IV, 2, 4; XXXVI, serm. I, 1; LXXVII, 3; LXXX, 2; XCVII, 3; CIII, serm. I, 13, *CC, 38,* 10, 14, 15, 336–38; *CC, 39,* 1067–68, 1122, 1374; *CC, 40,* 1485–86; *De fide et symbolo,* IX, 17, *CSEL, 40,* 18–20; *Soliloquia,* II, xi, 20, *PL, 32,* 894–96.

123. *De magistro,* XI, 36, Colleran, 175–76. See also VIII, 22; X, 33–35, *CSEL, 77,* 45–46, 30–32, 43–45. The idea that speech, for Augustine, has both indicative and commemorative functions has been noted by Paolo Rotta, *La*

(Augustine illustrates the commemorative function of speech in the *De magistro* in terms of two activities carried on by the Christian believer, prayer and the reading of Scripture. Speech in prayer, according to Augustine, is not used to convey information to God, Who has no need of this service. Rather, it is used for the benefit of men. It reminds them to Whom to pray and what to pray for. It recalls from their memories the reality of God as they believe Him to be, and encourages them to rededicate themselves willingly to Him.[124] Implicit in this interpretation of speech in prayer is the idea that the believer has an anterior knowledge of God, which his memory stores away for him. This previously acquired knowledge of God is also brought to bear on the believer's study of the Bible. Here again, notes Augustine, the words on the sacred page would have no meaning for the reader without his anterior faith.[125] He reads the Bible to deepen his knowledge of God. He already believes what he reads, but in order for faith to ripen into understanding, the believer depends on the intervention of Christ, teaching him from within. Augustine stresses that Christ distributes this illumination as He sees fit. But, he adds, underlining again the importance of morality to knowledge, only as much enlightenment is granted to each man as he is capable of receiving because of his good or bad will.) Before leaving this subject, Augustine also observes that it is necessary to believe many things even though one may not yet, or may not ever, attain to an understanding of them.[126]

---

filosofia del linguaggio nella Patristica e nella Scolastica (Torino, 1909), pp. 112–13. Irwin Lee Glatstein, "Semantics, too, Has a Past," *The Quarterly Journal of Speech, 32* (1946), 49–50, sees this function as solely indicative; K. Kuypers, *Der Zeichen- und Wortbegriff im Denken Augustins* (Amsterdam, 1934), p. 18, and Alberto Caturelli, *La doctrina agustiniana sobre el maestro y su desarrollo en Santo Tomás de Aquino* (Córdoba, 1954), p. 24, see it as solely commemorative.

124. *De magistro*, I, 2, *CSEL, 77,* 4–5.

125. Noted also by Caturelli, *La doctrina agustiniana sobre el maestro*, pp. 23–24. See also *Tractatus in I Ioannem*, XIII, *PL, 25,* 2004–05; *Enchiridion de fide, spe et charitate*, XXXI, 9, *PL, 40,* 247.

126. *De magistro*, XI, 37–38; see also XIII, 41, *CSEL, 77,* 46–47, 50.

The action of Christ, the Interior Teacher, assisted by the words of human teachers, is equally essential in cases where language functions indicatively. Here Augustine brings forward a knowing subject who is not a believer. Unlike the subject in Platonic dialectic, he has no anterior knowledge of God implanted in his soul from all eternity on which to draw. The speaker's words serve only to show him in what direction the realities they represent lie.[127] The subject will not become a believer by perceiving the sign, but by perceiving the reality. This can take place only if Christ wills to teach it to him from within. Nonetheless, human speech remains necessary. Its importance is commensurate to the kind of nonbeliever whom the speaker is addressing. All things that men know, states Augustine, are perceived either through the body or through the mind. With respect to the knowledge of God, the vast majority of men require large quantities of human speech to get them oriented in a Godly direction. The minority need not rely on sensory data in the perception of intellectual entities. They may acquire faith through the reception of God's Word in that inward speech which is personal meditation, rather than by listening at length to other people's descriptions of God.[128] This latter type of person will hence be dependent on an external human speaker to a far lesser degree than the former type, but he will still require some brief indications of Christian doctrine on which to begin his meditations.

In his discussion of Christ as the Interior Teacher, Augustine thus presents a theory of words as signs in the knowledge of God which specifies their status as true, though partial, representations of their objects, and which also clarifies their functions in conveying knowledge to two different kinds of subjects, believers and nonbelievers. Before leaving the *De magistro,* it may be noted that Augustine is so concerned here with emphasizing the links between verbal epistemology and

127. Ibid., X, 33–35, *CSEL, 77,* 43–45. See also *Enarratio in Psalmum* LXXXVII, 10, 13, *CC, 39,* 1215–16, 1218; *De utilitate credendi,* XIII, 28–XIV, 30, *CSEL, 25,* 38; *Epistola* CXLVII, i, 5; ii, 7–iii, 9; vi, 18; viii, 20–ix, 21; xi, 27; xiv, 35, *CSEL, 34,* pars 3, 278–79, 280–83, 289–92, 293–95, 300–02, 308–09.
128. *De magistro,* XII, 39–40; XIII, 41, *CSEL, 77,* 47–50.

57

the Incarnation that he assigns to Christ in this work a role that some Christian theologians accord to the Holy Spirit.

In the *De magistro,* as we have seen, Augustine touches on the Bible as a source of the believer's deepened knowledge of God. In the *De doctrina christiana,* his second major treatment of words as signs, he takes up the subject of the Bible at much greater length. There he sets forth the requirements for the biblical exegete and preacher. The work treats verbal signs as means of the discovery of the Word in the interpretation of the Bible, and as means of expressing the Word from the pulpit. As one would expect in any work of Augustine's dealing with epistemological matters, the whole discussion is set in the context of morality.

Before elaborating his version of the *modus inveniendi* and *modus proferendi* as applied to Scripture, Augustine introduces the distinction between use and enjoyment. Some things, he says, are to be used; others are to be enjoyed. The things that are to be used are not ends in themselves. They are used rightly only when they are ordered to the things that are to be enjoyed. Actually, Augustine only points to one reality that is to be enjoyed—God Himself. To the enjoyment of God, the exegete and preacher must direct all his knowledge and talent.[129] In order for him to do this it is necessary for him to purify his soul. In this connection Augustine inserts a résumé of the theology of salvation, concluding with a passage on the Church, in which, he holds, it is currently available.[130] The specific aspect of moral regeneration that he emphasizes here is the love of self and of other men rightly ordered to God. For the aspiring exegete and preacher, this virtue involves his commitment to serve God and his fellow man through his words. This task requires the dedication of all his technical skill to the study and teaching of Scripture and the recognition that his motive and the norm of his achievement must be charity, the only one of the theological

129. *De doctrina christiana,* I, ii, 3–ix, 9, *CC, 32,* 8–12.
130. Ibid., x, 10–xxi, 19, *CC, 32,* 12–16.

virtues that endures forever.[131] From the moral point of view, then, these are the principles which Augustine thinks should guide the minister of the Word.

The stage is now set for his unfolding of the linguistic principles on which the ministry of the Word likewise depends. The first question that Augustine takes up is the modus inveniendi, the method of acquiring a correct understanding of the Bible. Exegetical technique, he says, depends on the reader's recognition of the facts, events, and words that he finds in the text as signs of Divine realities, and, in turn, on his treatment of signification as a whole in verbal terms. At this juncture, Augustine provides a definition of sign reminiscent of Aristotle: "A sign is a thing which causes us to think of something beyond the impression that the thing itself makes upon the senses." [132] There are several kinds of signs, he states: natural, conventional, and linguistic. Of these kinds of signs, words can be applied most generally. Natural and conventional signs are susceptible of verbal description, but words cannot be described with equal success by signs of any other kind.[133] Thus, Augustine concludes, it is possible to reduce signification as such to verbal signification.

In the reading of Scripture, the exegete encounters signs and things. Things, according to Augustine, require no interpretation. They simply stand for themselves and do not signify anything else. Signs, he says, are essentially things, which, in addition to being things themselves, also refer to other things. Their original character as things remains more or less noticeable even while they are functioning as signs. The degree to which a *res significativa* noticeably retains its original character depends on whether it is a *signum proprium* or a *signum translatum*. The signum proprium signifies liter-

131. Ibid., xxii, 20–xl, 44, *CC, 32,* 16–32. A good discussion of the moral aspect of Augustine's theory of biblical exegesis can be found in T. S. K. Scott-Craig, "On Christian Instruction," *A Companion to the Study of St. Augustine,* pp. 128–29, 139–42.

132. *De doctrina christiana,* II, i, 1, *CC, 32, 32.*

133. Ibid., i, 2–iii, 4, *CC, 32,* 32–34.

ally. Signs in this category begin and end as words. In their capacity as things, words are sounds, but this original character is, on the whole, subsumed by their significative function. The signum translatum, on the other hand, signifies figuratively. In essence it is a nonverbal sign that is conceived in verbal terms by being treated as a metaphor, or a figure of speech with transferred meaning. In practice it retains a large measure of its original character, making the subject aware that it is an independent thing at the same time that it is acting as a sign of something else. Examples of signa translata in the Bible, cited by Augustine, are such symbolic objects and events as the lamb and the story of Abraham and Isaac, both of which refer to the Passion of Christ as well as to themselves.[134]

Augustine thinks that signa propria may best be understood by the study of languages and textual criticism.[135] Languages are also helpful in understanding signa translata, but even more important to the exegete here is a knowledge of arts, sciences, and institutions of all kinds. This factual knowledge will enable him to grasp the similarity between the reality to which the sign refers and the thing from which meaning has been transferred. The exegete is thus licensed to "spoil the Egyptians," to avail himself of the classical heritage, while of course remembering the end to which this knowledge is to be applied.[136] In finding the meaning of a passage in Scripture he should also make use of previous handbooks on hermeneutics, and here Augustine cites Tyconius, a contemporary Donatist exegete, with qualified approval. The principle of charity,

134. Ibid., I, ii, 2; II, x, 15, CC, 32, 7–8, 41. See also De civitate dei, X, 13, CC, 47, 287; De vera religione, L, 98, CC, 32, 250. A useful summary of this part of the De doctrina christiana is provided by Johan Chydenius, The Theory of Medieval Symbolism, Societas Scientiarum Fennica, Commentationes Humanarum Litterarum, 27, 2 (Helsingfors, 1960), 5–8. In our opinion, the discussion of Markus, "St. Augustine on Signs," Phronesis, 2, 70–76, is obscured by the author's tendency to try to make Augustine provide a general theory of signification.

135. De doctrina christiana, II, xi, 16–xv, 22; III, i, 1–iv, 8, CC, 32, 42–48, 77–82.

136. Ibid., II, xvi, 23–xli, 62, CC, 32, 48–76.

60

which Augustine may have derived indirectly from the exegetical tradition of Philo and Origin, is also invoked. One should not attribute immoral motives either to God or to holy persons, he states; nor should Old Testament figures be held accountable for behavior which enjoyed Divine sanction before the Christian era but which has since been proscribed.[137]

Augustine completes the *De doctrina christiana* with a discussion of the modus proferendi, the way of expressing one's knowledge effectively. For the most part this is a restatement of Ciceronian rhetoric, but with a new twist. While Cicero recommends the choice of one out of three styles, the elevated, the moderate, or the plain, depending on the content of one's speech, Augustine notes that Christian oratory always deals with subjects having to do with God, which are thus of equal or comparable grandeur. Hence, he recommends the selection of the style that will make the speaker comprehensible to the widest possible audience.[138] Cicero's stress on the necessity of persuasion is matched by Augustine's insistence on the preacher's apostolic mandate to teach, and his willingness in charity to subordinate elegance to effectiveness.[139] Classical rhetoric relates the orator's ethos to his eloquence, an idea that does not escape Augustine. Aware of the limitations of human language, both in the preacher's understanding of God's Word in Scripture and in his congregation's reception of the Word through his sermons, he concludes by advocating that the Christian teacher reinforce his technical competence with an exemplary moral character and with prayer.[140]

137. Ibid., III, x, 14–xxxvii, 56, *CC, 32,* 86–116.

138. Ibid., IV, vii, 11–xi, 26; xvii, 34–xxvi, 58, *CC, 32,* 123–35, 141–63.

139. Ibid., iv, 6–10; xii, 27–xiv, 31, *CC, 32,* 119–23, 135–38. As it has been well put by Baldwin, *Medieval Rhetoric and Poetic,* p. 60: "In the pulpit the sophistic heresy of art for art's sake becomes intolerable."

140. *De doctrina christiana,* IV, xv, 32–xvi, 33; xxvii, 59–xxxi, 64, *CC, 32,* 138–41, 163–67. Baldwin, *Medieval Rhetoric and Poetic,* p. 67, has noted Augustine's tendency to play on the word *oratio,* using it to mean "speech" and "prayer" at the same time.

61

The *De magistro* and the *De doctrina christiana* firmly anchor Augustine's theory of the function of words in the knowledge of God. As we have seen from our examination of these works, he holds that words may signify God truly, if partially, and that they may signify Him literally or figuratively. This signification is literal when the medium of knowledge is verbal in the first instance. It is figurative when the sign is originally nonverbal, but is "verbalized" by being treated as a metaphor. Whether literal or figurative, no word, for Augustine, conveys the knowledge of God to the subject by itself. The word may make the subject remember God, if he is already a believer; or it may orient the subject toward God if he is not a believer. Christ must act in the subject's mind if the speaker's words are to serve as a catalyst, either for his acquisition of faith or for a deeper understanding of what he already believes. By interpreting all signs as linguistic, Augustine makes it possible for himself to interpret all cognitive intermediaries between God and man as modes of verbal expression. This conception of knowledge as fundamentally verbal is a central principle of Augustine's theology, and, indeed, it is one of his major justifications for having become a theologian in the first place.

It would be quite possible to construct a verbal theory of knowledge, complete with epistemological guarantees and limitations, strictly on the basis of Christian doctrine. If one brought together, for example, the doctrine of the Incarnation as the guarantee that one's words may truly signify God, Christ's mandate to preach the Gospel to all nations, the Pauline idea that men know God on earth by faith, a partial form of knowledge acquired through human intermediaries, and the belief that faith is a gift of God, one would have in a nutshell both the apostolic motive for the expression of the Word and its methodological problems. Augustine does, in fact, bring these doctrines together. They are at the core of his verbal epistemology and those of his medieval successors. In compounding his sign theory and in formulating it in the mode of rhetoric, however, Augustine drew on the classical as well as the Christian tradition. We have already indicated by way of background the discussions of sign theory carried on by classical thinkers. Which aspects of this classical tradition did Augustine adopt? Through what channels did he acquire it? How did he combine classicism and Christianity in working out the sign theory which he analyzes in the *De magistro* and the *De doctrina christiana,* and which he illustrates so vividly in the *Confessiones?*

Judgments on Augustine's classical sources of sign theory must be largely conjectural. It has usually been inferred that Augustine, unlike his medieval successors prior to the twelfth century, was in possession of the greater Cicero rather than merely the *De inventione* and the *Rhetorica ad Herennium,* attributed to him, and that he was thus in a position to grasp the overall aims of Ciceronian rhetoric as well as its stylistic precepts. This assumption appears to be warranted, both in terms of the works that Augustine's training as a rhetorician would have made available to him, and on the basis of the analyzable tendencies of his own writings. This latter remark is particularly applicable to his *De doctrina christiana,* where, as we have seen, we find a picture of the Christian orator revealing a thorough knowledge and appreciation of Ciceronian rhetoric on Augustine's part.[141]

It remains to discuss the ways in which Augustine's noticeably Platonic and Aristotelian notions of language and knowledge found their way into his works. From Plato Augustine appears to have derived the idea that language, bound up in sensory, temporal existence as it is, may be contrasted with a purely spiritual and eternal way of knowing, involving unmediated communication between intellectual subjects and objects of knowledge. From Aristotle he could have acquired some reinforcement for his idea of signs as sensible, along with the confidence that signs really do signify their objects accu-

141. Baldwin, *Medieval Rhetoric and Poetic,* pp. ix, 54–55; Marrou, *Saint Augustin,* passim, and especially p. 407; Testard, *Saint Augustin et Cicéron,* passim.

rately, that signs are plausible indices of things that already exist. It is undeniable that Platonic and Aristotelian ideas on signs appear in Augustine's thought. How did they get there?

In the *Confessiones*, Augustine mentions having read Aristotle's *Categories* and "the books of the Platonists," which have universally been identified as Plotinus and Porphyry in the fourth-century Latin translation of Marius Victorinus. If we assume that Augustine's access to Plato and Aristotle was limited to these works, we would be at a loss to explain how Augustine acquired his command of Platonic and Aristotelian sign theory. The *Categories* contains nothing on this subject, and the Neoplatonists' treatment of Plato's epistemology is confined largely to the extrapolation of such principles as can be developed into an anatomy of mystical experience. We may perhaps tentatively resolve this difficulty if we begin by giving Plato, Aristotle, and Cicero equal treatment as potential sources. If we adopt the working norm that Augustine may be assumed to have read any works which were available to him and whose influence is apparent in his own writings, we may gain a hypothetical answer to the question of sources.

Aristotle's doctrine of signs, which is central to St. Augustine, is found mainly in his logical and rhetorical writings. It is true that these works were not accessible in Latin until Boethius translated some of them in the early sixth century. This fact does not in itself rule out the possibility that Augustine read them. By his own testimony, he learned Greek as a boy, although without much enjoyment.[142] Moreover, as a young man, he read Aristotle's *Categories,* which was available only in Greek until Boethius' translation. Now if Augustine could

142. *Conf.,* I, xiii, 20, *CSEL, 33,* 18. The whole question of Augustine's knowledge of Greek, and of his use of that knowledge, has undergone considerable scholarly discussion. The most recent review of the literature on this subject is provided by Gerald Bonner, *St. Augustine of Hippo: Life and Controversies* (Philadelphia, 1963), pp. 394–95. Bonner thinks that Augustine developed his childhood training in Greek to the point where he could use it to read works important for his theological and controversial writings. But, as Bonner's analysis of the bibliography shows, there is no consensus on this question.

read the *Categories* in Greek, there is no reason to suppose that he could not have read other works of Aristotle in Greek. Is this, in fact, how he gained his knowledge of Aristotle's definition of signs? We are inclined to argue that it is not. Unless Augustine was able to use pre-Boethian translations of Aristotle which are not now extant, we think it likely that Aristotle's doctrine of signs was transmitted to Augustine through the agency of Cicero. The relevant issue here, we feel, is not Augustine's knowledge of Greek, but rather the framework in which Augustine, Cicero, and Aristotle place their sign theories. As we have noted above, Aristotle subordinates rhetoric to logic, while Cicero subordinates logic, and signification altogether, to rhetoric. In this respect, Augustine has a Ciceronian orientation to signification, despite the fact that his conception of sign is demonstrably Aristotelian in terms of its ultimate provenance.[143] It is, of course, conceivable that Augustine might have read Aristotle in Greek, absorbed Aristotle's sign theory at the source, and then united it on his own initiative with Ciceronian rhetoric. But, given the accessibility of Aristotle's sign theory through Cicero, and given Augustine's extensive dependence on Cicero's rhetoric, we think that the indirect Latin route was more probably the real one.

The issue of Augustine's Platonism is more complex, because there are no known intermediaries who could have supplied him with the information he had. It is true that Augustine may well have received some generalized notion of Plato's epistemology through Cicero and Plotinus. However, neither of these authors presents in any detail those aspects of Platonic epistemology which were directly relevant to Augustine's linguistic concerns. In particular, the relevant topics involve signification in relation to the metaphysical status of sensible things, the possibility of direct intellectual perception of ideal

143. Hessen, *Augustins Metaphysik der Erkenntnis,* pp. 13–14, takes Cicero to be the main channel through which all classical philosophy, Platonic as well as Aristotelian, passed to Augustine. In our opinion, he underestimates the importance of the Aristotelian doctrine of signs in assessing these influences.

65

entities, and the cognitive function of memory. Of Plato's dialogues, the *Meno*, the *Phaedo*, and parts of the *Timaeus* were available in Latin in the fourth century in the translation of Chalcidius. A reading of the *Meno* would have provided Augustine with Plato's classic theory of memory. It is difficult to see how Augustine could have had a working knowledge of the remaining issues without some direct contact with Plato's other dialogues, especially the *Cratylus*. If we assume that a man capable of reading Aristotle's *Categories* in Greek is also capable of reading Plato's dialogues in Greek, however, we may have a tentative solution to this problem. It may perhaps be suggested that "the books of the Platonists" do not represent the sole access Augustine had to Plato's epistemology. It is, of course, possible that he acquired this information by means of the oral tradition of instruction, through *catenae*, translations, or compendia that have not survived, or through his reading of the Greek Fathers.[144] In any case, if it cannot be proved conclusively that Augustine actually did read Plato in Greek, it cannot be proved conclusively that he did not, and he seems to have an awareness of the implications of Plato's theory of knowledge transcending in its wholeness and circumspection that which is displayed by any of the extant intermediaries from whom he putatively derived it.

If it is rash to draw definite conclusions on the question of how Augustine acquired his knowledge of the Platonic and Aristotelian ideas relevant to his theory of words as signs, it also seems rash to rule out the possibility that Augustine may have consulted these philosophers directly, at least if there is no other known way in which he could have gained the knowledge of their ideas which he demonstrably possesses. In the absence of clear proof one way or the other, it would seem the better part of valor to leave the question open.

---

144. Courcelle, *Les Confessions*, p. 51, notes that Augustine was familiar with the myth of the cave appearing in Plato's *Republic*, adding that so was Gregory of Nyssa. Courcelle does not give an opinion on the means by which Augustine gained his knowledge of the myth.

Just as important as the sources of Augustine's classical ideas, however derived, are the uses to which he put them. It is here that the originality of Augustine is most clearly visible. All discussions of signification previous to his time, whether entrenched in a specific epistemology, as with Plato and Aristotle, or separated from epistemological considerations, as with Cicero, began by analyzing sensible data as signs. Words, as a species of sensible signs, were also analyzed by classical thinkers, but they were not held to be of primary importance. Augustine's theory of signification is the first to have concentrated exclusively on verbal signs.[145] His treatment of other kinds of signs is ancillary; he includes it in order to clarify his doctrine of verbal signification. While he retains Aristotle's definition of sign, therefore, he proceeds to reduce all signs to verbal signs. Furthermore, he seems to have used verbal signs, so conceived, to try to bridge the metaphysical and epistemological gap between Plato's two worlds. As the *Confessiones* testifies, Augustine eventually concluded that the Incarnation was the only viable bridge. His theory of sign as word is thus firmly correlated with his Christology, and it is on this basis that he unites those aspects of classical sign theory which he adopts with the Christian doctrines relating to redeemed speech. While, in some respects, this conjunction of ideas sets classical sign theory in a broader context, it also narrows and focuses its range. Since the objects of knowledge which interest Augustine and about which he theorizes are God and the human soul, he limits the application of his sign theory to religious knowledge. This is a type of knowledge which, for Augustine, is acquired less through the natural world as a whole than through man. Thus he did not intend his linguistic epistemology to be either a general theory of signs or a general theory of knowledge.[146] He created it explicitly to cope with

145. Kuypers, *Zeichen- und Wortbegriff*, p. 29; Markus, "St. Augustine on Signs," *Phronesis, 2*, 65.

146. Cf., on the contrary, Markus, "St. Augustine on Signs," *Phronesis, 2*, 69–70; Glatstein, "Semantics, too, Has a Past," *Quarterly Journal of Speech, 32*, 50; Caturelli, *La doctrina agustiniana sobre el maestro*, pp. 35 ff.

the knowledge and expression of the Word in and through human nature.

With the sign theory elaborated by Augustine in the *De magistro* and the *De doctrina christiana* clearly in mind, we may return to the *Confessiones,* where he brings it to bear on the pastoral activities which he shows himself performing after his ordination. In the *De doctrina christiana,* as we have seen, Augustine lays down his rules for the interpretation of the Bible. Scriptural exegesis is undoubtedly one of his favorite occupations, filling as it does the vast bulk of his collected sermons as well as a number of treatises and tracts. It is also one of the interests that he illustrates in the portion of the *Confessiones* devoted to his clerical career. The last three books of the *Confessiones* are largely given over to a literal and anagogical analysis of the first few chapters of Genesis. This text was evidently one of Augustine's favorites, or at least one that he considered problematic, for he commented on it on three separate occasions, in the *De Genesi adversus Manichaeos,* the *De Genesi ad litteram imperfectum,* and the *De Genesi ad litteram* in twelve books. In fact, Augustine's predilection for Genesis has enabled students of his hermeneutical technique to trace his gradual shift from a more to a less figurative type of interpretation.[147] In the books of the *Confessiones* devoted to Genesis, Augustine interprets it literally most of the time and is interested in showing that it may have more than one literal sense.[148] He does not neglect to note the commemorative function of language and the role of the Interior Teacher in the study of the Bible.[149]

147. See Maurice Pontet, *L'Exégèse de S. Augustin prédicateur,* Théologie: Études publiées sous la direction de la Faculté de Théologie S. J. de Lyon-Fourvière, 7 (Paris, 1944) ; Charles Donahue, "Patristic Exegesis: Summation," *Critical Approaches to Medieval Literature: Selected Papers from the English Institute, 1958–1959,* ed. Dorothy Bethurum (New York, 1960), pp. 67–68.

148. *Conf.,* XII, xxv, 34–xxxi, 42, *CSEL, 33,* 334–43. See also *De doctrina christiana,* III, xxvi, 37, *CC, 32,* 99; P. J. Llamas, "San Agustín y la multiplicidad de sentidos literales en la Escritura," *Religión y cultura, 15* (1931), 238–74.

149. *Conf.,* XI, i, 1; XII, xv, 18; xvi, 23; xviii, 27; xx, 29, *CSEL, 33,* 280, 321, 324, 327–28, 329.

Augustine's interpretation of Genesis in the *Confessiones* is also the setting for his famous discussion of time, a passage which, like the passage on memory, has often been regarded as profound but irrelevant to the work. His analysis of time, however, is clearly connected to his exegesis of Genesis, for it is designed to deal with the question "What was God doing before He created the universe?" Augustine answers that God lives in the eternal present, that time did not exist before the Creation, and that the question is hence beside the point. The way in which he arrives at this conclusion is characteristic of his stress on verbal explanations. The reason why the question of God's activities before the Creation occurs to people in the first place, he says, is because they think that time comes packaged in three parts, the past, the present, and the future. This preconceived idea is embedded in their minds at an early age, thanks to their linguistic training. As children in grammar school, they are taught that there are three tenses of the verb, past, present, and future. As a result, they assume uncritically that time itself is likewise tripartite. Actually, observes Augustine, all time is reducible to the present. The past, he says, is the soul's present remembrance; the present is the soul's present attention; and the future is the soul's present expectation. Since this is true for men, he concludes, it should not be so difficult to appreciate the idea of the eternal present when it comes to God.[150]

After interpreting Genesis literally, pausing to discuss the nature of time, Augustine continues with an anagogical treatment of the same text. The anagogical interpretation is one of the three figurative levels of meaning which patristic and medieval exegetes saw in the Bible, in addition to its literal or historical level.[151] The typological application of Augustine's

150. Ibid., XI, xii, 14–xxvii, 36, *CSEL, 33,* 290–307.

151. See, in general, Jean Daniélou, *From Shadows to Reality: Studies in the Biblical Typology of the Fathers* (London, 1960); Henri DeLubac, " 'Typologie' et 'Allegorisme,' " *RSR, 34* (1947), 180–226, and the same author's recent and magisterial *Exégèse médiévale: Les quatre sens de l'Écriture,* 4 vols. in 2, Théologie: Études publiées sous la direction de la Faculté de Théologie S. J. de Lyon-Fourvière, *41, 59* (Paris, 1959–64), especially *1,* part 1; Beryl Smalley, *The Study of the Bible in the Middle Ages* (Oxford, 1941).

theory of signification is clearly visible in cases where he adopts the fourfold method of scriptural exegesis.[152] In such interpretations, Augustine treats the persons, places, objects, events, and cryptic utterances found in the Bible as signa translata. There is only one basic difference between the ordinary run of Augustinian signa translata and his typological signs. Typological signs, like signa translata, involve the metaphorical transference of meaning from one thing to another. But typological signs also involve the transference of meaning across a span of time or from one mode of discourse to another. In the case of allegorical and anagogical interpretations, all that is involved is the transference of meaning in time. The allegorical method views persons, things, and events in the Old Testament as types of persons, things, and events that occur later, in New Testament times, with particular reference to the life of Christ. The anagogical method views persons, things, and events occurring in the Bible as types of the Church of the Saints at the end of time. In the case of the moral or typological method, both transference of meaning in time and the shift from one mode of discourse to another are involved. The moral state of the believer in the present time is the point of reference, and this is a state which is subject to change. Hence, there is a transference of rhetorical styles, usually from the expository to the hortatory.

Important as it is, Augustine does not see the Bible as the only means by which men can know God in the Christian life. Nor does he emphasize Holy Scripture to the extent of excluding other means of this knowledge, which he thinks should be associated with it. In the *Confessiones,* he links extrascriptural knowledge to cognition through Scripture by including them under the same verbal rubric. For Augustine, the reduction of signs to words or to figures of speech has an application that extends far beyond the science of hermeneutics.

152. This tendency is found throughout Augustine's exegetical works. A particularly explicit theoretical statement is found in *De mendacio contra mendacium,* V–VI, CSEL, 40, 419–27.

70

In fact, he holds that all of man's knowledge of God in the life of faith can be treated according to the very same principle of explanation. When communication between God and man takes place by means of what Augustine regards as words, as in prayer, meditation, intellectual intuition, Christian conversation, the writing and reading of theology, and the reception of the Gospel through preaching, he describes this communication as taking place literally. When the knowledge of God is expressed through things, persons, and actions, such as the mirror of the Trinity in the human soul, the sacraments, confessions of faith, and the witness of Christian example, Augustine regards it as operating figuratively. Whether literal or figurative, he holds, the verbal knowledge of God is correlative to the believer's moral transformation in Christ.

The anagogical interpretation of Genesis with which Augustine opens the last book of the *Confessiones* is thus a preface to his discussion of the moral and epistemological operations of the Church. Elsewhere he defines the Church as "the people of God throughout all nations, which is His body, in which are joined and numbered all the saints, who lived in this world even before His coming, and who believed that He would come, just as we believe that He has come." [153] According to Augustine, the function of the Church on earth is to transmit the Christian faith to mankind and to bring the faithful to a shared joy in the vision of God, through the medium of language.[154] As we have seen, his definition of language is a broad one. Thus, for Augustine, the Church, as the corporate extension of the Word into the present, provides a variety of agencies for the verbal interrelationship of God and man. These agencies are a résumé of the literal and figurative signs in the Christian life described above. This life, says Augustine, begins with faith and baptism, which incorporate the in-

153. *De catechizandis rudibus,* III, 6, *PL, 40,* 313–14.

154. *De libero arbitrio,* II, xiv, 38–xv, 39, *CSEL, 74,* 74–75; *Epistolae* CXL, ix, 25–x, 27; CXLVII, xxii, 51, *CSEL, 34,* pars 3, 175–78, 326–28; *Tractatus in Ioannem,* I, 2, 17–19; CI, 5; CXXIV, 5, *CC, 36,* 2, 10–11, 592–93, 683–86.

dividual into the Church.[155] Once enrolled in the Church, he gains access to a new language, with new modes of learning and expression.[156] Thus, in the Creed, the Christian can profess the faith that he holds.[157] He can deepen and share his faith through prayer, through biblical exegesis, and through theology, "interpreting, expounding, discussing, considering, blessing, and invoking You," [158] as well as in the communal sacrifice of the Eucharist.[159] This growth in knowledge, Augustine states, must be matched by moral purification, which should be manifested by a vital concern for the good of the Church, as a whole and in all her members. This concern should be expressed through charity, exemplary behavior, works of mercy, and the witness to God commensurate to one's vocation in the Church. All these practices, he says, strengthen the brethren and show forth to the world the things of God.[160] Christian virtue, he thinks, includes obedience to spiritual authority, in the sense of the norm of faith. The believer should submit willingly to it, says Augustine, even when he does not understand its contents.[161]

It will be noticed that there is nothing particularly unusual either in Augustine's ecclesiology or in his description of the attitudes and practices that make up the Christian life. What is new, however, is the fact that he interprets the various things that Christians say and do in expressing their knowledge and love of God as verbal signs of one kind or another.

According to Augustine, then, the whole of the life of faith provides man with the knowledge of God *per speculum in*

155. *Conf.,* XIII, xii, 13, *CSEL, 33,* 353–54.

156. *Enarratio in Psalmum* LXXI, 8, *CC, 39,* 977.

157. *De fide et symbolo,* I, i, *CSEL, 40,* 3–4.

158. *Conf.,* XIII, xxiii, 34, *CSEL, 33,* 373.

159. Ibid., xxiii, 34; xxvii, 42, *CSEL, 33,* 372, 380; *De civitate dei,* X, 9, *CC, 47,* 281–82; *De libero arbitrio,* III, x, 30, *CSEL, 74,* 115–16. On sacraments in general, see *De doctrina christiana,* II, iii, 4; III, ix, 13, *CC, 32,* 33–34, 85–86; *Enarratio in Psalmum* XVI, 5, *CC, 38,* 92; *Epistola* XCL, x, 27, *CSEL, 34,* pars 3, 177–78.

160. *Conf.,* XIII, xvii, 20–xxii, 32, *CSEL, 33,* 359–71.

161. Ibid., xxiii, 33, *CSEL, 33,* 371–72.

aenigmate.[162] Many "words," both literal and figurative, are at work in this process. But of all of them, he singles out one for very extensive treatment—the soul of man. Genesis, says Augustine, presents us with the doctrine of the Trinity, the most imponderable of all Christian beliefs. As an aid to the understanding of this mystery of faith, he adduces the soul of man, the most mysterious of God's creations.[163] This is a line of argument which Augustine touches on only briefly in the *Confessiones,* but which he develops at great length in the *De trinitate,* his most mature speculative work. From the point of view of Augustine's sign theory, the *De trinitate* bears comparison with the *De magistro* and the *De doctrina christiana,* even though it is a different kind of treatise from either of them. Each of these three works is important enough to warrant analysis in its own right. Also, each of them has a limited epistemological objective. In the case of the *De trinitate,* Augustine confines himself to the question of how God may be known through the Trinitarian analogies in the human soul. Concerned solely with religious knowledge, the *De trinitate,* like the *De magistro* and the *De doctrina christiana,* does

162. *Enarrationes in Psalmos* XXXVII, 15; XLVI, 1; XLVIII, serm. I, 5, *CC, 38,* 394, 529, 554; *Sermo LIII in Mattheum V: 3–8,* VI, 6; X, 10–11, *PL, 38,* 366, 368–69; *Tractatus in Ioannem,* I, 4; XIV, 8; XCVIII, 1; CII, 3; CXXIV, 6, *CC, 36,* 2, 146–47, 572–73, 595–96, 687; *De spiritu et littera,* XXIII, 38; XXIV, 41; XXVIII, 49, *CSEL, 60,* 191, 194–95, 204–05, *Retractationum,* I, xiii, 3, *CSEL, 36,* 67; *De civitate dei,* XIX, 27, *CC, 48,* 697–98; *Epistola* XCII, *CSEL, 34,* pars 2, 436–44.

163. *Conf.,* XIII, v, 6–xi, 12, *CSEL, 33,* 348–53. See also *De doctrina christiana,* I, xii, 12, *CC, 32,* 12; *De civitate dei,* XI, 26–28, *CC, 48,* 345–49; *Sermo LXXX in Mattheum XVII: 18–20,* passim, *PL, 38,* 493–98; *Tractatus in I Ioannem,* III, 7, 9, *PL, 25,* 2000–01, 2002; *Tractatus in Ioannem,* XIV, 7, *CC, 36,* 145–46. For a well-informed discussion of the pure or purified soul as a mirror of God in Greek patristic thought, with its classical and biblical sources, see Gerhart B. Ladner, *The Idea of Reform: Its Impact on Christian Thought and Action in the Age of the Fathers* (Cambridge, Mass., 1959), pp. 92–102, and, less recently, Hans Leisegang, "La connaissance de Dieu au miroir de l'âme et de la nature," *Revue d'histoire et de philosophie religieuses,* 17 (1937), 145–71; Johannes Behm, "Das Bildwort vom Spiegel I. Korinther, 13, 12," *Reinhold-Seeberg-Festschrift,* herausgegeben von Wilhelm Koepp (Leipzig, 1929), *1,* 315–42.

not try to present a general theory of language and signification.[164]

In the *De trinitate,* Augustine illustrates the strengths and
weaknesses of his chosen line of argument obliquely, through
the structure of the work, as well as directly. In the first fourteen books, working from the beliefs that man is made in the
image of God and that God is Triune, he argues that a study
of the created trinities in the human soul will enlighten us as
to the Uncreated Trinity which they signify. Then, in the last
book, after summarizing his previous arguments, he systematically breaks down all the Trinitarian analogies he has just
established, thereby emphasizing the idea that God transcends
all comparisons.

Augustine opens the *De trinitate* with a caveat, reminding
the reader of the difficulty of comprehending the changeless
Godhead through changeable human speech, and stressing the
need for faith, spiritual purification, and recourse to Holy
Scripture[165] Books I through VII are then given over to a
positive exposition of the doctrine of the Trinity, liberally
documented from the Old and New Testaments. After describing the nature of the Trinity *in se* and *quoad nos,* Augustine
devotes the rest of the treatise to the question of how the
Trinity can be known. The thesis of the *De trinitate* is that
man, since he is made in the image of God, can learn about
God by examining himself. Augustine supports this assertion
by outlining a series of Trinitarian analogies in the human
soul. The first one that he presents is the analogy of fraternal
love. We cannot love God unless we love our neighbor, Augus-

164. See, on the contrary, Chydenius, *Theory of Medieval Symbolism,* pp.
8–9; Markus, "St. Augustine on Signs," *Phronesis, 2,* 76 ff. Caturelli, *La doctrina
agustiniana sobre el maestro,* pp. 12–15, provides an accurate summary of Book
XV of *De trinitate.* Alfred Schindler, *Wort und Analogie in Augustins Trinitätslehre,* Hermeneutische Untersuchungen zur Theologie, 4 (Tübingen, 1965),
119–28, provides the most recent summary of the entire work and notes its
sources in Neoplatonism and Greek patristic thought, pp. 44–53.

165. *De trinitate,* I, i, 3; ii, 4; see also VIII, iv, 6–vi, 9, *PL, 42,* 821, 822,
951–56.

tine notes, and this love, though one, is also three: "Now love is the action of a lover; and, through love, something is loved. There are three things here: the lover, the beloved, and love. For what is love but a kind of life, which unites two beings or strives to unite them, namely, the lover and the beloved? . . . And thus there are three things: the lover, the beloved, and love."[166]

The terms of this trinity, love, the lover, and the beloved, are discernible when one loves another person. However, when one loves oneself, they would seem to be reducible to two, since in this case the lover and the beloved are identical. Now love of self, according to Augustine, may properly be charitable. A rightly ordered love of self is a precondition of the charitable love of others. But, how can love of self reflect the Trinity if it is not threefold? Augustine solves this problem by pointing to another Trinitarian analogy within the soul of man. Love of self, he says, can be understood in the interaction of the soul, its knowledge, and its love. The soul must know itself before it can love itself, and, concurrently, it must possess the desire of a lover in order to seek self-knowledge in the first place. A second Trinitarian analogy, that of *mens, notitia*, and *amor*, may thus be added to the first one.[167]

By elaborating this second analogy, Augustine provides a further elucidation of the Trinitarian lineaments of the soul's knowledge and love of itself. When the soul knows sensible things, he notes, it forms sensible images of them, which it then stores in the memory and recalls to mind when it wants to think or to talk about them. As an object of knowledge, however, the soul is not sensible. It gains knowledge of itself by intuition, by pure intellection, and it forms a strictly intellectual image of itself. Any self-knowledge which the soul wishes to convey to others it must express through sensible language. The term that Augustine applies to the soul's intellectual image of itself, or its image of any other object known

166. Ibid., VIII, x, 14, *PL, 42, 960.*
167. Ibid., IX, ii, 2–v, 8, *PL, 42,* 961–65.

by intuition, is *verbum mentis*. On the face of it, verbum mentis would seem to be a highly unlikely choice of terminology. For Augustine, as we have seen, words are sensible signs, occurring in time; and, conversely, all temporal knowledge is inexpugnably verbal. He holds intuition to be a mode of temporal knowledge; yet intuition is purely intellectual. What is one to make of the term "verbum mentis"? Augustine is aware that this term creates a problem. He explains that a verbum mentis, even though it is a verbum, is nevertheless not sensible. At this point, one well may wonder why Augustine has gone to the trouble to coin a phrase which involves him in a stated contradiction in terms. There is an excellent reason why he does this. One must bear in mind that he is discussing self-knowledge in a Trinitarian context, and that he has just illustrated the functional interplay of love and knowledge. Augustine uses the term "verbum mentis" because of the Trinitarian associations it conjures up in the mind of the reader. When the soul knows itself intuitively, when it forms an accurate verbum mentis of itself and is thus in a position to contemplate itself lovingly, it mirrors the relationship of the Three Persons of the Trinity in the eternal generation of the Word.[168] And, it might be added, when the soul communicates itself verbally to others, while retaining its internal verbum mentis, it mirrors the Trinity in the revelation of the Word made flesh.

The interplay of love and knowledge is Augustine's point of departure for his third Trinitarian analogy, that of *memoria, intellectus,* and *voluntas.* In practice, he observes, the memory, the intellect, and the will operate in and through each other; and the soul knows and loves itself through all of them. The soul, he says, gains knowledge of itself through the intellect; the soul retains knowledge of itself through the memory; the soul loves itself through the will. The life of the soul, he

168. Ibid., IX, vi, 9–xii, 18; X, i, 1–iv, 6, *PL, 42,* 965–77. Augustine's idea of *verbum mentis* should not be confused with the term as used by St. Thomas Aquinas. See below, pp. 172–73.

adds, is manifested integrally in the activities of its memory, intellect, and will. These three faculties are mutually contained in each other. With the memory, the soul remembers that is has memory, intellect, and will. With the intellect, the soul knows that it knows, remembers, and wills. With the will, the soul wills to will, to know, and to remember. Each faculty independently is hence fully equal to the other two, and each as a whole is equal to all three taken together. Thus, concludes Augustine, the three are one: one life, one soul, one essence.[169]

Up until this point in the *De trinitate,* Augustine has concentrated his attention on the soul's knowledge and love of other men and of itself. Now he goes on to note that the soul can also know and love the created universe and God. According to Augustine, the soul, for the most part, comes into contact with the created universe through sensory experience. He stresses that man's physical nature, unlike his spiritual nature, is not made in the image of God. Properly speaking, therefore, man's knowledge and love of physical objects through his physical senses cannot be treated as an analogy of the Trinity.[170] Nevertheless, Augustine finds it possible to suggest in the case of sensory experience two partial and very weak analogies which are Trinitarian, if only because they include three terms which function as one. In most empirical epistemologies, whether Aristotelian or Lockeian in derivation, the soul is seen to be passive with respect to the senses in the act of sense perception. Augustine, however, sees the soul as active with respect to the senses in the act of sense perception. In Augustine's theory of knowledge, both the affective and the cognitive faculties of the soul are employed when it lovingly grasps or lovingly contemplates a sensible object of knowledge. When the soul grasps a physical object, the will actively directs the senses to form a sensible image of it. The three terms here are the object, its sensible image, and the will.[171] When the soul

169. *De trinitate,* X, xi, 17–18, *PL, 42,* 982–84.
170. Ibid., XI, v, 8, *PL, 42,* 990–91.
171. Ibid., XI, i, 1–ii, 5; v, 9–vi, 10, *PL, 42,* 983–87, 991–92.

contemplates a physical object, the will actively evokes its sensible image from the memory, the three terms in this case being the sensible image, the memory, and the will.[172]

It is, however, in the soul's knowledge and love of God that Augustine sees its interrelated functions of memory, intellect, and will as the best possible analogy of the Trinity. Augustine defines the knowledge and love of God as wisdom (*sapientia*), in contrast to knowledge (*scientia*), a term which he applies to the knowledge and love of created things.[173] Wisdom and beatitude, he states, are correlative, and they are achieved through knowledge. The believer acquires them by virtue of the Incarnation, for God offers in Christ the perfect union between scientia and sapientia: "For Christ is our knowledge (*scientia*), and the same Christ is our wisdom (*sapientia*). He engrafts faith into us through temporal things; He shows forth the truth of eternal things. Through Him we proceed to Him; we aspire to wisdom through knowledge. But we do not depart from the one, same Christ." [174] As the believer grows in wisdom, as the image of God within him is progressively purified and enlightened, the temporal analogy of memoria-intellectus-voluntas is replaced by the eternal analogy of memoria Dei–intellectus Dei–amor Dei. This process represents the believer's transformation in Christ. For Augustine it is also identical to his faithful journey through words to the translinguistic vision of God, and of all things in God.[175] In the state of beatitude, then, the human soul resembles the Trinity as closely as anything can. The three interrelated faculties of the soul have God as their object, and, like the

172. Ibid., iii, 6–7; vii, 11–viii, 15, *PL, 42,* 988–90, 993–96.

173. Ibid., XII, xiv, 21–23; XIII, i, 1–2, *PL, 42,* 1009–11, 1013–14.

174. Ibid., XIII, xix, 24, *PL, 42,* 1033–34.

175. Ibid., XIV, ii, 4–iv, 7; xii, 15–xix, 26, *PL, 42,* 1038–41, 1048–58. As Burnaby, *Amor Dei,* pp. 80–81, has observed, the fact that Augustine sees the end of man as the vision of God in no way implies that the will is subordinate to the intellect or vice versa. Since Augustine uses the interrelationships of the faculties of the human soul to suggest the Trinity, his "absolutely co-equal Trinity imposes upon him a refusal of all 'subordinationism' in dealing with the spirit of man and its destiny."

Trinity, the soul in this condition knows and loves God through God Himself.

Having built up the foregoing analogies with great care and profundity, Augustine occupies himself with breaking them down in the final book of the *De trinitate*. His aim here is to restate the point that God is ineffable, and that He towers infinitely over anything men can say about Him. Our knowledge of God in this life, reaffirms Augustine, is partial and shadowy. It is the knowledge of faith, *per speculum in aenigmate,* and it is acquired and expressed through speech. Augustine's use of the term "aenigma" in this connection is quite important. It will be remembered that Cicero defined an aenigma as a figure of speech. At the close of the *De trinitate*, Augustine also reminds the reader that an aenigma is a rhetorical trope, one of the subdivisions within the category of allegory.[176] He describes aenigma as "a kind of simile, but obscure and difficult to understand," and adds, "by the terms 'mirror' and 'aenigma' we understand the apostle to have signified certain similes, which are accommodated to our understanding of God, in the way in which this is possible." [177]

As figures of speech go, aenigmata are admittedly difficult to grasp. But their very obscurity may also enable them to function as accurate signs. For Augustine, verbal signs, whether literal or figurative, represent truly, if partially, really existing things. While literal signification is a suitable way to express fairly straightforward realities, metaphorical signification is far better suited to express realities that are themselves intrinsically obscure and difficult to understand.[178] An aenigma, like any other figure of speech, and like speech itself, is designed to communicate information. Its built-in difficulties thus enhance, rather than reduce, its expressive power. In attempting to convey the infinite incomprehensibility of God, then, an aenigma is a most suitable *vox significans rem.*

176. *De trinitate,* XV, ix, 15–16, *PL, 42,* 1068–69.
177. Ibid., 16, *PL, 42,* 1069.
178. *Epistola* CLXXX, *CSEL, 34,* pars 3, 697–700.

The specific aenigma that Augustine has in mind here is, as we have seen, the human soul, with its various structural and functional similarities to the Trinity.[179] In the context of Augustine's sign theory, the soul, as an aenigma, can be treated as a signum translatum, a thing acting as a sign. Once he has conceived of it in this way, he can place the same limitations on the soul as an analogy of the Trinity as he places on words as signs of non-sensible realities. Hence, he circumscribes the soul as created, mutable, and temporal; it is inextricably bound up with the life of the body; it is subject to the gaps between meaning and being and between being and expression. The soul, he concludes, therefore cannot represent perfectly the eternal, uncreated Godhead, in Whom meaning and being, expression and existence, are simultaneous and identical.[180] But, notwithstanding these limitations, Augustine thinks that the aenigma of the human soul provides the fullest knowledge of God that is available in the earthly life, a knowledge, he hastens to add, which would remain extrinsic but for the action of God Himself within the knower. As a means of summarizing the powers and limits of speech in the knowledge of God, Augustine restates one of the central paradoxes in his theory of knowledge at the end of the De trinitate. We can know God as He is only if we become like Him, he says; and we can become like Him only by knowing Him. This appears to be a tautology, but, for Augustine, it is instead a dynamic opportunity, an opportunity which God makes possible by incorporating man into the life of the Trinity through the gift of the Holy Spirit.[181]

As his envoi to the reader of the De trinitate, Augustine poses once more the theologian's dilemma, which he also refers to at the beginning of the Confessiones. In view of the topic that he has set out to discuss, he confesses, he has said noth-

179. De trinitate, XV, x, 17–xi, 21; xx, 39–xxiii, 49, PL, 42, 1069–73, 1088–96.
180. Ibid., vi, 9; vii, 11, 13; xiii, 22–xvi, 26, PL, 42, 1063, 1065, 1066–67, 1075–79.
181. Ibid., xvii, 27–xix, 37, PL, 42, 1079–87.

ing of value. Still, he perforce must speak, and so he offers his words to God and to the reader, in a spirit of prayer.[182] Augustine's conception of the problem of expressing the Inexpressible, and his response to it, sum up his attitude toward redeemed rhetoric. In his own eyes, it would have been impossible for him to have been a theologian without the understanding of the ties between speech and knowledge which the exigencies of his personal life gave him. Once in possession of this understanding, he was moved to formulate it theoretically and to use it in practice in his writings. In doing this, he fused a classical conception of words, both literal and figurative, as the authentic, sensible signs of knowable realities, with the Christian belief that language, redeemed through the Incarnation, was both a necessary and an inadequate means to the knowledge of God. This constellation of ideas is basic to Augustine's epistemology, and it was to become authoritative to later medieval theorists on the knowledge of God. Augustine conceived this linguistic epistemology, and, at the same time, he exemplified it in the mode of rhetoric. In his theological writings, and in his very conception of himself as a theologian, St. Augustine typifies the Christian orator who interprets his vocation as an apostolic expression of the Word.

182. Ibid., xxviii, 50–51, *PL, 42,* 1097–98.

2 ST. ANSELM:
The Definition of the Word

The importance of the place occupied by St. Anselm in the history of medieval epistomology has never been contested. The first theological mind of the highest caliber to appear in Western Europe since the days of the Fathers, Anselm enjoys a prominence assured by the rigor and profundity of his thought as well as by the suddenness with which he seems to emerge in the eleventh century. Anselm's famous argument for the existence of God has usually been regarded as his principal contribution to Western thought. It is, thankfully, no longer necessary to belabor the point that this so-called ontological proof of God's existence is not at all ontological in the sense meant by Immanuel Kant, who invented this peremptory slogan, and who remains, along with St. Thomas Aquinas, the most widely cited opponent of the proof, at least as he understood it. Kant notwithstanding, however, Anselm's proof has managed to attract the attention of a variegated host of supporters and detractors, starting with Gaunilon, an eleventh-century monk of Marmoutiers, and continuing unabated well up to the present day.

Speaking as they do from a congeries of assumptions so ill assorted as to produce in some cases mutually exclusive arguments that nevertheless lead to the same conclusions about the validity or nonvalidity of the proof, most of these critics are united at least by their common tendency to interpret Anselm in anachronistic, and hence irrelevant, categories of thought. This frequently leads them to unhinge the relationships among Anselm's ideas as well as to misconstrue what he thought he was doing in formulating the proof. Anselm fastens on the existence of God in the opening section of the *Monologion*, his first major theological work. He compresses and refurbishes the argument in the first four chapters of the *Proslogion*, re-

82

stating it with some further refinements in his rebuttal of Gaunilon's objections. The attitude toward the cognitive status of theological statements which he adopts in these three works is quite consistent with remarks he makes on this subject in his other writings. Furthermore, an analysis of Anselm's method of argumentation, seen in the light of his wider intellectual aims, reveals that the style of his proof is integrally related to certain cultural developments peculiar to the eleventh century, a fact which also helps to explain why this method, and with it the medieval fortunes of the proof, declined in the decades after Anselm's death almost as rapidly as they had arisen during his lifetime. However, the fact that the proof may be found, already distilled, within the compass of a few easily accessible pages presumably explains why so many commentators seem to think that it can be understood without reference to Anselm's general ideas on theology and epistemology. This idea has, in some cases, progressed to the point where students of Anselm go so far as to abstract the proof from the very works in which the author placed it, thereby severely debilitating their own efforts to interpret its meaning through its location in context.

Anselm's proof, or, more accurately, his speculations on the theology of God's existence and nature, cannot be understood properly when they are approached in terms of anachronistic theological or philosophical categories. Nor can they be appreciated fully in isolation from the work of the man who developed them or from the intellectual milieu in which he labored and to which he spoke. Rather, the meaning of the proof and its place in medieval epistemology can only be grasped historically if they are seen in terms of what they meant to Anselm and to his contemporaries. In particular, it is the aim of this chapter to try to show that Anselm's conception of his famous argument reveals an attitude toward the knowledge of God influenced by the verbal theory of knowledge founded by St. Augustine.

It will be remembered that in this theory of religious knowledge words may represent really existing things truly, if partially, and that they function either commemoratively or indicatively in the subject's mind, depending on his previous relationship to the object. Although seen as an epistemological necessity, verbal signs are never held to be cognitive in the first instance. They must be energized by the action of God in the mind of the knower in order for them to conduce to the knowledge of their significata. These conditions obtain whether the subject be an infidel moving from unbelief to faith or a believer whose faith is deepening into an understanding of what he believes.

This Augustinian doctrine of the significative possibilities of redeemed speech, of the warrants and limitations of language with reference to God, and of its cognitive operations and restrictions on the level of the subject had been so thoroughly absorbed in Western Christian thought by Anselm's time that it became the implicit and unquestioned ambience in which religious epistemology was conceived. The received tradition of the trivium, moreover, although doubtless a pale imitation of the linguistic arts at Augustine's disposal, served nonetheless to make Anselm's conception of knowledge as ineluctably verbal as Augustine's was. At the same time, owing to the cultural developments, problems, and interests of post-patristic Europe, there was a gradual dissociation of Augustine's theory of signs from the rhetorical context in which he had expressed it. The theory was translated from rhetoric into the mode of grammar, a grammar derived originally from Donatus and Priscian, passed on in diluted form by Carolingian scholars, and growing increasingly rationalized in the eleventh century under the impact of a revived interest in Boethian-Aristotelian logic.

The real meaning and importance of Anselm's proof is rooted immovably in these facts of intellectual history. His general ideas of theology and of religious knowledge are derived from Augustine's verbal theory of signs; and the verbal medium in which Anselm himself thinks and works is grammar. Most of his writings, including those containing the proof, manifest his sense of the urgent need to adjust the current notions of grammatical signification to the new and disturbing insights of eleventh-century logic. This quasi-logical grammar is Anselm's basic theological tool; its peculiar, and, as events were to prove, highly transitory methods and presuppositions dictate the operative conditions of his thought as a whole. Like Augustine, then, Anselm's major epistemological concern is the theological problem of speaking about God. But, where Augustine sees the task of theology as the eloquent expression of the Word, Anselm sees it as the conscientious and faithful definition of the Word.

The need to survey the immediate intellectual background of Anselm's thought and to establish the contemporary meaning of his famous proof is impossible to deny. It becomes even more urgent when we survey the conflicting interpretations of Anselm which the anachronistic presuppositions of recent scholarship have provided. To place oneself in the hands of most twentieth-century exegetes is to plunge precipitously into a morass of contradictions, which do a fair job of illustrating some of the intellectual concerns of the twentieth, if not the eleventh, century. Categorizing the commentators into the friends and the foes of Anselm is no way out of the maze, because the reasons adduced in favor of the proof by some of Anselm's adherents are freely disparaged by other, equally vigorous, supporters, while those critics holding the proof untenable are as likely to betray antithetical grounds for rejecting it. It is extremely difficult to classify the views of Anselm scholars; this question has itself already become an issue of learned debate. Acceptance or rejection of Anselm's proof has become virtually meaningless as an index of opinion. It has recently been suggested that Anselm commentators fall into the two groups—or between the two stools—of exaggerated rationalism and exaggerated fideism.[1] While moderately helpful,

1. John MacIntyre, "Premises and Conclusions in the System of St. Anselm's Theology," *Spicilegium Beccense, 1* (Le Bec-Hellouin-Paris, 1959), 95–101.

this rationalist-fideist distinction is still an oversimplification. Before addressing ourselves to Anselm, then, it may be useful to give some indication of the range of modern points of view on his proof; the classical critiques of St. Thomas Aquinas, Locke, and Kant, on the one hand, and of Descartes, Leibniz, and Hegel, on the other, are too well known to warrant repetition here.[2] While the positions to be cited below are, in our opinion, defective in some way or other, they nevertheless do make some positive contribution to the understanding of Anselm. In most cases they err by perceiving only part of the picture and by mistaking the part for the whole. Notwithstanding the fact that this may lead to conclusions about Anselm so tangential as to be almost irrelevant, each of these commentators still manages to illuminate some central truth about him.

By far the largest group of commentators on Anselm is that whose philosophical or theological presuppositions may loosely be described as springing from the tradition of neoscholasticism. Whether agreeing or disagreeing with the proof, the members of this group possess a vocabulary and a conception of the nature of theological and philosophical problems which derive indirectly from the thirteenth century. Generally speaking, the neoscholastics can be divided into two broad subcategories. The first, who perceive correctly, and with much gratification, that Anselm deliberately tries to argue his proof on extra-scriptural grounds, see him in consequence as a "precursor of Aquinas" or as "the father of scholasticism" because of his alleged interest in proving the compatibility between revelation and reason, reason in this context being assumed to mean Aristotelian logic.[3] Anselm's proof thus

2. See Alvin Plantinga, ed., *The Ontological Argument, from St. Anselm to Contemporary Philosophers* (Garden City, N.Y., 1965), for a survey of these arguments.

3. M. T. Antonelli, "Il significato del Proslogion di Anselmo d'Aosta," *Rivista Rosminiana, 45* (1951), 260–68; Joseph Clayton, *Saint Anselm: A Critical Biography* (Milwaukee, 1933), pp. 136 ff.; Etienne Gilson, *A History of Christian Philosophy in the Middle Ages* (New York, 1955), pp. 130, 139; P. Enrico Rosa, *S. Anselmo di Aosta, Arcivescovo Cantuariense e dottore della Chiesa*

emerges as natural theology, as an exercise in pure philosophy. Exercises of this type are generally held by the neoscholastics to be cognitive. Anselm is therefore praised for having formulated a heuristic apology for the reasonableness of Christianity, such apologetic criteria being deemed normative for the work of the discursive theologian.[4] Paradoxically enough, this judgment is still capable of being harmonized in some cases with the standard Thomistic rejection of the proof.[5]

The second wing within the neoscholastic camp is composed of scholars who, while adhering to the canon of Aristotelian logic as the normative tool for discursive theology, still manage to grant a cognitive value to Anselm's proof, while simultaneously emphasizing the non-Aristotelian and nonlogical elements in it. This turnabout is accomplished by underlining the scholastic distinction between discursive and speculative theology. Although they do not admit Anselm to the ranks of the purely philosophical discursive theologians, these commentators readily underwrite the value of the proof, on grounds that Anselm is a mystic,[6] and ultrareal-

---

(Firenze, 1909), pp. 135 ff.; A. van Weddington, *Essai critique sur la philosophie de S. Anselme de Cantorbéry, Mémoires couronnés, 25* (Bruxelles, 1875), pp. 50 ff. and passim.

4. Antonelli, "Il significato del Proslogion," pp. 260–61; D. M. Cappuyns, "L'Argument de S. Anselme," *Recherches de théologie ancienne et médiévale, 6* (1934), 313–30; Clayton, *Saint Anselm,* pp. 136 ff.; F. C. Copleston, *A History of Philosophy* (Westminster, Md., 1957), *2,* 157–59; Le Comte Domet de Vorges, *Saint Anselme* (Paris, 1901), p. 134; Gilson, *History of Christian Philosophy,* p. 133; S. A. Grave, "The Ontological Argument of St. Anselm," *Philosophy, 27* (1952), 30–38; Adolf Kolping, *Anselms Proslogion-Beweis der Existenz Gottes im Zusammenhang seines spekulativen Programms Fides quaerens intellectum* (Bonn, 1938).

5. Fr. Spedalieri, "Anselmus an Gaunilo? Seu de recta argumenti sancti Doctoris interpretatione," *Gregorianum, 28* (1947), 54–77; "De intrinseca argumenti S. Anselmi vi et natura," *Gregorianum, 29* (1948), 204–12.

6. Anton Antweiler, "Anselmus von Canterbury, Monologion und Proslogion," *Scholastik, 8* (1933), 551–60; Charles Filliatre, *La philosophie de Saint Anselme: Ses principes, sa nature, son influence* (Paris, 1920), p. 50; Arrigo Levasti, *Sant'Anselmo: Vita e pensiero* (Bari, 1929), pp. 31–71; Julián Marías Aguilera, *San Anselmo y el insensato y otros estudios de filosofía* (Madrid, 1954), pp. 5–25; Renato Perino, *La dottrina Trinitaria di S. Anselmo nel quadro del suo metodo teologico e del suo concetto di Dio,* Studia Anselmiana

ist,[7] and/or a Neoplatonist.[8] While correct in noting the strongly devotional tendencies in Anselm, these scholars make the mistake of equating uncritically any and all kinds of religious experience with mysticism, and thus preserve the neoscholastic assumption that mysticism and logic, Platonism and Aristotelianism, are the only two alternatives for the Catholic theologian, and that they are parallel roads which never meet.[9]

The devotional timbre of Anselm's thought to which this latter wing of neoscholastics testifies links them with a second major group of commentators, who manifest neither the presuppositions nor the uniformities of neoscholasticism. Despite their heterogeneity, however, the members of this group are united in assuming the priority of experienced faith as the exclusive and irreducible criterion of all theological positions. They extend this assumption to Anselm either for philosophical or for theological reasons, and sometimes for both. We may find this presupposition expressed in the form of a strictly Kantian rejection of Anselm's proof, on the shopworn allegation that it is an ontological proof.[10] We may also find it

---

philosophica theologica edita a professoribus Instituti Pontificii S. Anselmi de Urbe, *29* (Romae, 1952), 28 ff.; Anselm Stolz, *Anselm von Canterbury* (München, 1937), pp. 37–39; " 'Vere esse' im Proslogion des Hl. Anselm," *Scholastik, 9* (1934), 400–06; "Zur Theologie Anselms im Proslogion," *Catholica, 2* (1933), 1–24.

7. Joseph Fischer, *Die Erkenntnislehre Anselms von Canterbury, Beiträge,* Band *10,* Heft 3 (Münster i. W., 1911), 40–42, 66–78; Robert G. Miller, "The Ontological Argument in St. Anselm and Descartes," *MS, 32* (1955), 344; Sofia Vanni Rovighi, *S. Anselmo e la filosofia del secolo XI* (Milano, 1949), pp. 71–72; Maurice de Wulf, *History of Mediaeval Philosophy* (London, 1935), *1,* 165.

8. A. Beckaert, "Une Justification platonicienne de l'argument a priori?," *Spicilegium Beccense, 1,* 185–90; Filliatre, *La philosophie de Saint Anselme,* pp. 20 ff.; Alexandre Koyré, *L'Idée de Dieu dans la philosophie de St. Anselme* (Paris, 1923), pp. vii, 60–99.

9. Paul Evdokimov, "L'Aspect apophatique de l'argument de Saint Anselm," *Spicilegium Beccense, 1,* 233–58.

10. Ferdinand Bergenthal, "Ist der 'ontologische Gottesbeweis' Anselms von Canterbury ein Trugschluss?," *Philosophisches Jahrbuch, 59,* Heft 2 (1949), 155–68; Georg Wendschuh, *Verhältnis des Glaubens zum Wissen bei Anselm von Canterbury: Ein Beitrag zu Anselms Erkenntnistheorie* (Weida i. Thür., 1909).

underlying the arguments of non-Kantian critics who accept the cognitive value of the proof. We have, for example, an Aristotelian who claims, by a somewhat non-Aristotelian distortion of the meaning of "empiricism" so that it is made to include data beyond the limits of the senses, that Anselm has provided an empirical a posteriori proof based on the evidence of his own psychic experience.[11] An analogous argument, without benefit of Aristotle and without sweeping claims, puts forth the view that the proof is valid on the basis of religious empiricism—valid, that is, on the level of knowledge, although noncommittal on the level of being.[12]

Emphasis on the preclusive authhority of individual religious experience and the certainty that it is an authentic guide to exterior realities is heaviest and most intense in the interpretations of scholars whose point of departure is *sola fide* Protestantism. The requirements of this position incline them to see Anselm as a "precursor of the Reformation" and encourage them to reject out of hand any explanation of the proof smacking of pagan rationalism.[13] In recent times, thinkers of this latter school have emerged who applaud Anselm's proof as a nonphilosophical, purely religious foundation for a new, constructive approach to Protestant theology.[14] Moving still farther afield, some of them claim Anselm as a "precursor" of contemporary neo-orthodox Protestant "crisis" theology, a position which, oddly enough, reaffirms fideism and excoriates philosophical arguments with a vengeance notwithstanding its own extensive reliance on categories of thought appropriated from Kant, the existentialists, and the phenom-

11. A. E. Davies, "The Problem of Truth and Existence as Treated by Anselm," *Proceedings of the Aristotelian Society,* n. s. 20 (1920), 167–90.

12. Henry G. Wolz, "The Empirical Basis of Anselm's Arguments," *PR, 60* (1951), 341–61.

13. Walter Betzendörfer, "Glauben und Wissen bei Anselm von Canterbury," *Zeitschrift für Kirchengeschichte, 48,* neue Folge, 11 (1929), 354–70.

14. Helmut Kimmerle, *Die Gottesbeweise Anselms von Canterbury: Ihre Voraussetzungen und ihre Bedeutung für die philosophische Theologie* (Berlin, 1961).

89

enologists. The leader of this movement is Karl Barth.[15] A similar reliance on Kantian epistemology may also be found, *mutatis mutandis,* in an interesting recent discussion of Anselm by Robert S. Hartman. Despite his debt to Barth, Hartman ends by denying the validity of Anselm's proof, terming it a *reductio ad absurdum.* Nevertheless, for Hartman the proof holds out the tantalizing possibility of being truly ontological, on the basis of an as yet undisclosed "meta-Anselmian axiomatic" matrix, which would make logical modes of prediction the criterion of God's existence.[16]

This, however, does not by any means bring our catalogue of critics to an end. The latest group of commentators to direct their attention to Anselm is one that generally derives its insights and assumptions from logical positivism and linguistic analysis, which, for the purposes of Anselm exegesis, may be treated as one movement. These philosophers are correct in noting the importance of grammar in Anselm's proof; this, indeed, explains why the proof has excited such interest within their ranks in the past few years. Although claiming to be epistemologists and speculative grammarians, the linguistic analysts tend to make insinuations about the real order, since, in virtue of the limitations which their point of view entails, they are forced to deny the authenticity of anything which proves recalcitrant in the face of their methodological assumptions. Some linguistic analysts reject Anselm's proof, usually conceiving it as an ontological proof, and, as such, inadmissible because ontologism would make existence a predicate. Their insistence on the idea that no existential proposition is

15. Karl Barth, *Anselm: Fides quaerens intellectum. Anselm's Proof of the Existence of God in the Context of His Theological Scheme* (Richmond, Va., 1960); Otto Samuel, *Über die Beweisbarkeit der Existenz Gottes: Konsequenzen des anselmischen Beweisverfahrens* (München, 1936). Support for this position on philosophical grounds is given by Hugh R. Smart, "Anselm's Ontological Argument: Rationalistic or Apologetic?," *RM, 3* (1949), 161–66.

16. Robert S. Hartman, "Prolegomena to a Meta-Anselmian Axiomatic," *RM, 14* (1961), 637–75.

true on the basis of its terms alone sounds remarkably like a restatement of the scholastic maxim *a nosse ad esse non valet consequentia*. Despite a shift in terminology, they conclude, as did St. Thomas, that Anselm's proof is a tautology.[17]

Similar presuppositions also inform critics from this school who support the proof. Their grounds are, simply, that linguistic analysis is concerned only with arguments and not with beings, and that, on the level of argument, Anselm's proof holds so long as it is suitably redefined in empirical, linguistic terms.[18] A peculiar variant of the linguistic analysts' position, finally, is one which holds that Anselm's proof is untenable, that it begs the question, but that it still may be meaningful, or at least useful. It may function either as a consolation to the believer, who is presumed not to need logic,[19] or as a means of making Kantians, logical positivists, and linguistic analysts realize that if they accept on principle that God's existence cannot be thought of as a logical necessity a priori, they must also accept the complementary principle that God's nonexistence cannot be thought of as a logical necessity a priori.[20]

There remain two other positions, both of which accept Anselm's proof, more or less, and neither of which fits into any of the categories previously discussed. Armando Cicchetti, interpreting the proof as ontological, upholds Anselm on the basis of "the new ontological idealism," a position to which he attaches the authority of St. Augustine and one which, the

17. R. E. Allen, "The Ontological Argument," *PR, 70* (1961), 55–56; William P. Alston, "The Ontological Argument Revisited," *PR, 69* (1960), 452–74.

18. Mario Dal Pra, "Il problema del fondamento del significato nella controversia fra Anselmo e Gaunilone," "Studi sul problema logico del linguaggio nella filosofia medioevale: I. 'Cogitatio vocum' e 'cogitatio rerum' nel pensiero di Anselmo," "Gaunilone e il problema logico del linguaggio," *Rivista critica di storia della filosofia, 9* (1954), 132–55, 309–43, 456–84.

19. Paul Henle, "Uses of the Ontological Argument," *PR, 70* (1961), 102–09; Norman Malcolm, "Anselm's Ontological Argument," *PR, 69* (1960), 41–62.

20. M. J. Charlesworth, "St. Anselm's Argument," *Sophia: A Journal for the Discussion of Philosophical Theology, 1* (1962), 25–36.

reader is not surprised to learn, he holds himself. Unfortunately, Cicchetti does not elaborate the nature of this new ontologism in any detail in his book on Anselm, but the philosophical bias he exhibits betrays his affinities to Hegelianism in its modern Italianate form.[21] Finally, Charles Hartshorne emerges as a qualified defender of the proof. He considers it heuristic, although he does not think that it exhausts God's reality. According to Hartshorne, the proof proves God's being without proving God. "God" is understood here as more than simple being; He is also, and preeminently, becoming.[22] This analysis is set in the context of a Whiteheadean metaphysics, in which the supreme reality is change and development; consequently God, for Hartshorne, can be grasped adequately, but only in part, through concepts that denote static absolutes. The grain of truth which lies all but concealed in these two interpretations is the fact that Anselm did think that, so far as he went, he was saying something accurate about God.

It is refreshing indeed to turn from Anselm as seen through the clouded filters of modern critics to Anselm as seen in the context of his own age. Paul Vignaux is quite correct in stating that "St. Anselm did not categorize his work according to our concepts." [23] The reason for this is the fact that Anselm's primary mode of thought is grammar. Just as the Middle Ages has been divided chronologically into an age of Vergil, an age of Horace, and an age of Ovid, so it may also be divided chronologically into an age of rhetoric, an age of grammar, and an age of dialectic, as the disciplines of the trivium gradu-

21. Armando Cicchetti, *L'Agostinismo nel pensiero di Anselmo d'Aosta* (Roma, 1951).

22. Charles Hartshorne, "The Logic of the Ontological Argument," *JP, 58* (1961), 471–73; "Introduction," St. Anselm, *Basic Writings* (La Salle, Ill., 1962), pp. 3–17. Hartshorne's position is most fully expressed in *The Logic of Perfection and Other Essays in Neoclassical Metaphysics* (La Salle, Ill., 1962), pp. 3–117; *Man's Vision of God, and the Logic of Theism* (Chicago, 1941).

23. Paul Vignaux, *Philosophy in the Middle Ages: An Introduction* (New York, 1959), p. 35.

ally replace each other in preeminence over the course of the centuries.[24]

The pervasiveness and importance of grammatical studies between the seventh and the twelfth centuries was a result of two major conditions. The first was the Germanic migrations and the struggle between Islam and Byzantium for the European shore of the Mediterranean. The Lombard conquest of Italy and the Muslim conquest of Spain and parts of southern France led to the waning of civic order and to the closing of the classical public schools in most of the heavily Romanized sections of southern Europe. The result was to shift Europe's intellectual center of gravity from the south to the north, particularly to the British Isles. In practical terms, this meant that, for the first time in early medieval history, the burden of culture after the seventh and eighth centuries fell on the shoulders of men to whom Latin was not a native language. Under these circumstances the immediate relevance of grammar was obvious. Grammar was the introductory subject in the trivium; it had to be mastered before the seals could be lifted from the books of the other arts and before any official business in Church or state could be transacted. Thus Rabanus Maurus in the ninth century stresses the importance of grammar in the contemporary curriculum: "Grammar is the science of interpreting the poets and the historians, and the method of writing and speaking correctly. It is both the source and the foundation of the liberal arts." [25] Early medieval educators were not innovators. Their tools for conveying the rudiments of the Latin language to the Germanic peoples were the grammatical compendia of the late imperial period, particularly those of Donatus and Priscian. Often enough the grammars of Donatus and Priscian proved to be too extensive and sophisticated for the uses to which they were put, and they

24. Charles Sears Baldwin, *Medieval Rhetoric and Poetic (to 1400) Interpreted from Representative Works* (New York, 1928), p. 91. Baldwin extends the age of grammar only through the tenth century.

25. Rabanus Maurus, *De clericorum institutione,* III, xviii, *PL, 107,* 395.

93

had to be condensed, abridged, and reformulated in scrupulously simple language. Grammar was the favorite topic among Carolingian textbook writers. Their educational efforts can be summed up as an attempt to preserve the grammatical traditions of Rome by progressive dilution,[26] a procedure dictated by the exigencies of the time.

A second reason why grammar outstripped rhetoric and dialectic after the age of the Church Fathers and transmitters lies in the fact that the principal purveyor of Latin letters in Western Europe up to the twelfth century was the Benedictine monastery. The *Rule* of St. Benedict presupposes literate monks, since one of their standard daily occupations, after the *opus dei,* is *lectio divina.* The meditative reading of Holy Scripture is to be supplemented by the perusal of scriptural commentaries and other edifying patristic works. These activities demand both a prayerful and contemplative attitude toward learning and a knowledge of how to read and to construe the texts. The monastic vocation may be presumed to have supplied the first requirement; for the second, the monks relied upon the classical discipline of grammar. The seven liberal arts were kept alive in the monastery, but grammar remained paramount. It was the means to the understanding of the sacred writings, and so it was intrinsic to the spiritual efforts of the monks. Grammar was even identified with the form of the writings composed by the inspired authors of the Bible. Rabanus Maurus makes this clear in the rhymed preface to his *De clericorum institutione:*

> Know, brethren, what the law requires
> Which fitly commands us to know the Word of God.

26. Martin Grabmann, "Die Entwicklung der mittelalterlichen Sprachlogik," *Mittelalterliches Geistesleben: Abhandlungen zur Geschichte der Scholastik und Mystik* (München, 1926), *1,* 109–13; R. W. Hunt, "Studies on Priscian in the Eleventh and Twelfth Century," *MRS, 1* (1941–43), 194–200; Charles Thurot, "Notices et extraits de divers manuscrits latins pour servir à l'histoire des doctrines grammaticales au moyen âge," *Notices et extraits des manuscrits de la Bibliothèque Impériale et autres Bibliothèques, 22,* 2ᵐᵉ partie (Paris, 1868), 60–64.

It asks that he who has ears, should hear
  What the Holy Spirit speaks in the Church.
Through grammar the Psalmist brings this to the peo-
    ple,
  Duly confirming their grasp of the law of God.
So, brethren, we should strive always,
  With eyes and ears intent, to learn the Word of
    God.[27]

During periods of monastic reform, such as the ninth century when Rabanus wrote this poem, "good letters" were
stressed because they were seen as essential to the main-
tenance or restoration of accurate texts of the Bible, the liturgical books, the Church Fathers, and the transmitters. Grammar, which included not merely the knowledge of the Latin
language but also the techniques of the gloss, the concordance,
and the allegorical method, was the necessary introduction to
the science of Holy Scripture. As such, it was quite natural
for it to become the basis of the monastic thinker's intellectual
style.[28]

Since this was so, it is not surprising to find early medieval thinkers applying explanations drawn from grammatical
modes of thought to their discussions of theology and other
topics of current interest. To be sure, some tendencies of the
earlier rhetorical method survived into the ninth century.
Thus, in the Eucharistic controversy between Paschasius Radbertus and Ratramnus Maurus, we find Paschasius supporting
his case in favor of the real presence of Christ in the sacrament by an argument that turns on a rhetorical figure, the
metaphor involving a transferred meaning. He compares the
relationship between the matter of the Eucharist, the bread
and wine, and its spiritual content, the Body and Blood of

27. Rabanus Maurus, *De clericorum institutione,* prologus, *PL, 107,* 293–94.
28. Jean Leclercq, *The Love of Learning and the Desire for God: A Study
of Monastic Culture* (New York, 1962), pp. 21–32, 44–56, 76–93, 116–51. This
work is an extremely valuable study of literature and spirituality in the medieval
monastery.

95

Christ, to the relationship between persons or events in the Old Testament that prefigure persons or events in the New Testament and their New Testament counterparts. Just as passages in the Old Testament may be allegorized in the light of the New Testament while still retaining their literal, historical meaning, he argues, so the matter of the Eucharist remains sensible in the sacrament notwithstanding the change in its spiritual content effected by the consecration.[29] Such rhetorical explanations, however, tend to disappear rapidly from view after the patristic period. More usual are grammatical elucidations of the Eucharist, and of other questions, as we shall see below.

In the tenth century, for example, Abbo of Fleury compiled a list of difficulties of all kinds in a volume entitled *Quaestiones grammaticales*. In *Quaestio* 21, Abbo deals with a problem in Trinitarian theology, the procession of the Holy Spirit. The Father is unbegotten; the Son is begotten; but the Holy Spirit is neither begotten nor unbegotten. How can this be? Abbo answers this question by first discussing the grammatical effects of negation. A negative statement, he explains, does not always denote unqualified privation. Some negations do signify the complete nonexistence of the things to which they refer. Thus, a man called "unjust" is never just of necessity; and a man called "blind" cannot see at all. But, he says, other negations are relative, and do not denote absolute privation by grammatical necessity. Thus, not everyone who does not see is blind; and not everyone who is not just is invariably unjust. Abbo's criterion for drawing this distinction seems to be that if a negative word, like *non*, is used in an adjectival phrase, the privative significance of the phrase is relative, but that if the adjective is itself grammatically negative, as in the case of *caecus* and *injustus*, it signifies complete privation necessarily. Now Abbo declares that the Holy Spirit is *nec genitum nec*

29. Paschasius Radbertus, *Liber de corpore et sanguine Domine, PL, 120,* 1280–81. Cf. the discussion of Paschasius in Beryl Smalley, *The Study of the Bible in the Middle Ages* (Oxford, 1941), pp. 65–66.

ingenitum. On the basis of the grammatical principle which he has just elucidated, he concludes that the Holy Spirit, although absolutely unbegotten, is also begotten in a relative sense, since He proceeds eternally from the Father and the Son.[30] Hence, far from being a digression in a book ostensibly given over to matters grammatical, the nature of the Holy Spirit is clearly a theological question which Abbo thinks can be explained by grammatical reasoning.

The tenth century provides us with additional evidence that grammar was called upon to play a role which we might ordinarily expect to find assigned to rhetoric or dialectic. In the year 964–65, one Gunzo, a noted Italian grammarian, was brought from Rome to Germany by the Emperor Otto I. During the month of January he stopped at the monastery of St. Gall. This visit provided the occasion for his *Epistola ad Augienses,* Gunzo's sole extant work and our only source of information about him.[31] It seems that one day Gunzo used an accusative instead of an ablative case ending, a faux pas which raised an outcry among the monks. One of the younger monks, or a student at the cloister school, decided to gloss the lapse in verse. His teacher forwarded this poem to Gunzo, who had already proceeded on his journey, thus beginning the literary feud between Gunzo and St. Gall which is contained in the *Epistola.* The *Epistola* may seem gratuitously turgid unless one perceives its underlying structure—it is a grammatical treatise converted to the uses of polemic. Although stressing pointedly at the outset that words and grammatical forms, unlike the sense and meaning of the thoughts they express, do not lead one to truth and wisdom, Gunzo nevertheless proceeds to combat his opponent's usage and to confirm his own accuracy in grammatical style. His principal method of argument is quotation. The *Epistola* is liberally sprinkled with choice passages from Servius, Donatus, Priscian, Vergil, Hor-

30. Abbo of Fleury, *Quaestiones grammaticales, PL, 139,* 533.
31. Gunzo, *Epistola ad Augienses,* ed. Karl Manitius, *MGH, QGM,* Band 2, Heft 1 (Weimar, 1958).

97

ace, Cicero, Plato, Aristotle, Boethius, Martianus Capella, the Bible, the liturgy, and Gregory the Great, to name only Gunzo's favorites. These extensive citations, in fact, form the bulk of the *Epistola,* and they are adduced to vindicate the correctness of Gunzo's usage. The author intrudes only to arrange the quotations in a plausible sequence and to comment on their contents. Lest the point escape the reader, he affirms in closing that grammar is the basic art. It would be difficult, however, to mistake Gunzo, for throughout the work he has applied the grammarian's technique of elucidating a grammatical usage by reference to hand-picked *exempla* drawn from the writings of unimpeachable stylistic authorities.

This intense interest in grammar continued into the eleventh century, as the incidence of contemporary commentaries on Priscian attests.[32] At the same time, grammatical thinkers were faced by a new problem, which was presented by a revival of interest in the Aristotelian *logica vetus* through the medium of Boethius' translations, or at any rate translations credited to Boethius. Recent scholarship on the part of Lorenzo Minio-Paluello, editor of the Boethian volumes in the *Aristoteles latinus* series, has shown that the *Categories* was translated from Greek to Latin in the tenth century, conjecturally in Italy, and that this tenth-century translation was widely circulated in Europe under Boethius' name after that time. In view of the fact that this tenth-century translation exists in a manuscript which is independent of the textual tradition of Boethius, Minio-Paluello considers its attribution to Boethius erroneous, a position that he documents in great detail.[33] For our purposes what is most important about this

32. Hunt, "Studies on Priscian," *MRS, 1,* 194–231.

33. Lorenzo Minio-Paluello, "The Genuine Text of Boethius's Translation of Aristotle's *Categories," MRS, 1* (1941–43), 157–77; "The Text of the *Categoriae:* The Latin Tradition," *The Classical Quarterly, 39* (1945), 70–74; "Les traductions et les commentaires aristotéliciens de Boèce," *Studia Patristica, 2* (Berlin, 1957), 361–64; Aristotle, *Categoriae vel praedicamenta,* ed. Laurentius Minio-Paluello, *Aristoteles latinus, 1,* 1–5 (Bruges-Paris, 1961), x–xxii, li–lii; A. van de Vijver, "Les étapes du développement philosophique du Haut Moyen-Age," *Revue Belge de philologie et d'histoire, 8* (1929), 425–52.

discovery is the fact that there was a translation of Aristotle's *Categories* from the Greek in the tenth century. This indicates that the Greek text was available in Western Europe, that there was a demand for such a translation, and that there was someone with the linguistic and philosophical competence to carry the project to completion at that time. While people may have been mistaken in thinking that this translation had issued from the hand of Boethius himself, it is nonetheless quite appropriate to describe the eleventh century, the heir to this newly discovered document, as an "age of Boethius," philosophically speaking.[34] It is not surprising, for example, that the eleventh century should witness the beginning of the realism-nominalism controversy, a problem suggested by Boethius' commentary on the *Isagoge* of Porphyry.

While the potential impact of a revival of interest in the *logica vetus* of Aristotle on philosophy is not difficult to appreciate, it is less immediately apparent why this revival should have created problems for grammarians. Yet, problems it did create, and they were serious ones. The issue centered in the fact that the *Categories* forcibly and inescapably introduced eleventh-century grammarians to the concepts of substance and accident, genera and species. The idea that a given thing might be looked at in a variety of ways called into question the classical definition of the part of speech used to denote a thing, the noun. Previous to this time, the noun had excited very little anxiety in Western Europe. Its definition was a fairly standard received tradition, originating in Donatus and Priscian and reiterated more or less coherently by Carolingian writers. Donatus on the noun reads: "The noun is a part of speech signifying the accidence of a thing whether properly or in general . . . The quality of a noun is twofold, for nouns may be proper or appellative."[35] Priscian recapitulates Do-

---

34. David Knowles, *The Evolution of Medieval Thought* (London, 1962), p. 100.

35. Donatus, *Ars grammatica,* ed. Heinrich Keil, *Grammatici latini*, ed. Heinrich Keil (Leipzig, 1864), *4,* 373.

natus: "The noun is a part of speech which distributes the quality of some subject, body, or thing, generally or properly." [36] He adds that "it is proper for the noun to signify substance and quality." [37]

This late classical definition was retained by ninth-century grammarians. Remigius of Auxerre tells us:

> The noun is used, in the first instance, to demonstrate a substance. . . . The definition [of the noun] includes several parts. It asks of what number, name, and substance a thing is. It is a part of speech under the surveillance of Latinity. Thus, the noun is defined. As we said above, the definition starts with the genus (*a genere*) and moves to the proper through species (*per species ad proprium tendat*).[38]

Alcuin proceeds more concisely: "The noun is a part of speech, according to the grammarians, which distributes quality to some body or thing generally or properly"; [39] and he adds that nouns may be proper or appellative.[40]

The grammarians, in short, assert that a noun defines a thing both substantially and accidentally, both generically and specifically. They lump these two types of designation together, without providing any insights into what changes nominal signification undergoes, if any, when it moves from the one to the other. Boethius, on the other hand, is quite precise in defining these distinctions. In his translation of the *Categories* it appears plainly that nouns do not all signify in the same way. If they signify with respect to accidents they cannot properly signify with respect to substance, and vice versa. He further elaborates in his translation of *De interpretatione*

36. Priscianus, *Institutionum grammaticarum libri XVIII,* ed. Martin Herz, 2.5.22, *Grammatici latini, 2,* 56–57.

37. Ibid., 2.4.15, 2.4.18, *Grammatici latini, 2,* 53, 55.

38. Remigius of Auxerre, *In Artem Donati minorem commentum,* ed. W. Fox (Lipsiae, 1902), pp. 8, 9–10.

39. Alcuin, *Grammatica, PL, 101,* 859.

40. Ibid., pp. 859–60.

that a noun must signify one or the other, but not both.[41] Hence the problem: Who is right, Donatus and Priscian or Boethius?

In general, we can say that the testimony of Boethius was accepted, but it was not allowed to overthrow the massive authority of grammar. The Boethian-Aristotelian concepts of substance and accident, genus and species, were integrated into Priscian's theory of the noun by commentators on the disciplines of the trivium in the eleventh century, despite the intellectual contortions which this occasionally required, and the peculiar amalgam of "categorized" grammar that resulted made its way thence into the intellectual gear of scholars and controversialists. It is no accident that the examples of scholarship and controversy most illustrative of the problems entailed by the new grammar of the eleventh century, and the uses to which it was put, are to be found in the works of Anselm, his teacher Lanfranc of Bec, and Lanfranc's principal opponent, Berengarius of Tours. The issues it raised were considered vital to the most outstanding minds of the age.

On the face of it, it is also no accident that eleventh-century monastic thinkers could have made this bizarre amalgam of logic and grammar in the first place. It is worth remembering that the practice of distinguishing rigorously among the seven liberal arts dates from the twelfth and thirteenth centuries, when individual scholars began to specialize in one, and only one, art. We can attribute this development not only to the wider range of classical materials which the renaissance of the twelfth century made available, but also to the fact that the most important centers of education had then become the burgeoning cathedral schools and universities. These new schools, which served an expanding urban population and which at-

41. Anicius Manlius Severinus Boethius, *In Categorias Aristotelis*, IV–V, *Aristoteles latinus, 1,* 1–5, pp. 48–54; *In librum Aristotelis de interpretatione,* I, *PL, 64,* 159–60, 162–63, 301. See also Thurot, "Notices et extraits," *Notices et extraits, 22,* 2me partie, 166. References to Boethius' translation of the *Categories* are drawn from the tenth-century vulgate text as established by Minio-Paluello.

tracted many foreigners, tended to be much larger than their monastic counterparts, and, unlike them, they were dedicated to full-time study and teaching. The instructors on their enlarged staffs were given specific curricular assignments, on which they were supposed to concentrate all their attention. These academic responsibilities, and their correlative limitations, usually paralleled the level of higher education that had been attained by the individual instructor, and his major field of interest as well. This was especially true of university education, the bachelor's, master's, and doctor's degrees being licenses to teach a particular subject at a particular level. Such a degree of academic specialization cannot be found in most eleventh-century monastic schools. Although, as we have seen, the monks required a certain amount and type of training, education was neither the exclusive nor even the primary function of the monastery as an institution. The average monastery could count itself lucky if it managed to attract or to develop educators with specialized talents; their presence in any number, however small, was by no means a foregone conclusion. While it is true that great houses such as Cluny tended to develop a comparatively large and distinguished staff of teachers, smaller and less eminent houses usually had to rely on the services of one or two instructors, whose responsibilities encompassed all of the arts that were taught.

In the case of the monastery of Bec, which had been founded in 1041 and which was just emerging from relative obscurity thanks to the patronage of several rising Norman barons [42] and the presence of Lanfranc, we find clear-cut distinctions among the arts absent. Lanfranc himself was generally acclaimed by his contemporaries for having relit the lamps of the liberal arts in the West. Even though his educational writings, the *Quaestiones Lanfranci* and the *De dialectica,* which are frequently listed in eleventh-century library catalogues but which are, unfortunately, no longer extant,

---

42. David C. Douglas, *William the Conquerer: The Norman Impact upon England* (Berkeley and Los Angeles, 1964), pp. 86, 116.

might lead us to assume that logic was his exclusive speciality, this is not the case. In actuality, he taught all the arts.[43] Anselm also falls into the category of the nonspecialist. If we were to draw inferences from his educational works alone, it would be easy to conclude that he, like Lanfranc, taught only logic. Yet we find contemporaries anxious to send their protégés to Anselm to be instructed in grammar.[44] The lack of academic specialization at the school of Bec is further attested by the description of it, and of Anselm as an educator, left by Ordericus Vitalis, Abbot of Mont Saint-Michel in the early twelfth century. At first, Ordericus seems to identify Anselm as a logician. He describes Lanfranc and Anselm in one breath as "profound sophists." [45] On the death of Abbot Herluin, he says, when Anselm, "plentifully imbued with a rich knowledge of letters," took over the monastic school, "clerics and laymen flocked to the counsel of the most worthy sophist." [46] However, when he judges the overall impact of Anselm on education at Bec, Ordericus does not give us much basis for assuming that his preeminence can be limited to any one of the arts:

> The fame of his wisdom was spread abroad by his teaching throughout the whole Latin-speaking world, and the Western Church was nobly intoxicated by the nectar of his good opinions. The distinguished seat of the liberal arts and sacred reading founded at the church of Bec by Lanfranc grew magnificently under Anselm, so that many learned doctors came thence, providing sailors and spiritual helmsmen, who were divinely commissioned by the Church as pilots to guide the course of this world. They diligently persevered in six disputations (*ser-*

43. R. W. Southern, "Lanfranc of Bec and Berengar of Tours," *Studies in Medieval History presented to Frederick Maurice Powicke* (Oxford, 1948), pp. 30, 32–33; *Saint Anselm and His Biographer: A Study of Monastic Life and Thought 1059-c.1130* (Cambridge, 1963), pp. 14, 16.

44. St. Anselm, *Epistola* XIX, Schmitt, *3*, 125–26.

45. Ordericus Vitalis, *Historiae ecclesiasticae,* ed. August Le Prevost, III, i (Paris, 1840), *2*, 14.

46. Ibid., IV, x, Le Prevost, *2*, 245.

monum) on sacred things, both mysterious (*aenigma-tum*) and useful, for the good practice of all the students at Bec, so that almost all of them were considered philosophers. And, from their own conversation, even those considered illiterates and called rustics among themselves could learn from each other how to be fluent grammarians.[47]

Given a habit of mind in which the liberal arts were not regularly compartmentalized, it is not difficult to see why Aristotelian ideas should be injected into grammar, and why logical as well as theological works should reveal a grammatical bias.

It has been observed that Berengarius and Lanfranc, two of the most important theological controversialists of the eleventh century, were grammarians at heart.[48] This fact has been brought into clear focus by R. W. Southern, in his valuable study of their conflict over the real presence of Christ in the Eucharist.[49] For our purposes, the most interesting aspect of this controversy is the opponents' style of argument, rather than their teachings on sacramental theology. Berengarius' case against the doctrine of the real presence is a manifest expression of the new Aristotelianized grammar. It turns entirely on the difference between nouns and pronouns, a distinction which the idea of substance and accidents had forced grammarians to accept. The current view was that a noun, with a nod to Priscian, signifies its object substantially and accidentally, but that a pronoun, *pace* Boethius, signifies its object only substantially. A pronoun has the grammatical function of

47. Ibid., pp. 245–46. Henri DeLubac, *Exégèse médiévale* (Paris, 1959–64), *1*, part 1, p. 94, note 3, supplies additional data on the contemporary educational repute enjoyed by Bec.

48. Jos. Ant. Endres, *Forschungen zur Geschichte der frühmittelalterlichen Philosophie, Beiträge*, Band *17*, Heft 2–3 (Münster i. W., 1915), 118; Southern, "Lanfranc and Berengar," *Powicke Studies*, p. 32; *Saint Anselm*, pp. 21, 23.

49. The following discussion of the conflict between Berengarius and Lanfranc, and the example illustrating the technique of equipollency, are drawn from Southern, "Lanfranc and Berengar," *Powicke Studies*, pp. 39–46; *Saint Anselm*, pp. 12–14, 20–26.

standing for a noun in a sentence. However, it does not share
the significative function of the noun which it replaces; in order to signify a thing both substantially and accidently, it
would have to be a noun itself. Since a pronoun is only a
grammatical substitute for a noun, it can signify the object
bequeathed to it by the noun it replaces only substantially,
but not accidently as well.[50]

Now what relationship does this theory of the pronoun have
to the Eucharist? Berengarius' whole argument turns on an
analysis of the formula which the celebrant uses to consecrate
the Eucharist during the mass, *"Hoc est enim corpus meum."*
Now "hoc" in this sentence is a pronoun, and its grammatical
function is to signify the Eucharistic bread on the altar. "Corpus," signifying Christ's body, is, to be sure, a noun. However,
it functions as a predicate nominative in the sentence, and, as
such, is controlled by "hoc," the subject of the sentence, with
which it must agree. Since the pronoun "hoc" has limited significative possiblities, good grammar dictates that these limitations must also extend to "corpus" in the context of the sentence. If, as the opposition claims, the substance of the bread
were actually changed into Christ's body during the consecration, the subject of the sentence would be annulled and de-
stroyed by its own predicate nominative, a manifest grammatical impossibility.

Formidable as this argument must have seemed to thinkers
well schooled in eleventh-century grammar, it did not daunt
Lanfranc. He developed on his own behalf a rebuttal of
Berengarius which is equally verbal in nature. This rebuttal is
particularly interesting as an index of Lanfranc's mentality.
While it is ostensibly logical, it is in fact based on grammar.
Logic, for Lanfranc, does not automatically connote the appa-
ratus of the syllogism. Instead, his argument employs a term
and a technique which he calls "equipollent propositions."[51]
Lanfranc is the first medieval thinker known to have used this

50. Thurot, "Notices et extraits," *Notices et extraits, 22,* 2me partie, 171–76.
51. Lanfranc, *Liber de corpore et sanguine Domine,* VII, *PL, 140,* 417.

term and mode of argument. Its ultimate provenance is thought to be Apuleius, a Platonist of the Middle Academy born about A.D. 125, whose work, according to Southern, was coming into use in the eleventh century. Equipollency means the detection of equivalent forms of a proposition. If equivalent forms can be produced, the initial proposition is conceded to have earned more cognitive weight than it had before. In an argument carried on by the use of equipollency, the speaker's aim is therefore to demonstrate this equivalency. He does this by taking a proposition and redefining it several times, each time expanding, focusing, or channeling the definition so that, when the final definition has been reached, the initial proposition has actually been converted into the one to which he wishes to prove it is equivalent. In short, this redefinition of a given proposition replaces it bit by bit with equivalent propositions, until it literally becomes what one is trying to prove it to be. The way in which an equipollent proof functions may be clarified by contrasting it with a diagram of the classic syllogistic proof. Where the syllogism would read:

All A is D
But B is A
Therefore all B is D

the equipollent proof would read:

$A = B = C = D$
Therefore $A = D$.

To the modern mind Lanfranc's method may appear to be no more compelling than Berengarius'. However, contemporaries found both arguments convincing, a fact which stems largely from the prominence of grammar in each proof. Berengarius, as we have seen, is dependent on the new theory of the pronoun conceived by eleventh-century grammarians under the impact of the *Categories*. Lanfranc is dependent on grammar in the more general sense of the word. His approach has

clear affinities to the monastic grammarians' method of elucidating a text or an individual word,[52] and he shares their confidence in the significative power of the noun by assuming that
definition in itself is somehow not only explanatory but intellectually convincing.

The controversy between Berengarius and Lanfranc was at
its peak when the young Anselm left his native Aosta and
went to Bec to study with Lanfranc. Anselm was thus in an
excellent position to familiarize himself with the methods of
both of the disputants, an opportunity which he did not waste.
Although he towers over Berengarius and Lanfranc in ability
and in theological importance, he learned a great deal from
both of them; it is thus incorrect to describe him as "a sudden
emergence, a Melchisedech without father or mother or gene-
alogy." [53] Southern has made the trenchant suggestion that
Anselm may be an even better source of examples of the
equipollency technique than Lanfranc, and that he shared
Berengarius' concern with developing proofs according to the
contemporary rules of language.[54] It is the suggestion that remains to be documented in detail. Anselm was a man of his
times; the problems of the new grammar were ones that he
studied and wrote about as an educator, and the methods it
provided were the tools he used in his famous proof and
throughout his theological writings as a whole.

We might begin by examining Anselm's educational works,
the *De grammatico* and the unfinished *De potestate et impotentia*. . . . Both are ostensibly logical treatises. Anselm himself describes the *De grammatico* as a discussion of problems
currently mooted among dialecticians, and as useful for students in that discipline; [55] elsewhere he recommends it as an
introduction to logic.[56] Eadmer, the monk of Canterbury who

52. Leclercq, *The Love of Learning*, pp. 77–83.
53. Knowles, *Evolution of Medieval Thought*, p. 99.
54. Southern, "Lanfranc and Berengar," pp. 35, 46; *Saint Anselm*, pp. 22–23, 25.
55. *De grammatico*, XXI, Schmitt, *1*, 168.
56. *De veritate*, praefatio, Schmitt, *1*, 173.

was Anselm's biographer, secretary, and close friend,[57] catalogues it in his list of Anselm's writings as a work which propounds and solves many dialectical questions.[58] Several modern scholars, however, have observed that the problem contained in the *De grammatico* is not purely logical, since it results from the impact of Boethius on Priscian's definition of the noun.[59] In fact both works are as much grammatical as logical, if not more so. This is true not only of the questions which they ask but also of Anselm's method of answering them. It is important to give particular attention to this method. The discipulus in the *De grammatico* requests the magister to prove his answers by necessary reasons;[60] and at the end of the dialogue he appears to be satisfied that his terms have been met. The work will thus begin to give us some idea of what Anselm thought necessary reasons were, a topic highly relevant to his epistemology and one to which we will have occasion to return in some detail below.

The basic question in the *De grammatico* is: "Whether a grammarian is a substance or a quality." This is an issue whose investigation promises at first glance to be as enervating as the redoubtable "How many angels can stand on the head of a pin?" and "How many steps did St. Denis take with his head tucked under his arm?," which used to be attributed regularly to medieval savants before the advent of revisionist historiography. The problem that the *De grammatico* raises is, however, both plausible and concrete. The discipulus asks this

---

57. *Epistola* CCVIII, Schmitt, *4,* 103.

58. Eadmer, *Vita Anselmi* (London, 1962), p. 28.

59. Filliatre, *La philosophie de Saint Anselme,* pp. 18, 147–61; Hunt, "Studies on Priscian," *MRS, 1,* 214–19; Desmond Paul Henry, "Saint Anselm's 'De grammatico,'" *The Philosophical Quarterly, 10* (1960), 115–26; *The De grammatico of St. Anselm: The Theory of Paronymy* (Notre Dame, Ind., 1964); "Why 'Grammaticus'?," *Archivum Latinitatis Medii Aevi, 28,* fasc. 2–3 (1958), 165–80; Southern, *Saint Anselm,* pp. 14–16; Thurot, "Notices et extraits," p. 166. There are, however, scholars who see the *De grammatico* as an exclusively logical work. See Perino, *La dottrina Trinitaria,* p. 17, note 15; Jean Rivière, "Saint Anselme logicien," *RSR, 17* (1937), 306–15.

60. *De grammatico,* I, Schmitt, *1,* 144.

108

question because he wants to know the denominative status of "grammarian" and words like it, a dilemma suggested to him by Boethius' *In Categorias Aristotelis,* where we read: "Denominatives are defined as those words that derive their appellation from the noun, with any single difference in case, as 'grammarian' from 'grammar' and 'strong' from 'strength.' " [61] The issue is located in the fact that the word "grammarian" is derived grammatically from the discipline of grammar. But it is equally true that grammarians are chronologically and logically derived from the human race, since it is necessary to be a man before one can become a grammarian, and "grammaticus" is a species of the genus "homo." Sensing that the discipulus will have difficulty understanding this logical relationship, the magister has recourse to a grammatical example in order to clarify it. The genus "homo" and the species "grammaticus," he points out, are related in logic the way that the adjective "hodiernum" and the adverb "hodie" are related in grammar.[62]

This still leaves open the status of the word "grammaticus" with respect both to man, on the one hand, and to grammar, on the other. Now words, Anselm states, represent things. What kind of thing does "grammaticus" represent? It represents a flesh and blood grammarian. This grammarian, according to Anselm, is a quality, and "grammarian" is therefore a *vox significans qualitatem.*[63] Quality, he adds, is one of Aristotle's accidents, and in order to explain what an accident is and how it compares with substance, he falls back once again on a grammatical analogy. Substance is to accident as a word which can either stand alone or be modified is to a word which is grammatically dependent on the word it modifies.[64] Words may signify either substantially or accidentally. Those signifying substantially are *voces significativae per se;* those sig-

61. Boethius, *In Categorias Aristotelis,* I, *Aristoteles latinus, 1,* 1–5, p. 47.
62. *De grammatico,* XIII, Schmitt, *1,* 159.
63. Ibid., IX, XVIII, Schmitt, *1,* 154, 163.
64. Ibid., XVIII, Schmitt, *1,* 163.

nifying accidentally are *voces singificativae per aliud*. The word "grammaticus" does not signify the human being occupied with the study of language and the agent whose name is derived from the discipline of grammar in the same way. It signifies the nominal derivative *per se* and the man *per aliud*. In the first case the word is properly significative; in the second case it is appellative.[65] For Anselm, thus, grammatical relationships are prior to, and more comprehensible than, logical and chronological relationships. The grammatical derivation of a word is substantial and independent, while the logical derivation remains accidental and dependent.

In the case of the *De potestate et impotentia* we find a similar tendency on Anselm's part to pose or to answer logical questions grammatically, although this is visible far less systematically than in the *De grammatico*. In one series of questions he takes up the implications of negation. What does not exist, he says, has no power at all. It has neither the power to be nor the power not to be, and hence, paradoxically, it is both necessarily nonexistent and necessarily existent. Anselm admits that this conclusion is absurd even though it is logically plausible.[66] Another series of questions deals with the problem of attributing negative or apparently privative terminology to God. We may say, Anselm notes, that there are some acts that are impossible to God, such as lying, or that some of God's characteristics are necessary, such as justice. However, impossibility connotes impotence and necessity connotes coercion, both of which are imperfections, and cannot therefore be attributed to God. If we say that He serves truth by His inability to lie and that He serves justice by coercion, this would mean that He can neither be truthful nor just freely, a conclusion which is plausible but which cannot be true because it conflicts with God's nature. If we try to avoid this conclusion by stating that, so far as God is concerned, necessity and im-

65. Ibid., XII, XV, Schmitt, *1*, 157, 161.
66. Franciscus Salesius Schmitt, ed., *Ein neues unvollendtes Werk des Hl. Anselm von Canterbury, Beiträge*, Band *33*, Heft 3 (Münster i. W., 1936), 24.

possibility signify perfections rather than defects, we are faced with the paradox of words that signify their opposites: "How," asks Anselm, "can this strength be designated by words signifying weakness?" [67] It would be interesting indeed to know how Anselm planned to find his way out of these difficulties. Unfortunately, this is an unfinished work, and the answers to these questions are not provided, although the questions themselves raise important issues.

Anselm's taste for explaining logical relationships in terms of grammatical relationships is also visible in the *De potestate et impotentia,* particularly with respect to causality. He compares causes to effects by analogizing them to nouns and predicate nominatives. As the noun governs the predicate nominative, he says, so the cause governs the effect.[68] In the case of efficient causality Anselm's illustrative example is drawn from metaphorical signification. The efficient cause, although it is not the effect, can still be affirmed of it, just as the foot, although it is not the eye, is figuratively speaking, the eye of a blind man.[69] In its fragmentary state, the *De potestate et impotentia* gives us much less to work with than does the *De grammatico.* Yet it is worthy of notice in that it provides us with some insight into the kinds of questions Anselm was asking, and it reinforces our impression of him as a man whose primary mode of thought was grammar.

The grammatical mode of thought is freely exploited by Anselm in his epistemological and theological works. It will be seen in the case of Anselm's theory of knowledge that he is in full command of the Augustinian view of the cognitive functions, possibilities, and limitations of words, and that he frequently explores epistemological relationships in terms of grammatical concepts. Like Augustine, Anselm sees a definite connection between love and knowledge, and his epistemology is formulated in such a way as to be applicable primarily, if

67. Ibid.
68. Ibid., pp. 27–28.
69. Ibid., p. 34.

111

not exclusively, to theological objects of knowledge. Anselm's epistemological preoccupations are fairly few in number. What concerns him most is the nature of truth, the tenability of proofs, and the cognitive function of proofs. These interests are explored, more or less respectively, in his dialogue *De veritate,* in his analysis of necessary reasons, and in his theory of *fides quaerens intellectum.* An understanding of these points is essential to an understanding of his views on the theology of God's existence in the *Monologion, Proslogion,* and *Contra Gaunilonem.*

The intimate connection between Anselm's theory of knowledge and his religious aims is made manifest in the prologue of the *De veritate,* the only one of his major works expressly devoted to epistemology. Here he states that the purpose of the dialogue is to aid the reader in the study of Scripture and to discuss the nature of truth, the things of which truth is ordinarily predicated, and justice.[70] At the outset, the discipulus poses the question of truth in the following terms: We believe that God is the truth. Yet, at the same time, there are many other things which we call true. Must we say that anything that is true is therefore God? This is an implausible notion in view of the fact that God is eternal, while other things are not. A definition of truth is hence required, which will explain in what sense the finite things we call true are true.[71]

The discipulus and magister accordingly turn their attention to the truth of signification, beginning with the significative function of statements. Their dialogue reveals Anselm's interest in both the relation of the sign to its significatum and the relation of the sign to the speaker.[72] There is, according to Anselm, an intrinsic, natural truth in speech, a *veritas enuntiationis,* in virtue of the fact that a statement signifies

70. *De veritate,* praefatio, Schmitt, *1,* 173.

71. Ibid., I, Schmitt, *1,* 176–77.

72. Martin Grabmann, *Die Geschichte der scholastischen Methode* (Darmstadt, 1956), *1,* 314, 320.

truly what its speaker means. This natural significative function pertains to all statements whether or not they are factually accurate. If they are in fact accurate in addition to expressing the intention of their speakers, they are accidentally true. It is this latter type of truth that Anselm dignifies with the name "rectitude." Statements that are intrinsically erroneous may yet be naturally true, but only statements which signify that what is, is, and that what is not, is not, possess both truth and rectitude. Rectitude, the correct relation of the sign to the thing it signifies, is the real criterion of its epistemological validity.[73] This being the case, it is clear that the hearer can perceive the rectitude of a sign only if he knows both the sign and the object it signifies. The sign, thus, does not bring to the hearer any knowledge which he does not already have. It is on the basis of his prior knowledge of the object that he judges the rectitude of the sign, the truth of a statement. This is completely consistent with Augustine's ideas on signification. The sign may be accurate, but it is not identical with its object. It is not cognitive in the first instance. Its objective accuracy is controlled by its object, and its subjective accuracy can be assessed only by a mind able to compare the sign with its object, which it already knows.

Anselm, like Augustine, begins with verbal signs: his explanation of rectitude is elaborated first with respect to the truth of statements and definitions. He then goes on to show that

---

73. *De veritate*, II, Schmitt, *1*, 177–80. The first scholar to notice the importance of Anselm's analysis of rectitude in the *De veritate* for his proof of the existence of God has been Etienne Gilson, "Sens et nature de l'argument de Saint Anselm," *AHDLMA*, *9* (1934), 5–51. Gilson has been followed by Miller, "The Ontological Argument," *MS, 32,* 341–49. More recently, rectitude has been studied as a general key to Anselm's works by George S. Heyer, Jr., *"Rectitudo* in the Theology of St. Anselm," Yale University Ph.D. dissertation, 1963; Robert Pouchet, *La Rectitudo chez Saint Anselme: Un itinéraire augustinien de l'âme à Dieu* (Paris, 1964). Pouchet gives a useful summary of the *De veritate,* pp. 55–67, and discusses the biblical and patristic sources of the term *rectitudo,* pp. 19–52. His discussion of the *Proslogion* proof, pp. 67–83, shows him in agreement with Gilson on the importance of *rectitudo* to it.

there are other types of signs which can be understood in the same way as statements.[74] After analyzing the truth of statements, he proceeds to discuss the truth of thought, the truth of will, the truth of action, the truth of the senses, and the truth of the essences of things. The same criteria which he applies to verbal signs are applied to these other types of signs. Thus, he notes, an idea may have rectitude if the thinker thinks that what is, is, and what is not, is not.[75] Just as the truth of thought lies in thinking what is right, so the truth of will lies in willing what is right, conforming the will to moral reality.[76] Moral rectitude includes truth of action, the doing of what is right. For Anselm, there is a direct parallel between the truth of statements and the truth of actions. Just as a statement may be naturally or accidentally true depending on whether it merely expresses the speaker's meaning or it also expresses realities accurately, so an action may be necessarily or unnecessarily true, depending on whether the agent merely exercises its given nature unconsciously, or it acts, or permits itself to be acted upon, with conscious reference to its moral objectives.[77] The truth of the senses is natural; to the extent that the senses are healthy, they provide the judgment with accurate data. The judgment may interpret sense data truly or falsely depending on how well informed it is on the science of sense perception. Thus, citing the conventional example of the straight stick that appears to be bent when seen through water, Anselm observes that an understanding of the physics of refraction will enable the judgment to correct for error and to retain the material truth of sensory data on the intellectual level.[78]

So far Anselm's discussion in the *De veritate* has shown that things which are not themselves eternal truth may still be

74. *De veritate,* IX, Schmitt, *1,* 188–89.
75. Ibid., III, Schmitt, *1,* 180.
76. Ibid., IV, Schmitt, *1,* 180–81.
77. Ibid., V, Schmitt, *1,* 181–83.
78. Ibid., VI, Schmitt, *1,* 183–85.

true insofar as they are signs that signify their proper objects with rectitude. There still remains the question of whether God is the truth of all true things. This point is taken up by Anselm in commenting on the truth of the essences of things. The essences of things exist and are true, he says, because they are derived from the supreme truth. They are true insofar as this truth is in them and they are in it; for they are what they are in relation to supreme truth.[79] This means that "what exists, is true"; but it does not necessarily follow for Anselm that "whatever is, is right and ought to be." Unlike most Neoplatonists, Anselm does not extricate himself from this difficulty by means of a privative theory of evil. Rather, he attacks the problem while achieving in effect the same thing, in grammatical form. The verb "ought," he states, may only be used properly in the active voice. Consequently, a knowledge of what is right obliges the agent to do it, but rectitude cannot be invoked as a justification of what happens to a person when he is acted upon.[80]

Supreme truth, however, is the basis for all other kinds of truth. Discourse, and by extension other kinds of signification, would have no rectitude unless its objects existed; and things exist only because God creates and sustains them. For Anselm, thus, truth is rectitude perceived with the reason; justice is rectitude sought consciously by the will and expressed in right action for the sake of, and by means of, justice itself.[81] The rectitude underlying all true signification is prior to its signs; it is independent of them and they cannot confer being upon it or withdraw being from it: "The rightness (*rectitudo*) therefore by which signification is called right does not acquire being, or any change, through signification, howsoever the signification itself may be changed." [82] This rectitude—God—is

79. Ibid., VII, Schmitt, *1*, 185.
80. Ibid., VIII, Schmitt, *1*, 188.
81. Ibid., IX–XII, Schmitt, *1*, 189–96.
82. Ibid., XIII, Schmitt, *1*, 198, trans. Richard McKeon, *Selections from Medieval Philosophers* (New York, 1929), *1*, 182.

115

the eternal truth toward which all other truths—truths of will, of intellect, of fact, of word, of action—are oriented.[83] This idea has very little to do with the exemplarism which some people find in Anselm.[84] It is, rather, a corollary of Anselm's belief that God is the creator of all things and the object of all human activity, and that He makes it possible for men to know and to love Him. For Anselm, as for Augustine, love and knowledge are correlative and inseparable. It is as impossible for Anselm to sever the cognitive from the affective faculties as to detach man's efforts toward intellectual and moral rectitude from God's initiative and assistance. "In Anselm's thought . . . the moral and intellectual virtues adumbrate an identical reality, and serve a single end." [85]

Anselm's second principal epistemological interest, necessary reasons, is somewhat more elusive, as it is a topic which he treats less extensively than the nature of truth. Nevertheless, the two ideas are inseparable. Anselm's notion of necessity is firmly embedded in the idea of rectitude which he elaborates in the *De veritate*; and the importance of necessary reasons to his theology as a whole is impossible to overlook. At the beginning of the *Monologion,* Anselm states that he intends to support his position with necessary reasons, which he defines as rational arguments acceptable even if they are not supported by the greater authority of Scripture and tradition.[86] Although the term "necessity" is used only twice in the *Proslogion,* it is invoked several times in Anselm's refuta-

83. *De veritate,* XIII, Schmitt, *1,* 199.

84. Cf. on the contrary Filliatre, *La philosophie de Saint Anselme,* p. 170; Heyer, *"Rectitudo,"* p. 29.

85. McKeon, *Selections, 1,* 145. See also Barth, *Anselm,* pp. 15 ff.; Filliatre, *La philosophie de Saint Anselme,* pp. 435 ff.; Grabmann, *Geschichte, 1,* 262–63; Heyer, *"Rectitudo,"* pp. 88 ff., 120 ff.; Gerald B. Phelan, *The Wisdom of Saint Anselm* (Latrobe, Pa., 1960), pp. 41–42; Vignaux, *Philosophy in the Middle Ages,* pp. 38, 40–41. On the other hand, Copleston, *History of Philosophy, 2,* 164, sees only the intellectual implications of rectitude. Anselm explores further the correlation between love and knowledge and their mutual end in beatitude in *Cur deus homo,* II, 1, Schmitt, *2,* 97–98.

86. *Monologion,* I, Schmitt, *1,* 14.

116

tion of Gaunilon.[87] in Anselm's own words, necessary reasons stand at the center of his proof of God's existence. It is therefore not surprising to find that scholarly opinions on the cognitive status of necessary reasons have sometimes been affected by scholarly conclusions as to the nature and validity of the proof.

There are a number of commentators who find some anomaly or imprecision in Anselm's conception and use of necessary reasons. Vignaux confesses his puzzlement. Necessary reasons, he states, are "not . . . merely probabilities for the use of this or that questioner, but rather [they] aspire to the universality of the true." Yet, Anselm employs them in writings that "leave aside the Incarnation but include the Trinity; they are not concerned with a philosopher's God"; [88] and, even stranger, their universal validating power is rather weak in practice in Anselm's arguments.[89] Knowles solves this dilemma by observing that in Anselm's thought, "the adjective *necessarius* means 'formally admissible,' 'probable,' rather than 'compelling.' " However, he finds an Anselmian paradox of his own. Notwithstanding the cognitive limits of necessary reasoning, Anselm, he holds, thinks that the human mind can perceive the "inevitability" of the truths of faith. This pecularity lies, according to Knowles, not so much in Anselm's presumed attempt to use necessary reasons in a manner which their nature does not warrant, as it does in his presumed failure to distinguish between "natural" and "supernatural" objects and modes of knowledge, a lapse not satisfactorily rectified until Aquinas, which therefore can be attributed to Anselm's philosophical naïveté.[90] While anxious, on the other hand, to assert that Anselm was no Pelagian of the mind, Heyer likewise concludes that Anselm uses necessary reasons unprofessionally because of the logical vagueness of his times.[91]

87. *Proslogion*, XXIII; *Contra Gaunilonem*, I, V, Schmitt, *1*, 117, 131, 135.
88. Vignaux, *Philosophy in the Middle Ages*, p. 36.
89. Ibid., p. 40.
90. Knowles, *Evolution of Medieval Thought*, pp. 101–02.
91. Heyer, *"Rectitudo,"* p. 85.

Besides tending to depict Anselm as fuzzy-minded and inconsistent, these opinions give rise to a major problem by focusing attention too exclusively on the function of necessary reasons in the proof of God. To be sure, Anselm's own statement of purpose is responsible for this emphasis, and we shall also make the proof the terminus of our discussion of his epistemology. However, one must recognize that the *Monologion* definition of necessary reasons is neither the only source of information about them, nor the only answer to all the relevant questions that they raise. In particular, two further questions remain to be settled: Where did Anselm get the idea of necessary reasons in the first place? What is Anselm's own criterion of necessity?

In answering the first question we are given substantial assistance by a helpful and strangely neglected article by A.–M. Jacquin, who traces the idea of necessary reasons to its ultimate source, the logic of Aristotle, and who gives us some notion of the filiation of this idea in the Latin Middle Ages up to Anselm's time. Aristotle talks about necessity most succinctly in his analysis of signs, which we have treated above. For Aristotle, it will be remembered, signs may be fallible or infallible. Infallible signs are proper to logic; they are used in syllogisms which entail scientific knowledge and necessary truth. Fallible signs are proper to rhetoric; they are used in enthymemes, which may be credited with probable, but not necessary truth. As Jacquin notes, this Aristotelian definition of probability and necessity was repeated by Cicero, Marius Victorinus, and Cassiodorus, its chief Latin transmitters. He thinks that Cassiodorus was most likely Anselm's source.[92] It must be emphasized that the works in which Aristotle expounds the syllogism-enthymeme distinction most thoroughly were not part of the logica vetus, and were thus not available in Latin until the second half of the twelfth century. Anselm

92. A.-M. Jacquin, "Les 'rationes necessariae' de Saint Anselm," *Mélanges Mandonnet: Études d'histoire littéraire et doctrinale du moyen âge* (Paris, 1930), 2, 68, 72–73.

was thus incapable of knowing the complete context of Aristotle's original idea of necessity. In his own conception of necessity, we note a significant shift in emphasis. Anselm is not at all concerned with the difference between probability and necessity. What does interest him is the fact that the derivative Latin discussions, in particular the discussion of Cassiodorus, emphasize the point that necessary reasons entail truth. Now, as we have seen, Anselm defines truth as rectitude, a quality indicating the accuracy of a sign vis-à-vis its object. It is not at all difficult for Anselm to assimilate the idea of necessity to the idea of rectitude, and this is precisely what he does. Thus, according to Anselm, an argument may be considered to have been proved by necessary reasons when it states that things are the way they really are, without invoking the support of a higher authority.[93]

Necessary reasons are therefore a mode of explaining the rectitude that exists between a sign and the object it signifies. They are not heuristic; their cognitive function is dependent on the hearer's prior knowledge of the object. In fact, the very same criteria apply to necessary reasons as apply to truth. All kinds of statements may be verified by means of necessary reasons. As we saw in the case of the *De grammatico*, they may be applied to purely academic questions. Apparently, their major practical limitation as epistemological tools seems to be the fact that they are usually grammatical in structure. In the case of theological questions, necessary reasons may likewise be used to verify statements about God, provided that these statements are consistent with God as He is. A concise definition of the nature, function, and limitations of necessary reasons may be found in the *Cur deus homo,* where Anselm, as magister, says to Boso, as discipulus:

> Since, in this inquiry, you take the place of those who
> are unwilling to believe anything not previously proved

93. Ibid., pp. 76, 78; Phelan, *Wisdom of St. Anselm,* pp. 29–32; MacIntyre, "Premises and Conclusions," *Spicilegium Beccense, 1,* 100.

by reason, I wish to have it understood between us that we do not admit anything in the least unbecoming to the Deity, and that we do not reject the smallest reason if it be not opposed by a greater. For as it is impossible to attribute anything in the least unbecoming to God; so any reason, however small, if not overbalanced by a greater, has the force of necessity.[94]

It is in this sense that Boso can say to Anselm at the end of the dialogue: "You prove that God became man by necessity."[95] Necessary reasoning, for Anselm, thus in no way implies that objects of knowledge can be altered, reified, or delimited by the human mind. What it does imply is that human words and ideas are validated and controlled by the objective realities they are designed to express, and that they can express these realities, in their own terms, with rectitude.

Necessary reasons are not only linked to rectitude. They are also linked to Anselm's third major epistemological preoccupation, the idea of fides quaerens intellectum. Fides quaerens intellectum sums up Anselm's epistemology. It presupposes and includes necessary reasons and the principle of rectitude, and it specifies his conception of the cognitive status of theological statements. Comment on this important question has usually been limited to its role in Anselm's proof of God's existence. As in the case of necessary reasons, there is good warrant for this; it is a well-known fact that Anselm entitled the *Proslogion* as *Fides quaerens intellectum* before giving it its later name.[96] It is, however, necessary to explore the meaning he attaches to fides quaerens intellectum in his other writings as well in order to appreciate fully what he means by this term in the proof.

An excellent source of information on fides quaerens intellectum is a series of letters which Anselm wrote to combat the

94. *Cur deus homo,* I, 10, Schmitt, *2,* 67, trans. Deane, pp. 200–01.
95. Ibid., II, 22, Schmitt, *2,* 133, trans. Deane, p. 287.
96. *Proslogion,* prooemium, Schmitt, *1,* 94.

Trinitarian doctrine of Roscellinus, a contemporary logician, whose nominalism inclined him toward tritheism. Anselm's attack on Roscellinus is the closest he comes to out-and-out polemic. In this rebuttal he rejects Roscellinus' position on two counts—the logician's faulty methodology and his faulty moral and intellectual attitude toward his subject. In connection with these two objections, Anselm reveals once again his grammatical orientation, and he has ample opportunity to develop his views on the role of arguments derived from human thought in theological speculation. He also gives a clear statement of his purposes in combatting Roscellinus, which provides a certain amount of insight into the epistemological functions he attributes to his own arguments.

When it comes to the actual content of Roscellinus' teachings, Anselm presents an objection derived bodily from the eleventh-century grammar with which, as we have seen, he was so deeply concerned. In fact, his argument is quite reminiscent of the *De grammatico*. He holds Roscellinus to be in error because his attribution of the names "Father," "Son," and "Holy Spirit" to the Persons of the Trinity, as Anselm understands them, is grammatically inaccurate. In Roscellinus' mouth, he states, these names are *flatus vocis,* because they are applied to God in the way that such terms as "white," "just," "king," and "grammarian" are applied to an individual man.[97] With our knowledge of *De grammatico* behind us, it is not difficult to appreciate Anselm's reasoning at this point. He deplores the confusion of the proper, substantial application of words to their objects with their improper and accidental applications. It is clear that Anselm's whole approach to this problem is verbal rather than logical. He understands Ros-

---

97. *Epistola de incarnatione verbi prior recensio,* II, IV, XI, Schmitt, *1,* 282-83, 290; *Epistola de incarnatione verbi,* I, Schmitt, *2,* 9. Precisely the same argument is offered by St. Bernard and his disciple, William of St. Thierry, in their objections to Peter Abelard's Trinitarian doctrine at the Council of Sens in 1142. See *Disputatio adversus Petrum Abaelardum ad Gaufridum Carnotensem et Bernardum,* II; *Disputatio catholicorum patrum adversus dogmata Petri Abaelardi,* I, *PL, 180, 253*-54, 290.

121

cellinus' position in terms of grammar rather than in terms of realism and nominalism.

Roscellinus' ideas are mistaken, according to Anselm. Even more noteworthy is his negative judgment on Roscellinus' moral and intellectual attitude. To Anselm it seems deplorable, almost inconceivable, that a man who is a Christian, and who thus may be assumed to know what he means when he uses the word "God," should have failed to ground his theological speculations on that knowledge. A Christian who speaks of the three Persons of the Trinity as if they were three *res* must be either grossly impious or so intellectually confused that he does not know what he is saying.[98] Roscellinus, along with the dubious "modern dialecticians" whom he represents, is clearly an intelligent man. Yet he attempts to reduce God to the dimensions of his own logic, to leap from thought to existence.[99] This would be a questionable procedure in any case, since rectitude demands that we employ the realities that we know as the criteria of our thoughts about them. It is an especially inappropriate procedure when it comes to God. In dealing with God, says Anselm, intellectual and moral rectitude demand our humble acknowledgment that He is a transcendent mystery and that He takes the initiative in our acquisition of whatever knowledge we have of Him: "By no means does God protect me if I dispute against the faith on how He does not exist. Through God's continual grace I believe, I love, I live for the disputation on how He does exist. If I am able to understand, I give thanks; if I cannot understand, I do not raise an outcry, but bow my head in worship." [100] In short, says Anselm, if one wishes to know God, one must first believe. Once firmly grounded in faith, the believer may investigate his beliefs with the greatest possible rigor; but this questioning is designed to explicate the rectitude of

98. *Epistola* CXXIX, Schmitt, *3, 272; Epistola de incarnatione verbi,* IV, Schmitt, *2,* 16–18.

99. *Epistola . . . prior recensio,* X, Schmitt, *1,* 289; *Epistola de incarnatione verbi,* IV–V, Schmitt, *2,* 16–19.

100. *Epistola . . . prior recensio,* IV, Schmitt, *1,* 282.

his beliefs, not to establish them in the first place.[101] This being the case, what value does Anselm attach to his own theological arguments against Roscellinus? His aims are limited; his comments are addressed to believers, as he puts it, "to confirm the faith of Christians." [102] Anselm explains what he means by this more fully in a letter written after Roscellinus' condemnation:

> Our faith should be defended by reason against the impious, not against those who rejoice in confessing the honorable name of Christian. For the latter, it is fitting that they be asked to search themselves regarding the admonitions given to them at baptism. For the former, the truth is shown rationally because they condemn us irrationally. Now a Christian ought to advance from faith to understanding. He should not approach by understanding, and, if understanding does not prevail, withdraw from faith.[103]

Judging from what Anselm has to say in this controversy, it might seem that he conceives of theology functioning exclusively as a series of correct statements about God, which, in showing the believer the rectitude of what he believes, serve to intensify his moral and intellectual appreciation of what he already knows by faith. It is undeniable that Anselm was an intramural theologian, and this is a fact which has been stressed by a number of scholars in their zeal to counteract the claims which others have made for the alleged apologetic character of his proof of God's existence. Most of the commentators who have advanced the purely intramural argument have cited the nature of Anselm's human environment to support their case. He lived, they note, in a world where atheism, skepticism, and religions other than Christianity were not well known enough to present a problem. Furthermore, he did most

101. Ibid., Schmitt, *1*, 284–85; *Epistola de incarnatione verbi*, I, Schmitt, *2*, 6–8.

102. *Epistola de incarnatione verbi*, I, Schmitt, *2*, 5.

103. *Epistola* **CXXXVI**, Schmitt, *4*, 280–81.

of his important theological work in the nondisputative, devotionally oriented atmosphere of the monastery.[104]

All of these conditions are real, and their significance should not be underestimated. However, in themselves they do not completely explain why Anselm thinks that theology can assist the believer; and they utterly fail to explain what Anselm thinks theology can do for the nonbeliever. It is necessary to point out that the nonbeliever exists in Anselm's writings. He is irreducibly there. It is probable, of course, that Anselm never met him in the flesh. One can only praise Weigel and Madden for their acute observation that

> the non-believer for Anselm is the non-believer of the order of Original Sin. Before that time [the Fall] man was in loving and familiar contact with God, and . . . would have seen the question [of God's existence and nature] lucidly. Of the man of pure nature, a later Scholastic conception, Anselm shows no awareness.[105]

We would certainly be the first to agree that Anselm saw the nonbeliever as a hypothetical straw man rather than as an organized contemporary threat to the Christian faith. On the whole, his controversial writings show that he was far more troubled by impiety and heterodoxy within the fold than by atheism. To the extent that he attacks individuals who disagree with him, he sees them not as Satanic intellects but as misguided Christians who have unaccountably gotten their heads screwed on backwards. Both in theory and in practice, Anselm's theology is weighted heavily in favor of the believer. Nevertheless, he does speak to, as well as about, the non-

104. Grabmann, *Geschichte, 1,* 282; Desmond Paul Henry, "The Proslogion Proofs," *The Philosophical Quarterly, 5* (1955), 147–51; Heyer, *"Rectitudo,"* pp. 80 ff.; Knowles, *Evolution of Medieval Thought,* p. 105; Leclercq, *The Love of Learning,* pp. 211–15; Southern, *Saint Anselm,* pp. 6–7, 47–49; "St. Anselm and His English Pupils," *MRS, 1* (1941–43), 29; Vignaux, *Philosophy in the Middle Ages,* pp. 39, 41–42; Gustave Weigel and Arthur G. Madden, *Religion and the Knowledge of God* (Englewood Cliffs, N.J., 1961), pp. 114, 115, 116–17.

105. Weigel and Madden, *Religion and the Knowledge of God,* p. 117.

124

believer, and he does think that the nonbeliever will be able to learn something from the argument of fides quaerens intellectum. It would be a gross mistake to overlook this fact, as it would prejudice one's understanding of Anselm's theory of knowledge from the outset. For Anselm, theological statements do not always function the same way. Their objective powers and limitations are permanent, for they are dictated by the intrinsic nature of correct signification. But their subjective powers and limitations are fluctuating; they are dictated by the moral and intellectual status of their audience with respect to their object, and are hence dependent on the individual and on God.

If we find in Anselm's *Epistolae* on the Trinity a case for intensive theology, his *Cur deus homo* provides us with a broader perspective. Here Anselm delineates the extensive role of theology as well and analyzes theological arguments by necessary reasons in relation both to their significata and to their hearers. He began to write the *Cur deus homo* when he was Archbishop of Canterbury and finished it during his Italian exile, which resulted from his conflict with King William II over lay investiture. This enforced travel may have widened Anselm's horizons; in any case, the preface of the work shows him to be quite serious about nonbelief. The *Cur deus homo,* he notes, is divided into two books:

> The first contains the objections of infidels, who despise the Christian faith because they deem it contrary to reason; and also the reply of believers; and, in fine, leaving Christ out of view, as if nothing had ever been known of Him, it proves, by absolute reasons (*rationibus necessariis*) the impossibility that any man should be saved without Him. Again, in the second book, likewise, as if nothing were known of Christ, it is moreover shown by plain reasoning and fact (*aperta ratione et veritate*) that human nature was ordained for this purpose, viz., that every man should enjoy a happy immortality, both in

125

body and in soul; and that it was necessary that this de-
sign for which man was made should be fulfilled; but
that it could not be fulfilled unless God became man, and
all things were to take place which we hold in regard to
Christ.[106]

Nonbelievers must be shown that Christianity is not irrational,
which demands arguments that do not depend on revelation.
Anselm thinks that arguments by necessary reasons will also
be useful to the believer faced with the task of answering the
objections of the infidel. He explains this point at further
length:

I have been often and most earnestly requested by
many . . . that I would hand down in writing the proofs
of a certain doctrine of our faith, which I am accustomed
to give to inquirers; for they say that these proofs
gratify them, and are considered sufficient. This they
ask, not for the sake of attaining to faith by means of
reason, but that they may be gladdened by understanding and meditating on those things which they believe;
and that, as far as possible, they may always be ready to
convince anyone who demands of them a reason of that
hope which is in us [I Pet. 3:15]. And this question, both
infidels are accustomed to bring up against us, ridiculing
Christian simplicity as absurd; and many believers pon-
der it in their hearts; for what cause or necessity, in
sooth, God became man . . . Therefore, since many desire to consider this subject, and, though it seem very
difficult in the investigation, it is yet plain to all in the
solution, and attractive for the value and beauty of the
reasoning; although what ought to be sufficient has been
said by the holy fathers and their successors, yet I will
take pains to disclose to inquirers what God has seen fit
to lay open to me.[107]

106. *Cur deus homo,* praefatio, Schmitt, 2, 42–43, trans. Deane, pp. 177–78.
107. *Cur deus homo,* I, 1, Schmitt, 2, 47–48, trans. Deane, pp. 178–79.

126

This is a very rich passage, and Anselm explores its implications at various points throughout the work. As he sees it, rational proofs can show the nonbeliever that Christian teachings are not absurd; but faith cannot be achieved by reason. Neither can reason dissolve the doubts of the faithful. Within the fold its task is to gladden the heart of the believer by helping him to understand the reason for his confidence, and to prepare him to defend the faith before nonbelievers.[108] In both cases, that of the believer and that of the nonbeliever, the same technique, argument by necessary reasons, is to be used.

According to Anselm, necessary reasons have several epistemological advantages. Like all signs possessing rectitude, they are accurate representations of their objects, so far as they go; and they are more useful than authoritative statements, which are not decisive for the nonbeliever.[109] They also have several epistemological limitations. Like all signs possessing rectitude, they are controlled by their objects. And, in the case of theology, statements cannot be correct or necessary if they attribute to God anything unjust, uncharitable, unfitting, lacking in harmonious proportions, or, in a word, inconsistent with His Divinity.[110] It must further be understood that, for Anselm, necessary reasons are auxiliary, but not essential, foundations of faith. Faith does not depend on rational proofs.[111] It is a gift of God; [112] and it is expressed sufficiently in the teachings of the Fathers of the Church. So embodied, it is the criterion of the necessity of any reasons invoked with respect to its contents. Finally, necessary reasons

108. A similar statement is made in *Cur deus homo,* I, 25, Schmitt, 2, 96, where Boso declares: "I come, not for this purpose, to have you remove doubts from my faith, but to have you show me the reason for my confidence" (trans. Deane, p. 238).

109. *Cur deus homo,* II, 13, Schmitt, 2, 113. See J. Bayart, "The Concept of Mystery according to St. Anselm of Canterbury," *Recherches de théologie ancienne et médiévale, 9* (1937), 165–66.

110. *Cur deus homo,* I, 3, 10, 12; II, 8, Schmitt, 2, 50–51, 67, 70, 104.

111. Ibid., I, 4, Schmitt, 2, 51–52.

112. Ibid., I, 1, Schmitt, 2, 48.

in theological questions are limited by the fact that their object cannot be known completely by the human mind; and, furthermore, that this object, God, must be loved in order to be known. Theological speculation, although true so far as it goes, must therefore combine moral and intellectual rectitude, and it can thus only be truly necessary if it reverently acknowledges its inadequacies in the face of Divine transcendence.[113]

We thus have in theological statements reasons which are necessary because they correspond to God, as previously known by faith on the part of the theologian. It should be noted that fides, for Anselm, means both the teachings of the Church as an objective norm of what is to be believed, and the subjective state of full, personal assent to it; there is no discrepancy between the two.[114] Intellectus is the believer's deepened awareness of the meaning of his faith, achieved by the quest for necessary reasons to fit the propositions of his creed. Intellectus fidei has been described as a form of contemplation which advances the believer on the road from faith to the vision of God.[115] A more complete definition of intellectus fidei would have to take into account the fact that it entails moral as well as mental transformation. Just as faith itself is a gift of God, so also intellectus fidei can take place only with the assistance of grace; its aim is beatitude, which is the consummation of the believer's love and knowledge of God.[116]

This aim, and the correlative method of fides quaerens intellectum, seem eminently plausible in the case of the believer.

113. Ibid., II, 17, Schmitt, 2, 126. Also noted by Bayart, "The Concept of Mystery"; Jacquin, "Les 'rationes necessariae,'" *Mélanges Mandonnet, 2*, 70; Vignaux, *Philosophy in the Middle Ages*, p. 38.

114. Hartman, "Prolegomena," *RM, 14*, 646, 647; Koyré, *L'Idée de Dieu*, pp. 24–26; Southern, *Saint Anselm*, p. 30.

115. Heyer, *"Rectitudo,"* pp. 80 ff.; Vignaux, *Philosophy in the Middle Ages*, p. 39.

116. *Cur deus homo*, I, 1; II, 1, 9, 22, Schmitt, *2*, 49, 97–98, 106, 133. See also Grabmann, *Geschichte, 1*, 283, 293 ff.; Jacquin, "Les 'rationes necessariae,'" p. 70; Weigel and Madden, *Religion and the Knowledge of God*, p. 116.

Anselm's confidence that it may plausibly be applied to the nonbeliever as well is based on the fact that the necessary reasons on which fides quaerens intellectum depends are not drawn from authority. Nonbelievers and believers are expected to listen to the same theological arguments. But they are not expected to profit from them in the same way. Necessary reasons cannot produce faith; the most they can do for a nonbeliever is to show him that Christian beliefs are not entirely incoherent. Anselm's preferred method for doing this, in the *Cur deus homo* as elsewhere, is by means of grammatical explanations,[117] although he also cites the persuasive power of the single argument.[118] For the believer, then, theology has an intensive and commemorative function; it gives him understanding and helps him to grow in the Christian life. For the nonbeliever, the same theology has a function which is purely indicative.[119]

In discussing the historical importance of Anselm, Southern has pointed out that "Augustine's thought was the pervading atmosphere in which Anselm moved. . . . Anselm, at his first appearance as a writer, was and claimed to be an *Augustinus minor;* but he was an Augustine formed by the logic, grammar and monastic life of the eleventh century." [120] From the point of view of the epistemology of theological statements,

117. The most extensive example is in *Cur deus homo,* I, 9, Schmitt, 2, 61–64.

118. Ibid., 24, Schmitt, 2, 94.

119. Jacquin, "Les 'rationes necessariae,'" p. 71. There has been some confusion on this point, to which Anselm himself contributes. Despite his clear statements in *Cur deus homo* to the effect that he is addressing nonbelievers as well as believers, his foil in the dialogue, Boso, is a Christian. Although Boso attempts to take the part of the man who will not believe unless he is convinced by reason (see, for example, I, 10, Schmitt, 2, 67), he is also, and more frequently, found in the role of the believer seeking to understand his faith (see, for example, I, 1, Schmitt, 2, 48–49). As far as scholarly comment on the intended intramural impact of Anselmian argument goes, Weigel and Madden, *Religion and the Knowledge of God,* pp. 114, 116, think that the force of the proof remains even if faith departs; and Heyer, *"Rectitudo,"* p. 74, thinks that the nonbeliever's willingness to listen testifies to an incipient faith on his part. We do not find anything in Anselm to support either of these interpretations.

120. Southern, *Saint Anselm,* pp. 32–33.

nothing could be more true than this observation. Working as he is in a different intellectual environment, with a much narrower range of antique sources, Anselm still manages to reiterate all of the salient aspects of Augustine's theory of signification—the accurate and yet limited status of signs in relation to their objects, and the differing subjective functions of signs, depending on the cognitive and affective status of their hearers vis-à-vis God—although he detaches the theory from its Augustinian framework of rhetoric, preferring to express it through grammar. Anselm's intellectual dependence upon and stylistic differences from Augustine have been noted in a variety of his works. They are nowhere more systematically revealed than in the three treatises which comprise his theology of God's existence; and it is to the *Monologion, Proslogion,* and *Contra Gaunilonem* that we now turn.

The first thing to be noticed about this series of works is their intention. The philosophical interest which they have aroused since the eleventh century has inclined people to focus attention on the proofs of God's existence which they contain. Strictly speaking, however, the *Monologion* and *Proslogion* are not exclusively, or even primarily, proofs of God's existence. A simple glance at the contents of these works should make this clear. The *Monologion* contains eighty chapters, of which I through IV deal with the existence of God; V through XXVIII deal with the nature of God and His relationships to the created universe; while chapters XXIX through LXXX, by far the largest portion of the work, deal with the Trinity. Among the twenty-six chapters of the *Proslogion,* I through IV discuss the existence of God; V through XXII, the bulk of the treatise, examine God's nature; XXIII is devoted to the Trinity; and XXIV through XXVI form a prayer directed to God as the end of man.

Anselm himself indicates what he thinks the *Monologion* and *Proslogion* are about in the prefaces of these two works. The *Monologion,* he states, represents his thoughts "regarding meditation of the Being of God, and on some other topics connected with this subject." [121] He describes the *Proslogion* as a continuation of the *Monologion,* a meditation "in the person of one who strives to lift his mind to the contemplation of God, and seeks to understand what he believes." [122] The similarities in subject and method are further visible in the titles he first selected for the two works, *Exemplum meditandi de ratione fidei* and *Fides quaerens intellectum.*[123] Nowhere in Anselm's work does he refer to the *Monologion* and *Proslogion* as proofs of God's existence. Rather, he sees them functioning together as attempts at Trinitarian speculation. In his *Epistola de incarnatione verbi,* he states that he wrote them so "that what we hold by faith of the Divine nature and His Persons, excepting the Incarnation, may be proved by necessary reasons (*necessariis rationibus*) without the authority of Scripture." [124] In his private correspondence, he further identifies the *Monologion* as a *De trinitate.*[125]

Certainly, Anselm's contemporaries shared his own views about his works. In discussing Anselm's writings, his biographer has this to say about the *Monologion* and *Proslogion:*

> Here [in the *Monologion*], putting aside all authority of Holy Scripture, he enquired into and discovered by reason alone what God is, and proved by invincible reason that God's nature is what the true faith holds it to be, and that it could not be other than it is. Afterwards it came into his mind [in the *Proslogion*] to try to prove by one single and short argument the things which are believed and preached about God, that He is eternal, un-

---

121. *Monologion*, prologus, Schmitt, *1*, 7, trans. Deane, p. 35.
122. *Proslogion*, prooemium, Schmitt, *1*, 93–94, trans. Deane, p. 2.
123. *Proslogion*, prooemium, Schmitt, *1*, 94. On the importance of meditation as a mental technique and the changes in the meaning of the term in the eleventh and twelfth centuries, see Southern, *Saint Anselm*, pp. 53–54.
124. *Epistola de incarnatione verbi*, VI, Schmitt, *2*, 20.
125. *Epistola LXXXIII*, Schmitt, *3*, 208.

changeable, omnipotent, omnipresent, incomprehensible, just, righteous, merciful, true, as well as truth, goodness, and so on; and to show how all these qualities are united in Him.[126]

Eadmer does not analyze the *Proslogion* any further, merely noting that after it was written a monk in a nearby monastery criticized it, and that Anselm had this critique and his reply to it attached to the body of the work.[127] Finally, in cataloging Anselm's theological contributions, Ordericus Vitalis notes: "At the requests of his friends, he piously wrote books of marvelous subtlety and profundity on the Trinity, on truth, on free will, on the fall of the Devil, and on why God was made man." [128] There is no mention of proofs of the existence of God.

As far as content, then, the "proof" is a *De trinitate,* which does not shrink from speculating on the most abstruse aspects of the Divine nature. From the point of view of method, Anselm specifies that necessary reasoning is to be the technique of argument, "in order that nothing in Scripture should be urged on the authority of Scripture itself, but that whatever the conclusion of independent investigation should declare to be true, should, in an unadorned style, with common proofs and with a simple argument, be briefly enforced by the cogency of reason *(rationis necessitas)*, and plainly expounded in the light of truth." [129]

There has been some confusion as to Anselm's meaning here, which arises from the fact that he cites the authority of St. Augustine's *De trinitate* immediately after he makes this statement.[130] Scholars, to be sure, have noticed Anselm's Augustinian tendency to argue the Trinitarian relations of the

126. Eadmer, *Vita Anselmi,* I, xix, trans. Southern, p. 29. Southern, p. 29, note 3, considers this an accurate assessement of Anselm's intention.

127. Ibid., pp. 30–31.

128. Ordericus Vitalis, *Historiae ecclesiasticae,* IV, x, Le Prevost, 2, 245.

129. *Monologion,* prologus, Schmitt, *1,* 7, trans. Deane, p. 35.

130. *Monologion,* prologus, Schmitt, *1,* 8.

Divine Persons on the analogy of the human mind as the image of God.[131] It is quite true that Anselm takes this style of argument, among others, from Augustine, not to mention his wholesale adoption of Augustine's epistemology of signs. However, it is important to understand exactly what kind of debt Anselm thought he owed to Augustine. When Anselm wrote the *Monologion*, he sent a copy to Lanfranc, then Archbishop of Canterbury.[132] Lanfranc's reaction was negative. He deplored the fact that Anselm had not documented the treatise with proofs drawn from scriptural and traditional authority. That Anselm was well aware of the fact that he was making a new departure is evident in the placatory tone he adopts when explaining his intentions in the preface to the *Monologion*.[133] He also answers Lanfranc's objection by pointing out that his work is not totally devoid of precedents, citing St. Augustine's *De trinitate:* "For, since this is how blessed Augustine proved his great disputations in his book *De trinitate,* I may argue in the same way, finding, as it were, my brief arguments in his sure authority." [134] It may seem strange to think of Augustine's *De trinitate* as a work proved by disputation. Anselm, however, clearly thinks that it is, and thus he uses it as a justification for his own method. He refers to Augustine not only because he is an authority in the Church, but also because he thinks that Augustine's style of argument in the *De trinitate* validates and confirms his own technique of argument by necessary reasons.

The specific kind of necessary reasons which Anselm employs in the *Monologion, Proslogion,* and *Contra Gaunilonem* tend to be grammatical in nature. His principal methods for implementing necessary reasoning in these three works are equipollent proofs and explanations turning on the grammati-

131. Grabmann, *Geschichte, 1,* 284 ff.; Heyer, *"Rectitudo,"* pp. 67–69; Southern, *Saint Anselm,* p. 50; Vignaux, *Philosophy in the Middle Ages,* pp. 36, 38; "Structure et sens du *Monologion," RSPT, 31* (1947), 197.

132. *Epistola* LXXII, Schmitt, *3,* 193–94.

133. *Monologion,* prologus, Schmitt, *1,* 8.

134. *Epistola* LXXVII, Schmitt, *3,* 199.

cal relationships among words. That equipollency is a sure path to the rectitude on which truth depends is underlined in the *De veritate,* where the discipulus at the beginning of the dialogue insists that the magister demonstrate his conclusions with a "definition of truth," as he had in the *Monologion.*[135] It has been appreciated that the *Proslogion* proof turns on the definition of a name,[136] and the importance of nominal definitions has also been noted in the case of the *Monologion.*[137] The use of definition is basic to these works in the sense of the quest for names of God that possess rectitude. To find these names, Anselm moves from one definition to another by equipollency.

Anselm chooses proof by definition as the style of the *Monologion* and *Proslogion* not only because he thinks of it as the most plausible expression of necessary reasoning, but also because he considers it the most appropriate style for the audience to which both works are addressed. Despite the intramural emphasis of these two works, they are both intended for nonbelievers as well as for believers. The statement in which Anselm explains that he wrote the *Monologion* because "certain brethren have often and earnestly entreated me to put into writing some thoughts that I had . . . regarding meditation on the Being of God" [138] is well known. Apparently less well known is the fact that he goes on to say, "It was their wish also, that I should not disdain to meet such simple and almost foolish objections as occur to me." [139] We find that at several points in the *Monologion,* Anselm has occasion to direct his attention to the "simple" and "foolish," who object to Christian teachings because of impudence, imprudence, falsehood, or impiety.[140] He also poses the problem

135. *De veritate,* I, Schmitt, *1,* 176. As Southern, *Saint Anselm,* p. 32, points out, definitions play an important role in Anselm's major works.
136. Heyer, *"Rectitudo,"* p. 71.
137. Vignaux, "Structure et sens," *RSPT, 31,* 200–01.
138. *Monologion,* prologus, Schmitt, *1,* 7, trans. Deane, p. 35.
139. Ibid., trans. Deane, pp. 35–36.
140. Ibid., IV, VI, VIII, XXII, Schmitt, *1,* 17, 19, 23, 31, 40.

of nonbelief at some length in the *Monologion,* explaining that his style of argument is tailored to the demands of that position.[141]

Similarly, in the *Proslogion,* we find Anselm repeating his intention of writing "at the solicitous entreaties of certain brethren," [142] a plausible audience in view of the extensive use of prayer which he makes in this work. At the same time, he chooses the famous nonbelieving fool of the Psalmist as the butt of his argument in Chapters II through IV. It is evident that these works have a twofold intention. This is a point which Anselm takes pains to re-emphasize in his *Epistola de incarnatione verbi,* when he discusses why he wrote the *Monologion* and *Proslogion:* "I set myself to answer on behalf of our faith those who, refusing to believe what they do not understand, make fun of believers, as well as to assist the religious study of those who humbly seek to understand what they already believe most firmly." [143]

The intensive and extensive functions of arguments by necessary reasons are thus visible in both the *Monologion* and the *Proslogion.* Here, as elsewhere, Anselm's confidence that the same arguments can function in two different ways for two different audiences at the same time is based on his concept of the cognitive strengths and weaknesses of linguistic, and particularly grammatical, signs. His frequent insistence on the necessity, truth, and persuasiveness of the arguments that he uses in these works, already noted, indicates his assurance that it is possible to speak about God with rectitude. The prayerful nature of the *Proslogion,* sometimes interpreted as a rejection of logic for devotion, is actually a refinement of Anselm's method. Just as he thinks that his proof in the *Proslogion* is enhanced because he has found a single demonstration to replace the several arguments for God's existence in the

---

141. Ibid., I, Schmitt, *1,* 13–14.

142. *Proslogion,* prooemium, Schmitt, *1,* 93, trans. Deane, p. 1. The dual function of the *Proslogion* has also been noted by Southern, *Saint Anselm,* p. 63.

143. *Epistola de incarnatione verbi,* VI, Schmitt, *3,* 20–21.

Monologion,[144] so the introduction of prayer in the later work should be seen as the decision to employ a research device that will result in a high degree of rectitude, considering the nature of the object of knowledge in question. As Anselm puts it: "Teach me to seek thee, and reveal thyself to me, when I seek thee, for I cannot seek thee, except thou teach me, nor find thee, except thou reveal thyself. Let me seek thee in longing, let me long for thee in seeking; let me find thee in love, and love thee in finding." [145]

With the proper attitude and technique, then, words about God can be true and thus necessary. At the same time, Anselm stresses, no statement about God can be totally accurate nor totally convincing. Anselm insists that his intention as a theologian is purely utilitarian. He formulates his speculations, he says, with an eye to their practicality.[146] Yet, at the same time, we find him protesting his ineptitude and voicing the hope that his work will soon be obsolete.[147] The nonbeliever, he thinks, can be persuaded by reason for the most part, but not completely; and the arguments by necessary reasons directed at him are not omnipotent, but provisional:

> And if, in this discussion, I use any argument which no greater authority adduces, I wish it to be received in this way: although, on the grounds that I shall see fit to adopt, the conclusion is reached as if necessarily, yet it is not for this reason, said to be absolutely necessary, but merely that it can appear so for the time being.[148]

In both the *Monologion* and *Proslogion,* we find Anselm building up proofs about God's nature on the analogy of human phenomena.[149] At a certain point, however, he sys-

---

144. *Proslogion,* prooemium, Schmitt, *1,* 93.
145. Ibid., I, Schmitt, *1,* 100, trans. Deane, p. 6.
146. *Monologion,* prologus, Schmitt, *1,* 7.
147. Ibid., pp. 7–8.
148. Ibid., I, Schmitt, *1,* 14, trans. Deane, p. 38. Noted also by Southern, *Saint Anselm,* p. 57.
149. *Monologion,* X, XXI, XXIX, XXXIII, XLVII–L, LIX–LX, LXII,

136

tematically breaks down these analogies in order to stress the uniqueness and transcendence of God. The functions of the human mind, human thought and language, he holds, must in the end stand abashed before God.[150] Both the building up and the breaking down of these analogies are Augustinian devices; and so are a number of the characteristics which Anselm analogizes to God, as we shall see below. The epistemological conclusions that Anselm reaches in the *Monologion* and *Proslogion* likewise reflect Augustine's view of the theological statement as an accurate, yet partial, *aenigma*. God is ineffable, Anselm agrees; yet we must speak about Him in order to know Him and to love Him.[151] And, by extension, we must also speak about God in order to inspire this knowledge and love in others. When he wishes to convey the simultaneous expressiveness and poverty of language, Anselm occasionally has recourse to the sensuous imagery of the mystics.[152] Still, he does not avoid the difficult question: Given God's transcendence, how can men possibly say things about Him that are valid? In answer, Anselm explains that theological statements may be valid without infringing on God's ineffability, so long as we remember that our words do not apply to God and to other things to which they may be applied in the same way. We know and express God, he says, through words, as through a reflection in a mirror:

> For often we speak of things which we do not express with precision as they are; but by another expression we indicate what we are unwilling or unable to express with precision, as when we speak in riddles (*aenigmata*). And often we see a thing, not precisely as it is in itself, but

LXVI–LXVII, LXX; *Proslogion*, VI–VII, XIII, Schmitt, *1*, 24, 36–38, 48–49, 52, 63–65, 70–71, 72, 77–78, 80–81, 104–05, 110.

ˈ 150. *Monologion*, XI–XII, XV–XVI, XXII, XXVI, XXVIII, XXIX, XXXVI, XXXVIII, LXIV–LXV; *Proslogion*, XV, Schmitt, *1*, 26, 29–30, 39, 44, 45–46, 47, 54–55, 56, 74–77, 112.

151. *Proslogion*, XXVII, Schmitt, *1*, 120–22.

152. Ibid., XVII, Schmitt, *1*, 113.

through a likeness or image, as when we look upon a face in a mirror. And in this way, we often express and yet do not express, see and yet do not see, one and the same object; we express and see it through another; we do not express it, and do not see it by virtue of its own proper nature.

On these grounds, then, it appears that there is nothing to disprove the truth of our discussion thus far, concerning the supreme Nature, and yet this Nature itself remains not the less ineffable, if we believe that it has never been expressed according to the peculiar nature of its own being, but somehow described through another.[153]

By its nature and in its operations, then, the human mind, for Anselm as for Augustine, is the most adequate *speculum Dei*.[154] Before meeting God in face-to-face vision, man may learn to know and to love Him by contemplating his own mind. The human analogies by which he does this, though they are only reflections in a mirror, are still the best aenigmata of God available in this life.[155]

A closer look at the *Monologion, Proslogion,* and *Contra Gaunilonem* will provide a clearer idea of how Anselm puts into practice his concept of the powers and limitations of theological statements, which we have just examined from a theoretical point of view. Let us begin with the *Monologion*, the earliest work in this series of three. In the *Monologion*, Anselm alternates between the use of equipollent proofs and explanations drawn from grammatical analysis, although he is also heavily indebted to arguments borrowed from St. Augus-

---

153. *Monologion*, LXV, Schmitt, *1*, 76, trans. Deane, pp. 129–30. Vignaux, "Structure et sens," *RSPT, 31*, 200–01, points out that superlatives in Anselm do not express God substantially, but refer to the relationship between God and not-God. Heyer, "*Rectitudo*," p. 71, holds that Anselmian statements do not refer to God substantially unless they are in the negative, a point which we find contrary to Anselm.

154. *Monologion*, LXVI–LXX, Schmitt, *1*, 77–81. See also *Epistola de incarnatione verbi*, XVI, Schmitt, *2*, 35.

155. *Monologion*, X, XXXI, LXII, Schmitt, *1*, 24–25, 48, 72.

tine. He establishes the proof of God's existence at the beginning of the work by equipollency. Anselm opens the treatise with the statement that all men naturally desire the things which they judge to be good. From this assertion he infers that all men should want to know the ultimate cause of the goods which they desire.[156] This sounds as if Anselm is laying the foundation for an a posteriori proof of God's existence. But such is not the case. Rather, his proof is based on a theory of participation and proportionality. One can discern sensibly and intellectually, says Anselm, that not all things are equally good. There are degrees of goodness, which we understand in terms of the quality of goodness itself; a thing is good insofar as it participates in goodness. Above and beyond degrees of goodness, he notes, it can also be seen that things are good in different ways. They must therefore be judged not only in terms of the extent to which they participate in goodness, but also by their relationship to goodness; that is, in terms of whether or not they promote goodness.[157] This reasoning depends on the existence of a quintessential good, which serves as the norm of other, lesser goods, a notion reminiscent of Platonic idealism. It is just at this point, however, that Anselm interjects a series of equipollent definitions into his argument, by means of which this Greek abstraction is translated into an entity capable of being equated with the God of Abraham, Isaac, and Jacob.

The first shift in definition is the almost imperceptible conversion of this supreme good into a being. Next, since this being is indubitably very good, and since all other goods exist through it and in relation to it, it must therefore be self-existent, assuming the absurdity of infinite regress. As self-existent, it is not merely very good, but supremely good. Anselm's third step is to redefine the supremely good as the supremely great, the highest of all existing things. Its very self-existence, he says, shows that it exists in the greatest degree of all beings; and, as such, it is not difficult for him to add that it

---

156. Ibid., I, Schmitt, *1*, 13–14.
157. Ibid., Schmitt, *1*, 14–15.

is unitary.[158] By the time Anselm has reached the end of Chapter IV, which terminates the proof of God's existence in the *Monologion,* he has managed to expand and to specify his definition considerably:

> There is, therefore, a certain Nature, or Substance, or Essence, which is through itself good and great, and through itself what it is; and through which exists whatever is truly good, or great, or has any existence at all; and which is the supreme being, being or subsisting as supreme, that is, the highest of all existing beings.[159]

Thus, by progressively redefining the idea of good, Anselm emerges with a Supreme Being, Who can be called a nature, substance, or essence, Who is great, one, and self-subsistent as well as good, and through Whom all goodness, being, and truth exist. With this definition well in hand, he has a solid basis for his further equipollent elaborations on the nature of this Being, and His relationships with the existents for which He is responsible.

Actually, Anselm has more or less inferred the proof *that* a Supreme Being exists. There is, for example, no particular reason to assume at the outset that the various goods which men desire on earth do, in fact, have a single cause. However, as we have seen, by redefining goodness, Anselm works out the unity of the Supreme Being, as well as His aseity and supremacy over all other beings. *That* such a Supreme Being exists is established by equipollency. When it comes to establishing the *how* of His attributes, Anselm has recourse to grammatical explanations of several kinds. In the case of existence per se, he unfolds the relationship between essence and existence in the Supreme Being by comparing it to the relationship between a noun and the infinitive and participle of the verb derived from it:

158. Ibid., I–III, Schmitt, *1,* 15–16.
159. Ibid., IV, Schmitt, *1,* 17–18, trans. Deane, p. 45.

> Finally, as to how it [the Supreme Being] should be understood to exist through itself, and to derive existence from itself, . . . it seems best to conceive of this subject in the way in which one says that the light lights or is lucent, through and from itself. For as are the mutual relations of the light and to light and lucent (*lux et lucere et lucens*), such are the relations of essence and to be and being (*essentia et esse et ens*). [160]

A second problem is that of creation *ex nihilo*. Its solution, according to Anselm, turns on the way in which the word "nothing" is understood. "Nothing," says Anselm, may be understood in three ways: as a *façon de parler,* when we mean that what we are talking about has never really existed; as a real entity, capable of action or passion; and as the negative of "anything." In the first case, he says, "nothing" may be true figuratively, but it is unintelligible when applied to real things literally. In the second case, "nothing" may have a natural truth in the sense that it expresses the intention of the speaker, but it is otherwise self-contradictory. If "nothing" is understood in the third sense, however, it may be said without inconsistency that the Supreme Being created the universe from nothing.[161]

In the next section of the *Monologion,* Anselm extends his discussion of the relations between the Creator and the creation. He continues to employ equipollency and grammatical arguments here, but he also displays an increased use of Augustinian devices, as well as an increased interest in the limitations to which human speech is subjected in reference to the Supreme Being. Pursuing further the mode of creation, Anselm states that created things had an existence in the mind of the Creator before they were made visible. He draws upon the Augustinian analogy of the formation of concepts in the

160. *Monologion,* VI, Schmitt, *1,* 20, trans. Deane, p. 49. Noted also by Vignaux, "Structure et sens," *RSPT, 31,* 202.
161. *Monologion,* VIII, Schmitt, *1,* 23.

human mind to explain this process. Just as a man has interior *locutiones mentis* before expressing himself in externally perceptible signs, he states, so the Creator has locutiones about the universe before He reifies it externally. Since this is so, the world exists in and through the creative expression of the Supreme Being.[162] Having noted this comparison, Anselm at once proceeds to depreciate the similarities between the operation of the human mind and that of the Creator, from which point he launches into an extensive discussion of the qualifications that must be made in speaking about the Supreme Being. He outlines three major limitations that pertain to the analogy based on human thought. Unlike men, says Anselm, the Creator needs no materials or images drawn from external sources in order to formulate His thoughts; He is absolutely original. Also, He can reify His thoughts at will. Finally, there is no gap in the Creator between either thought and expression or being and expression.[163]

The identity between the Creator and His *verbum mentis* means that man experiences the same general difficulties in trying to speak about either of them. These difficulties are considerable. The first one which Anselm attempts to solve concerns the sense in which different kinds of statements can be true of the Creator:

> I am now strongly impelled to inquire . . . which of all the statements that may be made regarding anything is substantially applicable to this so wonderful Nature. For . . . I should be surprised if, among the names or words (*nominibus vel verbis*) by which we designate things created from nothing, any should be found that could worthily be applied to the Substance which is the creator of all.[164]

162. Ibid., IX–X, XIII–XIV, Schmitt, *1,* 24–25, 27.
163. Ibid., XI–XII, Schmitt, *1,* 26.
164. Ibid., XV, Schmitt, *1,* 28, trans. Deane, p. 61.

He concludes that relative statements, that is, statements involving comparative adjectives, cannot be attributed properly to the Creator. Comparisons, such as "supreme," "greatest," or "highest," he says, imply the ability on the part of the subject they modify to suffer addition or diminution. They also imply the necessity of the creation in terms of which the Creator is supreme, whereas in truth His nature is not changed by the presence or absence of other beings. Thus, relative statements, whether positive or negative, do not describe Him substantially. On the other hand, Anselm holds that nonrelative expressions, such as infinitive statements, may be properly and truly applied to the Creator, so long as the characteristics which these statements attribute to Him are better than they are not. The accurate infinitive statement may be positive or negative, depending on its content.[165]

Anselm adds a series of further limitations to the strictures that he applies to relative and infinitive statements. These limitations pertain to the sense in which the terms "substance" and "quality" may be applied to the Supreme Being. Unlike other things, he observes, the Supreme Being is identical with His qualities. He does not participate in them, as this would entail the existence of entities prior to Him. Since He is simple, He is not a composite of His attributes, a condition which presupposes a whole made up of parts.[166] Anselm establishes these conclusions equipollently, by deductions from the definition of the Supreme Being at which he has already arrived. He employs redefinitions, grammar, and Augustinian arguments in explaining the categories of time and space as they apply to the Supreme Being. This Being, he says, is atemporal and aspatial, and is yet everywhere all the time. His atemporality is deduced from His self-subsistence, as well as from His status as truth. Nothing can precede Him, infers Anselm; and truth must be eternal in order for any

165. Ibid., Schmitt, *1*, 28–29.
166. Ibid., XVI–XVII, Schmitt, *1*, 30–32.

statement about eternity to be true.[167] Repeating his previous explanation of creation ex nihilo, Anselm notes that
here, too, "nothing" must be treated as the negative of "anything," rather than as a real entity, in order for the reader to
achieve a correct understanding of the statement that nothing
preceded the Supreme Being.[168]

The nature of time itself is a problem which Anselm solves
in an Augustinian fashion, although his speculations lack the
psychological profundity of the *Confessiones*. He notes that
time comes in three dimensions, past, present, and future,
which are understood in terms of the three tenses of the verb.
He further observes that the present tense is the only one
which really applies to the Supreme Being.[169] Similar considerations apply to space, but here it is the adverb whose nature Anselm scrutinizes.[170] In general, he concludes that the
Supreme Being transcends the categories of time and space.
We can speak correctly of time and space with respect to Him
only if we remember that they do not apply to Him substantially, but "according to the consistent truth of different
senses of the terms employed." [171] To complete his treatment
of the attribution of "substance" and "accident" to the Supreme Being, Anselm redefines atemporality and aspatiality
into immutability. From this vantage point he observes that
"accident" may not be properly attributed to the Supreme
Being, since He suffers no change.[172] "Substance" is also improper because it denotes something which can be affected by
accidents.[173] Strictly speaking, then, neither these nor other
words which we apply to the Supreme Being can be applied
substantially. Although we do apply them to Him, we must re-

167. Ibid., XVIII, Schmitt, *1*, 32–33.
168. Ibid., XIX, Schmitt, *1*, 33–35.
169. Ibid., XXI, Schmitt, *1*, 37–38.
170. Ibid., XXII–XXIII, Schmidt, *1*, 39–42.
171. Ibid., XXII, Schmitt, *1*, 41, trans. Deane, p. 81.
172. *Monologion*, XXV, Schmitt, *1*, 43–44.
173. Ibid., XXVI, Schmitt, *1*, 44.

member that He is unique and transcendent,[174] and "if He ever shares any name with other beings, doubtless a very different signification of that name is to be understood in His case." [175]

In the Trinitarian section of the *Monologion,* proofs based on the usage of words are absent, except where Anselm wishes to specify the limitations of language. Equipollency and Augustinian arguments predominate. Anselm begins his discussion of the Trinity by analyzing the Creator's verbum mentis, a definition already established. On the basis of this definition he deduces that the Word is one, coeternal, consubstantial, and coessential with the Creator.[176] The Word, he states, is not subject to the change and imperfection of the created universe, which is His image and which exists through Him; in short, the Word is related to the creation in exactly the same manner as the Creator is.[177]

When it comes to the relations of the Three Persons of the Trinity among themselves, Anselm relies extensively on the Augustinian triad of *intellectus-memoria-voluntas,*[178] although here, as in his discussion of time, his analysis is not particularly profound. According to Anselm, man's difficulties in knowing the Trinity spring from defective comprehension on man's part as well as from ineffability on God's part. It is impossible, he notes, for man to grasp precisely how God knows His creation.[179] It is even more difficult for man to grasp precisely how the Creator and His Word can be two and yet one, although, he thinks, the terms "Father" and "Son" have a high degree of rectitude.[180] Most difficult of all is the

174. Ibid., XXVIII, Schmitt, *1,* 45.

175. Ibid., XXVI, Schmitt, *1,* 44, trans. Deane, p. 86. I have substituted "He" for "it" in Deane's version.

176. *Monologion,* XXIX, XXX, XXXIII, XLIV, Schmitt, *1,* 47–48, 51–53, 60–61.

177. Ibid., XXXI, XXXV, XXXVII, Schmitt, *1,* 48–50, 54, 55.

178. Ibid., XLVII–LXIII, Schmitt, *1,* 63–75.

179. Ibid., XXXVI, Schmitt, *1,* 54–55.

180. Ibid., XXXVIII–XLIII, Schmitt, *1,* 56–60.

relationship among the Father, the Son, and the Holy Spirit. This problem impels Anselm to reinforce his caveat against applying human words to the Supreme Being substantially.[181] Still, he argues, the gaps in man's knowledge of the Supreme Being should not lead to despair and loss of faith. Anselm attempts to provide some consolation by elaborating some of the positive features of human nature, on the basis of his definition of the human mind as the best *speculum* of the Trinity. Man, he states, was created to know and to love God. He may do this partially in his earthly life. But, given the kind of being man is and the kind of being God is, Anselm can deduce the immortality and the potential beatitude of the human soul.[182] Given the possibility of eternal beatitude, he argues, men should be able to believe and hope in God, even though they cannot know Him completely in this life. Furthermore, they should love Him, which entails a faith living in good works.[183]

The process of redefinition, then, terminates in this point, apparent from Anselm's reasoning: "And so it is evidently expedient for every man to believe in a certain ineffable trinal unity, and in one Trinity." [184] But the real end of the *Monologion* is reached when Anselm states his final definition of the Supreme Being, in which he asserts that all the definitions and explanations that have gone before it, and the name itself, are true, proper, and necessary. "To this Supreme Being," he says, "the name *God* is properly given (*proprie nomen dei assignatur*)." [185] The whole treatise is a quest for a name of God that possesses rectitude.

Anselm carries on this quest for a name of God rather more concisely in the *Proslogion*. His principal technique in this work is equipollency, although there are a few important places where Anselm's point turns on the usage of words.

181. Ibid., LXIII, LXV, Schmitt, *1*, 73–74, 75–76.
182. Ibid., LXVI–LXXII, Schmitt, *1*, 77–82.
183. Ibid., LXXIV–LXXVI, LXXVIII, Schmitt, *1*, 82–84, 84–85.
184. Ibid., LXXIX, Schmitt, *1*, 85, trans. Deane, p. 142.
185. *Monologion*, LXXX, Schmitt, *1*, 86, trans. Deane, p. 143.

Augustinian proofs are absent, although the temper of the devotion in the treatise, particularly the prefatory *Excitatio mentis ad contemplandum deum,* has Augustinian overtones.[186] From the brevity of many of Anselm's arguments in the *Proslogion,* he seems to be presupposing that the reader has first studied the *Monologion,* where all of the same problems are analyzed in greater detail. As in the *Monologion,* he addresses the believer seeking to understand his faith. His aim here is to find necessary reasons which will explain that God is *what* we believe Him to be and *as* we believe Him to be; God's nature as well as His existence is to be considered. He also addresses himself to the fool who says in his heart, "There is no God." For Anselm, the question raised by the fool is not "Is he right?" but "Why is he wrong?" In explaining why the fool is wrong, he is able to show that his own definition of God, "that than which nothing greater can be conceived (*aliquid quo maius nihil cogitari potest*),"[187] possesses rectitude vis-à-vis the God of faith.

This name of God does not imply that either God's existence or His nature is contingent in any way on the powers of the human mind. Rather, Anselm intends the formula to indicate, first, that God is the greatest being and, second, that we can conceive of Him. By putting the definition in the negative, Anselm gains the advantage of being able to develop the first stage of his argument without having to prove that God is a being; he chooses this name because it is the simplest one he can find. From Anselm's point of view, the beauty of the name lies in the fact that it is a self-evident definition; it virtually proves itself. Only one major equipollent redefinition is needed to show that the name is an accurate designation of God. This step is based on the distinction between knowledge *in solo in-*

186. It has frequently been suggested that the *Proslogion* proof is Augustinian because Anselm's name of God resembles similar formulae found in Augustine's works. Augustine, however, cannot be thought of as Anselm's only probable source on this point. See Schmitt, *1,* 102, note; Jules Vergnes, "Les sources de l'argument de Saint Anselme," *RSR, 4* (1924), 576–79.

187. *Proslogion,* II, Schmitt, *1,* 101.

tellectu and knowledge *et in intellectu et in re*.[188] If "aliquid quo maius nihil cogitari potest" exists only in the mind, says Anselm, it does not conform to its definition. In order for it to be truly that than which nothing greater can be conceived, it must exist both in the mind and in reality.[189] Thus, the name proves the existence of the being which it defines.

According to Anselm, the reason why the fool is wrong is because he fails to make this distinction between esse in solo intellectu and esse et in intellectu et in re. He therefore confuses mental and extra-mental realities. He has in his mind the idea of God as "aliquid quo maius nihil cogitari potest," and he must know what this phrase means, otherwise it would not occur to him to reject it as false. However, he assumes that his negation of God's existence is an accurate statement about the world outside his mind.[190] It is not Anselm, but the fool, who makes an unwarranted leap from thought to being. What Anselm does, on the other hand, is to move from being to thought in the formulation of a name of God that does not contradict the nature of God as He is. The key to the fool's mistake lies in the fact that there are two kinds, or degrees, of truth in Anselm's epistemology. A word may have a natural truth when it accurately signifies the intention of the speaker, even when it is a *flatus vocis* with respect to existing things outside of the speaker's mind. A word may have both truth and rectitude if it correctly signifies its real object as well as the intention of the speaker.[191] "Non est deus," in the mouth of the fool, is an example of a sign with a truth that is merely natural. "Aliquid quo maius nihil cogitari potest," on the other hand, is a sign possessing both truth and rectitude. Rectitude cannot be divorced from being, but this is because rectitude is

188. Ibid., Schmitt, *1*, 101–02.

189. Ibid.

190. Ibid. According to Southern, *Saint Anselm*, pp. 60–61, and "St. Anselm and His English Pupils," *MRS*, *1*, 30, the fool uses words without understanding what they mean. It would be more accurate to say that the fool uses words with only a limited truth.

191. *Proslogion*, IV, Schmitt, *1*, 103–04.

148

dependent on being rather than vice versa. Anselm's name of God can be called *"verissimum"* because it conforms to its object, the being which exists most truly.[192]

Once having established the rectitude of the definition of God as "aliquid quo maius nihil cogitari potest," it is a fairly simple matter for Anselm to redefine this name equipollently so as to work out the salient attributes of God. Most of the argumentation here is an abstract of the same points in the *Monologion*. Thus, he shows God to be self-existent, the creator of the world ex nihilo, supremely good and hence just, truthful, and blessed, and, in short, whatever it is better to be than not to be.[193] God is consequently omniscient [194] and omnipotent. It is only on the subject of God's omnipotence that Anselm diverges from his equipollent arguments in favor of a strictly grammatical explanation. This explanation is identical to the discussion of relative and infinitive statements and their comparative applicability to God in *Monologion* XV, and the point at issue is reminiscent of the *De potestate et impotentia*, where he takes up the same problem but does not solve it. How, he asks, can we say that God is omnipotent when there are some things, namely evil things, which He cannot do? Are His inabilities in this respect a real curtailment of His power? Anselm answers that God's inability to do evil in no way qualifies His omnipotence, because *not* to be able to do evil is better than *to* be able to do evil, and is consequently true of God.[195]

Reverting to equipollency, Anselm further deduces that God is immutable and yet compassionate. This paradox can be explained, he says, by the fact that He is immutable *in se* but compassionate *ad nos*. His compassion extends to all, even to the wicked, because it operates in accordance with God's nature rather than being proportioned to our own just deserts.

192. Ibid., III, Schmitt, *1*, 103.
193. Ibid., V, Schmitt, *1*, 104.
194. Ibid., VI, Schmitt, *1*, 104–05.
195. Ibid., VII, Schmitt, *1*, 105–06.

This idea may seem difficult for men to understand, says Anselm, but it is true, because the reverse would be impious. In any case, he points out, justice, if necessary, can be redefined as the will of God, which effectively takes care of the problem.[196] Continuing to deduce attributes from his definitions, Anselm goes on to show that God is simple,[197] unbounded by time and space,[198] that He is light, wisdom, goodness, truth, eternal blessedness and blessed eternity, and finally that He is known and yet unknown, both because the human mind is dazzled by God's brightness and because it is darkened by its own intellectual and moral infirmities.[199] Anselm ends this section of the *Proslogion* with the affirmation that he has, in fact, proved that his original definition holds up under scrutiny: "Therefore, O Lord, thou art not only that than which a greater cannot be conceived, but thou art a being greater than can be conceived (*non solum es quo maius cogitari nequit, sed es quidam maius quam cogitari possit*)."[200] The importance of this final definition is that it recognizes God's unknowability as an integral part of His existence and nature.[201]

The remainder of the *Proslogion* is devoted, in effect, to a commentary on the known unknowability of God. For this reason there is a shift in method; the necessary reasons which best express this situation and the attitude which it demands are reverent statements rather than equipollent definitions. Consequently, Anselm makes practically no attempt to prove the assertion sets forth in Chapters XVI through XXVI. Instead, we find an extended prayer in which he catalogs Divine attributes, usually reiterating characteristics that he has already proved, in a tone of voice calculated to impress upon the reader the necessity of mental humility before God. He

196. Ibid., VIII–XI, Schmitt, *1*, 106–10.
197. Ibid., XII, XVIII, Schmitt, *1*, 110, 113–15.
198. Ibid., XIII, Schmitt, *1*, 110–11.
199. Ibid., XIV, Schmitt, *1*, 111–12.
200. Ibid., XV, Schmitt, *1*, 112, trans. Deane, p. 22.
201. Anton C. Pegis, "St. Anselm and the Argument of the Proslogion," *Mediaeval Studies, 28* (1966), 248–51.

begins with the point that God is incomprehensible,[202] then modulates into a mystic key by describing Him as ineffably beautiful, harmonious, fragrant, sweet, and pleasant.[203] God, continues Anselm, is atemporal, aspatial,[204] and transcendent;[205] He is wisdom, life, truth, blessedness, and eternity existing as one.[206] God is simply who He is. For Anselm, this implies the personal dimensions of Divinity best designated in the doctrine of the Trinity.[207] Paralleling his organization in the *Monologion*, Anselm ends the *Proslogion* by praising God as man's true delight, salvation, and eternal joy, by exhorting the reader to translate this conclusion into appropriate action, and by presenting himself as an example of one whose knowledge and love of God on earth inspire his hopes for the consummation of that love and knowledge in beatitude.[208]

Where the *Monologion* is an extended quest for a name of God that possesses rectitude, combined with a series of proofs which explain the nature of that rectitude, the *Proslogion* is a treatise in which the *rectum nomen* has already been found before the work begins. It is likewise written to explain the rectitude of the name.[209] Although less detailed and explicit than the *Monologion*, the *Proslogion* is in some respects a better demonstration, because of its greater economy and also because it illustrates Anselm's meaning by its shifts in form as well as by his use of equipollency and grammatical explanations. In this latter sense, one might consider the *Proslogion*, Anselm's most individual work, as more "Augustinian" in spirit than the *Monologion*, notwithstanding the fact that the

---

202. *Proslogion*, XVI, Schmitt, *1*, 112–13.

203. Ibid., XVII, Schmitt, *1*, 113.

204. Ibid., XIX, XXI, Schmitt, *1*, 115, 116.

205. Ibid., XX, Schmitt, *1*, 115–16.

206. Ibid., XVIII, Schmitt, *1*, 113–15.

207. Ibid., XXII–XXIII, Schmitt, *1*, 116–17.

208. Ibid., XXIV–XXVI, Schmitt, *1*, 117–22.

209. This point has been made by Henri Bouillard, "La preuve de Dieu et son interpretation par Karl Barth," *Spicilegium Beccense, 1,* 191–207; Pegis, "St. Anselm," *Mediaeval Studies, 28,* 228–67, although neither of these scholars relates the idea specifically to the concept of rectitude.

Monologion contains a larger number of overtly Augustinian arguments. In the *Proslogion,* however, the reader is placed in the presence of the theologian with his mind and heart at work. For the believer, this technique dramatizes the importance of the questions discussed and increases the persuasiveness of the solutions reached. Anselm's interest in moving his audience shows that he could find a place for rhetoric even in his grammatically oriented necessary reasoning.

Before leaving Anselm, we must consider Gaunilon's objections to the *Proslogion* proof and Anselm's rebuttal in the *Contra Gaunilonem.* Although neither of these works adds anything new to Anselm's epistemology of signs, both are nevertheless of interest. In Gaunilon of Marmoutiers we find a mind of high caliber, illustrating the high level of philosophical culture in the average Benedictine house of the late eleventh century.[210] Many of Gaunilon's arguments have served as the touchstone for later rejections of Anselm. As for Anselm, the *Contra Gaunilonem* gives him an opportunity to restate his proof, and it indicates that he has a thorough awareness of his own methodological presuppositions.

Gaunilon presents four major objections in his *Pro insipiente,* of which the first is by far the most important. It is based on the supposition that Anselm has started from the realm of thought, and that he is treating his definition of the name of God, and the proof which follows from it, as if they were heuristic. Assuming that this is the case, Gaunilon finds it impossible to follow Anselm's distinction between esse in solo intellectu and esse et in intellectu et in re. They are both in the mind; and if we begin with the mind, he asks, what grounds have we for claiming that the latter is extramentally real while the former is not? Furthermore, he argues, if this distinction were so obvious as Anselm makes it, there would be no fools. In general, Gaunilon's perspective leads him to the conclusion that the proof is a tautology.[211] Next, he chal-

---

210. Southern, in Eadmer, *Vita Anselmi,* p. 31, note 2.
211. Gaunilon, *Pro insipiente,* 2, Schmitt, *1,* 125–26.

lenges the idea that God is actually in intellectu. If God is un-known—and, after all, Anselm does say that He is not com-pletely knowable—how can His name tell one anything about him? The name is meaningless unless one knows what it sig-nifies.[212] Even if we assume that the name of God is in intel-lectu, this does not prove the existence of God in re, an argu-ment Gaunilon illustrates with the example of an imagined perfect island which has never been seen and whose existence cannot be proved on the basis of its intramental existence.[213] Finally, Gaunilon argues that it is possible to conceive hypo-thetically of the nonexistence of God, just as it is possible to conceive of the nonexistence of the self or of anything else.[214]

Anselm's response reaffirms his sense of audience and is in-tended to remind Gaunilon of it. His critic is a believer, and Anselm addresses him as such: "It was a fool against whom the argument of my *Proslogium* was directed. Seeing, how-ever, that the author of these objections is by no means a fool, and is a Catholic, speaking in behalf of the fool, I think it sufficient that I answer the Catholic." [215] This reproof is cushioned by a compliment; no fool, he observes, could have constructed objections as good as Gaunilon's.[216] Anselm be-gins by restating his proof verbatim, and then calls upon Gaunilon's faith and conscience to attest to its truth.[217] Having shown Gaunilon what his proper orientation should be, he follows by proceeding to answer his objections.

Anselm's first step is to establish his *Proslogion* proof all over again by translating it from the indicative to the subjunc-tive mood of the verb. No one who doubts or denies the exis-

212. Ibid., 4, Schmitt, *1*, 126–27.
213. Ibid., 6, Schmitt, *1*, 128.
214. Ibid., 7, Schmitt, *1*, 129.
215. *Contra Gaunilonem*, Schmitt, *1*, 130, trans. Deane, p. 153.
216. *Contra Gaunilonem*, I, Schmitt, *1*, 130.
217. Ibid. Weigel and Madden, *Religion and the Knowledge of God*, pp. 118–19, are correct in pointing out that Anselm addresses Gaunilon not as a natural philosopher but as a Christian. However, they are misleading in saying that he grounds his argument on faith and authority; this overlooks the fact that he argues by necessary reasons in the *Contra Gaunilonem*.

tence of a being than which nothing greater can be conceived, says Anselm, denies or doubts that *if it did exist,* its nonexistence, either in fact or in the mind, would be impossible; otherwise, it would not conform to its own definition.[218] It is difficult at first to see what Anselm has gained by pushing the argument a step backward into the realm of conjecture. However, by means of this subtle redefinition, he is able to prove that there is some point, at least, at which even the doubters and deniers are forced to admit that the extramental reality of "aliquid quo maius nihil cogitari potest" is possible. This conclusion deals in part with Gaunilon's first objection as well as giving Anselm a basis for his further redefinitions in the rebuttal. Taking up next the difficulty found by Gaunilon in the distinction between esse in solo intellectu and esse et in intellectu et in re, he points out that the intellect and reality cannot be thought of as locations where God may be found sometimes but not always. This argument is geared to God's known relationship to time and space; as Anselm points out, He exists *semper et ubique.*[219]

With respect to Gaunilon's second objection, Anselm maintains that words are intrinsically meaningful, in one way or another. Unless the person one is addressing does not comprehend the language, what one says to him will be in his understanding, and he will consequently understand it. Further, he notes, it is irrational to deny the existence of something just because one does not understand it completely; one can grasp statements in part about what one knows partially. Just as lesser goods resemble greater goods, so statements, even if defective, resemble the things they signify, and they therefore provide some positive knowledge about them.[220] Next, Anselm rebuts the third objection by observing that Gaunilon's example of the perfect island is an invalid one. All islands, however perfect, are created things. They are contingent;

---

218. *Contra Gaunilonem,* I, Schmitt, *1,* 131.
219. Ibid.
220. Ibid., II, VII–IX, Schmitt, *1,* 132, 136–38.

they come into being and pass away. It is not particularly difficult to contemplate the nonexistence of an island. However, he states, the same reasoning that applies to islands does not apply to God, since He is not contingent.[221] This same argument is also directed against Gaunilon's last objection. The self and all other beings that are not God are contingent, says Anselm, and they are thus eminently conceivable as nonexistent. However, nonexistence cannot be conceived of the being which exists in the highest degree, even hypothetically.[222]

Even more interesting than this point-by-point rebuttal of Gaunilon's objections are the overarching criticisms of Gaunilon's methodological presuppositions which Anselm makes in order to show that Gaunilon has failed to grasp his own. Anselm makes the trenchant observation that Gaunilon has misquoted him by understanding him to say that *if* something exists in the mind it *therefore* exists in reality.[223] He wishes to underline the view that the object is always the norm of its sign in the intellect. He also slices through Gaunilon's query of how, from a purely mental perspective, one would differentiate esse in solo intellectu from esse et in intellectu et in re. It is an irrelevant question: "This does not touch my argument, you see," he says.[224] The reason why the question is irrelevant to Anselm is because, once again, the reality guarantees the rectitude of our ideas about it; our ideas do not validate or reify their objects. Anselm leaves Gaunilon, after reasserting that his original proof has been demonstrated by necessary reasons, with the final principle that one must always attribute to God what it is better to be than not to be.[225] Whether Gaunilon was, in fact, brought around to an Anselmian way of thinking by these parting instructions we do not know. However, it may not be too much to assume that he

---

221. Ibid., III, Schmitt, *1,* 132–33.
222. Ibid., IV, Schmitt, *1,* 133–34.
223. Ibid., V, Schmitt, *1,* 134–36.
224. Ibid., VI, Schmitt, *1,* 136.
225. Ibid., X, Schmitt, *1,* 138–39.

considered himself answered. If Gaunilon took the trouble to criticize the *Proslogion* in the first place, he probably would have taken the trouble to criticize the *Contra Gaunilonem* had he not held himself refuted by it.

Gaunilon was the only contemporary thinker of a speculative temper who appears to have taken seriously Anselm's epistemology of signs in theological discourse. So far as we know, Anselm did not succeed in developing a school; despite his importance, his influence is traceable in only a small handful of rather insignificant disciples. They include Eadmer, his biographer; Gilbert Crispin, Abbot of Westminster ca. 1085–1117; Ralph, Abbot of Battle 1107–24; and Honorius Augustoduniensis. All of these men were English, with the possible exception of Honorius; most of them borrowed from Anselm in areas other than epistemology; and all were dead by 1130.[226] The waning of Anselmian influence can be partially reconstructed by a survey of the manuscript traditions of some of his major works. There are only nine extant manuscripts of the *Monologion,* seven of which date from the late eleventh and early twelfth centuries; by the end of the twelfth century, the textual tradition had died out altogether.[227] The tradition of the *De veritate* presents us with a similar story, although there are even fewer extant manuscripts in this case.[228] Of the nineteen extant manuscripts of the *Proslogion,* fourteen date from the eleventh and twelfth centuries, three from the thirteenth, and two from the fourteenth and fifteenth; already by the twelfth century people had begun to dismember the work, preserving only the first four chapters containing the proof of God's existence.[229]

To what can we attribute the dislocation and the rapid neglect of Anselm's works so soon after his death? The reason can be traced to a series of changes in intellectual history that

226. Southern, *Saint Anselm,* pp. 203–17; "St. Anselm and His English Pupils," *MRS, 1,* 3–34.

227. Schmitt, *1,* 3.

228. Ibid., p. 169.

229. Ibid., p. 91.

began to set in even while Anselm was still alive, which made his mode of argument, based as it is on the peculiar features of eleventh-century grammar, seem dubious, if not irrelevant. From the late eleventh century onward, internal developments within the sciences of grammar and logic, not to mention the shift from the monastery to the cathedral school and university and the general intensification of intellectual activity, expanded the content and altered the emphasis of these two disciplines, which in turn altered their mutual relations. The revival of classicism and the influx of Graeco-Arabic translations gave twelfth- and thirteenth-century grammarians and logicians much more to work with than their early medieval forebears had had, and tended to focus their attention on the distinctions rather than the similarities between their respective fields.[230] The grammatical interests of the post-Anselmian period differed sharply from those of the preceding age. Syntax now became a major concern.[231] There was a split along regional lines, whereby grammar tended to become an ancilla to disputation in France and an ancilla to jurisprudence in the *ars dictaminis* of Italy.[232]

By far the most striking new development in contemporary grammar was the emergence of speculative grammar in the late eleventh and early twelfth centuries. Its original exponents were the disciples of one Drogo, whose works are not extant. Our sole source of information about him is Anselm of Besate, one of his enemies, who provides some insight into the ideas of Drogo's school in the process of criticizing them. About Anselm of Besate we are more fortunate. According to his most recent editor, he was born around 1020 and was probably a cleric of Milan, but traveled widely in Italy, France, and Germany in search of further education. These peregrinations, rather than any philosophical inclinations he

230. Thurot, "Notices et extraits," *Notices et extraits, 22,* 2me partie, 129–30; Hunt, "Studies on Priscian," *MRS, 1,* 220 ff.

231. Thurot, "Notices et extraits," pp. 59, 212–14.

232. Grabmann, "Die Entwicklung," *Mittelalterliches Geistesleben, 1,* 109–13.

may have had, won him the cognomen "the Peripatetic." In 1045 Anselm went to Germany, where he became a scribe at the court of the Emperor Henry III; in 1047 he was promoted to the rank of imperial chaplain. It is not known exactly when Anselm died, but he is thought to have ended his days as chancellor to Opizo, Bishop of Hildesheim from 1054 to 1067.[233] Anselm's chief works are his *Rhetorimachia*, his *Epistola ad Drogonem*, and his *Epistola ad Droconem magistrum et condiscipulos*. Written in the late eleventh century, they achieved their widest circulation in the middle of the twelfth century,[234] although Anselm notes that Drogoism is already widespread in the Italy, France, and Germany of his own day.[235] Anselm's general objection to Drogo and his disciples is their alleged confusion between language and truth and their excessive verbal sophistry. Drogoism, he states, is marked by deliberate ambiguities,[236] flatus vocis,[237] a disrespect for traditional grammar,[238] "incantations" and meaningless digressions,[239] the use of distinctions and definitions so subtle that they cease to be helpful or even meaningful in terms of normal discourse,[240] and a variegated host of additional verbal sins. Drogo, in short, is a grammar-chopper.[241] His overrefined and jargonized grammar is not only useless but misleading, because he insists that it is the criterion of real existence.[242]

This grammatical abstractionism scorned by Anselm of

233. Karl Manitius, ed., Anselm of Besate, *Rhetorimachia, MGH, QGM,* Band 2, Heft 2, 61–74.

234. Ibid., p. 61.

235. Anselm of Besate, *Epistola ad Droconem magistrum et condiscipulos de logica disputatione in Gallia habita,* in *Rhetorimachia, MGH, QGM,* Band 2, Heft 2, 181.

236. Ibid.; *Rhetorimachia,* I, iii, *MGH, QGM,* Band 2, Heft 2, 57–58, 110.

237. *Rhetorimachia,* I, ix, *MGH, QGM,* Band 2, Heft 2, 120.

238. Ibid., xiv, *MGH, QGM,* Band 2, Heft 2, 128.

239. Ibid., xv, *MGH, QGM,* Band 2, Heft 2, 130.

240. Ibid., v, *MGH, QGM,* Band 2, Heft 2, 113.

241. Ibid., II, iv, viii, xii, *MGH, QGM,* Band 2, Heft 2, 148–49, 155, 161–62.

242. *Epistola ad Drogonem phylosophum,* in *Rhetorimachia, MGH, QGM,* Band 2, Heft 2, 103.

158

Besate aroused a great deal of antipathy in the twelfth and thirteenth centuries. Drogo and his later followers, in fact, have been identified as the "Cornificians" whom John of Salisbury excoriates so roundly in his *Metalogicon*,[243] although their ideas received the patronage of such a distinguished educator as Bernard of Chartres.[244] The criticisms of twelfth-century logicians were more pointed than John's plea for a balanced culture and for the union of wisdom and eloquence; Abelard and the school of dialecticians whom he trained rejected the epistemological claims of grammatical analysis as part of their general program of substituting logic for grammar in speculative thought.[245] The same note was sounded more strongly still in the thirteenth century, this time by the theologians. Speculative grammar had been applied to theology with disastrous results, they thought.[246] This, in part, inspired them to hasten the decline of grammar as a theological tool. Grammar was finally replaced by logic not only because of the excesses of the speculative grammarians; concurrently, the logicians were recovering the complete *Organon* of Aristotle, thus providing themselves with an epistemology which they considered to be far more thorough, precise, and reasonable than grammatical analysis.[247] Grammar had become too dry, too abstract, and too irrelevant; logic had to be invoked to "humanize" the thought of the thirteenth century.

In conditions such as these, a theology grounded so thoroughly in grammar as Anselm's had little chance of survival. The very qualities which had recommended it to Anselm and to his immediate contemporaries rendered it an obstacle to the

243. Edgar de Bruyne, *Études d'esthétique médiévale* (Brugge, 1946), 2, 166, 172, note 2; Grabmann, "Die Entwicklung," *Mittelalterliches Geistesleben, 1,* 109–13; Richard McKeon, "Rhetoric in the Middle Ages," *Speculum, 17,* 26–27.

244. M.-D. Chenu, "Grammaire et théologie aux XIIe et XIIIe siècles," *AHDLMA, 10* (1935), 13.

245. Baldwin, *Medieval Rhetoric and Poetic,* pp. 91–93; Meyrick H. Carré, *Realists and Nominalists* (Oxford, 1946), pp. 42–65; McKeon, "Rhetoric in the Middle Ages," p. 22.

246. Chenu, "Grammaire et théologie," pp. 10–17.

247. Ibid., pp. 19–20.

thinkers of the next two centuries. The problem of the impact of Boethius on Priscian ceased to be meaningful. But, despite this shift from grammar to a predominantly logical mode of thought after the eleventh century, the Augustinian epistemology of signs in theological discourse was retained. Having been dissociated from rhetoric and clothed in grammar by Anselm in the eleventh century, it was dissociated from grammar and re-emerged in the garb of logic in the thirteenth century.

3 ST. THOMAS AQUINAS: The Conception of the Word

It is a well-known fact that the thirteenth century marks an important milestone in intellectual history, as scholasticism became the dominant mode of thought in Western Europe. The shift to the university, the development of the full-time professional scholar, the reception of Graeco-Arabic translations, and the adjustment of thirteenth-century thinkers to a cultural environment broader than that known by their forebears—these innovations, occurring as they did in a period of political and social change, produced a situation of intense intellectual ferment in Western Christendom, as it strove to deal with a flood of new and sometimes alien ideas as well as with its own internal stresses and strains. Under these circumstances it is not surprising that the thought of the thirteenth century should witness a marked change in scope, emphasis, and style. Epistemology is one of the areas of thought in which this change is most apparent, particularly as it touches on the knowledge of God and on the problem of theological discourse.

It is an equally well-known fact that St. Thomas Aquinas is a leading exemplar of thirteenth-century scholasticism. This being the case, it may seem strange to find him placed in the same epistemological category as St. Augustine and St. Anselm. It is quite true that there are marked differences between St. Thomas and his patristic and monastic predecessors, differences too wide and deep to be explained by generalizing that Aquinas represents the triumph of Aristotelian analytics and empiricism over Augustinian "intuitionism" and Anselmian "apriorism." To be sure, Aristotelian logic, in its peculiar scholastic form, combined with the need to train professional theologians able to survive the disputative rigors of university life and to hold their own against heresy and

161

nonbelief, and the encyclopedic mentality characteristic of the age do give Thomas' thought a tenor which makes it impossible to confuse him with either Augustine or Anselm. However, it is necessary not to mistake form for content in dealing with the question at hand. Despite his cosmological emphasis, despite the deliberate impersonality of his style, despite the fact that by utilizing the intellectual vocabulary of his century he was forced to express his views on the role of signs in the knowledge of God in the context of a general epistemology that was in some respects poorly suited to this purpose, Thomas nevertheless retains the salient features of the verbal theory of religious knowledge which we have already found in Augustine and Anselm. Translated into the mode of a logic originally formulated to analyze and to organize conceptually the structure and function of the sensible universe, this theory is interpreted by Thomas so as to stress ideas, and to some extent the created universe, as the principal *signa Dei*. Like Augustine and Anselm, Thomas is preoccupied with the task of finding the most suitable terms in which to express man's knowledge of God, and he is interested in the reasons why these terms make different subjective impressions on different audiences. However, he is fascinated above all by the conception of the Word, by the attempt to understand how the knowledge of God enters the human mind.

Since Thomas conceives the Augustinian theory of signs in logical terms, it is necessary to devote some attention to the kind of logic he used. During the late twelfth and thirteenth centuries there was a marked revival of interest in Aristotelian logic. Beginning with Abelard and his school and acquiring momentum as the *Organon* became available during the second half of the twelfth century, this movement was quite successful in popularizing Aristotle and in winning for logic the priority over grammar and rhetoric which it enjoyed in the thirteenth century.[1] As taught in the arts faculty of the Uni-

1. See above, pp. 157, 159, 160; M.-D. Chenu, "Grammaire et théologie aux XIIe et XIIIe siècles," *AHDLMA, 10* (1935), 19–21; Richard McKeon, "Rhet-

versity of Paris, this logic was only partially representative of logic as Aristotle himself had taught it. Purely formal, concerned only with modes of predication and prescriptive rules of argument, scholastic logic shared with Aristotle the view that logic is not a total epistemology, and that logical rules are not psychological rules. At the same time, by disavowing interest in the application of logic to all philosophical questions, a task which the arts professors left to their colleagues in the higher faculties, this scholastic logic tended to overlook the fact that Aristotelian logic is essentially a methodology of science, and thus they abstracted it from its original context.[2]

There were three principal exponents of formal logic at Paris in the thirteenth century, the Englishman William of Shyreswood, who died after 1267, his probable pupil Lambert of Auxerre, who flourished ca. 1250, and, most famous of all, Peter of Spain, who died in 1277 as Pope John XXI, and whose *Summulae logicales,* the first systematic compendium of scholastic logic, was a standard authority for the next three centuries. There are two aspects of their work which are especially noteworthy for our purposes. One is the fact that their logic is almost exclusively syllogistic in emphasis; to all intents and purposes, they reduce argument as such to syllogism.[3] Beyond this, however, they recognize that not all syllogisms have the same probative force. Shyreswood distinguishes three types of syllogisms: the demonstrative syllogism, which begins with the necessary and certain causes of the conclusion and which produces scientific knowledge, the dia-

---

oric in the Middle Ages," *Speculum, 17* (1942), 22–23. This movement also fostered a more dialectical style of preaching. See Brother S. Robert, "Rhetoric and Dialectic according to the First Latin Commentary on the Rhetoric of Aristotle," *NS, 31* (1957), 484–98.

2. Marjorie Grene, *A Portrait of Aristotle* (Chicago, 1963), pp. 69–70; Thomas Gilby, *Barbara Celarent: A Description of Scholastic Dialectic* (London, 1949), p. 32; Ernest A. Moody, *Truth and Consequence in Medieval Logic* (Amsterdam, 1953), pp. 1, 14–15.

3. Philotheus Boehner, *Medieval Logic: An Outline of Its Development 1250-c.1400* (Manchester, 1952), p. 5; C. Prantl, *Geschichte der Logik im Abendlande* (Leipzig, 1867), *3,* 92.

lectical syllogism, which begins with probable causes and produces tentative conclusions, and the sophistic syllogism, which begins with what appear to be probable causes and whose aim is not knowledge but glory or triumph in discussion.[4] In practice, the sophistical syllogism comes into play very little. The dialectical syllogism bears a striking resemblance to the Aristotelian enthymeme, which pertains to rhetoric and which is distinguished from the syllogism in the writings of the Stagirite. Although Shyreswood and his successors emphasize the difference between demonstration and dialectic, they insist that both can be handled syllogistically. It is important to bear in mind this shift in the use of terms. When we encounter probable arguments in Aquinas' works, the fact that they are arranged or described syllogistically should not mislead us into thinking that their conclusions are invariably scientifically necessary.

Secondly, although these thirteenth-century logicians were in possession of the complete corpus of Aristotelian logic, their works do not follow Aristotle's order, nor do they reproduce the full contents of the *Organon*. They treat only six of the subjects discussed by Aristotle: propositions, predicables, categories (which Shyreswood omits), syllogisms, topics or *loci communes*, and fallacies.[5] Notwithstanding their omissions, they make some additions to the logical canon, which they elaborate in great detail. One of these contributions, which does not particularly concern us, was the treatment of syncategorematic signs, that is, words such as "every," "neither," "both," "if," "unless," etc.[6] The other contribution, which does concern us, was the theory of supposition. The theory of supposition, as expounded by Peter of Spain, provides a somewhat more complex method of explaining signification

4. Etienne Gilson, *A History of Christian Philosophy in the Middle Ages* (New York, 1955), pp. 318–19; Gilby, *Barbara Celarent*, pp. 5–6, 33.

5. Boehner, *Medieval Logic*, pp. 77–78; Moody, *Truth and Consequence*, pp. 3–5.

6. Boehner, *Medieval Logic*, pp. 19–26; Moody, *Truth and Consequence*, p. 5; Prantl, *Geschichte, 3*, 19–26.

than we have encountered before. It also shows the logicians' tendency to intellectualize the process of signification, for they inject a conceptual stage between the mind's conception of a sign and its acknowledgment of the sign as such. Supposition theory draws a distinction between words as sensible signs of things and words as logical signs of things in propositions. In the case of a word that stands for a thing we have signification; in the case of a verbal sign that is part of a proposition we have supposition. The term "supposition" implies that the subject knows what he means by the word when he uses it in a proposition and that he can form a judgment about it, whereas the word as a sign is simply a sense datum. Signification and supposition are logically distinct, although supposition depends on signification.[7] The principal accomplishment of this theory is to shift the discussion of the truth conditions of propositions from signs, which are more or less automatically accurate, to supposita, whose use involves an intellectual judgment of truth.

This is a notion which is new to the Middle Ages, since it was created by scholastic logicians. But, in some respects, it is familiar. Despite the differences in terminology and in the epistemic process that it is designed to elucidate, the distinction between signification and supposition bears some resemblance to Anselm's distinction between natural truth and rectitude, if we omit the moral implications of rectitude. For both Peter and Anselm, when the mind and the senses are working normally and the things to be signified are not in themselves confusing, the spoken word signifies its object with an automatic truth. This truth is real for Peter, because it denotes the resemblance between the word and the existing thing it represents; it is intentional for Anselm, because the word represents the meaning of the speaking subject. In the case of supposita and words possessing rectitude, we have words that are

7. Boehner, *Medieval Logic*, pp. 32–36; Moody, *Truth and Consequence*, pp. 5, 18–25; Prantl, *Geschichte, 3*, 10–18. Prantl seems to be alone in the view that this theory is derived from the Byzantine logician Psellus.

true both really and intentionally; each is commensurate with extra-mental reality, and each is correctly judged to be so by the subject. The differences between the two theories lie in their epistemological direction. Where the Anselmian judgment of rectitude starts with the mind of the speaker and moves to the acknowledgment that his words correspond to exterior reality, the step from signification to supposition indicates that a real thing has entered the mind of the subject by means of its similitude, that the subject has achieved a correct knowledge of what the sign represents, and that he is capable of relating it to other things which he knows. What is interesting about this comparison, outside of the perhaps unexpected similarities that it reveals, is the thirteenth-century emphasis on the question of how the outside world gets into the mind, as contrasted with Anselm's interest in determining how statements can be judged to be objectively true. The logic to which Peter is committed makes it a very short step to the full-blown scholastic identification of signs as concepts, whereby the world is signified in the mind by ideas which are formed from the intelligible species of things, and words are required to signify these ideas only insofar as one wishes to communicate them to others.[8]

As we have noted, the professional logicians of the thirteenth century adhered to a strictly formal logic. At the same time, members of the theological faculty at Paris, who had occasion to concern themselves with a broader range of problems and who were conversant with a wide selection of works translated from the Greek and Arabic, did not hesitate to study Aristotelian logic on their own and to apply it to epistemological and metaphysical questions. Since they had all been trained in formal logic as undergraduates, it was natural for them to use it, and, for the most part, they are correspondingly syllogistic in method.[9] Aquinas reflects this general

8. Gilby, *Barbara Celarent*, pp. 50–53; Alfons Nehring, "A Note on Functional Linguistics in the Middle Ages," *Traditio, 9* (1953), 433–34.

9. Boehner, *Medieval Logic*, p. 5; Prantl, *Geschichte, 3*, 92.

adoption of formal logic as the *modus sciendi;* he uses the term "logic" more or less interchangeably with "reason" and employs syllogistic techniques for both demonstration and dialectic.[10] In the process of adapting logic to their own purposes, the theologians undoubtedly imbued it with many speculative connotations and ambiguities; their fourteenth-century nominalist critics claimed that they had confused logic with metaphysics.[11] Perhaps they supplied logic with too much context to compensate for the fact that the logicians had supplied it with too little.

In any event, the theologians were intensely interested in logic, as well as in other works making up the Aristotelian corpus. This fact is attested by the large number of new translations of and commentaries on Aristotle's works that were made in the mid-thirteenth century. In some cases this can be explained by the fact that previous translations were inaccurate, or were clouded by the extrapolations of intermediary critics, as was true of the Averroized *Metaphysics.* However, Aristotle's logical works were also restudied, even though they had already been translated satisfactorily for the most part and had been incorporated into the logical curriculum for decades. The majority of these new commentaries on logic were made by theologians rather than logicians, and quite a few of these theologians were friars.[12] Dominican contributions to this effort, which were extensive, began about 1240. This apparently reflects the order's loosening of restrictions on secular studies, as well as the interest of its leading members in gaining an insight into Aristotle more suited to philosophical and theological problems than that purveyed by contemporary logicians.[13]

10. L. Lachance, "Saint Thomas dans l'histoire de la logique," *Études d'histoire littéraire et doctrinale du XIIIe siècle, 1* (Paris, 1932), 61–103.

11. Moody, *Truth and Consequence,* pp. 5–6.

12. Fernand van Steenberghen, *Aristote en occident: Les origines de l'aristotélisme parisien* (Louvain, 1946), pp. 62–63, 98–102.

13. M.-D. Chenu, *Introduction à l'étude de Saint Thomas d'Aquin* (Montréal-Paris, 1954), 173–75.

Highly prolific in this vein was Albert the Great, the teacher of Thomas Aquinas, who produced eleven commentaries on various logical works of Aristotle in the course of commenting on most of the Aristotle that was available in Latin in his time. One of the noteworthy features of Albert's logical commentaries is his tendency to stress Neoplatonic and Arabic interpretations, either because they made sense to him or because they were more readily available to him than representatives of the Stoic and Megaritic traditions of Aristotle exegesis.[14] Thomas contributed two logical commentaries, on the *Analytica posteriora* and on part of the *Perihermenias*, in addition to his treatises on Aristotelian ethics, physics, metaphysics, and politics. The logical commentaries, written between 1268 and 1272, are works of his maturity. They became justly famous in his own day for the easy familiarity with Aristotle's thought and the critical use of previous commentaries which they reveal, and for Thomas' comparative objectivity, remarkable as thirteenth-century commentaries go, in interpreting both the literal sense and the intention of his author.[15]

The caliber of these works indicates that Thomas had a thorough and integral knowledge of Aristotle's logic, and a good idea of its context. At the same time, he was open to Platonic influences, both through other works upon which he commented, and through the Neoplatonic elements in the interpretations and commentaries of his teacher. Thomas produced a commentary on the *Liber de causis*, a work attributed to Aristotle in the thirteenth century, but which was actually written by an Arabic author who derived most of his ideas from Proclus. He also wrote a treatise explaining Boethius' *De hebdomadibus*, an essentially Platonic work. Probably most important is the fact that both Thomas and Albert regarded

---

14. Boehner, *Medieval Logic,* pp. 2–5.

15. Martin Grabmann, "Die Aristoteleskommentar des heiligen Thomas von Aquin," *Mittelalterliches Geistesleben, 1* (München, 1926), 266–313; Chenu, *Introduction,* pp. 175–92.

Dionysius the Areopagite as an authority. Thomas commented on Dionysius' *De divinis nominibus,* and Albert wrote an exposition of all of the Areopagite's writings, which Thomas cites extensively in his own theology.[16] Platonic and Neoplatonic ideas thus found their way into Thomas' thought and affected his epistemology at the points which concern us, as well as did an Aristotelianism somewhat broader and more inclusive than the formal logic of the arts faculty.

Aquinas made use of this inheritance in formulating his views on the role of signs in the knowledge of the Christian universe. The term "Christian *universe*" is apposite here because Thomas, unlike Augustine, was interested in knowing the world as well as God and the soul, a concern for which he found both logical and theological warrants. While Aquinas has a theory of signs and some definite ideas on the nature of the universe, he does not have a systematically articulated epistemology. As George Lindbeck has well put it, if Aquinas had a systematic philosophy at all, he never wrote it down.[17] Thomas' views on the subject of knowledge must be pieced together, for the most part out of passages in his writings where he discusses the operations of the human mind by way of illustrating some other question. The only works in which he confines himself to epistemological questions are his commentary on Dionysius' *De divinis nominibus,* which takes up the cognitive status of names of God, and his *Quaestiones disputatae de veritate,* which deals with the truth of man's knowledge. However, in this latter work he devotes far more

16. Chenu, *Introduction,* pp. 192–96.
17. George Lindbeck, "Participation and Existence in the Interpretation of St. Thomas Aquinas," *Franciscan Studies, 17* (1957), 108. See also David Knowles, *The Historical Context of the Philosophical Works of St. Thomas Aquinas* (London, 1958); Anton C. Pegis, *The Middle Ages and Philosophy: Some Reflections on the Ambivalence of Modern Scholasticism* (Chicago, 1963), pp. viii–xiv, 26–29, 43–60, 69–81; *St. Thomas and Philosophy* (Milwaukee, 1964), pp. 19, 26–46, 80–82; Josef Pieper, *Introduction to Thomas Aquinas* (London, 1963), pp. 156–59; *The Silence of St. Thomas: Three Essays* (New York, 1957), pp. 69–71; Paul Vignaux, *Philosophy in the Middle Ages: An Introduction* (New York, 1959), pp. 116–17.

space to the metaphysical and theological than to the epistemological aspects of truth.

The fact that most of Thomas' teachings on knowledge are
scattered through the body of his thought is rarely suggested
by his commentators, many of whom are anxious to extrapo-
late a "Thomistic epistemology" by wrenching his ideas out of
the contexts in which he originally placed them. This is unfor-
tunate, since these contexts are frequently illuminating. Probably the most misleading consequence of this procedure, outside of the fact that it conveys the impression of a system
where one does not exist, has been to foster the misapprehen-
sion that the world Thomas was interested in knowing was a
purely philosophical or scientific Greek world, rather than a
Christian one. This has resulted in a highly intellectualistic
interpretation of Thomas' epistemology, which overemphasizes
the certainty and extensiveness of man's knowledge of nature.
In a few cases, scholars interpret this intellectualism in a Platonic vein.[18] Most commentators, however, place Thomas in
Aristotle's epistemological universe, and do not shrink from
attributing to Thomas Aristotle's unbounded confidence that
the world is totally intelligible and that the human mind is
perfectly adequate to it.[19] The effect of this point of view on

18. Arthur Little, *The Platonic Heritage of Thomism* (Dublin, 1949); Josef
Santeler, *Der Platonismus in der Erkenntnislehre des heiligen Thomas von
Aquin* (Leipzig, 1939). R. J. Henle, *Saint Thomas and Platonism: A Study of
the 'Plato' and 'Platonici' Texts in the Writings of Saint Thomas* (The Hague,
1956), cites Platonic epistemological texts mainly to show how extensive
Thomas' rejection of them was.

19. Meyrick H. Carré, *Realists and Nominalists* (Oxford, 1946), pp. 79–81,
86; Bernard Lonergan, "The Concept of *Verbum* in the Writings of St. Thomas
Aquinas," *TS, 7* (1946), 349–92; *8* (1947), 35–79, 404–44; *10* (1949), 3–40,
359–93; Richard McKeon, "Thomas Aquinas' Doctrine of Knowledge and Its
Historical Setting," *Speculum, 3* (1928), 425–44; Bruno Nardi, *Studi di filosofia
medievale* (Roma, 1960), 193–207; Gaston Rabeau, *Species. Verbum. L'Activité
intellectuelle élémentaire selon S. Thomas d'Aquin* (Paris, 1938); K. E.
Skysgaard, "La connaissance humaine d'après Saint Thomas d'Aquin," *Classica
et Medievalia, 2,* 1 (1939), 86–120; Edward F. Talbot, *Knowledge and Object*
(Washington, 1932), pp. 33–49; Viktor Warnach, "Erkennen und Sprechen bei
Thomas von Aquin: Ein Deutungsversuch seiner Lehre auf ihrem geistes-

the analysis of signification is to produce an interpretation of Thomas' signs in which they have full cognitive powers but no cognitive limitations. In some instances scholars have gone so far as to claim that Thomistic signs are identical with their significata,[20] although, if pushed to its logical conclusion, this view would have to countenance either the assimilation of the mind to the world or the assimilation of the world to the mind.

The main ingredients in this overly confident construct of the powers of Thomistic signs are quite easy to assemble. There is substantial agreement on it among most scholars, and it can be located at will by consulting any standard study of Aquinas.[21] In outline, this theory is an explanation of how the exterior world comes to be known by the knowing subject. So far as it goes, it can be documented from Thomas without

geschichtlichen Hintergrund," *Divus Thomas, 15* (1937), 189–218, 263–90; *16* (1938), 161–96; "Das äussere Sprechen und seine Funktionen nach der Lehre des hl. Thomas von Aquin," *Divus Thomas, 16* (1938), 393–419; Paul Wilpert, *Das Problem der Wahrheitssicherung bei Thomas von Aquin: Ein Beitrag zur Geschichte der Evidenzproblems, Beiträge,* Band *30,* Heft 3 (Münster in Westfalen, 1931); Paul Wyser, "Die wissenschaftstheoretischen Quaest. V. u. VI in Boethium de Trinitate des hl. Thomas von Aquin," *Divus Thomas, 25* (1947), 437–85; *26* (1948), 74–98. An unusual entry in the class of philosophical comparisons is Alfons Hufnagel, *Intuition und Erkenntnis nach Thomas von Aquin* (Münster in Westfalen, 1932), who thinks that Thomas was a proto-Husserlian. On Aristotle, see John Herman Randall, Jr., *Aristotle* (New York, 1960), pp. 5, 7, 98.

20. The most exaggerated example of this tendency is Pierre Rousselot, *L'Intellectualisme de Saint Thomas* (Paris, 1908), passim, and especially p. 22. See also Ritamary Bradley, "The Mirror of Truth according to St. Thomas," *MS, 31* (1954), 314; Peter Hoenen, *Reality and Judgment according to St. Thomas* (Chicago, 1952); Hugo Lang, *Die Lehre des hl. Thomas von Aquin von der Gewissheit des übernatürlichen Glaubens* (Augsburg, 1929), pp. 18–19; William W. Meissner, "Some Aspects of the *Verbum* in the Texts of St. Thomas Aquinas," *MS, 36* (1958), 1–30; Gerald B. Phelan, "Verum sequitur esse rerum," *Mediaeval Studies, 1* (1939), 17.

21. M. C. D'Arcy, *Thomas Aquinas* (London, 1930), pp. 76–77, 81–84, 88–92, 102–03, 216–17, 224–26; F. C. Copleston, *A History of Philosophy* (Westminster, Md., 1959), *2,* part 2, 109–12; Etienne Gilson, *The Christian Philosophy of St. Thomas Aquinas* (New York, 1956), pp. 218–22, 223–34; *The Philosophy of St. Thomas Aquinas* (St. Louis, 1941), pp. 57, 250, 263–74. The following discussion is based on these references.

forcing the texts. Thomas, like Aristotle, begins with the assumption that the world is so constructed as to be knowable by the human mind, that the mind is able to gain true knowledge of the world, and that the mind is primarily passive in doing so. Knowledge of the world, for Thomas, begins with sensation. Sense impressions automatically signify the objects they represent; falsity occurs only accidentally, when the object happens to resemble something it is not. An accurate sensible sign, or phantasm, is formed out of sensory impressions; it is then transformed into an intelligible sign by a faculty of the mind which Thomas calls the active intellect. The active intellect in a sense distills the significative content out of the phantasm by abstracting from it its intelligible species, that is, the aspect of the phantasm which is capable of being conceptualized. The intelligible species is then impressed on the possible intellect, or the mind insofar as it can know all things, and the possible intellect responds by forming a *verbum mentis,* or conceptual sign of the original object. This verbum mentis is directly analogous to the phantasm. It is produced automatically and is naturally free from error unless the intelligible species of its object happens to be confusingly similar to something else.[22] It is primarily the conceptual level of signification with which Thomas is concerned. While concepts are dependent on phantasms to supply the raw materials out of which they are constructed, sensory data themselves do not really begin to play an effectual role in cognition at large until they have been processed to permit the extraction of their intelligible components.

It will be noted that Thomas uses the Augustinian term "verbum mentis" to describe a mental sign. However, this term, in Thomas' hands, undergoes a change of meaning. For Augustine, a verbum mentis is the sign of a purely intellectual object of knowledge, such as the soul and other non-sensible

22. St. Thomas Aquinas, *Comp. theol.,* I, 37–38, 40; *In VII Met.,* lect. 1, c. 1253; *De pot.,* I, q. 1, a. 1, ad 10; q. 2, a. 1; *Der ver.,* q. 1, a. 11–12; *ST,* Ia, q. 17, a. 2; q. 85, a. 1.

things which are known by intuition. He uses this term to indicate that even intuitive knowledge is mediated in this life by signs, as well as for the sake of the Trinitarian connotations which the term arouses.[23] While Thomas, as we shall see below, draws frequently on the verbum mentis when casting about for analogies of the Trinity, he does not confine its significative function to any particular kinds of objects of knowledge on principle.[24]

The presence of an accurate conceptual sign in the mind in the form of a verbum mentis represents only the first step in Thomas' theory of signification. The subject cannot use the sign coherently in any kind of logical construction unless he is able to acknowledge that it is, in fact, accurate. This requires another ideational step, the formation of a judgment on the object by means of the sign. The validity of the sign must be judged and its truly representative character accepted before the mind can willingly employ the sign in composing negative or affirmative propositions concerning the object. This point is often overlooked by Thomists. In itself, the judgment is also a conceptual sign of the object, although it may also function as the significatum of a verbal sign should the subject wish to express his knowledge externally. The intentionality of the judgment makes it capable of being true on a conscious level, above and beyond the automatic signification of the verbum mentis. This means that the subject, in a sense, has epistemological responsibilities when he makes a judgment. He must be simultaneously aware of the object and of the contents of his mind. His judgment will be true only if it affirms that what is, is, only when it corresponds or is adequate to the thing it signifies. In the act of judgment, the mind ceases to be passive; and it must render an accounting of itself. The subject does this, not by measuring the object against the yardstick of his intellectual sign of it, but by measuring the sign against the

23. Cf. above, p. 68.
24. Meissner, "Some Aspects of the *Verbum*," *MS, 36,* 1–30; Lonergan, "The Concept of the *Verbum*," *TS, 7,* 349–92; *8,* 35–79.

yardstick of its object. As in the theory of signification we have already noted in Augustine and Anselm, the beings signified, for Thomas, are the criteria of the correspondence, and hence the truth, of the ideas that men have about them.[25]

According to Thomas, then, we can come to a true knowledge of things through conceptual signs. What limitations, if any, are there on the extent of this knowledge? In the conventional picture of Thomist epistemology, natural objects are so constructed as to enable the mind to acquire scientific knowledge of them by demonstrative logic. This scientific knowledge is perfect, because it affords a knowledge of the essential nature of a thing. In knowing the quiddity of a thing, one knows it in itself and in relation to its cause; one can form a precise sign of it, a definition of its intrinsic being and place in the universe.[26] Thomas' confidence in the ability of logic to perceive the proper structure of the world is shown by his frequent explanations of the relations between things in nature by means of logical relationships.[27] It would seem, from this analysis, that man is limited in his knowledge of the universe only by the fact that there are a finite number of things in nature to be known.

This, however, is not all that there is to be said about the powers of concepts and their logical arrangements in the knowledge of the world in the thought of Thomas Aquinas. The difficulty with the conventional approach is that it tends

25. *De pot.*, I, q. 1, a. 1, ad 6; q. 3, a. 17, ad 27–29; *De ver.*, q. 1, a. 1–3, 8–9, 11–12; *In II Met.*, lect. 2, c. 298; *In IV Met.*, lect. 17, c. 736; *In IX Met.*, lect. 11, c. 1896–97; *In I Sent.*, d. 2, q. 1, a. 3, ad 2; *De anima*, a. 3, ad 1; *ST, Ia*, q. 5, a. 2; q. 10, a. 3, ad 3; q. 16, a. 1–2, 5; q. 17, a. 1; q. 21, a. 2. Xavier Maquart, "La Causalité du signe: Réflexions sur la valeur philosophique d'une explication théologique," *RT, 32,* n. s., 10 (1927), 40–60, notes that Thomas sees signs as measured by their significata, but he thinks that this is relevant primarily to sacraments rather than to theology as a whole or to general epistemology.

26. *De ente et essentia,* II; *In I Met.,* lect. 1, c. 29, 34; *In III Met.,* lect. 6, c. 400; *In VII Met.,* lect. 2, c. 1537, 1541; *ST,* IIa IIae, q. 9, a. 1, ad 1.

27. *De pot.,* I, q. 3, a. 1, ad 6; *ST,* IIa IIae, q. 8, a. 1; q. 9, a. 2. See also Phelan, "Verum sequitur esse rerum," *Mediaeval Studies, 1,* 13–14; John K. Ryan, "The Problem of Truth," *Essays in Thomism* (New York, 1942), pp. 72–73.

to stop here. In order to gain a complete picture of the nature of Thomistic signs, it is necessary to point out that there are, for Thomas, some definite limitations to the power of signs. His theory is far less intellectualistic than most treatments of his epistemology would indicate. In contrast to the blandly objective realism which is frequently attributed to him, Thomas makes it perfectly plain that intellectual signs, however far advanced on the road to demonstrative knowledge they may be, are different from their objects. Men, he states, do not know natural objects perfectly, even those objects accessible to the senses, since they have made and can make mistakes about them.[28] The mind of man, he observes, runs into even more obstacles in attempting to know objects which are not sensible, such as the universal causes of things. These "separate substances," that is, entities devoid of matter, are the most actual, the least potential, and therefore the most intrinsically intelligible things in the universe. But they are the least known things as well. Since science and speculation require a knowledge of things through their causes, difficulties in the cognition of these causes cannot but have a deleterious effect on our knowledge of other, less general things. Yet, because these separate substances are not sensible, it is impossible to know them perfectly in their essences.[29] The first principles upon which all science rest are themselves nondemonstrable; they are either intuited or presumed to exist because of their explanatory power.[30]

The limitations of the human mind with respect to its natural objects are also clearly implied in Thomas' analysis of judgments of truth. He repeatedly states that things which are known are known according to the mode of the knower.[31] At the same time, he affirms that things are the criteria of the

28. *Comp. theol.*, II, 18; *SCG*, IV, 1, 3.

29. *De anima*, a. 16; *In II Met.*, lect. 1, c. 282–85; *SCG*, III, 41–43, 45; *ST*, Ia, q. 88, a. 1–2; Ia IIae, q. 3, a. 6.

30. James F. Anderson, "Is God's Knowledge Scientific? A Study in Thomism," *An Etienne Gilson Tribute*, ed. C. J. O'Neil (Milwaukee, 1959), pp. 4–6; Randall, *Aristotle*, p. 98.

31. See, for example, *De ver.*, q. 19, a. 1.

truth of men's thoughts about them. Being is evidently prior to knowing. Being is also evidently different from thought; one of Thomas' most frequent assertions is that the order of being is not the same as the order of knowing.[32] The human mode of knowing is by means of sensible things. This makes the mind better adapted to the knowledge of inferior beings than to the knowledge of superior beings; the more intelligible a thing is, the higher its grade of being, the less the mind can know about it. Intelligibility is a property of things in themselves; it is not a property of things which they acquire when they exist in the human mind and under no other circumstances. This raises some interesting questions: If men know whatever they know in terms of their limited, sense-bound mode of knowledge, how can they know that a mode of being exists which is different from their mode of knowledge? If man's judgment of truth, of the adequation of the mind to its object, is itself a conceptual sign, how can the subject perceive the accuracy of another mental sign by means of it?

The answer to these questions can be found if we avoid either a radically objectivist or a radically subjectivist interpretation of Thomistic signs.[33] Thomas shares with Augustine and Anselm a metaphysical bias. Before he starts to theorize he knows a great deal more about the universe than his insistent empiricism would immediately lead one to suspect. In the case of the knowledge of nature, he has a large selection of presuppositions about reality, which permit him to measure the adequacy of a given intellectual sign to its object.[34] He should not be confused with post-medieval empiricists who assert that sense data, and/or ideas derived from them, are not only what we know first, but that they are all we know. The Augustinian theory of signs which Thomas adopted avoids these problems by insisting that we begin with existing

32. See, for example, *In VII Met.*, lect. 2, c. 1300–05.

33. Martin Grabmann, *Thomas Aquinas: His Personality and Thought* (New York, 1928), pp. 72–73, 82.

34. *De pot.*, I, q. 3, a. 17, ad 29.

things, that we assent that the signs men make of them may be true, but incomplete, and that we can judge this fact by comparing the sign with the original. For Thomas, sensibly derived intellectual signs do not leave the knower trapped within his own mind. Neither does the priority of being render human cognition irrelevant. Signs are true, so far as they go, and the knower is capable of judging that they do not go the whole way.

Beyond the philosophical reasons for the limitations under which Thomistic signs labor, there are a host of qualifications on their powers which are a consequence of the Christian dimensions of both Thomas' universe and his knowing subject. It is in their failure to give adequate emphasis to this fact that the conventional commentaries go farthest afield in attempting to depict Thomas' epistemology. After perusing the literature on Aquinas, one is given the impression that most writers are primarily interested in delineating, organizing, and even extending in some cases the areas of knowledge in which man is supposed to be able to operate on his own. Presumably, they do this in the attempt to show that Thomas' Christianity does not prevent him from being a philosopher. In our view, this is a totally lopsided picture of Thomas Aquinas. It is achieved by editing and rearranging his ideas in a manner which fails to show the true nature of his aims. It is necessary to state strongly that Aquinas was first, last, and always a theologian.[35] He was a philosopher only incidentally, and his philosophical statements cannot be isolated from their theological contexts and treated independently. This is a point on which even some of the most eminent authorities are confused.[36]

35. This point has been made by such eminent authorities as Jacques Maritain, *The Angelic Doctor: The Life and Thought of Saint Thomas Aquinas* (New York, 1931), p. 51; and Pegis, *The Middle Ages and Philosophy,* pp. viii–xiv, 26–29, 43–60, 69–81; *St. Thomas and Philosophy,* pp. 18–19, 26–46, 80–82; *Saint Thomas and the Greeks* (Milwaukee, 1943), pp. 1–2. But it deserves to be made again.

36. Cf. Gilson, *Christian Philosophy of Thomas Aquinas,* p. 9, where he says that conclusions not presupposing revelation may be abstracted from their

The "autonomy of philosophy" approach to Thomas is predicated on a rigid distinction between nature and supernature, and on the styles of knowledge which are considered appropriate to these levels of being, each of which is assumed to be fundamentally self-contained. It is well to keep in mind that the idea of pure nature is not found in the works of Thomas Aquinas. It is an interpolation which appears to have been introduced into Thomism by Cardinal Cajetan in the sixteenth century.[37] The knowledge of nature in Thomas is not discrete; it is part of a theological and epistemological whole. It is also something which he talks about in different ways, depending on what he hopes to accomplish at the particular point where he is discussing it. A full consideration of the limits as well as the aptitudes of signs will clarify Thomas' perspective on the role of logic in knowledge.

As we have seen, there are philosophical contraints on the exhaustiveness of Thomistic signs, based on his view that the origins of man's knowledge are empirical. In the process of formulating signs, in the judgment of truth, and in the acquisition of scientific knowledge of nature through signs, human concepts are further bounded for Thomas by the fact that both the knower and the world he knows are dependent on God. God operates in the human intellect, since He is the source of all intellectual power. Man is part of the creation;

---

contexts and treated philosophically, and p. 14, where he states that Thomas was not interested in safeguarding the autonomy of philosophy but in explaining how theology could use it without destroying the unity of theology; and his *History of Christian Philosophy*, p. 365, where he says: "Thomas changed the water of philosophy into the wine of theology. Thomas always considered himself a theologian."

37. Copleston, *History of Philosophy, 2,* part 2, 36. This point has been studied in detail by Henri DeLubac, *Augustinisme et théologie moderne* (Paris, 1965), pp. 136–281; and *Le mystère du surnaturel* (Paris, 1965), passim. In the first volume, he treats the development of the idea of pure nature, its definition in the sixteenth and seventeenth centuries, and its implications for theologians at that time on the doctrines of man's natural desire for God, beatitude, and man's primal state. In the second volume, he treats the broad theological implications of the idea of pure nature in general.

he owes everything he has to God. The natural light of his mind is given to him and sustained in him by God.[38] Thomas describes the active intellect, the mental faculty which abstracts the intelligible species from the phantasm and makes it possible for the mind to form a conceptual sign of its object, as a participation of God: "If we posit that the active intellect is a kind of power participated in our minds, as it were a kind of light, it is necessary to posit another external cause from which this light is participated. And this we call God, Who teaches from within." [39]

As the final words of this quotation indicate, Thomas shares with Augustine the doctrine of God as the Interior Teacher. While human teachers, he thinks, may assist a student in his acquisition of knowledge by proposing examples, by strengthening his mind through intellectual discipline, and even by causing him to know things by means of demonstrations, their assistance is purely external. It is God who implants in the student's mind the light of reason and the power to know; and it is God who uses the teacher instrumentally as a proximate cause in the student's instruction.[40] The principal difference between Augustine and Thomas here is that Augustine is exclusively concerned in his *De magistro* with the transmission of religious truths through preaching, while Thomas has in mind the acquisition of knowledge about the natural world through the agency of the university lecturer.[41] It should be clear from the above discussion, however, that what Thomas means by "natural knowledge" is not knowledge which man

38. *De pot.,* I, q. 3, a. 7; *In Boeth. de trin.,* q. 1, a. 1, ad 2; *ST,* Ia, q. 79, a. 4; q. 89, a. 1; q. 105, a. 3–4; q. 117, a. 1, ad 1; Ia IIae, q. 68, a. 2; q. 109, a. 2.

39. *De anima,* a. 5, ad 6.

40. *De ver.,* q. 11, a. 1; *ST,* Ia, q. 117, a. 1.

41. Cf. Alberto Caturelli, *La doctrina agustiniana sobre el maestro* (Córdoba, Argentina, 1954); Wilhelm Schneider, *Die Quaestiones Disputatae de Veritate des Thomas von Aquin in ihrer philosophiegeschichtlichen Beziehung zu Augustinus, Beiträge,* Band 27, Heft 3 (Münster in Westfalen, 1930), 24–26. Thomas does not perceive this distinction between himself and Augustine. See *De ver.,* q. 11, a. 1, ad 6.

can acquire without the "intervention" of God, for there is no such thing, but rather, simply, the knowledge which the creature, man, has about the rest of creation.

In judging the truth of its ideas, the mind, for Thomas, must also rely on God, and in more than one way. Truth, according to Thomas, is not only an epistemological condition. It is also a metaphysical transcendental, which is convertible with being. All things have truth to the extent that they have being; and their truth and being are dependent on God. As the supreme Being and the supreme Truth, God is the ground and the cause of the truth and the being of the various things which exist in nature; and they, in turn, are the criteria of the truth of men's ideas about them.[42] This notion is highly reminiscent of Anselm's idea of truth.[43] The parallel does not end here. Anselm's definition of truth as rectitude bears with it moral implications; it entails rectitude of the will as well as rectitude of the intellect vis-à-vis the object. Truth also has a moral aspect for Thomas. He discusses truth as a virtue as well as a metaphysical and epistemological fact. When truthfulness is simply the adequation between the sign and its significatum, it is related to God as the supreme Truth epistemologically and metaphysically. But when truthfulness is what prompts a man to speak what is true, to be a witness to the truth, it is a virtue by which he is related to God as the supreme Good morally.[44]

Having acquired a true, if partial knowledge of things with the assistance of God, men are still faced with the task of discovering the essential natures of things and their places in the universe. Since it is a Christian universe, scientific knowledge, and even speculative understanding, fall short of the perfection and exhaustiveness which they enjoy in an Aristotelian universe. The ultimate in knowledge for Aristotle is a knowl-

42. *Comp. theol.,* I, 129; *SCG,* I, 60–62; Martin Grabmann, *The Interior Life of St. Thomas Aquinas* (Milwaukee, 1951), p. 25; Phelan, "Verum sequitur esse rerum," *Mediaeval Studies, 1,* 12; Ryan, "The Problem of Truth," *Essays in Thomism,* p. 67; Schneider, *Die Quaestiones Disputatae,* pp. 6–15.

43. See above, pp. 112–16, 119–20, 122–23, 127, 128, 134, 135, 136, 145, 146, 147, 148–49, 155.

44. *ST,* IIa IIae, q. 109, a. 1.

edge not just of things, but of the nature and interrelationships of the causes of things and of the universe known through its causes. This, Thomas agrees, is accessible to man by the light of reason in signate form, but it is perfect only up to a point. Beyond that point lies the knowledge of the universe as it really is. It is a world created in the pattern of Christ and restored to God through Christ.[45] It is a world that is ordered by the providence of God, Who disposes all things and directs them to their rightful ends.[46] Prior to the world we know, to the extent that we can know it, is the world as it exists in the mind of God. In order for men to know the real world perfectly, it would be necessary for them to know perfectly Christ, God's providence, and God's ideas. This is impossible, even to the blessed in Heaven, for Christ, providence, and the prototypes of creation in God's mind are identical with God. To know them perfectly would be to know God perfectly, and this is possible only to God Himself.[47] In this sense, a world created by God and endowed with its nature and purpose by God always retains some of God's own inscrutability, which is not so much a darkness as a brightness that makes it too dazzling to be seen.[48]

The fact that the world is created by God, as well as the epistemology to which Thomas is committed, makes it imperative for him to proclaim the importance of the knowledge of nature. Epistemologically, as we have seen, he holds that all knowledge, with the exception of intuited first principles, enters the mind through the senses. One must therefore study natural objects in order to acquire an understanding of their universal causes. Far more important than this purely philosophical interest in nature are Thomas' theological motives for understanding the universe so far as is possible. The most accurate vision of the world, although it may employ philosophically obtained knowledge, is a vision which is dependent

45. *De ver.*, q. 3, a. 1; *In I Sent.*, prologus. See Bradley, "The Mirror of Truth," *MS, 31,* 311–12.

46. *SCG,* IV, 1, 3.

47. Ibid., III, 56; 57, 7, 9; *ST,* IIIa, q. 92, a. 3.

48. Pieper, *The Silence of St. Thomas,* pp. 57–67, 69–71.

on God, not only because God is the reason why the world exists as it is and why it can be known by man, but also because the world is part of the Divine economy. According to Thomas, one would misinterpret the true nature and value of the universe unless one were to recognize this fact. The investigator must thus have a prior knowledge of God in order to appreciate fully the importance of the world.

In addition, the world, for Thomas, resembles God and provides men with a means of acquiring knowledge about Him. On the level of philosophy, this may be said to be true insofar as effects resemble their causes, and serve as an a posteriori way of knowing these causes. Theologically, however, this is true because God has expressly constructed the world to be more or less like Him, and to provide a set of signa Dei for man. Such signs are aids in the restoration of a correct relationship between man and God,[49] a relationship which is obstructed by man's sin and lack of faith. Where the person to whom these signs are addressed is a believer, they can help to deepen his understanding of what he believes. In this connection, Thomas frequently quotes St. Paul's dictum: "The invisible things of God are clearly seen, being understood by the things that are made" [Romans 1:20].[50] It is important for Thomas, then, that we know the world accurately; otherwise we might misconstrue the nature of God. For this reason, one may "spoil the Egyptians" of their science, while at the same time recognizing that the first cause of the philosophers is not the God of salvation, Who can be known as such only by faith.[51]

This view is based on Thomas' acknowledgment that the knowledge of God required for salvation comes from faith. Faith is addressed to, and has consequences for, the whole

49. *Comp. theol.,* I, 3, 18–36; *In Boeth. de trin.,* prologus; *SCG,* I, 3, 2; 7, 2; II, 2, 4; *ST,* Ia, q. 12, a. 12; IIa IIae, q. 1, a. 5, ad 3.

50. See, for example, *ST,* Ia, q. 2, a. 2; q. 88, a. 3.

51. *In Boeth. de trin.,* q. 1, a. 1, ad 7; a. 2; a. 4; *In I Sent.,* d. 2, q. 1, a. 4; d. 3, q. 1, a. 4; *In III Sent.,* d. 24, a. 3, sol. 3; *SCG,* I, 1; 3, 2–3; 8, 1; III, 38–39; *ST,* Ia IIae, q. 3, a. 6, 8; IIa IIae, q. 1, a. 5; a. 8, ad 1. See also Copleston, *History of Philosophy, 2,* part 2, 13–14, 29–31; Gilson, *Christian*

man, and not just the intellect.[52] For Thomas, faith is not
merely a revealed metaphysics, which endows the intellect
with a set of facts that it would not otherwise possess. Faith
is, rather, a bond between God and man, initiated by God as a
gratuitous gift,[53] which demands a moral as well as an intellectual response from man. These conditions are entailed both
by the fact that God is the object against Whom man's judgment of faith is to be measured, and by the manner in which
the human mind functions. In religious knowledge, as in
knowledge of all other kinds, the object is always the criterion
of what may be known about it. Even in the philosophical sciences, Thomas notes, different methods of cognition and degrees of certitude apply to different sciences, depending on
what they deal with.[54] Now faith deals with God. Since God
is the supreme Good as well as the supreme Being and the supreme Truth, man cannot form an adequate judgment of Him
in the act of faith unless he apprehends Him morally, ac-
knowledging God as the object of his will as well as the object
of his intellect. God's nature, in itself and as the final beatitude of man, demands that men love Him as well as know
Him.[55] Anything less would reflect a conception of God lacking a true adequation to God as He is.

Actually, the metaphysical bias we have observed in Thomas

Philosophy of Thomas Aquinas, p. 21; History of Christian Philosophy, pp.
366–67; Philosophy of St. Thomas, pp. 46–48; Grabmann, Thomas Aquinas,
pp. 90–91; Ghislain Lafont, Structures et méthode dans la Somme théologique
de Saint Thomas d'Aquin (Paris, 1961), p. 493; Pieper, Introduction, pp. 147 ff.;
Vignaux, Philosophy in the Middle Ages, pp. 123–26; Victor White, Holy
Teaching: The Idea of Theology according to St. Thomas Aquinas (London,
1958), p. 11.

52. See, in general, Lang, Die Gewissheit des übernatürlichen Glaubens, pp.
34–70, on faith.

53. De ver., q. 14, a. 2; In III Sent., d. 23, q. 3, a. 1; SCG, III, 151, 2; ST, Ia
IIae, q. 62, a. 3; IIa IIae, q. 2, a. 3, ad 2; a. 9, ad 3.

54. In II Met., lect. 5, c. 335–37; In VI Met., lect. 1, c. 1149; SCG, I, 3, 1;
Anthony A. Nemetz, "Logic and the Division of the Sciences in Aristotle and
St. Thomas Aquinas," MS, 33 (1956), 91–109.

55. Comp. theol., I, 1, 104, 143, 149; De ver., q. 14, a. 10; In Boeth. de trin.,
q. 6, a. 4, ad 5; SCG, III, 116, 118; ST, Ia, q. 12, a. 4–5; Ia IIae, q. 4, a.
1–2, 4; q. 5, a. 6; q. 6, a. 2; IIa IIae, q. 2, a. 3.

is a corollary of his God-centeredness. He sees knowledge of the world and knowledge of God as both regulated by God, although in different ways, depending on the metaphysical distance between God and the particular object to be known. In the case of His creation, God is the criterion of man's knowledge generally and relatively. In the case of God Himself, and of the creation as it is known through Him, His initiative and control are specific and absolute. In the latter case, God, as both the object known and the intrinsic cause of that knowledge in men, may grant or withhold Himself at will in a particular case. In the economy of redemption, to be sure, He appoints apostles, teachers, and preachers to spread the knowledge of God through the world. These intermediaries may be compared at some points with teachers in the field of natural knowledge, in that they are both extrinsic instruments of God in transmitting information to other men.[56] In both instances, they labor, but it is God Who gives the increase. However, the teacher of natural knowledge may enact his role without necessarily realizing that he is, in fact, God's instrument, whereas the commissioned teachers and preachers of Christian truth are generally cognizant of the fact that they have been called and ordained for their work. Further, they may be aware that God has given them special graces, which enable them to interpret correctly the truth that they are expected to communicate, and to express it with an eloquence sufficient to touch the minds and hearts of their audiences.[57] In addition, while the student addressed by the teacher of natural knowledge actually appropriates the information put before him by the teacher by means of his God-given rational powers, these are powers in which all men share by definition. On the other hand, an individual in the audience of an ordained teacher or preacher of God's Word is able to recognize the truth of what he hears, or to gain a deeper insight into it if

56. See, on this comparison, *In Boeth. de trin.,* q. 1, a. 1, ad 2; q. 3, a. 1, ad 4.

57. *SCG,* I, 6, 1; III, 54, 9–13, 19; *ST,* IIa IIae, q. 9, a. 1, ad 2; q. 177, a. 1.

184

he is a believer, solely through a gift of God's grace to him in particular, whether it be a preparatory grace which sows the seeds of a future conversion, the gift of faith itself,[58] or, for the believer, the gifts of the Holy Spirit, which enable him to penetrate further into the mysteries of God, to perceive their theological interrelations, and to become aware of their practical applications.[59] This specific and individual character of the inner workings of grace is attested by the fact that, although all men are potentially believers, not everyone actually does believe. Some men before whom Christian teachings are expounded receive the gift of faith and some do not. Nor do all believers receive the gifts of the Holy Spirit to the same degree or in the same particulars. On the contrary, all men with the same intellectual aptitude are potentially teachable to the same degree about nature. Furthermore, in accordance with the fact that different objects of knowledge are at issue, the successful student will become a knower and will grow in the perfection of his intellect, while the successful hearer of the Word will become a witness or will grow in his witness, thus expanding in the perfection of his whole being.

Faith, and the understanding of one's faith, entail love and knowledge not only because they are signs of God which must correspond to His nature, but also because of the way in which the human mind operates. In analyzing the mind in general, Thomas observes that the intellect and the will are functionally interrelated. It is necessary to know something in order to desire it as good, he says; and the desire to know must precede the act of knowing.[60] These interrelations are assumed in all mental operations. But in some cases Thomas gives priority to one or the other faculty. He thinks that scien-

58. *In III Sent.*, d. 23, q. 2, a. 2, sol. 2, ad 3; *SCG,* I, 6, 1; III, 152, 4; 154, 20; *ST,* IIa IIae, q. 1, a. 9; q. 6, a. 2.

59. *De anima,* a. 16, ad 3; *In Boeth. de trin.,* q. 1, a. 2; *ST,* IIa IIae, q. 6, a. 2, ad 1; q. 8, a. 2; q. 9, a. 1, ad 2; q. 45, a. 1, ad 2.

60. *De ver.,* q. 20, a. 1; q. 22, a. 12; *SCG,* I, 5, 2; *ST,* Ia, q. 16, a. 4, ad 1; q. 82, a. 4. See also D'Arcy, *Thomas Aquinas,* p. 130; Lang, *Die Gewissheit des übernatürlichen Glaubens,* pp. 52–53.

tific knowledge, for example, is primarily the work of the intellect. This is so because the necessary truth of demonstrative conclusions rules out the need for choice. Scientific conclusions constrain the mind to accept them; the mind is not really free to weigh them or to reject them.[61] There is thus no need for the will to encourage the intellect to assent to demonstrations.

In the case of faith, however, the will plays a much more important role. The will finds no difficulty in attaching itself to God as the good. The fact that this good cannot be grasped completely is no obstacle, since the quality of yearning for an unfulfilled desire is basic to the will. The intellect, on the other hand, is more demanding. It hesitates to accept as true something which it cannot know quidditatively, and which it cannot verify empirically. One may wonder at this point why the intellect has such a problem when it comes to God, since it readily accepts as self-evident first principles which cannot be demonstrated. Thomas' reasoning here is essentially descriptive and is geared to the exigencies of theological polemic. In actual fact, he thinks, few people have difficulty with first principles. On the other hand, there are many people to whom God is not at all self-evident. There are also some who assert that God is self-evident to them, but Thomas takes pains to derogate this view by asserting that this self-evidence is merely customary and unexcogitated.[62] It may, of course, be true that this judgment represents Thomas' considered opinion of persons he knew who argued that God was self-evident to them. However, a stronger imperative for disclaiming this position is that, if one subscribes to it, one has no means of rebutting the objections of those to whom God simply is not self-vident.

Stayed from action by the demands of an intellect geared to scientific knowledge, the unbelieving mind is unable to acquire the perspective which would help it out of its dilemma.

61. *In Boeth. de trin.,* q. 3, a. 1, ad 4; *ST,* IIa IIae, q. 2, a. 9, ad 2.
62. *SCG,* I, 10–12; *ST,* Ia, q. 2, a. 1.

186

The believer, according to Thomas, is aware that faith transcends science. Faith, after all, deals with the noblest possible object of knowledge; it opens to the knower an infinitude of truth and goodness; and it is absolutely certain. The mind toying with belief, however, can only see that faith represents partial knowledge, a knowledge which cannot be verified in a manner leading to scientific certainty.[63] It is to overcome these intellectual scruples that the will now intervenes, silencing the doubts of the intellect. In the completed act of faith, the will supplies what is lacking to the intellect, carrying the mind into a realm which the intellect cannot chart, yet making the mind cling to the unknown God with a firm adhesion.

The act of faith is thus accomplished by the intellect through the agency of the will.[64] While grace must be present to move both intellect and will,[65] it does not constrain the believer as does a scientific demonstration, which forces assent. The reason for this, according to Thomas, is that faith is a virtue, as well as an epistemological condition.[66] In fact, his most extensive discussions of faith in his works of general theology, the *Summa theologiae,* the *Summa contra gentiles,* and the *Compendium theologiae,* are found under the heading of virtue. Since faith is a virtue, it requires both an infusion of Divine grace, without which man cannot do what is good nor even undergo a preparatory change of heart, and the freedom of man to accept or to resist grace. If faith were forced into the mind by grace under constraint, it would cease to be a virtue. Belief, then, is proper to both the will and the intellect because of their functional correlation in the act of faith, and because faith has moral as well as epistemological characteristics and implications. Again, although faith, once received, may degenerate into a purely intellectual condition which ren-

63. *De ver.,* q. 14, a. 2; *In III Sent.,* d. 23, q. 2, a. 2, sol. 3, ad 1; *ST,* Ia IIae, q. 67, a. 4, ad 1; IIa IIae, q. 2, a. 1; ad 1; a. 3, ad 3; a. 5; q. 4, a. 1, 8.

64. *De ver.,* q. 14, a. 1; *In Boeth. de trin.,* q. 1, a. 2; *In III Sent.,* d. 23, q. 2, a. 2, sol. 1–3; d. 24, a. 1, sol. 2; *ST,* IIa IIae, q. 2, a. 9.

65. *In Boeth. de trin.,* q. 3, a. 1, ad 4.

66. Ibid.; *ST,* IIa IIae, q. 2, a. 9, ad 2.

187

ders it barely adequate to shoulder its religious weight, it is through the will, under the influence of grace, that faith achieves its proper "form" in becoming a living faith infused by charity.[67]

The interaction of love of God and knowledge of God which Thomas posits conserves the basic outlines of the Augustinian and Anselmian positions on this subject. One is impressed, however, by Thomas' comparative lack of straightforwardness in expounding it. In part this is a result of his use of an epistemology and a doctrine of mental faculty which perhaps unnecessarily complicate his description of the act of faith by forcing him to milk texts of Aristotle of implications which are foreign to Aristotle's mind. That Thomas does manage to maintain this fundamentally Christian position, despite the intellectual contortions that it sometimes requires, attests to his simultaneous commitment to both Christianity and Aristotle, or his realization that Aristotelianism was the only language in which his contemporaries would hear him, if not both.[68]

In the light of Thomas' teaching on the superiority of the believer's love and knowledge of God to the philosopher's knowledge of the first cause as an adequate sign of God, it is clear why faith rather than philosophy should provide the normative relationship between man and God. Yet, despite this fact, Thomas is by no means averse to the use of philosophical arguments in theology, nor does he shun logic in the elaboration of his teachings. It is necessary to indicate the precise sense in which Thomas admits the use of human reason, as well as the reasons why he makes these admissions. It is equally important to indicate the kind of emphasis that he gives to reason in the various contexts in which he employs it. This is a question that requires the elucidation of Thomas'

67. *De ver.*, q. 14, a. 3, 5; *In III Sent.*, d. 23, q. 3, a. 1; *ST*, IIa IIae, q. 4, a. 3.

68. M.-D. Chenu, "La psychologie de la foi dans la théologie du XIIIe siècle," *Études d'histoire littéraire et doctrinale du XIIIe siècle* (Paris, 1932), 163–91.

188

conception of theology: its aims, its methods, his view of the cognitive status of theological arguments, and the ways he expects them to affect particular audiences.

Thomas' reliance on logic is so obvious that it is unnecessary to belabor the point. His use of the *quaestio* form in the vast majority of his works gives him ample opportunity to employ syllogisms of various kinds in his *sed contras* and in his responses to the objections in each article. Deduction is his ordinary method of proof, and he uses it in the discussion of every kind of topic, including those having to do with the nature of God. In addition, he is strongly committed to the principles of contradiction, identity, and excluded middle, and he uses these and other logical rules freely as explanations of God's operations.[69]

More problematic, however, is Thomas' use of philosophical proofs of the existence of God. Such proofs are found in the *Compendium theologiae,* the *Quaestiones disputatae de potentia,* the *Summa contra gentiles,* and the *Summa theologiae,* the famous "five ways" in the latter work being their classical locus. What kind of accuracy as signs of God does Thomas attribute to the conclusions of these proofs, and why does he use them? It must be admitted that the majority of commentators on the proofs do not contribute very much to the discovery of Thomas' intentions. On the whole, they either confine themselves to expositions of the five ways which try to establish the priority of one or another of them,[70] or, insisting that the

69. *Comp. theol.,* I, 102, 106, 129; *De pot.,* I, q. 1, a. 3, ad 7; a. 4, ad 5; a. 5–7; q. 2, a. 3, ad 6; q. 3, a. 19; II, q. 5, a. 2; *In III Sent.,* d. 1, q. 1, a. 1; *SCG,* I, 84; *ST,* Ia, q. 25, a. 3–4; IIIa IIae, q. 14, a. 4; q. 16, a. 4, ad 6.

70. Mary Annice Donovan, *The Henological Argument for the Existence of God in the Works of St. Thomas Aquinas* (Notre Dame, Ind., 1946); L.-B. Geiger, *La Participation dans la philosophie de S. Thomas d'Aquin* (Paris, 1942), pp. 152, 295, 360, 373; Gilson, *Christian Philosophy of Thomas Aquinas,* p. 81; *History of Christian Philosophy,* pp. 369–72; Frank R. Harrison, III, "Some Brief Remarks concerning the Quinque Viae of Saint Thomas," *Franciscan Studies, 21* (1961), 80–93; Charles A. Hart, "Participation and the Thomistic Five Ways," *NS, 26* (1952), 266–82; Charles Lemaître, "Quarta Via: La preuve de l'existence de Dieu par les degrés des êtres," *Nouvelle revue*

ways are fully heuristic, they try to show that Thomas solves
in advance most of the major problems of post-medieval philosophy.[71] A recent variant of this latter tendency has been the
attempt to translate the ways into the terminology of symbolic
logic, presumably to make them more palatable to the modern
mind.[72] In general, one can say that this approach to the
proofs reflects the interest shared by many modern Thomists
in abstracting the philosophical texts of Aquinas from their
theological contexts. The impression one receives from much
of their work is that they are trying to make Thomas vindicate the autonomy of metaphysics.

théologique, *54* (1927), 321–39, 436–68; James B. Nugent, *The Fundamental
Theistic Argument in the Metaphysical Doctrine of Saint Thomas Aquinas*
(Washington, 1961); Joseph Owens, "The Conclusion of the *Prima Via*," *MS,
30* (1952–53), 33–53, 109–21, 203–16; E. Rolfes, "Zu dem Gottesbeweise des hl.
Thomas aus den Stufen der Vollkommenheit," *Philosophisches Jahrbuch der
Görres-Gesellschaft, 26* (1913), 146–59.

71. Mortimer J. Adler, "The Demonstration of God's Existence," *The
Maritain Volume of the Thomist* (*The Thomist, 5* [1943], New York, 1943),
188–218; Patterson Brown, "St. Thomas' Doctrine of Necessary Being," *PR, 73*
(1964), 76–90; Thomas Kevin Connolly, "The Basis of the Third Proof for
the Existence of God," *The Thomist, 17* (1954), 280–349; Léon Elders, "Justification des 'cinq voies,'" *RT 61* (1961), 207–25; P. Geny, "A propos des
preuves thomistes de l'existence de Dieu," *Revue de philosophie, 24* (1924),
575–601; C. Henry "Histoire des preuves de l'existence de Dieu au Moyen âge,
jusqu'à la fin de l'apogée de la scholastique," *RT, 19* (1911), 1–24, 141–58;
Dermot O'Donoghue, "An Analysis of the *Tertia Via* of St. Thomas," *Irish
Theological Quarterly, 20* (1953), 129–51; Jean Paulus, "Le caractère métaphysique des preuves thomistes de l'existence de Dieu," *AHDLMA, 9* (1934),
143–53; José Maria Sánchez-Ruiz, *Las pruebas de la existencia de Dios en el
Tomismo* (Turin, 1957); Matthew Schumacher, *The Knowableness of God:
Its Relation to the Theory of Knowledge in St. Thomas* (Notre Dame, Ind.,
1905); Fernand van Steenberghen, "La problème de l'existence de Dieu dans le
'Scriptum super Sententiis' de saint Thomas," *Studia Mediaevalia in honorem
admodum Reverendi Patris Raymundi Josephi Martin* (Bruges, 1948), pp.
331–49. A formerly conventional commentator, Gilson has recently changed his
mind. He now argues, in his *Christian Philosophy of Thomas Aquinas*, pp. 82–
83, that the proofs do not prove God's existence and that they are not a
posteriori proofs from creatures to God at all, a view prompted by the exigencies
of his "existential" version of Thomism.

72. Jan Salamucha, "The Proof 'Ex Motu' for the Existence of God: Logical
Analysis of St. Thomas' Arguments," *NS, 32* (1958), 334–72.

Nothing, however, could be further from Thomas' true intention. His aim, on the contrary, is to show that philosophical proofs, although they may have their uses, are fundamentally inadequate signs of God. It is important to note here that the amount of emphasis which Thomas places on the respective utility and inferiority of these proofs has a great deal to do with the nature of the works in which he locates them. Thus, in the *Compendium theologiae,* a straightforward piece of positive theology, organized under the headings of faith, hope, and charity and dedicated to a believer, one friar Raymundus, Thomas gives one proof of God's existence: Aristotle's argument from motion to a prime mover. The proof is located at the beginning of the work under the heading of faith. In stating his reasons for including it, Thomas simply says that God's existence must be affirmed before anything else can be affirmed of Him, and that reason can prove this.[73] The *Compendium* is in no sense apologetic; Thomas merely wishes to observe that reason provides an extrinsic support for faith.

A similar intention is visible in the *Quaestiones disputatae de potentia,* although here the discussion is set in a much more academic context. Thomas begins by posing the question whether anything can exist which is not created by God. His answer is predictably negative, and he lets his case rest on the *sed contra* by quoting St. Paul: "From Him and through Him and to Him are all things" [Romans 11:36]. In his response, he goes on to observe that a number of pre-Socratic philosophers attempted to locate the universal cause in matter. This is an approach which he deplores, and he indicates his disapproval by citing with evident appreciation three post-Socratic proofs which involve an immaterial universal cause. The first is derived from Plato and others, by way of Augustine, and is based on the inference of unity from multiplicity. The second is Aristotle's *primum in aliquo genere* argument. The third proof also comes from Aristotle, by way of Avicenna, and stresses the possibility of reducing effects to causes until one

73. *Comp. theol.,* I, 3.

reaches unparticipated pure act. The function of these three proofs is both to beat the Greeks with their own stick and to provide a bit of orchestration for the dominant theme already provided by St. Paul; Thomas' conclusion is: "For thus it is demonstrated by reason and held by faith that all things are created by God." [74]

The case of the *Summa contra gentiles* is rather a different story. This work, while not expressly addressed to non-Christian readers, was written for the instruction of Dominican missionaries faced with the task of spreading the Word in Muslim Spain. The *Summa contra gentiles* is an excellent example both of the acute sensitivity that Thomas has to the exigencies of theological apology and of the fact that he looks at Toledo with Parisian spectacles. He sees Islam as a doctrine constructed out of philosophical arguments, rather than as a revealed religion whose believers revere the testimony of the Bible. Nor is he aware of the Koran. Thus, in stating the cardinal principle that errors should be disproved from authorities accepted by one's opponents, he concludes that with Muslims one must depend on natural reason.[75] This conclusion notwithstanding, Thomas does not mince words about the limitations of his suggested approach. He states quite plainly that although reason can know God as the first cause, there is a great deal more to be said about Him.[76] Faith, he adds, compensates for these limitations, as well as aiding the lazy and the intellectually inept in acquiring even the knowledge of God as first cause.[77]

Thomas' principal aim in the *Contra gentiles* is to refute what he holds are Muslim errors by showing that the teachings of the Christian faith are not opposed to reason.[78] Having made a clear distinction between truths that apply to God as the first cause and truths that apply to Him as the God of

74. *De pot.*, I, q. 3, a. 5.
75. *SCG*, I, 2, 3.
76. Ibid., 3, 3.
77. Ibid., 4–6.
78. Ibid., 2, 4; 7–8.

faith, he considers it expedient to emphasize the former in the first three quarters of the work. It is in this context that he proceeds to prove the existence of God, after proving God's provability, as a necessary basis for what is to follow in Books I through III. Thomas cites only one major proof of God's existence, Aristotle's argument from motion. Actually, he devotes much more attention to the impossibility of infinite regress of causes, on which this argument is based, than to the proof itself.[79] The importance of proving God philosophically in the *Summa contra gentiles* is a consequence of the apologetic burden of the work. Philosophy, Thomas thinks, is the only way to reach the Muslims. Since he assumes that they are all thoroughly grounded in the teachings of the Greeks, he also assumes that a missionary would be foolish to assert either that God's existence is self-evident or that it cannot be proved.[80] The Muslims, he thinks, know as well as he does, and possibly even better, that the existence of the first cause can be proved. The situation is not hypothetical; the first cause already *has* been proved by philosophers using only the light of natural reason.[81] Thomas wants to make certain that his pupils give proper weight to this fact; if they do not, they are in danger of being booted out of Spain as illiterates.

It is only when we reach the fourth and last book of the *Summa contra gentiles* that the intrinsic, as opposed to the ad hoc, value of such philosophical proofs is explained. Here, in the context of exploring the truths which may be known only by faith, Thomas emphasizes the fruitlessness of reason, rather than its cognitive possibilities. Imperfect even in the acquisition of natural knowledge, reason must be supplanted by faith in the acquisition of the truths needed for salvation, of which it can catch only a vague and momentary glimpse.[82] Extensive as Thomas' exploitation of the philosophical stance

79. Ibid., 13.
80. Ibid., 9–12.
81. Ibid., 13, 2.
82. Ibid., IV, 1.

is in the *Summa contra gentiles,* the overall impression he leaves with the reader is a theological one; even in the books dedicated to the treatment of Christian doctrines by natural reason, the organization follows the theological movement from God to creatures rather than the philosophical movement from creatures to God.[83]

Thomas' treatment of proofs of God in the *Summa theologiae* is somewhat more subtle; it is, even, initially ambiguous. This is not a work designed primarily to confute non-Christians, but rather the text of an introductory course in divinity given by Thomas to students in the theological faculty at the University of Paris. It is safe to assume that these students would not have been working for degrees in theology unless they were already believers. The *Summa* seems to begin harmlessly enough, but it suddenly brings the reader up short. Although the first article of the first question of the first part of the work is ostensibly designed to prove the inadequacy of philosophy and the need for revelation and faith, it does this by proclaiming not only that there are truths about God which can be known by reason, but also that only the lethargic, preoccupied, and slow-witted need know them by faith.[84] The impression that Thomas places a high value on the knowledge of God acquired by philosophy is fortified when one turns to the second question of the first part, there to discover that it contains not one, not three, but five proofs of God's existence drawn from philosophical reasoning, more proofs, in short, than are found even in the overtly apologetic *Summa contra gentiles.*

It may seem, at the outset, that the *Summa theologiae* does provide a case for Thomistic metaphysics after all. Closer scrutiny, however, uncovers some details which do not square with this view. The amount of space which Thomas devotes to

83. Cf. M. B. Crowe, "Saint Thomas against the Gentiles," *Irish Theological Quarterly, 29* (1962), 93–120, who considers the genre of the work problematical on the basis of its organization.
84. *ST,* Ia, q. 1, a. 1. See also q. 2, a. 2; IIa IIae, q. 1, a. 5, ad 3.

philosophical truths about God is proportionately smaller in the *Summa theologiae* than it is in either the *Summa contra gentiles* or the *Compendium theologiae,* and the proofs themselves are presented in a rambling, intellectually flabby manner which scarcely resembles Thomas' characteristically incisive style. One is inclined to wonder why he chose to enlist the aid of philosophy if he intended to give it such languid and summary treatment.

The answer to this question lies in the function which the *Summa theologiae* was designed to serve for Thomas' students. This involves some understanding of the temper of Thomas' intellectual environment, since his intentions here are not as outspoken as they are in the *Summa contra gentiles.* The *Summa theologiae* aims at preparing incipient doctors of divinity to cope with the kinds of problems they are likely to encounter in their work as professional theologians. While it is true that thirteenth-century theologians often ended their careers in high posts in the ecclesiastical hierarchy, they rarely acquired these posts by working their way up from the level of the parish priesthood. Most of the time they lived out their lives as university professors, preoccupied with academic rather than pastoral concerns. If they became Dominicans or Franciscans, they were subsidized by their orders, without having to go to the trouble of securing benefices and supervising them in absentia. Thomas' students thus looked forward to an existence devoted to study, lecture, and debate, in an environment electric with theological conflicts. Although the theologians with whom they expected to lock horns were believers, many of them regarded some of Thomas' teachings and, more important, his very approach to theology, as radical and dangerous. In addition, the atmosphere was by no means devoid of philosophically motivated heresy, agnosticism, and nonbelief. Thomas himself had helped to lay down the lines that most of the conflicts took in thirteenth-century Paris, and it is understandable that he should want to pass on his point of view to his students. His students, on their part, were anx-

195

ious to follow in his footsteps; otherwise they would have chosen a different professor.

Now one of the quarrels in which Thomas was involved was the dispute over whether or not God's existence needs to be proved rationally, and whether it can be so proved. This was a hotly contested question among Parisian theologians. For Thomas, what was at stake was the *aggiornamento* of theology; in the minds of his opponents, among whom were ranged many of the members of the conservative university establishment and a number of prominent friars, what was at stake was devotion to the older ways, the dignity of revelation, and, in some cases, the vindication of a mystical rather than logical epistemology.[85] While the *Summa theologiae* in itself is not an apology for Christianity, it is an apology for Thomas' theology. His theological organization of his material, which moves from God to creatures, does not prescind from the fact that the style and method of the *Summa* give every article, in effect, an apologetic structure and tone. Thomas shows his interest in silencing philosophers' objections. But it is largely the objections of his fellow Christians that he has in mind. The structure and arrangement of the work, as well as the fact that Thomas is arguing against a fairly wide range of philosophical and theological opponents, give the *Summa theologiae* an intramural ad hoc character.

The principal reason for the inclusion of the proofs, then, is didactic; [86] it is to train his students to cope with Thomas'

85. Jean F. Bonnefoy, *La Nature de la théologie selon Saint Thomas d'Aquin* (Paris, 1939), pp. 72–79; M.-D. Chenu, *La théologie comme science au XIIIᵉ siècle* (Paris, 1957), pp. 26–32; "Les 'Philosophes' dans la Philosophie chrétienne médiévale," *RSPT, 26* (1937), 27–40; P. Hadelin Hoffmans, "Roger Bacon. L'Intuition mystique et la science," *Revue néoscolastique, 16* (1909), 370–97.

86. Antoninus Finili, "Is There a Philosophical Approach to God?," *Dominican Studies, 4* (1951), 86–87; Edward Sillem, *Ways of Thinking about God: Thomas Aquinas and Some Recent Problems* (London, 1961), pp. 35–39; White, *Holy Teaching,* pp. 7–8; "The Prolegomena to the Five Ways," *Dominican Studies, 5* (1952), 134–58. In this latter work, White sees the didactic aim of the *Summa* as confined only to the training of apologists. Cf. Per Erik Persson, "La plan de la Somme théologique et le rapport 'Ratio-Revelatio,'" *RPL, 56* (1958), 545, who sees no pedagogical importance in the work.

critics. Some of these critics oppose him as philosophical ag-
nostics, heretics, and nonbelievers, rejecting the need for revelation. To this group, Thomas wishes to prove the plausibility
and necessity of theology as a science learned through revelation rather than through metaphysics. Further, he wants to
show that the first principles of theology, although undemon-
strable, are not opposed to reason.[87] Insofar as the philosophers may be dislodged from their complacent rationalism,
such an array of truths about God proved philosophically may
serve as *praeambula fidei;* their prejudices may be shaken if
they are encouraged to see the harmony between reason and
revelation where it exists.[88]

Many of the opponents whom Thomas envisages, however,
are his own confrères who claim that God's existence is self-
evident, or who think it impossible or impious to try to prove
it. In general, they wish to exclude the new philosophy from
the theological enterprise. Thomas' approach here is to make
his points while indicating that he shares their reverence for
revelation and for the mystery of God. He begins by giving
his assurances that faith transcends philosophy and that God
in Himself is supremely self-evident.[89] However, he goes on
to show the absurdity of the statement that God's existence
cannot be proved by natural reason. He does this by indicating that it has already been done, and that it has been done by
thinkers using natural reason and natural reason alone. It is in
this connection that Thomas cites the five ways, beginning
from motion, efficient causality, contingency, *summum in
aliquo genere,* and purposive order, and arriving at a necessary, intelligent, supreme being, which is the prime mover and
the final cause of the universe.[90] We have encountered some
of these arguments before in other works of Thomas. None of
them is original. Nor are they meant to be. The fact that they
would be familiar to anyone conversant with thirteenth-cen-

87. *ST,* Ia, q. 1, a. 1.
88. Lafont, *Structures et méthode,* p. 41, sees no apologetic aim in the proofs.
89. *ST,* Ia, q. 2, a. 1.
90. Ibid., a. 3.

tury philosophy is precisely why Thomas employs them. In this manner, he hopes to point out to his objectors that rational proofs for God's existence are not only possible but actual. Even before he thus insinuates the obviousness of what they deny, he proposes a further justification for rational proofs of God, based on the fact that they use a posteriori arguments. Rather than taking this occasion to stress the resemblances between God and creation in order to validate the use of proofs that work from effect to cause, an idea to which Thomas alludes with respect to rational proofs of God in other contexts, he displays his apologetic intent here, stating that a posteriori arguments for God's existence give witness to God's otherness, by affirming that man cannot know God as He is in Himself, but only through lesser, human ways of knowing.[91]

Thomas' conclusion that God is not self-evident to man is thus designed to accomplish several things at once. It is an argument against what he holds to be obscurantism, against his critics' failure to recognize the existence and the tenability of well-known philosophical demonstrations. It is also a plea for the rejection of a support for faith whose contrary is incontrovertible. Finally, it is a statement of the view that philosophical reasoning about God does not necessarily reflect impiety. This latter point is just as essential an ingredient in Thomas' position as the former two. In the context of his proofs for the existence of God, he stresses it once more, emphasizing the gap between God and man by asserting that men should not confuse their own fuzzy apperceptions, desires, and verbal intentions with facts.[92]

It is in this connection that Thomas restates and condemns Anselm's *Proslogion* proof. He rejects it because he is unaware of its nature.[93] This leads him to misconstrue the aim of the

91. Ibid., a. 2.
92. Ibid., a. 1. Cf. *SCG*, I, 10–11.
93. Anton C. Pegis, "St. Anselm and the Argument of the Proslogion," *Mediaeval Studies, 28* (1966), 228–30, 261–67; Gustave Weigel and Arthur G. Madden, *Religion and the Knowledge of God* (Englewood Cliffs, N.J., 1961), p. 124.

author of the proof. Thomas mistakenly thinks that Anselm is trying to provide a philosophical demonstration in terms of the truth criteria of first principles. He is unwittingly put off by the fact that he has a different conception of definition from Anselm. For Anselm, definition is a grammatical notion. It refers to the name of a person or a thing; it is, in short, simply a noun or a nominal phrase. His aim in the *Proslogion,* as we have seen, is to find and to explain a *rectum nomen* for God, with all that rectitude implies. On the other hand, a definition, for Thomas, is a judgment which signifies a quidditative grasp of its object, and which can be used as a term in a demonstrative syllogism. It is thus out of the question, for Thomas, to try to define God. One of the most interesting paradoxes in Thomas Aquinas is that he argues the bulk of his own theology along lines resembling Anselm's more than he realizes, as will become clear below, although his logical bent of mind prevents him from perceiving this fact.[94]

The proofs of God's existence in the *Summa theologiae* are not ends in themselves. Thomas' mode of presenting them is conditioned by the fact that he is trying to address and to convince several groups of critics simultaneously, some orthodox and some heterodox, some rationalist and some antirationalist. As in the *Summa contra gentiles,* Thomas does not wish to leave the impression that the ad hoc presentation at the beginning of the first part of the *Summa theologiae* is all that there is to be said. In the second part of the *Summa,* where he treats things from a faith-oriented perspective, he indicates his overall views on the values and limits of the proofs. Philosophical knowledge of God, he states, is valid to some extent, but only because it is participated from the knowledge of God by faith.[95] Even though it is possible to

94. Sillem, *Ways of Thinking about God,* p. 54, sees the proofs for the existence of God as a form of Anselmian *fides quaerens intellectum.* While the *intellectus fidei* approach does pertain to Thomas' theology, as will be seen below, it does not apply to the proofs or to any of the truths about God that Thomas thinks can be known by natural reason.

95. *ST,* Ia IIae, q. 3, a. 6.

know some things about God by reason, he says, it is better to know them by faith. Faith is more certain than reason, and, more importantly, faith is a virtue which reflects a right relation to God. Now the only truly virtuous motive for believing in God is the acceptance of the preambles of faith because they are proposed on God's authority. If one believes for this reason, one's faith has merit. The merit that attaches to this assent, however, does not attach to an assent to truths about God in the category of praeambula fidei which are held on the authority of reason. Since what is known demonstratively is not believed, at least not by the same person at the same time, philosophical knowledge of God thus detracts from the merit of faith, in that it reduces the number of preambles of faith which are believed on God's authority. A believer who goes out of his way to demonstrate the rationality of the rationally knowable preambles of his faith therefore does himself a disservice, although this does not apply to the attempt to understand the beliefs he already possesses. But, the greatest demerits go to persons who refuse to believe what they cannot understand scientifically by demonstrative proof.[96]

Surveying in general Thomas' conclusions on the values and limits of philosophical knowledge of God as a sign of God, it appears that he considers it most useful in an apologetic context. Elsewhere it may provide extrinsic support for things that are believed. The prevailing impression one gets from the *Summa theologiae* is that such knowledge is valuable not only apologetically but also to counteract current theological approaches which Thomas thinks would make Christian faith appear irrelevant or indefensible to the *litterati*. On the whole, despite their uses, he maintains that a posteriori proofs of God's existence drawn from reason are weaker than they are strong. They bear only a shadowy resemblance to their object, both because the mind cannot know perfectly the creatures on which they are based, and because the creatures themselves fall infinitely short of God. In any case, according to Thomas,

96. Ibid., IIa IIae, q. 2, a. 5; a. 10, ad 2.

it is possible only for a believer to recognize the existence and the extent of the resemblances between God and creatures,[97] and hence only a believer can judge the accuracy of philosophical proofs of God.

Helpful as these signs may be as praeambula fidei for the nonbeliever, Thomas does not neglect to note that they are purely external and indicative. The real and intrinsic praeambula fidei are the preparatory graces which God gives to a person whom He intends to convert,[98] without which the potential believer would be unable even to take these proofs seriously as indicative signs. And, finally, proofs of God's existence by natural reason cannot even achieve the heuristic, demonstrative status which they claim on their own basis. All judgments, for Thomas, require the knower's awareness of the thing to which his mental sign is to be compared. In order to make an existential judgment about something, one has to have some prior knowledge of its nature: "But we know that we cannot know whether a thing is unless we know in some way what it is, whether by perfect cognition or, at least, by confused cognition." [99] These conditions apply to God as well as to other things. In fact, they are especially applicable to God because He is supremely simple; His essence and existence are one. God's nature can be known, not, to be sure, perfectly, but in part, *per speculum in aenigmate*. But this is the knowledge of faith, not of philosophy. Notwithstanding Thomas' frequent assertions that philosophical knowledge is a preparation for faith, in the last analysis it appears to be not only extrinsic to faith but ex post facto. The kind of knowledge that would make the proofs work rests on faith.[100]

Although a great deal of emphasis is traditionally placed on such rational usages as the proofs of God's existence as characteristic of the theology of Thomas Aquinas, in actual prac-

97. *Comp. theol.,* II, 8–9; *SCG,* I, 7, 2; 8, 1.
98. *De ver.,* q. 24, a. 15; *ST,* Ia IIae, q. 109, a. 6; q. 112, a. 2.
99. *In Boeth. de trin.,* q. 6, a. 3.
100. R. A. Markus, "A Note on the Meaning of *Via*," *Dominican Studies,* 7 (1954), 241–45.

tice they play a very minor role in it. The vast majority of Thomas' work does not consist in the application of demonstrative reason to the world in order to induce truths about God, but rather in the deduction of conclusions from the truths of faith by dialectical reasoning. This is a procedure which Thomas calls *sacra doctrina*. Sacra doctrina must be carefully distinguished from metaphysics, or natural theology.[101] Although they both use reason, they employ it in different ways, to a different extent, and with different results. For our purposes, the most important consequence of this distinction is that sacra doctrina, or the science of theology, is concerned with signs of God which are more complete and accurate than those produced by natural reason. Also, where the function of philosophical signs in religious knowledge is largely indicative, the function of signs that are, strictly speaking, theological, is largely commemorative.

For Thomas, the science of theology is a science because it employs rational arguments and syllogisms. However, it is essential to note that Thomas uses the term *scientia* in a variety of ways: as the absolutely certain knowledge produced by demonstrative syllogisms, as the firm possession of certain knowledge, and as a gift of the Holy Spirit.[102] It is in the latter two senses, with a qualified admixture of syllogism, that Thomas considers theology a science. It is not a science in the strict Aristotelian sense of the word.[103] The science of theol-

101. Alexander M. Horváth, "Der wissenschaftliche Charakter der Apologetik," *Divus Thomas,* 25 (1947), 29–52, 117–91, 345–408; Siegfried Neumann, *Gegenstand und Methode der theoretischen Wissenschaften nach Thomas von Aquin aufgrund der Expositio super librum Boethii de Trinitate* (Münster in Westfalen, 1963), p. 66; Gerald F. Van Ackeren, *Sacra Doctrina: The Subject of the First Question of the Summa Theologica of St. Thomas Aquinas* (Romae, 1952), fail to make this distinction.

102. Roy J. Deferrari, *A Latin-English Dictionary of St. Thomas Aquinas* (Boston, 1960), s.v. "Scientia"; Gilson, *History of Christian Philosophy,* pp. 316–17.

103. The best work on this subject is Chenu, *La théologie comme science.* See also J.-F. Bonnefoy, "La théologie comme science et l'explication de la Foi selon saint Thomas d'Aquin," *Ephemerides Theologicae Lovanienses, 14* (1937), 412–46, 600–31; *15* (1938), 491–516; A. Gardeil, "Le donné théologique," *RT,*

ogy, like other branches of science, is grounded on first principles, which are not demonstrable. In the case of the philosophical sciences, the first principles are not demonstrable because they are self-evident; in the case of theology, the first
principles are not demonstrable because they are articles of
faith which cannot be known by reason.[104] Sacra doctrina
does not deal with the kind of articles of faith which may be
known philosophically as praeambula fidei. Instead, it works
with beliefs concerning the Trinity and the Incarnation, which
are accessible only by faith. Thomas also includes in the category of sacra doctrina the problem of whether the universe is
eternal, because he does not think that it can be solved philosophically.[105]

Scientific theology, as defined above, was not something
new to Thomas. It was a development which began around
1130, with the arrival of Aristotle's *logica nova* in Western
Europe.[106] The second half of the twelfth century shows the
gradual displacement of scriptural commentaries using grammatical techniques of exegesis, which up until this time had
been the dominant style of theology, by the new discipline.
The growing use of *quaestiones* at this time indicates the
emergence of a more logical approach to theology, as does the
shift in the meanings of some key words. *Sententiae,* for example, which traditionally had been statements of the Church
Fathers used as the basis for glosses, or as the contents of

---

17 (1909), 385–405; Gilson, *Christian Philosophy of Thomas Aquinas,* p. 21;
History of Christian Philosophy, pp. 366–67; *Philosophy of St. Thomas,* pp.
46–48; Grabmann, *Thomas Aquinas,* pp. 90–91; Kuhn, "Glauben und Wissen
nach St. Thomas," *Theologische Quartalschrift, 42,* 2 (1860), 273–340; Lafont,
Structures et méthode, p. 493; A. R. Motte, "Théodicée et Théologie chez S.
Thomas d'Aquin," *RSPT, 26* (1937), 5–26; Pieper, *Introduction,* pp. 147 ff.;
Sillem, *Ways of Thinking about God,* pp. 41–48; Vignaux, *Philosophy in the
Middle Ages,* pp. 123–26.

104. *In Boeth. de trin.,* q. 1, a. 4; q. 2, a. 2–3; q. 5, a. 2; *In I Sent.,* prologus,
q. 1, a. 3, sol. 2; d. 2, q. 1, a. 4; *ST,* Ia, q. 1, a. 1–2; a. 5, ad 2.

105. *De pot.,* I, q. 3, a. 17; *SCG,* II, 131–38; *ST,* Ia, q. 46, a. 1.

106. The following is dependent on Chenu, *La théologie comme science,* pp.
18–57; Lang, *Die Gewissheit des übernatürlichen Glaubens,* pp. 147 ff.

florilegia, came to be systematically arranged compilations of theological interpretations. The standard work in this genre, the *Sentences* of Peter Lombard, became in turn the subject of innumerable commentaries in the thirteenth century. In general, the emergence of theology as a science marked a separation between speculative theology and biblical exegesis. Most of the progressive theologians began to use extra-scriptural modes of proof; logical skill, rather than the extensive citation of authorities, came to dominate theological treatises.

There were some thirteenth-century opponents to these developments. Robert Grosseteste and Roger Bacon held out for a more scriptural emphasis, and the conservative secular theologians at the University of Paris were disturbed. However, by 1220, William of Auxerre had formulated at Paris the classic scholastic statement of the rights of reason in theology in his *Summa aurea.* William begins by affirming the priority and independence of faith. At the same time, he employs rational methods to develop his conclusions. He sees three different uses for reason in theology: to augment and to confirm the faith of believers, to convince heretics of error, and to incline the ignorant toward faith. William justifies his position by taking St. Paul's definition of faith as the *argumentum non apparentium,* as well as Aristotelian logic, as a warrant. This new view attained wide popularity in the years following the publication of the *Summa aurea,* particularly among the friars now making their way to Paris. Such prominent theologians as Eudes Rigaud, Simon of Tournai, the Franciscans Alexander of Hales and St. Bonaventura, and the Dominicans Albert the Great, Robert Kilwardby, and Thomas Aquinas adhered to it. The proponents of theology as a science in the thirteenth century all believed that its technique in no way altered the nature of theology as *sapientia,* as a quest for communion with God, and as an activity integrally related to the personal piety of the theologian, although some, with Bonaventura, emphasized the affective side of the theological enterprise more than others. None of them believed that the proofs used in scientific theology were conclusive demonstrations.

204

Thomas is an inheritor of this tradition, but he elaborates and refines it somewhat. The most noticeable difference between his own interpretation of theology and William's is Thomas' distinction between demonstration and dialectic, which goes back to scholastic logic. For Thomas, demonstration has no place in a science based on faith because demonstrative proofs can either be verified empirically or referred to self-evident first principles. However, God, the object of faith, is not available for empirical tests, and is not, in Thomas' view, self-evident to men. Therefore, he selects dialectics as the appropriate type of reasoning for theology, its function being to find probable arguments.[107] Within the general category of theological arguments, however, not all are dialectical. Some conclusions are only deducible from faith on Divine authority, whether it be through Scripture or through another article of faith. These proofs, he states, are extremely convincing for the believer. They are more potent than scientific demonstrations, because the believer holds the first principles of faith with more certainty than he holds philosophical first principles.[108] One of Thomas' most frequently used types of the argument from Divine authority is the argument from theological suitability. He employs this proof in discussing God in general,[109] but more often in connection with the Trinity[110] or the Incarnation.[111] Its basic criterion is the

107. *In Boeth. de trin.,* q. 6, a. 1; *In I Sent.,* prologus, q. 1, a. 3, sol. 2; *SCG,* I, 8, 1; *ST,* Ia, q. 1, a. 8, ad 2; IIa IIae, q. 1, a. 5, ad 2.

108. *SCG,* IV, 1, 10; *ST,* Ia, q. 1, a. 8; IIa IIae, q. 11, a. 5, ad 2.

109. *De pot.,* I, q. 1, a. 1–2; q. 2, a. 2; q. 3, a. 15, ad 16; a. 17, ad 8; *In I Sent.,* d. 8, q. 2, a. 1–2; d. 35, q. 1, a. 1; d. 37, q. 2, a. 2–3; d. 42, q. 1, a. 1; *In III Sent.,* d. 1, q. 2, a. 3; *SCG,* I, 29, 5; *ST,* Ia, q. 25, a. 1.

110. *De pot.,* II, q. 5, a. 6; q. 6, a. 6, ad 5; q. 9, a. 9; ad 1; q. 10, a. 1, ad 6; *In I Sent.,* d. 31, q. 2, a. 1; q. 3, a. 1; *ST,* Ia, q. 29, a. 3; q. 31, a. 2, q. 36, a. 1; q. 39, a. 7; ad 8; q. 43, a. 4–5, 7.

111. *In III Sent.,* d. 1, q. 1, a. 2; a. 3, ad 3; a. 4; q. 2, a. 2; d. 12, q. 3, a. 1–2; d. 15, q. 1, a. 1; d. 21, q. 1, a. 2–3; q. 2, a. 1–4; d. 22, q. 2, a. 1; *SCG,* IV, 42, 45–46, 54–55; *ST,* IIIa IIae, q. 1, a. 3, 5–6; q. 3, a. 1–2, 8; q. 4, a. 5–6; q. 5, a. 4; q. 6, a. 3; q. 7, a. 1; q. 8, a. 1; q. 14, a. 1; q. 21, a. 3; q. 22, a. 1; q. 23, a. 1–2, 4; q. 27, a. 2; q. 28, a. 2–3; q. 32, a. 1; q. 45, a. 1; q. 50, a. 1; q. 51, a. 1; q. 52, a. 1; q. 53, a. 2; q. 54, a. 4; q. 55, a. 2; q. 57, a. 1; q. 58, a. 1. Appropriateness to God as a norm of Thomas' theological proofs is also noted

norm of what is fitting to God, in terms of what one already knows about His nature and operations by faith. This is something that a believer, and only a believer, can judge.

Thomas' second major source of arguments is the dialectical syllogism. Its conclusions are less probable than those derived from Divine authority, but they can be accepted both by believers and nonbelievers. It is because of their wide appeal that Thomas advocates public debates on theology employing dialectical syllogisms before a heterogeneous audience. The rules he lays down for this kind of debate put one back in the intellectual world of the thirteenth-century university town. They also exemplify Thomas' concern for the social responsibilities of the theologian. One is struck by the level of dialectical skill he demands in his theologians. Although limited to the use of probable arguments, the theologian, says Thomas, may not convey the impression that the articles of faith are themselves doubtful. His stated reason for arguing, outside of *jeu d'esprit,* is to refute error, but he must do this without suggesting that his refutations have been demonstratively proved, for if he did this he would hold the Christian faith up to the ridicule of objectors capable of detecting such a logical faux pas.[112] His probable arguments also avail to the consolation of the faithful.[113] But here, Thomas notes, the theologian must exercise prudence and discretion, lest he bewilder and demoralize rather than edify. Thomas notes that the literate believer, who can be counted on to be theologically sophisticated, will enjoy the disputation and will profit from it. But in the case of weak or poorly instructed brethren, the theologian must rapidly discover whether they are beset by nonbelievers trying to corrupt their faith. If this is so, he must take the risk that they will be confused by theological debate; if not, it is best to leave them undisturbed.[114]

by Chenu, *Introduction,* pp. 153–58; Gilson, *Philosophy of St. Thomas,* pp. 48–49.

112. *In Boeth. de trin.,* q. 1, a. 1; ad 1–3; a. 2, ad 4; q. 2, a. 3.

113. *SCG,* I, 9, 2; *ST,* IIa IIae, q. 2, a. 9, ad 1.

114. *In Boeth. de trin.,* q. 2, a. 4; *ST,* IIa IIae, q. 10, a. 7.

In addition to the needs of the people whom the theologian is commissioned to serve, he has personal requirements to meet in his work. According to Thomas, theology has an important practical side, but it is primarily a speculative science, which aims at beatitude.[115] Both the public and the private goals of theology make it essential that it be a living dialogue between the contemplator and God, and not merely an abstract discipline. Practical and speculative theology alike demand that the theologian's work be wedded to his spiritual life. The grace of God, piety, and personal holiness are required for the deepening of his understanding of what he believes,[116] an exercise of *fides quaerens intellectum* that contributes both to his external effectiveness and to his own contemplation. As an instructor, Thomas notes, the theologian needs the gifts of knowledge and understanding, which teach him how to make the faith known.[117] If he is a preacher, he also needs the gift of speech, in order to carry out successfully the Augustinian mission to teach, to delight, and to persuade.[118] Man's cognitive powers, Thomas observes, are affected by his moral status.[119] Since the end of contemplation is the vision of God, the theologian must strive to grow in wisdom and virtue. *Intellectus fidei,* as well as faith itself, demands the functional interaction of love and knowledge,[120]

---

115. *In Boeth. de trin.*, q. 2, a. 1; ad 1–3; a. 2, ad 4; *In I Sent.*, prologus, q. 1, a. 3, sol. 1; *SCG*, I, 1–2; *ST*, Ia, q. 1, a. 4–6; IIa IIae, q. 180, a. 4.

116. *ST*, IIa IIae, q. 2, a. 10; ad 2; q. 6, a. 2, ad 1; q. 8, a. 1; ad 2.

117. Ibid., q. 9, a. 1, ad 2.

118. Ibid., q. 177, a. 1. On Thomas' theology as a form of Dominican *sacra praedicatio*, see White, *Holy Teaching*, pp. 21–22.

119. *ST*, IIa IIae, q. 15, a. 3.

120. Bonnefoy, "La théologie comme science," *Ephemerides Theologicae Lovanienses, 15,* 492–503, 516; Chenu, *La théologie comme science,* pp. 12–13, 37–53, 78; John F. Dedek, *"Quasi experimentalis cognitio:* A Historical Approach to the Meaning of St. Thomas," *TS, 22* (1961), 357–90; J. Durantel, *Le Retour à Dieu par l'intelligence et la volunté dans la Philosophie de S. Thomas* (Paris, 1918), pp. 210–379; A. Gardeil, *Le donné révélé et la théologie* (Juvisy, 1932), pp. xxi, 319–58; Martin Grabmann, *The Interior Life of St. Thomas Aquinas* (Milwaukee, 1951), pp. 12, 29–31; Scientific Cognition of Truth: Its Characteristic Genius in the Doctrine of St. Thomas Aquinas," *NS,*

and the grace of prayer [121] as well as the faculty for finding probable arguments.

For Thomas, the knowledge of God acquired through a deepened faith is the most adequate sign of God, short of mystic rapture, that is available to man in this life. Yet, he states, all knowledge by faith is essentially partial and confused. Theological speculation is just that: the knowledge of God *per speculum in aenigmate*.[122] It is in this context, the context of sacra doctrina, that Thomas considers a final species of sign, which brings into sharp focus the tension between man's God-given ability to speak about God and the impossibility of his ever saying anything truly commensurate with Him. One of the tasks of the theologian, Thomas states, is to provide likely similitudes about God, for the purpose of clarifying the Divine truths which he teaches.[123] These similitudes must bear a resemblance to God, otherwise they are useless. They cannot be

---

13 (1939), 1–30; *Die theologische Erkenntnis- und Einleitungslehre des hl. Thomas von Aquin auf seiner Schrift "In Boethium de Trinitate" im Zusammenhang der Scholastik des 13. und beginnenden 14. Jahrhunderts dargestellt* (Freiburg in der Schweitz, 1948), pp. 45–100; *Thomas Aquinas,* pp. 50–52; M.-M. Labourdette, "La Vie théologale selon S. Thomas," *RT, 60* (1960), 364–80; James Coleman Linehan, *The Rational Nature of Man with Particular Reference to the Effects of Immorality on Intelligence according to Saint Thomas Aquinas* (Washington, 1937). Cf. Reginald Garrigou-Lagrange, "La foi éclairée par les dons," *La Vie Spirituelle, 64* (1946), 657–66; Dermot O'Keefe, *Theology and Contemplation according to St. Thomas Aquinas* (Romae, 1952); George van Riet, "Y a-t-il chez saint Thomas une philosophie de la religion?" *RPL, 61* (1963), 44–81, who hold that piety is irrelevant to theology in St. Thomas. On theology as fides quaerens intellectum in Thomas, see Johannes Beumer, "Thomas von Aquin zum Wesen der Theologie," *Scholastik, 30* (1955), 195–214; Pierre Germain, "La théologie de saint Thomas d'Aquin, science de la foi," *Revue de l'Université d'Ottawa,* section spéciale, *28* (1958), 174*; Martin Grabmann, "Il concetto di scienza secondo S. Tommaso d'Aquino e le relazioni della Fede e della teologia con la filosofia e le scienze profane," *Rivista di filosofia neoscolastica, 26* (1934), 127–55; Lafont, *Structures et méthode,* p. 484; White, *Holy Teaching,* pp. 8–9.

121. *Comp. theol.,* I, 2.

122. Ibid., I, 105; II, 1; *De ver.,* q. 10, a. 11, 13; q. 14, a. 1; *In Boeth. de trin.,* q. 1, a. 2; *ST,* Ia, q. 12, a. 11; IIIa IIae, q. 3, a. 3. Gilson, *Christian Philosophy of Thomas Aquinas,* pp. 24–25; Grabmann, *Thomas Aquinas,* pp. 137–38.

123. *In Boeth. de trin.,* q. 2, a. 3.

anything but probable, because they are to be dealt with under the heading of sacra doctrina rather than natural theology. The problem of locating signs such as these was one that both Augustine and Anselm had to face. For Thomas, the quest was even more difficult, because he was obstructed by his logical habits of mind and by the scholastic method of his theology from finding the easiest solution to it. Where Augustine and Anselm respond with apt figures of speech, and are able to specify the paradox posed by the assignment of discussing the known yet unknown God in the programmatic arrangement of their works, Thomas is blocked by the impersonality and argumentativeness of the *quaestio* style and by the fact that his epistemological predilections incline him to replace figurative language with literal and discursive speech wherever possible. It is not that Thomas' poetic sensibilities were atrophied. His liturgical verse shows him a master at that art. But his poetic style is one of highly intellectualized verbal conceits and multiple layers of connotation rather than metaphor.[124] Given the problem of dealing with transferred meanings, Thomas' response was analogy. Analogy is his attempt to make logic do what can be done much more easily by metaphor, in speaking about God from the limited vocabulary provided by human ways of knowing.

Analogy, for Thomas, is essentially a *façon de parler*. It is necessary to state this quite plainly, for the prevailing approach on the part of commentators has been to regard Thomistic analogy as a metaphysical doctrine. In doing this, they have placed more weight upon analogy than it was designed by Thomas to carry. It is not our intention here to enter the intramural disputes among Aquinas scholars on analogy; for our purposes, most of them have asked the wrong questions.[125] Before proceeding further, however, it may be

---

124. Walter J. Ong, "Wit and Mystery: A Revaluation in Mediaeval Latin Hymnody," *Speculum, 22* (1947), 310–41. I would like to thank Father John R. Cavanaugh, C.S.B., for this reference.

125. Some commentators, adhering to the traditional metaphysical emphasis, content themselves with giving an exposition of analogy in order to show its usefulness in systematic philosophy and theology. George P. Klubertanz, *St.*

useful to state the traditional conceptions of Thomistic analogy and to indicate why we think that the subject requires an approach different from those usually accorded it.

It should be noted at the outset that analogy is a device used by Thomas to explain how we can think about two or more things that are not quite the same and yet not entirely different, and which thus cannot be thought of either univocally or equivocally. Thomas is very unsystematic about analogy, which is the best he can do in trying to rationalize ambiguities while keeping them ambiguous at the same

Thomas on Analogy: A Textual Analysis and Systematic Synthesis (Chicago, 1960), presents a thorough assemblage of texts and a helpful bibliography on analogy. See also Nicolas Balthasar, *L'Abstraction métaphysique et l'analogie des êtres dans l'être* (Louvain, 1935); F. A. Blanche, "L'Analogie," *Revue de philosophie, 23* (1923), 248–70; W. Esdaile Byles, "The Analogy of Being," *NS, 16* (1942), 331–64; D'Arcy, *Thomas Aquinas,* pp. 125–26, 131–32; J. Fehr, "Offenbarung und Analogie: Ihr Verhältnis in dialektischen und thomistischen Theologie," *Divus Thomas, 15* (1937), 291–307; B. Landry, "L'analogie de proportion chez saint Thomas d'Aquin," *Revue néoscolastique de philosophie, 24* (1922), 257–80; "L'analogie de proportionnalité chez saint Thomas d'Aquin," *Revue néoscolastique de philosophie, 24* (1922), 454–64; *La Notion d'analogie chez saint Bonaventure et saint Thomas d'Aquin* (Louvain, 1922), pp. 35–68; Hampus Lyttkens, *The Analogy between God and the World: An Investigation of Its Background and Interpretation of Its Use by Thomas of Aquino* (Uppsala, 1952), pp. 244 ff.; Armand Maurer, "St. Thomas and the Analogy of Genus," *NS, 29* (1955), 127–44; George McLean, "Symbol and Analogy: Tillich and Thomas," *Revue de l'Université d'Ottawa,* section spéciale, *28* (1958), 193*–233*; Joseph Owens, "Analogy as a Thomistic Approach to Being," *Mediaeval Studies, 24* (1962), 303–22; Eleuthère Winance, "L'Essence divine et la connaissance humaine dans le Commentaire sur les Sentences de Saint Thomas," *RPL, 55* (1957), 171–215.

Most commentators spend their time trying to decide which of the various kinds of analogy is "properly Thomistic," which generally involves a dispute over whether Suarez or Cajetan was correct in interpreting Thomas. For the Suarezian approach, see F. A. Blanche, "La notion d'analogie dans la philosophie de S. Thomas d'Aquin," *RSPT, 10* (1921), 169–93; "Une théorie d'analogie," *Revue de philosophie,* n. s., *3* (1932), 37–78; Thomas Marguerite Flanigan, "The Use of Analogy in the *Summa contra gentiles,*" *MS, 35* (1957), 21–37; Ralph J. Masiello, "The Analogy of Proportion according to the Metaphysics of St. Thomas," *MS, 35* (1958), 91–106; Ch. de Moré-Pontgibaud, "Sur l'Analogie des noms divins," *RSR, 19* (1929), 481–512; *20* (1930), 193–223.

Some hold a nominally Suarezian position, but on other grounds, usually Platonic. See John S. Dunne, "St. Thomas' Theology of Participation," *TS,* time.[126] He does not limit analogy to the relationships between God and creatures. Therefore, not all the analogies that can be found in Thomas' works are directly relevant to the problem of theological discourse, although attention has usually been directed to those analogies which Thomas thinks can be used for this purpose. A second point that should be kept in mind is that there are two approaches to analogy in

---

18 (1957), 487–512; Lindbeck, "Participation and Existence," *Franciscan Studies, 17,* 1–22, 107–25; Little, *The Platonic Heritage of Thomism; Thomas* Prufer, *Sein und Wort nach Thomas von Aquin* (München, 1959).

The Cajetanians are, on the whole, more numerous, and tend to claim more authority for their position. See James F. Anderson et al., "Some Basic Propositions concerning Metaphysical Analogy," *RM, 5* (1952), 465–72; Copleston, *History of Philosophy, 2,* part 2, 73–78; Gilson, *Christian Philosophy of Thomas Aquinas,* p. 106; Antoine van Leeuwen, "L'analogie de l'être: Genèse et contenu du concept d'analogie," *Revue néoscolastique de philosophie, 39* (1936), 293–320; George P. Klubertanz, "The Problem of the Analogy of Being," *RM, 10* (1957), 553–79; Jacques Maritain, *Distinguish to Unite, or the Degrees of Knowledge* (New York, 1959), Appendix 2, pp. 418–21; Ignatius O'Brien, "Analogy and Our Knowledge of God," *Philosophical Studies, 6* (1956), 91–104; M. J. L. Penido, *Le Rôle de l'analogie en théologie dogmatique* (Paris, 1931); Gerald B. Phelan, *St. Thomas and Analogy* (Milwaukee, 1943); Schumacher, *The Knowableness of God.*

Lately, some Cajetanians have taken to translating their position into the terminology of modern symbolic logic and linguistic analysis. See I. M. Bochenski, "On Analogy," *The Thomist, 11* (1948), 424–47; William Bryar, *St. Thomas and the Existence of God: Three Interpretations* (Chicago, 1951); James F. Ross, "Analogy as a Rule of Meaning for Religious Language," *International Philosophical Quarterly, 1* (1961), 468–502.

A recent trend has been for scholars to consider some, or all, of the kinds of analogy logical rather than metaphysical. See David Burrell, "A Note on Analogy," *NS, 36* (1962), 225–32; "Religious Language and the Logic of Analogy: Apropos of McInerny's Book and Ross' Review," *International Philosophical Quarterly, 2* (1962), 643–58; Ralph McInerny, "The Logic of Analogy," *NS, 31* (1957), 149–71; *The Logic of Analogy: An Interpretation of St. Thomas* (The Hague, 1961); Bernard Montagnes, *La Doctrine d'analogie de l'être d'après saint Thomas d'Aquin* (Louvain, 1963); Herbert Thomas Schwartz, "Analogy in St. Thomas and Cajetan," *NS, 28* (1954), 127–44; Wilbur Marshall Urban, *Language and Reality: The Philosophy of Language and the Principles of Symbolism* (London, 1939), Appendix IV, pp. 748–50; C. J. F. Williams, "Existence and the Meaning of the Word 'God,'" *Downside Review, 77* (1958–59), 53–71.

126. M. S. O'Neill, "Some Remarks on the Analogy of God and Creatures in St. Thomas Aquinas," *Mediaeval Studies, 23* (1961), 215.

Thomas, the theoretical and the practical. Virtually all the commentary on this subject has been confined to the theoretical level. It has thus concentrated on what Thomas says about analogy. No attempt has been made to examine in detail the kinds of analogies that Thomas actually uses when he wants to elucidate the nature of God by reference to creatures. As we shall see, Thomas' use of analogy in practice goes a long way toward explaining his doctrine of analogy in theory.

Although a variety of different kinds of analogy have been found in Thomas' writings by the assiduous scholarship of his disciples,[127] the debates of the commentators have focused on two kinds, the analogy of attribution and the analogy of proper proportionality. In the analogy of attribution, a characteristic, such as being, is attributed to two or more entities, each of which bears a relationship to being that is different from the others. The prime analogate possesses being properly and intrinsically, while the secondary analogates possess being extrinsically, by attribution from the prime analogate. In the analogy of attribution, then, being is regarded as intrinsically one, and as relatively diverse. Being is present in the various analogates *per prius et posterius*. The classic example used to illustrate the analogy of attribution is drawn from Aristotle: an animal, urine, and medicine are all called healthy. The health involved is the same in each case, but each of the analogates is related to it in a different way. Health is an attribute proper to an animal. Urine may be "healthy," since it is a sign of health; and medicine may be healthy because it is conducive to health. In general, the analogy of attribution tends to stress the similarities among the analogates rather than their differences. Scholars who follow Suarez on Thomistic analogy and those who wish to emphasize the Neoplatonic aspects of Thomism are inclined to consider the analogy of attribution the basic kind of analogy in Thomas, since it

127. Klubertanz, *St. Thomas on Analogy,* is the fullest and most recent attempt to catalog the various types of analogy in Thomas.

can be utilized in a participationist type of metaphysics more easily than can other kinds of analogy.

The chief contender for the title of basic Thomistic analogy is the analogy of proper proportionality. The analogy of proper proportionality sets up a four-term proportion. The classic example of such a proportion is: man's being: man as God's Being: God. In contrast to the analogy of attribution, being is proper here to each of the analogates. In the case of both man and God, the mode of being in question is intrinsic to the entity in question, although the two modes of being are not equal to each other. As opposed to the analogy of attribution, the analogy of proper proportionality presents us with a situation in which being is regarded as intrinsically diverse, and only relatively one. The analogy of proper proportionality thus tends to emphasize the differences between the analogates rather than their similarities. Scholars who stand with Cajetan on Thomistic analogy are inclined to reject the claims of all kinds of analogy except proper proportionality to be truly Thomistic.

The prevailing trend in analogy scholarship has been reductionism. It is the foregone conclusion of most of the commentators that there must be one, and only one, kind of analogy that is "properly Thomistic." On this point there is almost universal agreement; the debate among the commentators centers on whether the one, true Thomistic analogy is the analogy of attribution or the analogy of proper proportionality. There is a variety of reasons why scholars argue for the one or the other. They range from metaphysical preference to the adding up of all the instances where Thomas cites analogy and the conclusion that the analogy which appears most frequently is the "properly Thomistic" one. In reaction against reductionism, M. C. D'Arcy has urged that it is a mistake to emphasize either kind of analogy at the expense of the other. If we adhere too rigidly to attribution, he states, the result is pantheism; and if we adhere too rigidly to proper pro-

213

portionality, the result is relativism.[128] Others have sought to
heal the breach by arguing that analogy describes similarities
which lie "halfway between equivocity and univocity." [129]

These positions, despite their differences, all reveal a fundamentally unhistoric approach to the interpretation of
Thomas. Scholars whose preference for one kind of analogy
or another rests on metaphysical grounds show their willingness to base their views on traditional sixteenth-century Thomistic authorities, often at the expense of the text of Thomas,
or on their equally traditional unwillingness to believe that
Thomas could have employed both Aristotelian and Neoplatonic ideas on analogy without choosing decisively between
them on principle. Some think that one or another kind of
analogy should be put forth as "properly Thomistic" because
it permits them to solve problems in post-thirteenth-century
philosophy or theology to which they think Thomism provides
an answer. Those who attempt to discover which type of analogy is "properly Thomistic" on the basis of a statistical or
chronological study of Thomas' works make the mistake of attributing too much system to his thought.

George P. Klubertanz has quite rightly observed that
Thomas only discusses analogy in specific contexts, vis-à-vis
specific objections.[130] This insight leads to the conclusion
that the frequency with which Thomas refers to a particular
kind of analogy has more to do with the frequency with which
he feels called upon to rebut particular objections than with
his personal preference for one kind of analogy as opposed to
another. Here, as elsewhere in Thomas' thought, it is necessary to remember that the structure of scholastic argument
creates an apologetic tone that is not present to the same degree in other philosophical styles. It has been noted that the
analogy of attribution inclines more toward a univocal concept

128. D'Arcy, *Thomas Aquinas,* pp. 131–32.

129. Klubertanz, *St. Thomas on Analogy,* p. 138. See also Lyttkens, *The
Analogy between God and the World,* p. 389.

130. Klubertanz, *St. Thomas on Analogy,* p. 3.

of being and that the analogy of proper proportionality inclines more toward an equivocal concept of being. Thus, the respective plausibility of these two approaches depends on whether one looks at the relationship between God and creatures from the point of view of nonbeing or from the point of view of being.[131] If one looks simply at the Being of God vis-à-vis the being of creatures, one has to deal with two radically different modes of being. The analogy of proper proportionality is most useful in this context, because it stresses the differences rather than the similarities between the analogates. On the other hand, compared with nonbeing, both God and creatures possess being, although in different ways. The analogy of attribution is most useful in this context, because it stresses the similarities rather than the differences between the analogates.

Having said this, it is irrelevant to ask how often Thomas stresses the similarities between God and creation by means of the analogy of attribution and how often he stresses the differences between God and creation by means of the analogy of proper proportionality. It is sufficient to state that Thomas believes that both similarities and differences exist; thus, he employs both kinds of analogies. His reason for citing one of them in a particular context usually depends on the nature of the objection it is designed to refute. Thomas tends to use the analogy of attribution, and, in general, a participationist type of argument, to combat thinkers who see nothing in common between God and creation.[132] Thomas opposes this view because he holds that, if it were permitted to stand, it would result in agnosticism, for both philosophical and theological reasons. As an empiricist, and as a firm supporter of the idea that causes and effects resemble each other, Thomas is philosophically certain that the world resembles God, its first cause.

131. D'Arcy, *Thomas Aquinas*, p. 127; Lyttkens, *The Analogy between God and the World*, p. 269.

132. For a particularly clear example, see *ST*, Ia, q. 13, a. 5; and for some other good examples, see *Comp. theol.*, I, 27; *In I Sent.*, prologus, q. 1, a. 2, ad 2; d. 2, q. 1, a. 3; *ST*, Ia, q. 4, a. 3.

This belief is basic to his view that the world can provide man with information about God through a posteriori reasoning. As a Christian, Thomas takes seriously St. Paul's assertion that the invisible things of God can be seen through the visible things of His creation. Both philosophy and theology, for Thomas, proclaim the existence of some resemblances between God and creation, however weak. Both philosophy and theology provide warrants for the doctrine that God can be known to some degree from creation, according to human ways of knowing. Now for Thomas human knowledge operates by means of ideas derived from sense data, which are provided by creation. But if the creation in no way resembles God, it cannot tell man anything about God. Man has no alternative but agnosticism. It may be noted that Thomas here omits faith as a possible means of knowledge about God in default of a creation that resembles Him. This is because faith, for Thomas, is given through created intermediaries; it is proposed to men by the words and deeds of other men. If nothing that is created, whether it be the laws of nature or the words of preachers, resembled God, man would have no access whatever to the certainty that God is God.

On the other hand, Thomas uses the analogy of proper proportionality when he wants to combat thinkers who, he holds, find too much in common between God and creation.[133] Insufficient discrimination between God and creation, he thinks, leads to pantheism or monism. Pantheism and monism are mistaken positions primarily because they obliterate the transcendence of God. They also fail to do justice to the uniqueness of created beings, particularly human beings. Thus, Thomas tends to use the analogy of proper proportionality in dealing with opponents who, he thinks, are overly emanationist in their metaphysics, and against proponents of the Averroist view of the unity of the intellect.[134] He finds just as many philosophical and theological warrants for stressing the differ-

133. For a particularly good example, see *De ver.,* q. 2, a. 11; and for some others, see *SCG,* I, 34; *ST,* Ia, q. 3, a. 5, ad 2; q. 13, a. 5.

134. *ST,* Ia, q. 88, a. 1; IIIa, suppl., q. 92, a. 1.

216

ences between God and creation as for stressing their similarities. The same Aristotelianism which assures him that causes can be known through their effects provides him with the conviction that causes are always greater than their effects, and that they are never identical with them. And, the same theology which asserts that the creation proclaims the Creator also asserts that it falls infinitely short of Him.

Attention to context, then, solves one of the difficulties in which many commentators on Thomistic analogy needlessly embroil themselves. Another problem, touched on at the outset of our discussion of analogy, results from the tendency of many scholars to treat Thomistic analogy as a metaphysical doctrine. According to this view, being is intrinsically analogous. Therefore, concepts about being must also be analogous. Analogous concepts tell us the truth about beings. It is thus possible to discover something about God through analogous concepts derived from creation. Further, analogous concepts derived from creation can tell us that God is transcendent over creation, and that He possesses any perfections that we may find in creation in an absolutely preeminent way. This position on analogy contains two accurate perceptions about Thomas' epistemology: the priority of being over knowing and the idea that concepts based on sense data can be accurate signs of their objects. However, proponents of the view that analogy is a metaphysical doctrine fail to integrate these two notions successfully, thus confusing the order of being in Thomas with the order of knowing. This position, therefore, results in a paradox. Its supporters argue that analogical concepts are simply the intelligible representations of intrinsically analogical facts, and that God possesses the characteristics being analogized in a unique and supreme way. At the same time, they argue that the analogical way of knowing moves from creation to God, since men derive the ideas on which analogies are based from their inspection of created things. This sounds like an attempt to eat one's cake and have it too. If, for Thomas, our knowledge were truly limited to what we can know by means of sense data, it would be impossible for us to know that God possesses His analogated attributes in a radically different way from sensible creatures. The argument that analogy can show us a transcendent God would thus fall. At the same time, if we begin with the mode of being instead of the mode of knowing, asserting that God's Being transcends the being of creatures on the basis of metaphysical or theological first principles known by intuition or faith, the argument that analogical concepts can tell us something about God and creation that we did not already know would also fall. This notion of analogy, which demands that we begin with creation and work up to God, but which depends on God's movement down to creatures for its validity, is, in effect, a tautology.[135]

It would be a tautology, that is, if Thomistic analogy really were a metaphysical doctrine, or if Thomas actually thought that his analogies of God provided heuristic foundations for a constructive metaphysics. The case, however, is quite otherwise. Analogies are never intended by Thomas to bring anyone to a knowledge that he does not already have.[136] Rather, they are a means of showing forth the relationships between things that are already known by faith, and are hence a species of intellectus fidei. To establish this point with the firmness that it deserves, it is necessary to underline three basic qualifications which Thomas applies to analogy. The first of these qualifications stems from the general limitations which Thomas places on all concepts, whether logical or analogical, as signs of non-sensible objects. The second can be deduced from his placement of analogical arguments in his works, which tells us whether or not he considers them demonstrative proofs from effects to causes. The third concerns the aspects of Deity for which Thomas seeks analogies, and the nature of the analogies that he finds for them. With these latter two qualifications we move from the realm of analogical theory to the realm of analogical practice.

135. Cf. William L. Reese, "Analogy, Symbolism, and Linguistic Analysis," RM, 13 (1960), 447–68.

136. ST, Ia, q. 13, a. 10.

218

For Thomas, as we have seen, true concepts are accurate but partial signs. They always have cognitive limitations vis-à-vis their objects. The more immaterial the object, the more extensive the limitations, for the human mind is so constructed that its ideas, with the exception of intuited first principles, derive from sense data. These conditions apply to analogical concepts no less than to logical concepts. It is just as necessary in analogical as in logical reasoning for the subject to have a prior knowledge of the object in order to be able to judge the truth of the analogy, its adequation to what it signifies. In this sense, no true judgment, whether logical or analogical, ever tells the subject something of which he was previously ignorant. Analogies are signs; so far as their adequation to their objects goes, they are no weaker nor stronger than other kinds of signs. But, for Thomas, analogies have a special advantage. Because of their structure, they are able to signify the relationships between things as well as the things themselves.

Analogies, then, are not heuristic. In fact, if we examine Thomas' practical use of analogies, it appears that they have even fewer capacities for demonstrative use than do ordinary arguments about God. As we have noted earlier, Thomas employs both demonstrations and probable arguments in his theology. The vast majority of his arguments are probable ones. This is because he assigns to probable arguments a very large task, the discussion of articles of Christian doctrine which can be known only by faith. The number of such doctrines far outstrips the number of those which he thinks can be known by natural reason. Probable arguments fall under the purview of sacra doctrina, in which conclusions are deduced from theological principles. On the other hand, Thomas assigns to demonstration a comparatively small task, the discussion of God's existence and some of His primary attributes. Demonstration is responsible for the conclusions about God which natural philosophers have been able to prove about God by accurate induction. Demonstrative conclusions about God fall into the category of praeambula fidei. With this distinction in mind, we may ask whether Thomas uses analogical arguments in sacra doctrina, in the praeambula fidei, or in both. The answer is quite simple. There are no arguments from analogy whatever in those sections of Thomas' works devoted to the treatment of praeambula fidei. Analogical arguments appear only as a means of explaining those truths of the Christian faith which, according to Thomas, must be known by faith. It is thus impossible to regard analogy as a kind of philosophical demonstration from effects to causes, or to place it in the same category as Thomas' proofs for the existence of God. Rather, analogy should be regarded as a kind of probable argument, by means of which Thomas deduces conclusions from articles of faith according to the norm of theological appropriateness, and whose resemblance to God can be judged only by believers.

Still greater insight into the uses to which Thomas puts analogy can be gained if we consider the specific articles of faith for which he formulates analogous arguments, and the nature of the analogies which he chooses for this purpose. As we have seen, Thomas employs the theory of analogy in different contexts, depending on the objections he wants to refute and on the kind of relationship between God and creatures that he wants to stress. Despite his heavy emphasis on the idea that we derive analogical concepts about God from nature at large, when he is faced with the practical problem of finding likely similitudes of God, he has recourse to only one kind of analogy: the mind of man. He uses analogies drawn from human nature primarily in passages dealing with Trinitarian theology. Thus, in practice, Thomas emphasizes psychology over cosmology; and he does not shrink from analogizing man's mental processes to the deepest mystery of the Christian faith. He compares such phenomena as the interactions of man's mental faculties, the process of concept formation, and the relationship between man's inner ideas and his external expression of them to the relations among the Persons of the

220

Trinity,[137] the procession of the Word,[138] and the Incarnation.[139] In fact, it is in the course of discussing these Trinitarian doctrines that Thomas develops a sizable proportion of his teachings on the operations of the human mind.

Both Thomas' methods and his examples are quite conventional. They follow faithfully the tradition of Augustine and Anselm. Equally conventional is Thomas' construction of analogies between God and the mind of man. He begins by building up the analogy, underlining the similarities between God and man. Then, he breaks down the analogy, illustrating the immense gap between God and man. Analogy, like man himself, has both strengths and weaknesses as a sign of God. The human mind, which resembles God more closely than any other created thing, cannot represent Him fully, even in the state of beatitude. Only Christ is the perfect image of God.[140] So analogy, which combines univocity and equivocity, adumbrates the mysterious relationship between two mysterious entities, God and man. The imprecise nature of analogy enables it to display the impenetrable as impenetrable.

For Thomas, then, analogical knowledge of God is one species within the general category of conceptual signs of God. Like all signs of God, analogies refer to a reality Whose nature is already known in part by faith. Analogy is more serviceable than are straightforward names of God in displaying the doctrine of the Trinity because it can signify relationships as well as things and because it can elucidate the relationships between things that are both similar and different without

137. *De ver.*, q. 10, a. 1; *In I Sent.*, d. 10, q. 1, a. 1; a. 2–3; d. 12, q. 1, a. 3; *SCG,* IV, 11–12, 19; *ST,* Ia, q. 14, a. 8; a. 11, ad 1; a. 12; q. 19, a. 1; q. 27, a. 3, ad 3; a. 4; q. 36, a. 1–2; q. 37, a. 1; q. 45, a. 6; a. 7; q. 93, a. 6; ad 4; a. 7; a. 8.

138. *De pot.*, I, q. 2, a. 1; q. 3, a. 16, ad 5–7, 10; III, q. 8, a. 1; *De ver.*, q. 4, a. 1; ad 10; a. 2; ad 4–6; *In I Sent.*, d. 10, q. 1, a. 4; d. 27, q. 2, a. 1; *SCG,* IV, 11–12, 19.

139. *Comp. theol.*, I, 216; *De pot.*, I, q. 2, a. 4, ad 7; a. 6, ad 3; III, q. 9, a. 5; *Der ver.*, q. 4, a. 1; ad 10; a. 2; ad 4–6; *SCG,* IV, 11–12, 19; *ST,* Ia, q. 27, a. 1; a. 2; ad 2; q. 34, a. 1; ad 2–3; a. 2; ad 1; a. 3; q. 44, a. 3, ad 1.

140. *ST,* Ia, q. 93, a. 1.

221

identifying the similarities or making polar opposites of the differences. Analogies of God, for Thomas, are *aenigmata*. The lack of mathematical precision in his doctrine of analogy, his failure to state just how similar and just how different the analogates in his analogies are, his disinterest in systematizing his theory of analogy, and his disinclination to tell the reader which, if any, of his types of analogy is "properly Thomistic" are hence deliberate. An aenigma by nature signifies through its obscurity rather than through its clarity and precision. Thomistic analogy is a pillar of cloud, not a pillar of fire.

As a theorist on the role of signs in the knowledge of God, Thomas Aquinas is in some respects harder to lay hands on than either Augustine or Anselm. Despite the extensive amount of space he devotes to topics related to this problem, Thomas never compiles all the relevant materials into one work, nor does he put forth his theory with either economy or overtness. Clearly, the question of signs did not interest Thomas as much as it interested Augustine and Anselm; and his efforts to harmonize Aristotle with Augustine on this point are not always felicitous. But, when there is a contest, it is generally Aristotle who is made to cede. For all Thomas' differences from Augustine and Anselm, it is possible to see that he agrees with the basic Augustinian theory of signs on all the important points. For Thomas, concepts, and by extension words, represent real things. They represent them truly but partially. This applies to all the signs he treats, from judgments about natural objects to God as represented by demonstration, dialectic, and analogy. In all cases, he sees the object as the criterion of the truth of its sign. The more adequately these signs signify God, the less they rely on reason, and the more closely correlated to the mystery of the Godhead they become. In the cognition of their objects, however, signs always remain extrinsic. No sign is perfectly heuristic in the first instance. All signs are appropriated mentally as representations of their objects on the basis of God's activity, in one way or another, in the mind of the subject, whether God's in-

222

trinsic causality be reflected in the light of the intellect, the gift of faith, the gifts of the Holy Spirit, or, ultimately, the light of glory. There are some Thomistic signs which are primarily indicative, such as inductions from nature to the first cause, and there are others which are primarily commemorative, such as deductions from faith as performed by sacra doctrina, although there is some degree of overlapping between these two types. And, finally, Thomas retains the Augustinian stress on the interrelationship of love and knowledge in the signification of God per speculum in aenigmate, in his analysis of the functions of the human mind, in his definition of faith, and in his notion of the nature and aims of theology.

4 DANTE: Poet of Rectitude

The linguistic epistemology which is the subject of this study was, as we have seen, both resilient and adaptable. Capable of assuming the garb of rhetoric, grammar, and dialectic in response to the shifting intellectual climates of the Middle Ages, it retained its Augustinian amalgam of classical sign theory and the theology of the Incarnation despite these permutations and their attendant shifts in emphasis. The durability of this theory during the Middle Ages can be explained not only because it bore Augustine's authoritative stamp, but also because it appeared to satisfy the needs of theologians as diverse as Augustine, Anselm, and Aquinas for an explanation of how human powers of thought and expression could achieve and communicate the knowledge of God. This was a concern which appealed primarily to the professional theologians of the Middle Ages. Yet, if we confine ourselves exclusively to the history of theology, we will be unable to appreciate fully the range and flexibility which this theory attained. The Augustinian conception of words as signs in the knowledge of God was, in fact, applied to a number of forms of expression other than that of theological discourse. One of these forms of expression, which we propose to examine here, was poetry.

The extension of Augustinian sign theory to poetry can be seen in the poetics of Dante Alighieri and its consummation in the *Divine Comedy*. Our selection of Dante for this purpose does not necessarily imply that he is representative of all phases of medieval poetics. Nor is it meant to suggest that his view of poetry can be applied retroactively to his literary predecessors at all points. It may certainly be argued that Dante's poetics is original in conception and unique in accomplishment. Yet, Dante's theory of poetry is related to traditional medieval poetics and to his immediate poetic back-

224

ground, the *dolce stil nuovo,* both by way of acceptance and by way of reaction. For Dante, the poet is a prophet and teacher. Poetic beauty becomes the means whereby he communicates God to man. Dante's treatment of poetry as an epistemic method thus parallels the rhetorical theology of Augustine, the grammatical theology of Anselm, and the dialectical theology of Thomas Aquinas, and it is based on the same fundamental conception of words as signs.

This attribution of cognitive and didactic functions to poetry springs in part from the subject matter of the *Divine Comedy* and from the heavenly inspiration which Dante believes warranted his writing it. It is derived also from his assimilation of poetics to rhetoric. This assimilation, a common practice among medieval educators, was perpetuated by Dante, although he departs from the tradition in several important respects, as we shall note below. Now the linguistic epistemology of the Middle Ages was also set in a rhetorical context, at least in its original Augustinian manifestation. Given a tradition in which poetry was treated from the point of view of rhetoric, and given the wide availability of Augustine's works, it would not be difficult for a medieval poet and intellectual to put them together, especially if he saw himself as a reformer with a message for his times. This, we maintain, is what Dante does. Appropriating for Christian poetry the role that Augustine entrusts to Christian rhetoric in the knowledge of God, Dante develops a poetics which aims to teach, to delight, to persuade; a poetics which, in attempting to express the Word and to move men toward God through its aesthetic, moral, and intellectual rectitude, retains the functional interrelations between wisdom, virtue, and eloquence assigned by Augustine to redeemed speech.

Given the retention of this interrelationship by Dante, it must be stressed that he sees the content and the corollaries of wisdom, virtue, and eloquence in a manner both broader and more specific than any of the thinkers whom we have already examined. For Dante, the pursuit of wisdom and virtue de-

225

mand that he take an attitude toward the Europe of his own day. This attitude entails a thoroughgoing reform of Christian society at all its levels, from the most universal to the most particular. The need to unite wisdom and virtue is the focus around which Dante organizes his views on ethics, doctrine, ecclesiastical and political theory. Out of this complex of ideas he posits an ideal of intellectual and moral rectitude, which correlates the salvation of the individual with the restoration of right order in Church and state. Wisdom and virtue, in turn, must be related to eloquence. This Dante accomplishes by attaching his moral and intellectual ideals to a literary ideal, which entails a reform of language and the invention of a poetry of rectitude, and by expressing them in a poem which meets his own linguistic and literary criteria.

Dante's poetic epistemology, while grounded in the Augustinian tradition, is thus specified, as were its grammatical and dialectical counterparts, in terms of the conditions and needs of a particular historical environment as perceived by a particular mind. Dante's theories on human nature, the state, the Church, language, and poetry, his interpretation of his own poetic development, his local and European loyalties, are fused aesthetically in the *Divine Comedy*. This work, then, in its conception, contents, and execution, is the specific mode in which Dante resets and re-expresses the Augustinian doctrine of signs.

In attempting to demonstrate this assertion, our first task is to set forth the poetic theory of Dante, to explain its development in his early works up to the *Divine Comedy,* and to ascertain the nature and extent of his debt to medieval poetics before his time. As one would expect in the case of an author who has been commented on unremittingly from his own age to the present, there exists a wide variety of interpretations of Dante's poetic theory. These variations, to the extent that they deal with Dante's relationship to medieval poetics, result in part from the fact that what is commonly regarded as medieval poetics is actually made up of several ingredients,

226

which do not necessarily blend consistently into one coherent theory. There are theories of poetry expressed in textbooks on the liberal arts, and these may be taken to represent the school tradition. There are also theories of poetry put forth by figures whose contributions lie primarily in fields other than the writing and teaching of poetry. Both must be contrasted with attitudes toward poetry implicit in medieval poems whose authors were not interested in issuing theoretical analyses of their art.

When these various approaches are taken into account, several different views of poetry emerge. All of them possess classical antecedents. All of them contain the implicit idea that poetry, as a form of communication, can be judged according to rhetorical canons, although the type of rhetoric in each case may differ. Thus, medieval poetics can assume a sophistical, or purely technical orientation, in which primary stress is placed on decoration and style. Or, it can assume a broader, antisophistic orientation in which the good, the true, and the eloquent are linked and applied to poetry, by way of criticizing existing poetry or by way of establishing norms for the poetry that ought to be written. Some medieval theorists hold the view that poetry is wholly or partially false or fictitious, an interpretation which implies that poetry is didactic and persuasive. Thus, some of them regard the characters, plot, or stylistic accoutrements of a poem as fictitious veils which stand between the reader and an edifying inner core. These fictitious veils may be pulled aside by literary analysis or left clothing the core of the poem, depending on the literary astuteness of the reader. For the less sophisticated reader, the veils may be regarded as a lure, a sugar coating over the pill within, which makes the edification provided by the poem more palatable. The more skillful reader will regard the veils as a series of obstacles, and his enjoyment of the poet's message will be enhanced by his feeling of success in having met and solved them. Alternatively, the fictitious veils may be thought of as a shield protecting an esoteric inner truth from

227

profane eyes, ensuring that it will be detected only by initiates whose intellects are equal to the task of penetrating the veils. Finally, following the tradition established by Plato when he ejected the poets from his *Republic* and seconded by Augustine in his *Confessiones,* some medieval theorists thought that poetry was entirely false and fictitious in the ideas and attitudes it put forth, and that it was dangerously seductive on account of its beauty. It must be kept in mind that when most medieval theorists said "poetry" they were referring to classical poetry, that is, to poetry written by pagans, which contained references to pagan gods and religions. The truth of such poetry could be treated in several ways. Although all of these approaches could be related to rhetoric, medieval poetic theory was by no means a homogeneous tradition. In constructing and exemplifying a specifically Christian poetic theory, Dante accepted some aspects of it while rejecting others.

Both the distinction between poetry and rhetoric and the tendency to assimilate the former to the latter can be traced to classical literary theory. Greek and Roman educators treated poetry and rhetoric as two separate arts requiring two different styles of composition. Where poetry utilized an imaginative mode of organization involving an emotional progression from image to image, rhetoric utilized an intellectual mode of organization involving a logical progression from idea to idea. Thus, each demanded its own technique of composition.[1] For centuries rhetoric and poetic were kept apart. During the Augustan age, however, there was a marked tendency to conflate them, to the detriment of poetry's autonomy. This development has been attributed to the fact that Cicero and his contemporaries regarded rhetoric as the most important type of literature. This led them to treat poetry as an ancilla to rhetoric and to conceive of poetry in rhetorical terms. Thus, in his *Pro Archia,* Cicero defends poetry by arguing that it has didactic value and that it is a useful means of commemorating

1. Charles Sears Baldwin, *Ancient Rhetoric and Poetic Interpreted from Representative Works* (New York, 1924), pp. 1–3.

228

the great deeds of famous men. Poetry, like rhetoric, he holds, should instruct as well as delight the reader.[2]

The rhetorical attitude toward poetry dominated Roman criticism from Cicero's day until the end of the classical era. It is expressed most completely in Horace's *Ars poetica*. Horace, as J. W. H. Atkins describes him, succeeded in "applying to poetry a doctrine which by this time had become standard in the rhetorical schools."[3] The very title of *Ars poetica*, which was given to Horace's treatise by Quintilian, was perpetuated by grammarians who scarcely saw poetry as a separate technique. This indicates the degree to which poetry had become assimilated to rhetoric, for there is very little in this work that does not apply equally to Ciceronian prose.[4] Horace defines the aim of poetry as didactic and pleasurable; it should uplift the reader morally as well as delight him. Horace upholds Cicero's emphasis on persuasion and teaching, at the expense of pleasure if necessary. He also stresses the educational function of poetry, envisioning it as a civilizing agency in the broadest sense. Cicero's preoccupation with suiting the style of the oration to its subject matter is paralleled by Horace's ideal of congruity between the poem's theme, its organization, and its stylistic finish.[5]

The impression that Roman men of letters were merging poetry into rhetoric of a deliberately antisophistic sort is strengthened by a consideration of Plutarch. Plutarch stresses pointedly that the didactic and ethical aspects of poetry should be the poet's first concern. It is not enough, according to Plutarch, for a poem to produce pleasure in the reader. The real aim of the poet is to elevate the reader's character, to move him to follow the good, and to bring ethical principles to

2. J. W. H. Atkins, *Literary Criticism in Antiquity: A Sketch of Its Development* (New York, 1952), 2, 37.

3. Ibid., p. 100; Mary A. Grant and George Converse Fiske, "Cicero's *Orator* and Horace's *Ars Poetica*," *Harvard Studies in Classical Philology, 35* (1924), 1–74.

4. Baldwin, *Ancient Rhetoric and Poetic*, p. 246.

5. Ibid., pp. 246–47; Atkins, *Literary Criticism in Antiquity, 2*, 76–77.

229

bear on his daily life. Plutarch emphasizes this idea to the point where he strains the Ciceronian harmony between wisdom, virtue, and eloquence by conceiving of the pleasing function of poetry in a purely utilitarian light, thus subordinating it rigorously to its moral ends.[6]

Late Latin critics, who were responsible for transmitting classical literary theory to the Middle Ages, preserved this assimilation of poetry to rhetoric. One way in which they did this can be seen in their treatment of Vergil. The Antonine rhetor Florus entitles a fragmentary work *Virgilius orator an poeta*. Donatus and Macrobius lend their authority to the rhetorical treatment of Vergil; and the minor rhetoricians of the Roman Empire follow suit, repeatedly citing passages from Vergil to illustrate the rhetorical usages which their works outline.[7] The assimilation of poetry to rhetoric was also susceptible of more synthetic treatment at the hands of Cassiodorus, who restates the principle that the poet can speak according to the rules of rhetoric. The poet's aim, according to Cassiodorus, is to move the conscience of the reader. It is not his subject matter but his technique which differentiates him from the orator.[8]

Scholars have frequently noted that this classical confusion between poetry and rhetoric was carried over into the medieval school tradition.[9] In part this was simply the result of the perpetuation of the ideas of Cicero and Horace by late classical critics, whose textbooks became the basic channels of literary education. In part it was the result of the fact that rhetoric tended to lose its forensic orientation during the Middle Ages. Except for its application to preaching, rhetoric was

6. Atkins, *Literary Criticism in Antiquity, 2,* 315.

7. Ernst Robert Curtius, "Neue Dantestudien," *Gesammelte Aufsätze zur romanischen Philologie* (Bern und München, 1960), pp. 319 ff.

8. Edgar de Bruyne, *Études d'esthétique médiévale* (Brugge, 1946), *1,* 46.

9. For general statements on this point, see Ernst Robert Curtius, *European Literature and the Latin Middle Ages* (New York, 1953), p. 480; Joseph A. Mazzeo, *Medieval Cultural Tradition in Dante's 'Comedy'* (Ithaca, N.Y., 1960), p. 3.

generally treated as a science of literary style. Latin poetry was also studied as a rhetorical production, and thus it was an easy matter to fuse the methods of these two arts.[10] Poetry, it is true, was taught as part of the grammatical curriculum, as it had been in classical times; in his definition of grammar Rabanus Maurus states that its concern is to interpret the poets and historians.[11] Yet, in practice, rhetorical canons of style came to be imposed upon poetry. Many medieval teachers of poetry concentrated on the *colores rhetorici*. Poetry, for them, was the study of style. They were chiefly interested in illustrating how to apply the appropriate stylistic decoration to poetic works, and extended rhetorical norms of literary decorum and beauty to poetic decoration.[12]

Scholars of late have frequently cited many examples of the application of rhetoric to poetics in the Middle Ages. In the seventh century, we find Isidore of Seville treating poets and rhetors as stylists, under the same general heading. According to Isidore, both poets and orators must suit their style to their audience. Thus, he passes on to poetry the Augustinian redefinition of Cicero's three modes of discourse, the elevated, the middle, and the low. Poetry, like rhetoric, is a form of narration, which may also have didactic functions. Isidore adds that figurative language contributes to the beauty and decorum of poetry, just as it ornaments rhetoric.[13] The transference of the three Ciceronian styles to poetry is also evident in the writings of Bede in the eighth century and of Alcuin in the late eighth and early ninth; the Carolingian scholar Lupus of Ferrières repeats this principle and illustrates it from Vergil.[14] An anonymous Carolingian commen-

10. Baldwin, *Medieval Rhetoric and Poetic*, p. ix; Edmond Faral, *Les Arts poétiques du XIIe et du XIIIe siècle: Recherches et documents sur la technique littéraire du moyen âge* (Paris, 1924), pp. 55–103.

11. Baldwin, *Medieval Rhetoric and Poetic*, pp. x, 130–32. See above, p. 93.

12. Michele Barbi, *Life of Dante* (Berkeley and Los Angeles, 1954), pp. 42–43; Faral, *Les Arts poétiques*, pp. 93–97; Edgar de Bruyne, *L'Esthétique au moyen âge* (Louvain, 1947), p. 49.

13. De Bruyne, *Études d'esthétique médiévale, 1*, 92 ff.

14. Baldwin, *Medieval Rhetoric and Poetic*, pp. 131–32, 144–45.

tator on Horace's *Ars poetica* reiterates the idea that the aim of poetry is to charm and to instruct, while adding a new twist to the theory. The author assumes a normative point of view, affirming that the true poet ought to depict a moral ideal. The poem will be useful to the extent that it contains moral truths and moves the reader toward them. Only truth, according to the author, will really delight the audience. The charm of the poem thus depends on the wisdom of the poet as well as on his literary artistry. The most important criterion of a poem is the degree to which it conforms to the good, the true, and the beautiful. The style of the poem is thus assimilated to its content; the content itself determines the ability of the poem to please the reader. This interpretation marks a correlation of style to content new to the tradition of rhetorical poetry. The Carolingian anonymous, however, does not develop it systematically, for, in restating the Ciceronian rule of the three styles, he reverts to the view that the poet should adjust his style to the level of the audience.[15]

The early medieval tendency to equate poetry with rhetoric was carried forth in the twelfth and thirteenth centuries by commentators on poetry almost without exception.[16] Poetry was still taught as a part of grammar, but although many writers, like John of Salisbury, Alexander of Villedieu, and Éverard of Béthune, discuss it under the rubric of grammar, they conceive of it in rhetorical terms.[17] And it is analyzed in rhetorical terms even by authors who treat it as an art in its own right. This approach has been noted in Vincent of Beauvais. Despite the fact that he devotes a separate section of his *Speculum doctrinale* to poetry, Vincent affirms that its function is to rouse the minds of its readers to emulate or to reject the ideas which the poet puts forth in images.[18] The ethical emphasis of a Vincent of Beauvais or a John of Salisbury,

---

15. De Bruyne, *Études d'esthétique médiévale, 1,* 223–38.
16. Ibid., *2,* 14–49; Faral, *Les Arts poétiques,* passim.
17. Baldwin, *Medieval Rhetoric and Poetic,* pp. 157–64, 184.
18. Ibid., p. 175.

however, is not always typical of this period. In the numerous *artes poeticae* which now begin to appear, there is a marked tendency to move away from a didactic interpretation of poetry toward an almost preclusive stress on technique, which leads most of the poetic theorists to underline the stylistic and decorative applications of rhetoric to poetry rather than its moral or educational functions. A transition figure in this regard is Alain de Lille. Alain was a product of the school of Chartres, whose members in the twelfth century looked at poetry as a vehicle for philosophy.[19] Alain himself is well known for his lengthy, allegorical, didactic poems. In uniting poetics to rhetoric, however, it is not the didactic side of rhetoric which he stresses. Rather, he sees rhetoric primarily from the point of view of adornment.[20] Allegory is a kind of rhetorical trope, and Alain's rhetoric, in the words of Baldwin, "is not operative as composition, but only as style after the fact . . . His diffuseness arises from the idea that *poetica* involves decorative dilation by those *colores* of which Cicero and Vergil are equally patterns." [21] The idea, prevalent in the twelfth and thirteenth centuries, that the chief concern of poetic theory was to communicate the technique of decorative dilation by applying the colores rhetorici to poetry is traced by Baldwin through the *artes poeticae* of Matthew of Vendôme, Geoffrey of Vinsauf, Éverard the German, and John of Garland.[22] The only significant modification of this approach occurs in the *Poetria* of John of Garland. John appears to be the only figure on Baldwin's list who takes account of the contemporary revision of rhetoric in the *ars dictaminis*. This, however, does not prevent him from giving both poetry and dictamen surveillance over the three styles, illustrated from Vergil and sanctioned by citations from Horace's *Ars poetica*

19. De Bruyne, *Études d'esthétique médiévale, 2,* 397; H.H. Glunz, *Die Literaturästhetik des europäischen Mittelalters* (Bochum-Langendreer, 1937), pp. 268–69.

20. Baldwin, *Medieval Rhetoric and Poetic*, pp. 172–74.

21. Ibid., p. 174.

22. Ibid., pp. 185–96. See also Faral, *Les Arts poétiques*, passim.

and the *Rhetorica ad Herennium.* The only distinction John draws between dictamen and poetry is one of quantity. The style of dictamen, he says, should be brief; that of poetry should be diffused by means of coloristic dilation.[23]

In the tradition we have been describing, two basic applications of rhetoric to poetry have emerged. Some writers carry over antisophistic principles to poetry, thus endowing the poet with the power and the duty to express the true and the good and to move the reader toward them. Others concentrate instead on the technical aspects of poetic decoration, borrowing from rhetoric its figures, allegories, tropes, and colors, and applying them to poetry as canons of adornment. The members of this latter group manifest comparatively little interest in the uses of poetry; they are preoccupied mainly with establishing rules on how to write it. These two approaches rarely occur unmixed with each other between the seventh and the thirteenth centuries. However, in the twelfth and thirteenth centuries, they seem to be drawing further apart. During these two centuries, the school tradition, as represented by the *artes poeticae,* tends to emphasize a poetics of purely decorative technique, while the contemporary proponents of a poetics joined in some way to wisdom or virtue are drawn on the whole from the ranks of the practicing poets or the critics and summarizers of culture.

The rhetorical idea of poetry as a medium of education and as a moral stimulus was also retained by medieval commentators who, following the Platonic tradition, thought that the truth of poetry was either covered with fictitious veils or nonexistent. This view can often be found paralleling the more technical or positive attitudes toward poetry described above, and sometimes these divergent approaches coexist in the writings of the same author. Thus, Isidore of Seville, in analyzing poets and rhetors as stylists, describes them in the same breath as fabricators of fables. In so doing he cites the standard classical criticisms of the truth of poetry, derived from

23. Baldwin, *Medieval Rhetoric and Poetic,* pp. 191–93.

Platonism, that are put forth by Victorinus, Priscian, Diomedes, and Varro. Poems, according to Isidore, contain fables. Yet they may also contain some truths and may serve a didactic function. Poetic fictions are a way of making delightful to the reader moral or natural truths which he might otherwise find distasteful. Thus, the role of the poet is to present these truths obliquely, by decorating his works with rhetorical figures. Poetry, for Isidore, is a method of indirect discourse; poetic fictions, figures, and coloristic decorations are a decoy to the reader and are extrinsic to the poet's message.[24]

Carolingian scholars perpetuated the theory of poetic fiction. The Carolingian anonymous, in commenting on Horace's *Ars poetica,* takes as his point of departure the view that Horace's intention is to treat poetry as the art of composing fables. The author makes a strong effort to relate this idea to his didactic theory of poetry. He thinks, as we have seen above, that the poem should communicate truths and that its pleasing character depends on the truth and goodness of its content. Although poetry is fiction, he argues, it is the kind of fiction that imitates truth, for the best fictions are those possessing verisimilitude.[25] In this way, the commentator tries to prevent poetic fable from undermining poetic truth, by stressing a mimetic rather than an imaginative conception of fiction. John the Scot reiterates the idea of poetry as fiction, arguing that although it is not really right for an author to depict deliberate falsehoods, poetic fictions are admissible because they may contain natural or moral truths. John thus agrees with the Carolingian anonymous that the poet must be learned in these matters as well as artful.[26]

In the twelfth and thirteenth centuries the idea of poetic fiction underwent some modifications and was supplemented by a strong scholastic stress on the falsity of poetry. Many twelfth-century writers expressed the view that poetic fiction

24. De Bruyne, *Études d'esthétique médiévale, 1,* 92–98.
25. Ibid., pp. 223 ff.
26. Ibid., pp. 227–30; De Bruyne, *L'Esthétique au moyen âge,* pp. 53–55.

should be true to life, a tradition deriving from the Horatian principle *ut pictura poesis.*[27] The question of poetic allegory also excited a good deal of attention during these two centuries. Allegory was viewed not merely as a mode of decoration, correlated or not with the didactic and moral aims of poetry, but also as a method of literary criticism. Thus, John of Garland, in his *Poetria,* argues that the Christian reader can neutralize the dangerous falsehoods he encounters in pagan literature by allegorizing the offending doctrines.[28] Even more noticeable in the thirteenth century is the tendency to treat allegory as a scriptural and theological method that is incompatible with profane literature, an idea linked with the general denigration of poetry on the part of the scholastics. The view that poetry has no claims to truth was quite popular. It can be found in the works of the Franciscans Robert Grosseteste and St. Bonaventura, as well as in the works of the Dominicans Albertus Magnus and Thomas Aquinas. However, it is usually Aquinas' dicta on poetry that have been cited to illustrate this scholastic position. Aquinas places poetry on the lowest plane of logic. Poetry is regarded as subrational, as incapable of signifying truth. Poems cannot be grasped by the discursive reason because they deal with fables and illusions, not with realities. Hence, he says, poets use an allegorical or symbolic method. This allegorical method, as used by poets, is by no means to be confused with the symbolic language and techniques employed by theologians and exegetes. Speculative theology may use a symbolic method because its object transcends discursive reason. Scriptural exegesis may use the allegorical method because God Himself has placed several levels of meaning in the Bible, and allegory is simply the way in which exegetes discover what is already in the inspired text. On the other hand, concludes the scholastic argument, when similar techniques are applied to poetry, they are being used

27. De Bruyne, *L'Esthétique au moyen âge,* p. 55.
28. De Bruyne, *Études d'esthétique médiévale, 2,* 321–27.

236

either improperly or by default, because of the false and in-frarational nature of this art.[29]

Despite its relatively late appearance on the medieval scene and the fact that it was professed mainly by scholastic theologians rather than by practicing poets or textbook writers in the school tradition, this depreciation of poetry has achieved the status among many modern scholars of a representative or even a normative medieval poetics. The net effect of this interpretation has been the conclusion that Dante was forced to sever himself radically from the tradition of medieval poetics, for a poetics so conceived could give no place to a professedly theological poem in which the allegorical method of the theologians is deliberately adopted as a principle of construction. This theory fails to take into account the antisophistic didacticism of much of medieval poetic theory or the existence of figures like Peter Riga, who wrote biblical poetry in the late twelfth and early thirteenth centuries in the belief that God was inspiring him.[30] Some scholars, in their desire to prove that Dante was not a Thomist, feel it sufficient to rest their case on the very fact that he was a poet.[31]

29. This idea has been discussed repeatedly. See, for example, ibid., *3*, 313–18, 344; Ernst Robert Curtius, "Medieval Basis of Western Thought," *Gesammelte Aufsätze*, pp. 34–35; Glunz, *Die Literaturästhetik*, pp. 189–97; Nancy Lenkeith, *Dante and the Legend of Rome* (London, 1952), pp. 34–36; Johan Chydenius, *The Typological Problem in Dante: A Study in the History of Medieval Ideas* (Helsingfors, 1958), pp. 41–43; Charles Donahue, "Patristic Exegesis," *Critical Approaches to Medieval Literature,* ed. Dorothy Bethurum (New York, 1960), pp. 77–80; Hugh Pope, "St. Thomas as an Interpreter of Holy Scripture," *St. Thomas Aquinas: Being Papers Read at the Celebration of the Sixth Centenary of the Canonization of Saint Thomas Aquinas Held at Manchester, 1924* (Oxford, 1925), pp. 134–39. These scholastic strictures do not alter the fact that classical poets, especially Ovid and Vergil, were interpreted allegorically during the Middle Ages. See Henri DeLubac, *Exégèse médiévale* (Paris, 1959–64), *2*, part 2, 233–62.

30. Curtius, "Medieval Basis of Western Thought," *Gesammelte Aufsätze*, pp. 34–36; Glunz, *Die Literaturästhetik*, pp. 279–81, 372; Lenkeith, *Dante*, pp. 34–42.

31. Ernst Robert Curtius, "Dante und das lateinische Mittelalter," *Romanische Forschungen, 57*, Heft 2–3 (1943), 171; "Medieval Basis of Western Thought,"

Poetics in the Middle Ages can be derived not only from the school tradition and the scholastic theologians. One must also take into account the religious poetry that was produced in abundance during this period. Religious poetry was, on the whole, detached from the decorative canons of the school tradition and from the scholastic derogation of the truth of poetry. The religious poets would not have written so much and with such unabashed confidence unless they had thought that poetry was capable of communicating theological and moral truths and of moving the hearer toward God. Curtius has made the point that the poetics of Dante is best understood in terms of the literature of the Middle Ages, not through its scholastic philosophy.[32] Baldwin adds that the school tradition, preoccupied as it was with style, gives us little insight into the *Divine Comedy*. Rather, he urges, it is medieval hymnody which provides the best introduction to Dante's view of poetry.[33] Baldwin dates the emergence of a specifically Christian poetic in the fourth century, with the hymns of St. Ambrose, and sees it as a direct analogue of Augustine's Christianization of Ciceronian oratory. "As Augustine redeemed rhetoric," he states, "so Ambrose transformed poetic, by new motives." [34] According to Baldwin, this new Christian poetic has two main characteristics. In the first place, Christian hymns are lyrics, but their authors expand lyricism from the expression of individual emotions to the expression of a shared faith, aspiration, worship, and fellowship. This communal orientation stems from the fact that Christian hymns were written to be used in public worship, and to in-

---

Gesammelte Aufsätze, p. 36; Cesare Foligno, "Dante: The Poet," *Proceedings of the British Academy,* 10 (1921), 3–18; Joseph A. Mazzeo, *Structure and Thought in the 'Paradiso'* (Ithaca, N.Y., 1958), pp. 40–41; Daniel Sargent, "Dante and Thomism," *The Thomist, 5* (1943), 256–64.

32. Curtius, "Dante und das lateinische Mittelalter," *Romanische Forschungen, 57,* 153–85.

33. Baldwin, *Medieval Rhetoric and Poetic,* pp. 205, 261, 269–71.

34. Ibid., p. 123. See also F. J. E. Raby, *A History of Christian-Latin Poetry from the Beginnings to the Close of the Middle Ages* (Oxford, 1953), for a general study of Christian hymnody.

struct and inspire a congregation. A second new feature of hymnody is its treatment of physical reality as the first step toward eternity; it aims at an expansion of human consciousness, beginning in the here and now, which is to culminate in the beatific vision. This point of view of course reflects the theological and devotional content of the hymns. But, out of these practical, communal, theological necessities there developed a new literary aesthetic. Poetry, in the hymns, is not regarded as a means to an end. The hymn is not regarded as theology in verse. Rather, the theological aspirations and corporate ideals of the poet coalesce with the form of the poem. The content, style, and function of the poem become an aesthetic unit.[35]

In the twelfth and thirteenth centuries, religious poetry retained the communal character of early medieval hymnody, as well as its aesthetic unity, while developing a number of stylistic modifications. Symbolism is used extensively, particularly by the Victorines. But the symbols of an Adam of St. Victor differ from the figures of poetry as conceived by the textbook writers. They are "not decoration, not epithets or paraphrases used instead of proper names, but immediate lyrical approaches" to the theological realities presented by the author.[36] Some religious poets in this period, like Thomas Aquinas, apply a more intense level of contemplation to the subject matter of their hymns than is evident in early medieval hymnody, while the Franciscans develop a technique of sublimation, starting from concrete images with a high emotional content.[37] The Franciscan style was carried over into the vernacular in the thirteenth century, and its chief Italian exponent, Jacopone da Todi, is thought to have influenced Dante.[38]

35. Baldwin, *Medieval Rhetoric and Poetic,* pp. 123–25.

36. Ibid., pp. 263–64.

37. Ibid., pp. 204–05; Walter J. Ong, "Wit and Mystery: A Revaluation in Mediaeval Latin Hymnody," *Speculum,* 22 (1947), 310–41.

38. Thomas G. Bergin, *Dante* (New York, 1965), p. 56; Luigi Tonelli, *Dante e la poesia dell'ineffabile* (Firenze, 1934), p. 213.

In considering the various influences which affected Dante and in terms of which he forged his own poetics, accepting some aspects of his background and rejecting others, we may take a clue from Dante himself and address ourselves to the figures and traditions to which he avows his indebtedness. At the head of this list we must place Vergil, whom Dante acknowledges in the *Comedy* as the light and honor of the other poets, his master and author, and the source of his own style, and whom he takes as his guide through Hell and Purgatory. As we shall have occasion to note below in another connection, Vergil enjoyed an extensive and variegated reputation in the Middle Ages. This stemmed in part from popular legendary tradition and in part from the frequency with which his works were cited as poetic exemplars in the grammatical curriculum. Dante was familiar with both aspects of the medieval tradition of Vergil. In the *Comedy* he freely borrows Vergilian characters, topographical details, and even phrases. Far more important than this, however, is the fact that Dante thinks of himself as a second Vergil. His conception of himself as a poet is thus based to a significant degree on his conception of Vergil as a poet. Whether or not Dante's conception of Vergil actually corresponds with Vergil's poetic theory, that conception is highly relevant to any study of Dante's poetics, for Vergil provided him with an authoritative classical model which he believed he was following in writing the *Divine Comedy*. Dante sees in Vergil the singer of the glory of the Roman Empire, whose medieval analogue he himself was trying to refurbish and restore. He sees Vergil as the reformer and unifier of the Italian dialects of his time, a burden which Dante lays on his own shoulders. He sees Vergil as a prophet of Christ, serving, in this capacity, as a link between the Rome of Caesar and the Rome of Peter. The image of Vergil as a prophet, seer, and sage, instructing his audience through the story of a hero who takes a pilgrimage through the other world, is one that Dante adopts for himself. He has but to translate the wis-

240

dom and inspiration expressed through the poet's prophetic voice into Christian terms, and to make himself the hero of his own didactic epic.

Vergil, as we have noted, was available to Dante partly through the school tradition. This tradition was represented for Dante more fully by the *ars dictaminis* and by the rhetoric of Brunetto Latini, whom he greets in the *Inferno* as a father and of whom he says, "You taught me how man makes himself eternal." [39] The ars dictaminis taught Dante the canons of approved Latin style, to which his Latin works adhere.[40] Though attached to jurisprudence and public affairs, and hence strongly concerned with persuasion, the ars dictaminis of Dante's day had also recovered the Ciceronian correlation between eloquence, wisdom, and virtue.[41] Brunetto Latini was thoroughly familiar with the ars dictaminis, and in his *Trésor* he reiterates and intensifies its union of ethics, politics, and rhetoric. At the same time, he draws upon the contemporary *artes poeticae* in elaborating the techniques of rhetoric, applying rhetorical canons of decoration to poetry as well as to *dictamen.*[42] Thus, several strands of medieval poetics converge in Brunetto's *Trésor.*

Brunetto indicates his debt to Cicero not only by his heavy reliance on the latter's *De inventione* and *De officiis,*[43] in his

39. *Inf.,* XV, 85, English translation by J. A. Carlyle, Thomas Okey, and P. H. Wicksteed, Temple Classics Edition, quoted by permission of E. P. Dutton & Co., Inc., and J. M. Dent & Sons Ltd. Subsequent quotations from the *Divine Comedy* are taken from this edition.

40. See the appendix on the *cursus* in Paget Toynbee's edition of Dante's *Epistolae* (Oxford, 1920), pp. 224–47; also Toynbee's "The Bearing of the *Cursus* on the Text of Dante's De vulgari eloquentia," *Proceedings of the British Academy, 11* (1923), 1–19.

41. André Pézard, Le *"Convivio" de Dante* (Paris, 1940), pp. 51–52; Helene Wieruszowski, *"Ars Dictaminis* in the Time of Dante," *Medievalia et Humanistica, 1* (1943), 95–108.

42. Baldwin, *Medieval Rhetoric and Poetic,* pp. 179–81.

43. Thor Sundby, *Della vita e delle opere di Brunetto Latini* (Firenze, 1884), pp. 187, 195.

repetition of Cicero's definition of signs,[44] but also in his arrangement of the contents of the *Trésor*. The *Trésor* is divided into three books. The first contains a mélange of subjects, including cosmology, theology, history, astronomy, geography, economics, and natural history. The second deals with ethics, while the third treats rhetoric and politics.[45] Brunetto follows Cicero in insisting that eloquence is necessary for the proper conduct of political life: "Tully says that the highest science of governing the city is rhetoric, that is, the science of speech. For if there were no speech, neither cities, justice, nor human society would be established; it was for these things that speech was given to all men." [46] Rhetoric, Brunetto continues, deals not merely with the science of speaking, but with the art of speaking well. It is "full of noble teaching; and teaching is nothing but wisdom; and wisdom is the understanding of things as they are." Wisdom joined to eloquence engenders goodness.[47] In primitive times, Brunetto explains, when men were devoid of civic institutions, there were certain wise and well-spoken men, who taught and counseled their fellows about the greatness of the soul and the dignity of reason. These sage, eloquent men were the first to promote law and justice and to restrain the savagery of primitive man; it was through their leadership that civil society was established.[48]

In discussing the competence of rhetoric, Brunetto states that it has cognizance of matters both private and public. It is used "to induce belief (*por faire croire*), to praise and to

44. Brunetto Latini, *Trésor*, III, i, 50, p. 540.

45. André Pézard, *Dante sous la pluie de feu* (Paris, 1950), pp. 87–130, presents a résumé of Book III of the *Trésor*. He also presents the ingenious thesis that Dante places Brunetto in Hell not merely because he is a sodomite, but because, despite the valuable contents of the *Trésor*, Brunetto has committed a sin against language by writing in French instead of Italian. Brunetto's interrelation of rhetoric and politics, according to Pézard, explains why Dante puts him in a region of Hell shared by Priscian and Accursius, who, following this argument, are guilty of the abuse of speech and law.

46. *Trésor*, III, i, 1, pp. 467–68.

47. Ibid., pp. 468–69. See also 2, p. 470.

48. Ibid., i, 1, p. 469.

blame, and to hold counsel on any needful matter, or about anything that requires judgment." [49] Anything can be dealt with by rhetoric so long as it is written or spoken; thus rhetoric covers prose, poetry, and the ars dictaminis.[50] In setting forth the technique of rhetoric, thus broadly conceived, Brunetto follows the Ciceronian sequence of invention, organization, decoration, memorization, and delivery. Decoration consists in applying ornamental figures to one's speech, letter, or poem. In this connection Brunetto cites the Horatian dictum *ut pictura poesis,* while altering its usual emphasis. Rhetoric is like painting, he says, not because they both aim at the imitation of nature, but because both are colorful, rhetoric adding its *colores* to prose and poetry alike.[51]

In the second part of Book III of the *Trésor,* which deals with politics, Brunetto defines his subject as "the noblest and highest science and the noblest office on earth, for politics generally comprehends all the arts necessary for human society." [52] All political dominion and honor, he says, come from God. God ordains that human governments be firmly established on the three pillars of justice, reverence, and love. By justice, the ruler gives to each subject his due; by reverence, the subjects give honor to the ruler; and by love, the ruler and the ruled give their mutual attention to the needs of the common weal.[53] After laying down these general definitions, Brunetto devotes the rest of this part of Book III to the two kinds of commonwealths, those with officials elected by the people and those with permanent rulers who appoint the officials.[54] He places greater emphasis on and gives more space to the former kind of commonwealth, since it is more directly applicable to the situation in contemporary Italy. He goes into considerable detail in outlining the qualities that the electorate

49. Ibid., 2, p. 471.
50. Ibid., 10, 16–23, pp. 471, 481, 492–505.
51. Ibid., 3, 10, pp. 473–74, 482.
52. Ibid., ii, 1, p. 575.
53. Ibid., 2, pp. 577–78.
54. Ibid., 1, pp. 576–77. See also Sundby, *Brunetto Latini,* pp. 195–96.

should seek in candidates for public office,[55] the method of their election,[56] and the ways in which the officials should receive and administer their public charge.[57]

Brunetto's *Trésor* is an important work, which exerted considerable influence on Dante. While he adheres to a poetics concerned with decoration, derived from the medieval school tradition, Brunetto also combines poetics with a rhetoric firmly attached to didactic, ethical, and political concerns.[58] The Middle Ages, as we have seen, had a tradition of didactic poetry, carried on side by side with the tradition of poetic decoration. But none of the medieval exponents of didactic poetry had detailed its moral mission in so broad and yet so explicit a sense as Brunetto. Brunetto links rhetoric, including poetry, to wisdom and virtue, and also to a specific kind of political morality which flows from a specific set of political institutions, those of the Italian city-state of his own day. What Dante takes from Brunetto is his didactic, rhetorical idea of poetry and some of its particular political connotations. The idea of poetry as decoration, however, he abandons. Nevertheless, Dante did not have to break away from all of the poetic theory available at his time in order to write didactic poetry.[59]

In addition to the influences put forth by Vergil and by the school tradition, as represented by the writings of Brunetto Latini, contemporary vernacular lyric poetry must also be taken into account as part of Dante's immediate background. It is a well-known fact that Dante made a contribution of fundamental importance to this tradition, which encompasses the Provençal lyrics of southern France and their Italian sequels in the *dolce stil nuovo*. Dante is well aware of his links to this

55. *Trésor,* III, ii, 3, pp. 578–81.
56. Ibid., 4–5, pp. 581–84.
57. Ibid., 6–33, pp. 585–620.
58. Bergin, *Dante,* pp. 56–57; Sebastiano Scandura, *L'Estetica di Dante, Petrarca e Boccaccio* (Acireale, 1928), pp. 77–78.
59. Cf. on the contrary Baldwin, *Medieval Rhetoric and Poetic,* pp. 196, 261, 269–71, 280; Lenkeith, *Dante,* p. 33.

movement. In the *Purgatorio* he greets with obvious respect two eminent practitioners of the vernacular lyric, the Provençal Arnaut Daniel and the Italian Guido Guinizelli.[60] At another point he speaks with an earlier author of Italian lyrics, Bonagiunta, explaining to him how the art of poetry has been transformed since his day.[61] Dante also places two lyric poets in the *Comedy* for political reasons—Sordello, in whose mouth he puts a series of judgments on the princes in his circle of Purgatory after his own eloquent diatribe against the current corruption of Italy,[62] and Bertran de Born, whom he consigns to the *Inferno* as an evil counselor and a fomenter of rebellion.[63]

At this point it may be well to set forth some of the main features of troubadour and dolce stil nuovo poetry. Both employ rhyme, meter, and a refined and elaborate stanza structure. This latter characteristic is particularly marked in the intellectualistic and even recondite Provençal *trobar clus*. The obscurity of trobar clus is replaced in the dolce stil nuovo by a more logical method of organizing the stanza and a firm grasp of syntactical connections between words.[64] The aims of these lyric poets are to celebrate the virtues of an ideal lady, to praise the ennobling effects of love, and to lament the sufferings of unrequited love. Marcabru is virtually unique in this school for voicing cynical and misogynous views about love. The idealized lady is sometimes treated as an inaccessible *princesse lointaine;* she is also often compared with God. The Provençal authors frequently apply feudal terminology to the lady, describing her as a *domina* who commands the loyalty and service of the lover. The Italians further rarefy the image of the lady, treating her as a quasi-celestial figure.[65] This par-

60. *Purg.,* XXVI, 112–48.

61. Ibid., XXIV, 49–63.

62. Ibid., VI, 74–150; VII, 85–136.

63. *Inf.,* XXVIII, 131–42.

64. Erich Auerbach, *Dante: Poet of the Secular World* (Chicago, 1961), pp. 38 ff.

65. Bergin, *Dante,* pp. 46–48, 52–55.

ticular usage is not original. It reflects a tradition visible in medieval lyrics from the Carolingian period onward, in which tropes drawn from Christian Latin hymns are applied to the objects of love poems.[66] Thus, the tendency of thirteenth-century lyricists to analogize the lady and the emotions that she inspires in the lover to biblical concepts and states of mind, and their treatment of her virtues as secularized versions of the biblical counsels of perfection, should be seen as the formalization of existing practices.

Dante adopts many of these ideas in his early love poems and they are evident in his *Vita nuova*. At the same time, this work reflects a modification of the dolce stil nuovo attitude toward the lady, and it is the first attempt on Dante's part to make a statement about the nature of poetry. His effort to clarify what he is doing in the *Vita nuova* can be seen by examining the structure of the work, which is composed of poems followed by explanatory prose passages. This genre derives immediately from Provençal poetry, especially that of Bertran de Born, but it is taken ultimately from the style of Boethius' *Consolation of Philosophy*.[67] The incisiveness and power of Dante's lyrics is enhanced by the fact that he expresses his state of mind through a concrete event rather than through a rhetorical mood.[68] His treatment of the lady, Beatrice, shares in the tendency of his school to attribute almost a Divine or salvific quality to the lady, a point underlined by Dante in his playing on the verbal similarity between Beatrice's name and beatitude. Scholars interpreting the Beatrice of the *Vita nuova* from the point of view of the Beatrice of the *Divine Comedy* have argued that Beatrice is a Christ figure

66. James J. Wilhelm, *The Cruelest Month: Spring, Nature, and Love in Classical and Medieval Lyrics* (New Haven and London, 1965), pp. 88–258; see also Jefferson B. Fletcher, "The Philosophy of Love of Guido Cavalcanti," *Annual Report of the Dante Society, Cambridge, Mass.,* 22 (1904), 22–24.

67. Bergin, *Dante,* p. 81; Nicola Zingarelli, *La vita, i tempi e le opere di Dante* (Milano, 1931), *1,* 119.

68. Auerbach, *Dante,* pp. 38 ff.

for Dante from the very first.[69] This interpretation, we feel, is erroneous, since it applies a later idea retroactively to an earlier period of Dante's thought. It also fails to take sufficient account of the traditional use of religious tropes in medieval lyrics and the refinement of this technique by Provençal and dolce stil nuovo poets. A far more significant shift in Dante's treatment of the lady is the fact that in the *Vita nuova* he always portrays Beatrice in a social context, in the company of other people. This is a major departure from the ordinary Provençal and dolce stil nuovo practice, where the lady is always alone.[70]

In the *Vita nuova* Dante is also interested in setting forth an idea of poetry. This poetic theory contains certain features which remain permanent in Dante's poetics and which he retains up through the *Divine Comedy*. Other aspects of the view of poetry which he expresses in the *Vita nuova* he later modifies or drops altogether, as his conception of poetry changes and develops. As we have seen in discussing the Augustinian theory of signs in earlier portions of this study, its exponents hold that speech is capable of signifying real objects truly and also that verbal signs are not identical with their significata. Words are thus accurate but imperfect indices of their objects. Further, they hold that speech has a necessary but a purely instrumental role in teaching and moving its audience. Dante reiterates both of these points in the *Vita nuova*. He seeks an authority outside of himself to validate what he is saying; his words, he notes, are dictated by love, a

69. See, for example, Jefferson B. Fletcher, "The Allegory of the *Vita Nuova*," *Modern Philology, 11* (1913), 19–37; J. A. Scott, "Dante's 'Sweet New Style' and the *Vita Nuova*," *Italica, 42* (1965), 98–107; James E. Shaw, *Guido Cavalcanti's Theory of Love: The Canzoni d'Amore and Other Related Problems* (Toronto, 1949), pp. 126–27; Charles S. Singleton, *An Essay on the Vita Nuova* (Cambridge, Mass., 1949), pp. 4, 24, 56. This view has been contradicted by E. R. Vincent, "The Crisis in the *Vita Nuova*," *Centenary Essays on Dante by Members of the Oxford Dante Society* (Oxford, 1965), pp. 132–42.

70. Philip H. Wicksteed, *From Vita Nuova to Paradiso: Two Essays on the Vital Relations between Dante's Successive Works* (Manchester, 1922), p. 76.

force which he personifies and converses with in the body of the work.[71] Outside of the truthfulness which his words derive from love's inspiration, speech in general, according to Dante, is an authentic sign of preexisting realities. In a frequently quoted statement, he cites the maxim "Nomina sunt consequentia rerum." [72] This dictum has been identified as a commonplace of Roman law.[73] More important, it is a clear expression of the Augustinian principle that the object is prior to its verbal sign, and that the sign must be judged true or false in terms of its object. This principle must be grasped in order to understand Dante's attitude toward poetic style. To speak, for Dante, means to write poetry.[74] Poetic language and form must thus be commensurate with the subject matter of a poem in order for the poem to possess rectitude and to be able to move its readers toward true and worthy ends. According to Dante, it is clear in the *Vita nuova* that words which signify worthy objects have persuasive force and moral power. His praise of his lady, he says, possesses beatitude.[75] One who speaks with her, he adds, cannot come to a bad end.[76] Putting the idea more strongly still, he affirms that his love poems have the power to make people feel love, and thus to acquire its ennobling virtues.[77]

In describing how the beloved lady communicates these ennobling virtues to the lover, Dante effects an important change

71. *Vita nuova*, XIII, 1.

72. Ibid., 4.

73. Bruno Nardi, *Dante e la cultura medievale* (Bari, 1949), pp. 218–23; "Due capitoli di filosofia dantesca: I. La conoscenza humana; II. Il linguaggio," *Giornale storico della letteratura italiana*, miscellanea dantesca, suppl. *19–21* (Torino, 1921), 246–47; *La filosofia di Dante* (Milano, 1952), pp. 44 ff. This maxim has also been noted by Bergin, *Dante*, pp. 83–84; Francesco d'Ovidio, *Dante e la filosofia del linguaggio* (Napoli, 1892), p. 6; *Studii sulla Divina Commedia* (Milan-Palermo, 1901), pp. 487–88; Paolo Rotta, *La filosofia del linguaggio nella Patristica e nella Scolastica* (Torino, 1909), p. 174.

74. Jefferson B. Fletcher, "The 'True Meaning' of Dante's *Vita Nuova*," *Romanic Review, 11* (1920), 98–99.

75. *Vita nuova*, XVIII, 8.

76. Ibid., XIX, 10.

77. Ibid., 4–5.

in a standard lyric trope, the eyes and smile of the lady. Dolce stil nuovo poets advert frequently to these features of the beloved. The eyes, traditionally, are the windows of the soul. By looking into the lady's eyes, the dolce stil nuovo poet sought to discern whether she possessed a gentle heart, whether she was a fitting object of his love and of his song. The lady's smile is a sign of her regard for the poet. Dante also treats the lady's eyes and smile as signs, but he interprets them metaphorically as means of verbal communication. Love's words are smiles, he says.[78] The lady's eyes are bearers of love, of pity; her smile is love's image.[79] The eyes and smile of the lady are thus, for Dante, actual channels through which she transmits to the poet the goodness, truth, and moral power of love, of which she is a messenger.

While words, in the literal sense of speech and poetry, and in the figurative sense of the lady's eyes and smile, are true and persuasive for Dante, he does not neglect the other side of the Augustinian theory. He observes in the *Vita nuova* that speech and poetry also have limitations as signs of their objects. On several occasions in this work he notes that his words are too weak to convey the true glory of his lady, and that they are defective signs of his own feelings about her as well.[80] The marvel of Beatrice's smile cannot be grasped fully by his mind nor expressed fully by his words; her very salutation makes the tongue fall silent.[81] Dante's best known statement of the limits of poetry in the *Vita nuova* comes at the end of the work, where he says that he must hold his peace until he is able to write a poem truly worthy of Beatrice, a task which he regards his art as now inadequate to perform.[82]

Above and beyond Dante's interest in specifying the powers and limits of poetry, he is also concerned in the *Vita nuova* with describing the uses of vernacular poetry. In this work,

78. Ibid., XXIV, 7.
79. Ibid., XIX, 11–12; XXI, 2; XXXVII, 8; XXXIX, 3, 10.
80. Ibid., XIX, 6; XXVII, 2; XXVIII, 2; XXXI, 15.
81. Ibid., XXI, 4; XXVI, 5.
82. Ibid., XLII, 1–2.

Dante takes the position that the sole function of poetry in the *volgare* is to speak of love. In fact he vigorously opposes those who argue that it can serve in any other capacity.[83] Vernacular love poetry, he adds, is patterned after Latin lyrics, both in terms of its subject matter and in terms of its style. It is necessary to use the vernacular for love poetry, he states, because this poetry is addressed to women who cannot be expected to understand Latin.[84] However, since vernacular love poetry has the same aims as Latin love poetry, it may be accorded the same stylistic usages; any rhetorical figures or colors conceded to the Latin "poets" must also be conceded to the vernacular "rhymesters." In the *Vita nuova,* Dante thus remains within the decorative approach to poetry, viewing the style of vernacular lyrics in the context of a poetics of ornamentation.[85] His justification of the vernacular in this work is a purely rhetorical one, going back to the principle that one must choose the style that one's audience can best understand. There is also present in the *Vita nuova* a trace of the medieval view that poetry contains an inner core of truth hidden by poetic veils. In the course of the work, Dante sets before the reader a series of enigmatic or metaphorical statements and situations, which he gradually explains as the work progresses. He regards this technique as an extension of the right of the vernacular poet to use personification and other rhetorical tropes, but he feels it necessary to explain their meaning himself.[86] The most interesting feature of this method is that the reader's enlightenment is provided both through Dante's exegesis of his lyrics and through Dante's own progressive enlightenment as the protagonist of the *Vita nuova.* He thus takes a twofold point of view—that of the central character in a series of events, who learns and grows through his experi-

83. Ibid., XXV, 6.

84. Ibid., 6–8; Fletcher, "True Meaning," *Romanic Review, 11,* 95.

85. Barbi, *Life of Dante,* p. 42.

86. *Vita nuova,* XXV, 8–10. See also Jefferson B. Fletcher, *Dante* (New York, 1916), pp. 33, 36; Domenico de Robertis, *Il libro della "Vita Nuova"* (Firenze, 1961), p. 9.

ence, and that of a commentator analyzing his previous states of mind retrospectively.

The *Vita nuova* presents us with a theory of poetry that is inchoate and not entirely consistent. On the one hand, Dante adopts a didactic view of poetry. Poetic speech and its metaphors, such as the lady's eyes and smile, convey information and moral benefits to the lover, and, through him, are capable of teaching and moving the reader. Along with the intrinsic significance of language and the authority which the poet derives from love's inspiration go the significative limitations which apply to speech. On the other hand, Dante tends to derogate the didactic function of poetry by confining its vernacular use to love poetry alone, and by contrasting the vernacular "rhymesters" in a derogatory sense with the Latin "poets." His view of poetic style as essentially ornamental is ill assorted with his careful construction of the *Vita nuova*, with its shifts in tone as he first speaks in his poems to Beatrice and then about her, an approach which reflects the idea that his poetic style at any given point in the work must correspond to his level of understanding of Beatrice's importance for him.

The features of Dante's poetic in the *Vita nuova* which he retains in his later works are the idea of language as an accurate yet inadequate sign, the notion that poetry is didactic and persuasive, the view that style must reflect the content of the poem and must be adjusted to the audience, and the technique of instructing the reader through the development of the poet as a character within the work. The limitations that Dante places on the use of the vernacular and the ornamental approach to poetry in the *Vita nuova*, however, tend to drop from view in Dante's later works.

In Dante's next work, the *Convivio*, he develops the idea of poetry expressed in his *Vita nuova* and broadens its context considerably. The *Convivio* follows the same general pattern as the *Vita nuova*. It is composed of four books, the last three of which are commentaries on *canzoni* at their heads. The in-

251

fluence of Boethius' *Consolation of Philosophy* is visible not
only in its structure, but also in the fact that the lady whose
praises the poet sings is Philosophy. Dante employs Boethian
terms in describing Philosophy and tells us that he was moved
to become her devotee by reading Boethius and Cicero.[87] By
orienting his art to the love of wisdom, Dante is here clearly
enlarging the scope of his literary didacticism; he widens it
still further to include the Ciceronian correlation of wisdom,
virtue, and eloquence by devoting a large portion of the work
to the nature of true nobility, which he analyzes in a moral
and a political context.

Dante also makes use of the Ciceronian triad of teaching,
persuasion, and pleasure in elaborating the powers and limitations of speech. In the *Convivio,* even more than in the *Vita
nuova,* he stresses the didactic strand of medieval rhetorical
poetics. He also expands the scope of the vernacular. The
Convivio, Dante tells us, aims to move men to wisdom and
virtue; to this end the author sets forth his knowledge of these
subjects for the benefit of others who may have been deflected
from seeking them by public and private cares.[88] He has no
doubts that literature is capable of bringing errant humanity
back to the right path (*diritto calle*); he states in Tractate IV
that this is the purpose of the *canzone* preceding it, and that
the canzone not only presents the truth but refutes error.[89]
Speech, affirms Dante, can transform the behavior of the
hearer; "words . . . are like seeds of action."[90] This power
is based on the fact that language is the means by which one

---

87. *Convivio,* II, xii; xv, 1–2. The influence of Boethius on the *Convivio* has
been noted by Vincenzo Grasso, *Il De Consolatione Philosophiae di Boezio in
Dante, Petrarca, Chaucer: Contributo allo studio delle loro fonti* (Catania,
1923), pp. 13, 17, 18, 55–56; Edward Moore, *Studies in Dante: First Series*
(Oxford, 1896), pp. 282–88; Rocco Murari, *Dante e Boezio: Contributo allo
studio delle fonti dantesche* (Bologna, 1905), pp. 211–54; Howard Rollin Patch,
The Tradition of Boethius: A Study of His Importance in Medieval Culture
(New York, 1935), pp. 6, 43, 91–92.

88. *Convivio,* I, i, 5–12; ix, 7; IV, xxii, 1–2.

89. Ibid., IV, i, 9; ii, 14–16.

90. Ibid., ii, 8.

man expresses his thoughts to others.[91] The particular language that Dante chooses for this purpose is Italian. He justifies his use of the vernacular on the rhetorical grounds that it enables him to reach a wider audience than Latin.[92] He also stresses that the vernacular is the pathway to the knowledge which is man's final perfection, and that it allies one with his family and his fellow citizens.[93]

In describing the importance he attaches to his own work, Dante analogizes his tractates to the sun, the symbol of God, and does not scruple at comparing his own literary efforts to Christ's miraculous multiplication of the loaves:

> This commentary shall be that bread . . . with which thousands shall be filled; and baskets full of it shall remain over . . . This shall be a new light and a new sun, which shall rise when the old sun shall set, and shall shine on those who are in darkness and mist because of the old sun which gives no light to them.[94]

Dante attributes to the vernacular rhetoric of his *Convivio* a political significance and a moral and an almost religious power. The importance of his objectives, he says, justifies the mention which he makes of his own life in the work, since this is done strictly for didactic purposes, as in Augustine's *Confessiones*.[95] His style involves persuasion and pleasure. Dante does not subordinate his task of teaching and convincing his readers to the task of pleasing them. The two, he indicates, go hand in hand. In his analysis of the canzone "Voi che 'ntendendo il terzo ciel movete" in Tractate II, he states that the third heaven of the canzone corresponds to Venus and to rhetoric, for rhetoric is "the pleasantest of all the Sciences,

91. Ibid., I, v, 12.
92. Ibid., vii, 12–ix, 11.
93. Ibid., xii, 5; xiii, 5.
94. Ibid., xiii, 13, Jackson, p. 66. On God as symbolized by the sun, see III, xii, 6–8.
95. Ibid., I, ii, 13–14.

253

inasmuch as its chief aim is to please." [96] By pleasing the reader, the author can convince him: "In every kind of discourse the speaker ought chiefly to be intent upon persuasion, that is on charming his audience, for this is that kind of persuasion which is the beginning of all others, as every rhetorician knows." [97]

Dante clearly agrees with Augustine that rhetoric can have a potent effect on man's knowledge and moral behavior, and he applies this view to poetry along with a variety of rhetorical tropes.[98] He also expresses the Augustinian view that one's ability to learn through speech is conditioned by one's moral state.[99] In the *Convivio,* as in the *Vita nuova,* Dante treats speech in a figurative as well as in a literal sense, and, when he does so, he fastens on the same metaphors, the eyes and smile of the lady. The lady in the case of the *Convivio* is an abstraction, Philosophy, which heightens the metaphorical character of her eyes and smile in contrast to those of Beatrice in the *Vita nuova.* In the *Convivio,* however, Dante is more precise about the nature and functions of the lady's eyes and smile than he is in the *Vita nuova.* He defines the eyes of the lady as "her demonstrations, which, when directed into the eyes of the intellect fill with love a soul that is free in her conditions." [100] The mouth, like the eyes, reflects the soul of the lady; laughter is the "coruscation of the soul's delight," and the smiles of the lady are her persuasions.[101] Dante's addition of another level of metaphor to his description of the lady's eyes and smile does not alter the fact that the lady is assuming for him an increasingly didactic role in the *Convivio,* in accordance with the change in her nature from a real per-

96. Ibid., xiii, 14, Jackson, p. 108.

97. Ibid., II, xi, 6, Jackson, p. 90. On rhetoric as persuasion in the *Convivio,* see Pézard, *Le "Convivio,"* pp. 85–86.

98. James E. Shaw, *The Lady "Philosophy" in the Convivio* (Cambridge, Mass., 1938), p. 17, notices Dante's application of rhetorical tropes to poetry but not his appropriation of didactic rhetoric.

99. *Convivio,* I, i, 1–4.

100. Ibid., II, xv, 4, Jackson, p. 117. See also III, xv, 2, 19–20.

101. Ibid., III, viii, 11; xv, 2, 19–20.

son, as in the *Vita nuova,* to a personalized abstraction. While Dante has before his eyes the figure of Boethius' Lady Philosophy, and while he can explain his own personification of Philosophy as the application of a rhetorical figure to poetry,[102] he still describes her in dolce stil nuovo terms as "the beatitude of the intellect." [103] More significantly, he still tends to see a love relationship between himself and a lady, symbolic or otherwise, as the context in which he, and by extension, the reader, acquires wisdom and virtue.

Dante, as we can see, retains and amplifies in the *Convivio* the ideas on the powers of speech which he expresses in the *Vita nuova;* this is no less true for his treatment of the limitations of speech. At various points in the *Convivio* he states that his mind is not able to grasp nor his tongue express the things to which he is currently referring.[104] More importantly, Dante limits the truth of poetry in a way that breaks down his previously stated rhetorical union of didacticism and pleasure by recourse to an ornamental view of poetry. He does this by distinguishing the beauty of the first canzone from its goodness. Its beauty, he says, consists in its stylistic adornments, while its goodness consists in its meaning. Dante does not regard the meaning and the way in which it is expressed as two inseparable functions of a unitary work of art; rather, he urges the reader to enjoy the beauty even if he does not understand the meaning.[105] Furthermore, he derogates the truth content of such beautiful poetic decorations as allegories. In his discussion of the fourfold method of literary analysis, he distinguishes the theological use of allegory from the poetic:

> Writings can be understood and ought to be expounded chiefly in four senses. The first is called literal, and this is that sense which does not go beyond the strict limits of

102. Ibid., ix, 2; x, 6.
103. Ibid., xiii, 2. See also viii, 20.
104. Ibid., Canzone II, ll. 9–18; III, ii, 1; iii, 15; iv, 1–3, 4, 9–12; viii, 15; IV, xxi, 67.
105. Ibid., II, xi, 9.

the letter, the second is called allegorical, and this is disguised under the cloak of . . . stories, and is a truth hidden under a beautiful fiction (*bella menzogna*) . . . Theologians indeed do not apprehend this sense in the same fashion as poets; but inasmuch as my intention is to follow here the custom of poets, I will take the allegorical sense after the manner which poets use.

The third sense is called moral; and this sense is that for which teachers ought as they go through writings intently to watch for their own profit and that of their hearers . . .

The fourth sense is called anagogic, that is, above the senses; and this occurs when a writing is spiritually expounded, which even in the literal sense by the things signified likewise gives intimation of higher matters belonging to the eternal glory.[106]

He adds that the literal sense should always be established first, since the other three senses depend on it.[107] Dante's definition of the literal, moral, and anagogical senses is perfectly traditional. What he has done with the allegorical sense has been to replace it with the theory of the poetic veils. While poetry still has a core of truth, according to this view, the figures through which this truth is put forth are lies, although beautiful ones. This theory widens the gap Dante posits between his canzone's good inner meaning and its beautiful exterior style. It reinforces the poetic of decoration and undermines the aesthetic and didactic unity which Dante sees as a feature of rhetoric, and by extension, of poetry. Thus, the limitations he applies to poetic speech in the *Convivio* do not square with the powers he grants it in the same work.

Notwithstanding this inconsistency, Dante goes on in the fourth tractate to explore the connections between eloquence, wisdom, and virtue. He does this largely by discussing at some

106. Ibid., i, 2–6, Jackson, pp. 73–74.
107. Ibid., i, 8–15.

length the nature of true nobility. In order to prove his own position and to refute the reverse, Dante also includes a long section on political theory, centering on the need for a universal empire and the nature of its authority. The political ideas that Dante expresses in the *Convivio* present us in germ with his later position in the *De monarchia*. But this is not their only importance. They must not be regarded as a digression in the *Convivio*. Dante begins with a definition of nobility attributed to the Emperor Frederick II, who, he says, described nobility as consisting in inherited wealth and fine manners.[108] In order to disprove this definition, Dante finds it necessary to define the authority of the emperor, with the aim of showing that the emperor has no right to define nobility. Also, the juxtaposition of nobility and political theory indicates Dante's view that morality and political life cannot be divorced, an Aristotelian principle which he affirms obliquely by referring to Aristotle several times in the tractate as the "master of human life," [109] the leader of human reason,[110] whose philosophy must be considered as "almost Catholic opinion." [111]

With this orientation of the problem in mind, Dante proceeds to outline the need for a universal empire. Human life, he begins, is ordered toward the end of happiness. No one can achieve this end by himself, since man is by nature social; he cannot attain happiness, nor can he satisfy his needs without the family, the neighborhood, and civil society at all its levels from the city to the empire. If man is naturally social, continues Dante, he is also naturally greedy. This tendency leads men to develop territorial ambitions, which in turn lead to wars among kingdoms, a situation which has a deleterious effect on all aspects of social life and which prevents men from reaching the goal of happiness. But, Dante argues, if there were one empire, wars and their causes would cease, for if one

108. Ibid., IV, iii, 6–9.
109. Ibid., xxiii, 8, Jackson, pp. 210–11.
110. Ibid., vi, 6–8; ii, 16.
111. Ibid., vi, 16, Jackson, p. 213.

man possessed all territorial dominion, there would be nothing left for him to covet. Omitting to notice that this would not prevent other men from being jealous of the emperor, he concludes that if there were one universal ruler, he would be able to institute a lasting peace. Thus, men would be able to live happily and to achieve their end.[112]

Having made this point, it remains for Dante to explain why this universal dominion should be vested in the Holy Roman Emperor rather than in some other prince, especially since the power of Rome was initially acquired by force. Dante argues that the choice of the Holy Roman Emperor as the one best prince was ordained by God. Thus, the empire gained its power by Providence, not by force; force was only the instrumental cause. God chose the Romans, whom Dante does not distinguish from the current German emperors, on account of their virtues, since these virtues were needed in order for the empire to fulfill the mission assigned to it by God.[113] This mission is the reconciliation of God and man. It is for this reason that God became incarnate during the Roman era. As further proof of Rome's authority, he states that the birth of David and the foundation of Rome occurred simultaneously, which clearly reveals God's special interest in the establishment of the Roman Empire. God, for Dante no less than for Augustine, oversaw the entire history of Rome, inspired its rulers and citizens with virtues human and Divine, and is responsible for its most outstanding accomplishment, universal peace. Thus, Dante concludes, Rome is worthy of special reverence.[114]

Dante now moves to the discussion of the nature of imperial and philosophical authority. The imperial authority derives, as Dante has indicated, from God. But he is also interested in the etymological derivation of the term from the Latin and Greek. Authority, he states, flows from the activity proper to

112. Ibid., iv, 1–7.
113. Ibid., 8–14.
114. Ibid., v.

an *auctor;* it also bespeaks the quality of being worthy of trust and obedience, an idea which Dante extracts from the Greek by way of the contemporary jurist Uguccione. He has comparatively little to say about philosophical authority, contenting himself with the judgment that it pertains above all to Aristotle. Dante advocates the cooperation of philosophical and imperial authorities for the good of the commonwealth, a piece of advice which he urges the Italians to take to heart.[115]

With these principles before the reader, Dante now rebuts the view that true nobility is based on wealth, ancestry, and manners. He begins his attack on Frederick II's definition by discussing briefly the nature of worthiness. Worthiness, he says, entails reverence, which he defines as the acknowledgment of one's subjection to both princely and philosophical authority.[116] This reverence, however, is not unlimited, particularly as it applies to the emperor. The empire, argues Dante, was invented for the perfection of human life. Thus, the emperor's jurisdiction extends justly over all those human activities which can be described as voluntary, since it is in terms of man's voluntary choices that he achieves or rejects his end. The emperor justly regulates these activities by law, and his authority also covers certain technical matters like marriage, slavery, military affairs, and the laws of succession. But God has imposed limits upon the jurisdiction of the emperor. The emperor has no authority over those things which the human will does not direct, such as nature, supernature, and mathematics. Since true nobility is a natural faculty,[117] whose ultimate source is God alone,[118] it follows for Dante that the emperor does not have a legitimate right to define the nature of true nobility.[119]

This disposes of the right by which Frederick II issued his dictum on the subject. Dante now proceeds to criticize the

115. Ibid., vi.
116. Ibid., viii.
117. Ibid., ii, 11.
118. Ibid., xx.
119. Ibid., ix, 16–17.

content of Frederick's definition. The difficulties that Dante
sees in attributing nobility to lineage and inherited wealth are
manifold. Riches are irrelevant to nobility, he argues, since a
man who is noble remains noble even after he loses his
wealth.[120] In any case, riches produce worldly cares and corrupt their owner, making him greedy for more. Greed pro-
motes conflict and instills in the wealthy the irrational desire
for perfect wealth, which is self-defeating since it cannot be
achieved. Riches thus cause evil and deprive their owner of
good. They make him envious, fearful of loss, and insecure.
Furthermore, these attitudes distract men from their chief
end, God.[121] Ancestry is no key to nobility either. The fact
that the men of one generation may be noble should not lead
us to extend this judgment uncritically and automatically to
their descendants.[122] This view is erroneous, according to
Dante, because it assumes that people cannot change for better or for worse, an idea which forces us to posit two aborigi-
nal ancestors of the human race, one base and one noble, from
whom two different breeds of men are descended, instead of
one common ancestor, Adam.[123] Neither are manners a criterion of nobility; they are the effects, not the causes, of nobility.[124]

Moving to the positive side of his argument, Dante now defines nobility as anything perfect in its own nature.[125] Since
perfection is the end of the moral life, nobility is related to

120. Ibid., x.
121. Ibid., x–xiii.
122. Ibid., vii.
123. Ibid., xiv–xv.
124. Ibid., viii, 8–9; x.
125. Ibid., xvi. For a good summary of Dante's idea of nobility, stressing its
Christian and Aristotelian features, see Gino Dallari, "Sul concetto della nobilità
nella terza canzone del 'Convivio' Dantesco," Reale Istituto Lombardo di
scienze e lettere, *Rendiconti,* serie 2, *61* (1928), 572–80. On the other hand,
see Eduard Jourdan, "Dante et l'idée de 'virtù,'" *Mélanges sur Dante: Publiés
par la Nouvelle revue d'Italie à l'occasion du sixième centenaire de la mort du
poète* (Rome, 1924), pp. 79–92, who argues that Dante has a Renaissance idea
of virtù.

virtue. Dante cites with approval several classical virtues derived from Aristotle, reserving highest honors for justice as the most distinctively human of them.[126] Each virtue, he says, is subject to two vices, on the side of excess and on the side of defect; virtue can be described as the mean between the two. The virtuous life may be active or contemplative, although Dante voices an Aristotelian and biblical preference for the latter.[127] Nobility, Dante adds, is wider and more inclusive than the moral virtues. It also encompasses the intellectual virtues, piety, and religion, praiseworthy emotions like shame and pity, and physical excellences like health, strength, and beauty. Still, none of these is the sine qua non of nobility, since it can be found in persons like women and children who do not possess all of these characteristics.[128] The addition of these qualifications may appear to muddy the waters of Dante's analysis, but, in any event, he ends by making the covering statement that it is God alone Who confers true nobility and that it is beyond the range of human reason to know precisely how He does this.[129] Finally, Dante applies his idea of nobility to the three Aristotelian divisions of the soul—the vegetative, animate, and intellectual—and to the four stages of life—adolescence, youth, old age, and decline— illustrating each aspect of the soul and each age with its appropriate virtues.[130]

The *Convivio* is a rather disjointed and unbalanced work, the result, probably, of the fact that Dante never completed it. Nevertheless, it is interesting for several reasons. It presents a theory of poetry stressing didacticism intertwined with aesthetic pleasure. It adds much weight to Dante's growing stress on the vernacular and on the powers of poetic speech. In it he employs his favorite device, an idealized lady, as the channel through whom he acquires the insights which he sets

126. *Convivio,* I, xii, 5.
127. Ibid., IV, xvii.
128. Ibid., xviii–xix.
129. Ibid., xx–xxi.
130. Ibid., xxiii–xxviii.

before the reader. While somewhat inconsistently linked to a view of the limits of poetry which treats its aesthetic strategy as a bella menzogna, Dante's poetics in this work shows his increasing tendency to envision eloquence in the context of ethics and politics. Although his treatment of nobility in the *Convivio* is neither particularly original [131] nor entirely lucid, Dante relates it, along with the discussion of the Holy Roman Empire which it entails, to the love of wisdom and to an elevated view of literature as a vehicle of truth and a spur to moral action.

Dante's most elaborate theoretical statement on the subject of poetry is found in his *De vulgari eloquentia*. This work, which sets the discussion in the context of an analysis of the nature and origin of language, includes an extensive treatment of Italian dialects and the norms of poetic style. In it Dante joins verbal epistemology and literary theory to his ethical and political concerns in the quest for a new Italian vernacular capable of unifying Italy linguistically and of serving the ideals of wisdom, virtue, and eloquence.[132] Dante begins by point-

131. Barbi, *Life of Dante,* pp. 47–49; Wieruszowski, *"Ars Dictaminis,"* *Medievalia et Humanistica, 1,* 108. Cf. on the other hand Giovanni Getto, *Aspetti della poesia di Dante* (Firenze, 1947), p. 26.

132. Treatments of the *De vulgari eloquentia* break down in two main types: those which are more or less satisfied with summarizing Dante's ideas on language and those which go on to note the relationship in this work between language, literature, ethics, and politics. The latter approach is best represented by Giorgio Petrocchi's excellent *Il "De Vulgari Eloquentia" di Dante* (Messina, 1961). See also Alessandro Passerin d'Entrèves, *Dante politico e altri saggi* (Torino, 1955), pp. 39, 97–113; Karl Witte, *Essays on Dante* (London, 1910), p. 386; Zingarelli, *La vita, 1,* 568. Giulio Bertoni, "La lingua di Dante," *Nuova antologia, 68,* fasc. 1462 (1933), 481–90, retains this view but interprets it in the light of the fascist sublimation of the individual into the group. Among those summarizing Dante's views on language without setting them in a broader context are Karl Otto Apel, *Die Idee der Sprache in der Tradition des Humanismus von Dante bis Vico* (Bonn, 1963), pp. 98–99, 104–23; J. Cremona, "Dante's Views on Language," *The Mind of Dante,* ed. U. Limentani (Cambridge, 1965), pp. 138–62; Nardi, *Dante,* pp. 235–47; "Due capitoli," *Giornale storico della letteratura italiana,* suppl. *19–21,* 245–64; *La filosofia di Dante,* pp. 44–51; Ovidio, *Dante,* pp. 8–33; Pézard, *Dante,* pp. 151–200, 223–52; Karl Vossler, *Mediaeval Culture: An Introduction to Dante and His Times* (New York, 1929), *1,* 162–65.

ing out that speech is distinctively human and essential to men, since they require a discursive mode of knowing and of expressing their thoughts to others.[133] "Language," he says, "is as necessary an instrument of our thought as a horse is of a knight." [134] Men, according to Dante, need language because speech, like human nature itself, is both rational and sensible. Words are signs in both their sensible and their rational aspects. They are sensible signs of things insofar as they are sounds; Dante, in the tradition of classical sign theory, stresses the sonic character of language.[135] Language is also a rational sign insofar as it signifies the ideas or intentions of the speaker and communicates them to the hearer, but it must do this through a sensible medium.[136] Dante's emphasis on the need for a sensible medium reflects the view that sense perception is the beginning of human knowledge,[137] and the idea that sensible signs can represent non-sensible referents adequately.

In surveying the current linguistic situation, Dante notes that there are many different languages. He interprets the fact of linguistic diversity in a moral context. The variety of languages is a consequence of man's sin. Following a lengthy patristic and medieval tradition which had been reiterated by Brunetto Latini,[138] Dante holds that speech originated in the

133. *De vulg. el.,* I, ii.

134. Ibid., II, i, 8, Howell, p. 67.

135. Guglielmo Bilancioni, *Il suono e la voce nell'opera di Dante* (Pisa, 1927), pp. 17–18; Luigi Malagoli, *Linguaggio e poesia nella Divina Commedia* (Genova, 1949), pp. 104–09.

136. *De vulg. el.,* I, iii, 2–3.

137. See *Convivio,* II, iv, 17; v, 1–5.

138. *Trésor,* III, i, 1. Noted also by Petrocchi, *Il "De Vulgari Eloquentia,"* pp. 8–10. A thorough analysis of this tradition can be found in Rotta, *La filosofia del linguaggio,* passim; Roger Dragonetti, *Aux frontières du langage poétique: Études sur Dante, Mallarmé, Valéry* (Gent, 1961), pp. 7, 9, 10, 17–18, 19 ff., 75, 95; and Willy Krogmann, "Die Mannigfaltigkeit der Sprache in der Sicht Dantes," *Die Metaphysik im Mittelalter: Ihr Ursprung und ihre Bedeutung, Vorträge des II. internationalen Kongresses für mittelalterliche Philosophie, Köln, 31. August–6. September 1961* (Berlin, 1963), pp. 136–43. On the other hand, A. Ewert, "Dante's Theory of Language," *Modern Language Review, 35* (1940), 358, sees this idea as original with Dante.

garden of Eden. Unlike speech after the Fall, which was a cry of woe, Adam's first statement was an act of worship, the recognition of God's sovereignty.[139] The harmony between man and the rest of creation in the Earthly Paradise is also symbolized by Adam's naming of the animals in the garden, which shows in turn the natural affinity between rightly ordered speech and reality. According to Dante, all men spoke the same language, Hebrew, until they built the tower of Babel. The building of the tower was an act of human presumption against God, and God punished man for it, dividing the human community by the introduction of different languages, which cut men off from God and from each other by hampering their mutual communications.[140] Since Babel, speech has varied from place to place and has also been subjected to changes in time, as words die out or are altered over the course of the years.[141]

The idea that diverse languages signalize a sinful state of human disunity prefaces Dante's analysis of the languages of Europe, the differences between the vernacular and Latin, and the attempt to establish norms for an Italian vernacular which will raise it to the level of a literary language capable of expressing important subjects of all kinds. Dante first draws a distinction between grammar and the vernacular. By grammar he means the Latin language, as well as the stylistic rules that govern its literary use. The dignity and preeminence of grammar, Dante explains, lie in the fact that it lays down unchanging concepts of language, in contrast to the fluctuating character of the vernacular, which permit people to translate other languages into their own and hence to maintain contact with their past and with other men who live outside of their immediate locality.[142] Despite the commanding position possessed by Latin, Dante holds that the vernacular is intrinsically

139. *De vulg. el.,* I, iv–v.
140. Ibid., vii, 3–7.
141. Ibid., ix, 6–11. See also *Convivio,* I, iv, 7–10.
142. *De vulg. el.,* I, ix, 11.

nobler than grammar. It is natural, not artificial; it is the first speech that men employ; and it is used by everyone, although in different forms.[143] Notwithstanding the natural superiority of the vernacular, it labors under a cultural disadvantage. This being the case, Dante takes as his mission the raising of the vernacular, especially that of Italy, to the dignity of grammar, and he invokes Christ the Word at the beginning of the *De vulgari eloquentia* to aid him in this task.[144] The establishment of the unified Italian language which Dante projects in this work is linked to moral and intellectual rectitude, the pursuit of the Good and the True. A unified Italian vernacular, he thinks, will also foster a sense of community among all Italians. In addition, the erection of stylistic norms in the Italian language will enhance the literary culture of the country, as well as serving Dante's own needs as a poet.[145] This fusion of Dante's personal aims with his broader ethical and political objectives, which we have noted in Dante's earlier works, is his underlying motive in the *De vulgari eloquentia*.

The work now moves rapidly into a technical discussion of dialects. Dante subdivides the languages of Europe into three groups, those of the North, which use *iò* for yes, those of the South, which use *oc, oïl,* and *sì,* and those of Eastern Europe and parts of Asia, which Dante associates with Greek.[146] He confines himself to the Southern group, and within it, to Italian, enumerating fourteen different Italian dialects and discussing their regional peculiarities.[147] Dante thinks that each of these dialects is flawed in some way, which prevents it from serving as his ideal vernacular. The very fact that Dante finds it possible to judge each of these dialects presupposes

143. Ibid., i, 3–4.
144. Ibid., 1.
145. Petrocchi, *Il "De Vulgari Eloquentia,"* pp. 6–7, 35.
146. *De vulg. el.,* I, viii. Cf. *Trésor, III,* i, 1, where Brunetto Latini sets forth a tripartite subdivision of speech, on somewhat more sophisticated linguistic grounds than Dante, into oriental (gutteral), Greek (palatial), and Italian (dental).
147. *De vulg. el.,* I, x–xv.

that there is a normative Italian language which can be used as a criterion. Dante explains that this criterion may be established according to the principle of simplicity: "Everything considered as belonging to a kind becomes measurable by that which is simplest in that kind." [148] Thus, the ideal vernacular is somehow present in all the Italian dialects and can be derived from them by abstraction. However, this normative Italian language cannot be identified with the Italian spoken anywhere in contemporary Italy. The ideal vernacular is simultaneously everywhere and nowhere. Dante does not hesitate to analogize the simplicity and omnipresence of his linguistic ideal to God:

> Now the supreme standards of those activities which are generically Italian are not peculiar to any one town in Italy, but are common to all; and among those can now be discerned that vernacular language which we were hunting for above, whose fragrance is in every town, but whose lair is in none. It may, however, be more perceptible in one than in another, just as the simplest of substances, which is God, is more perceptible in a man than in a brute, in an animal than in a plant, in a plant than in a mineral . . .
>
> Having therefore found what we were searching for, we declare the illustrious, cardinal, courtly, and curial vernacular language in Italy to be that which belongs to all the towns in Italy but does not appear to belong to any one of them, and by which all the municipal dialects of the Italians are measured, weighed, and compared.[149]

The pan-Italian yet nonfunctional description of the ideal vernacular is carried over by Dante into his discussion of its four attributes. In exploring the nature of the illustrious, cardinal, courtly, and curial vernacular, the *De vulgari eloquentia* shows a marked expansion of the competence of the vernacu-

---

148. Ibid., xvi, 2–3, Howell, pp. 54–55.
149. Ibid., 4–6, Howell, pp. 55–56.

lar in comparison with the *Convivio* and the *Vita nuova*. The ideal vernacular is called cardinal, explains Dante, because it is the head, chief, and father of all the Italian dialects. It is called courtly because it pertains to the common ruler and meeting place of the people. "If we Italians had a court, it [the courtly vernacular] would be spoken at court." Since there is no court, the courtly vernacular "wanders about like a wayfarer." The curial vernacular, on the other hand, pertains to ethics in general and to the supreme court of justice in particular. It is called curial, says Dante, "because 'curiality' is nothing else but the justly balanced rule of things which have to be done. . . . Whatever in our actions has been well balanced is called curial." While the balancing of man's ethical life is presumably possible under any circumstances, Dante points out that Italy has no supreme court. Although the members of such a court currently exist, he notes, at present they can be unified only by abstracting them rationally from their local institutional settings; they are not unified by the existence of a single prince or governmental system.[150] Dante's distinction of the vernacular into cardinal, courtly, and curial shows that he regards it as a suitable medium for the handling of ethics, law, and public affairs, which he in turn sees as correlatives of each other. Yet, his definitions of these three forms of the vernacular place an implicit limitation on it; it appears to be either a hypothetical Romance *ur-Sprache* or a technical legal and administrative vocabulary which does not exist in fact because the institutions that it might serve do not exist.

However, in discussing the illustrious vernacular Dante gives the distinct impression that his ideal vernacular does exist. In fact he names several famous authors who use it, including Cino da Pistoia, Bertran de Born, Arnaut Daniel, and Giraut Borneil,[151] and asserts that it can be found in all parts

---

150. Ibid., xviii, Howell, p. 61. See also Petrocchi, *Il "De Vulgari Eloquentia,"* pp. 55–57.

151. *De vulg. el.,* I, xvii, 3 ; II, ii, 9.

of Italy.[152] Furthermore, he attributes to the illustrious vernacular a range of topics which enable it to subsume and outstrip the other subdivisions of the volgare. The illustrious vernacular is the language of literature, and it is no accident that its powers are so broad. Literature, for Dante, is capable of encompassing the problems of ethics, public life, and religion, and is thereby capable of reforming and unifying the Italian people even in the absence of the institutional and legal unity upon which the courtly and curial vernacular depend.

In explaining the nature of the illustrious vernacular, Dante draws upon the literary theory which he expresses in his earlier works, but carries it much further. The literary theory of the *De vulgari eloquentia* includes both prose and poetry. Thus we find in Dante's treatment of the illustrious vernacular his predictable identification of rhetoric and poetics.[153] Dante applies many rhetorical norms, derived both from classical rhetoric and from the ars dictaminis, to his treatment of poetic technique,[154] and cites Vergil as a stylistic authority in the manner of the school tradition.[155] The rhetorical approach, both sophistic and Ciceronian, is visible in his definition of the illustrious vernacular. It is illustrious, he says, because of the skill it demands, because of its power to move men's hearts, and because it confers fame on authors who use it.[156] He indicates that in poetry, as in prose, there are levels of style and form, and that each has its appropriate subject matter.[157] He goes so far as to say that "poetry . . . is nothing else but a rhetorical composition set to music." [158]

Still more important is Dante's inversion of the traditional assimilation of poetics to rhetoric. Dante's poetics, to be sure,

152. Ibid., I, xix, 1–2.

153. R. Weiss, "Links between the 'Convivio' and the 'De Vulgari Eloquentia,'" *Modern Language Review, 37* (1942), 156–68.

154. Fletcher, "True meaning," *Romanic Review, 11,* 99; Glunz, *Die Literaturästhetik,* pp. 414–16.

155. Zingarelli, *La vita, 1,* 579 ff.

156. *De vulg. el.,* I, xvii, 3; Petrocchi, *Il "De Vulgari Eloquentia,"* p. 52.

157. *De vulg. el.,* II, iii–iv.

158. Ibid., iv, 2–3, Howell, p. 77.

result from the absorption of certain rhetorical aims and techniques by poetry. But, in his handling of the relationship between prose and poetry in the *De vulgari eloquentia,* Dante insists that poetry is prior to prose and that prose should be patterned after the norms that he lays down for verse.[159] Thus, the stylistic counsels and the epistemological and didactic functions which poetry once borrowed from rhetoric have become so identified with poetry in Dante's mind that he thinks that prose style can model itself after the strategies of poetry, which he delineates in some detail. In point of fact, Dante does not delineate prose style in the same detail. The *De vulgari eloquentia* is an unfinished work, which leaves off before the author gets up to prose. While of course circumstantial, the truncation of the work can, however, be justified in terms of Dante's poetic priorities. Considering the manner in which rhetoric and poetics originally came together in classical Rome, one might say that Dante has out-Ciceroed Cicero.

The essential characteristic of poetry in the illustrious vernacular is rectitude. Rectitude, for Dante, has the same implications that it has for Anselm. It entails an adequate intellectual and moral attitude on the part of the poet, which is related to the subject that he is writing about. Concerned as he is with literary style, Dante adds to these canons a series of formal, aesthetic, and linguistic norms in terms of which the fitness of a poem vis-à-vis its object can be assessed. He begins by defining the kinds of persons who should use the illustrious vernacular and the kinds of subject matter they may treat. The illustrious vernacular entails skill and poetic power; therefore, says Dante, it should be used only by men possessing poetic genius and knowledge who will use it to express the worthiest thoughts. There are degrees of worthiness, he points out, analogous to the three Aristotelian divisions of the soul: the vegetative, the animate, and the rational. The subjects which pertain to these three aspects of the soul are the useful

159. Ibid., i, 1.

(*utile*), the pleasant (*delectabile*), and the right (*honestum, rectum*). Each of these categories provides subject matter in its own right. Although the honestum or rectum might seem to be the most specifically human of the three, the delectabile and the utile are seen as ends in themselves, not as means to other ends. The worthiest thoughts of all are those directed toward rectitude, which man seeks insofar as he is rational; virtue is hence the most fitting subject for poetry, which may also deal with the other two parts of the soul, the animate and the vegetative. Worthy thoughts may be directed to the pleasant, which man seeks insofar as he is animate, and which finds as its subject love. Finally, the poet may direct himself worthily to the useful, which man seeks insofar as he is vegetative, and which finds as its subject matter safety, by which Dante means warfare and the exercise of arms. He notes that the best poets have written on rectitude, love, and war, citing several Provençal troubadours and practitioners of the dolce stil nuovo as examples.[160]

By defining the scope of poetry written in the illustrious vernacular in this fashion, the *De vulgari eloquentia* shows Dante in the process of developing a theory of poetry going far beyond his ideas on this subject in the *Convivio* and the *Vita nuova,* a theory which is beginning to look capable of sustaining a work like the *Divine Comedy*. Safety, love, and virtue may sound quite narrow as topics suitable for vernacular poetry, but they are potentially quite broad. They have both personal and community characteristics. Safety can be expanded to include the peaceful as well as the warlike aspects of civic life. Love can address itself to a beloved who supplies the lover with eternal as well as earthly delights. Virtue can take in the natural and the theological virtues, thus linking earthly love and civic life to the love of God and the community of saints. Moreover, this is a theory containing built-in ethical and philosophical dimensions. Since it is rooted in the

160. Ibid., ii; Petrocchi, *Il "De Vulgari Eloquentia,"* pp. 60–61.

soul of man, as Dante understands it, it is thus as wide and deep in its scope as human nature itself.

Since words must correspond to things, the excellent subject matter expressed in the illustrious vernacular is worthy of an equally excellent form. This leads Dante to address himself to the canzone, which he thinks is the noblest of poetic forms. It should therefore be used for the worthiest subjects; indeed, he notes, it has been so used by the best poets.[161] The canzone has a set form, which can be learned and produced as an act of good literary craftsmanship. Dante places much stress on craftsmanship, and in fact devotes a sizable part of the *De vulgari eloquentia* to the formal and linguistic rules for good canzoni, including such topics as meter, the length of lines, syllables, sentence structure, vocabulary, stanza structure, rhyme, and musical setting, and lists abuses to be avoided as well as good examples to be emulated.[162] Perhaps most interesting in Dante's assortment of rules, for our purposes, is his discussion of different kinds of words, the childish, feminine, masculine, sylvan, and urban, the urban being further subdivided into glossy, rumpled, combed-out, and shaggy. Dante places words in one or another of these categories on the basis of how they sound. Feminine words, for example, have many liquid vowels, while sylvan words have harsh consonants, often doubled.[163] This stress on the way words sound as the basis for the appropriateness of their use in particular literary contexts underlines Dante's interest in the sensible quality of language. It brings man's physical nature as well as his soul into the framework of literary theory, while indicating the need for a fitting sensible medium in the process by which words communicate the things they signify.

Literary craftsmanship also involves the selection of a subject that the poet is capable of handling, an insight which

161. *De vulg. el.,* II, iii.
162. Ibid., v–xiii.
163. Ibid., vii.

Dante borrows from Horace's *Ars poetica,* and the choice of an appropriate genre, which is related both to content and to style. Dante defines three basic genres: elegy, comedy, and tragedy. Elegy is written in the style of the wretched and may use only the lowly vernacular. Comedy is written in a mean-to-low style and should use the middle or low vernacular. Tragedy is written in an elevated style; it employs the illustrious vernacular and should use the canzone form. It alone is worthy of dealing with the most elevated subjects: safety, love, and virtue.[164] These subjects, Dante insists, demand unflagging effort, practice, and craft, and not merely poetic genius. By supplying poets with the rules of their craft, he hopes to make the vernacular a truly literary language, and its poetry the equal of Latin poetry. Returning to the theme struck at the beginning of the *De vulgari eloquentia,* he argues that the main difference between the Latin and the vernacular poets is that the former proceed according to rules and the latter proceed haphazardly.[165] To reform the vernacular, to make it a medium truly fitted for the discussion of great questions, vernacular poets should imitate the regularity of classical poetry by developing and applying to their own art rules appropriate to their own native language.

In the *De vulgari eloquentia,* Dante goes a long way toward working out the theory of poetry which he ultimately expresses in the *Divine Comedy.* As we have seen, he broadens extensively the scope of the vernacular. The linguistic reform that he projects is closely related to ethical and political reform, involving as it does the healing of at least some of the linguistic breaches caused by human sin as well as promoting a more unified Italy. Dante's quest for the ideal Italian vernacular is also closely related to literary reform and the development of a theory of literature stressing the priority of poetry while according to it the significative functions attrib-

164. Ibid., iv, 4–9.
165. Ibid., 1–3.

uted to rhetoric by the Augustinian tradition. Dante bases his theory, as we have noted, on the nature of man, and, from this vantage point, makes it competent to deal with the major problems and interests of mankind. The one aspect of the poetics of the *De vulgari eloquentia* which Dante later alters in the interests of the *Divine Comedy* is his limitation of the worthiest subjects—war, love, and virtue—to the tragic style and his insistence that the canzone is the only suitable form in which to write about them. He is forced to change his mind on this point in order to make the treatment of the theme of salvation in the *Comedy* plausible. Nevertheless, his notion that the comic genre may use a moderate style containing a mixed vocabulary is one that Dante does carry over into the *Comedy*. Certainly the *Comedy* vindicates Dante's argument in the *De vulgari eloquentia* that both craftsmanship based on rules and poetic genius are necessary if the vernacular is to assume its rightful place by the side of Latin as a literary language.

The development of Dante's linguistic and literary answers to current problems in the *De vulgari eloquentia* is matched by his elaboration of a political solution to the same problems in his *De monarchia* and political letters. Dante's political ideas have excited a good deal of interest on the part of scholars.[166] Outside of a brief interlude in the twentieth century, during which the exigencies of the moment inspired fascist and antifascist interpretations of them,[167] the prevailing approaches have been two in number, paralleling the critical treatments of the *De vulgari eloquentia*. Some scholars are content to abstract Dante's strictly political ideas from his

166. Pino da Prati, *La politica e la filosofia nella "Monarchia" di Dante* (Sanremo, 1963), pp. v–xvii, gives a useful survey of criticism on the *De monarchia*.

167. A fascist interpretation is put forth by Arrigo Solmi, "La 'Monarchia' di Dante," *Nuova antologia, 70,* fasc. 1513 (1935), 321–31, who sees in Dante a precursor of Mussolini's attempted reconstruction of the Roman Empire. This view is expressly contradicted by Maurice Vallis, "Dante et l'apologie de l'Empire," *Mercure de France, 287* (1938), 586–91.

works,[168] while others take account of the fact that Dante's political ideas occur in an ethical and religious context.[169] This latter point of view is by far the more plausible, since Dante's arguments throughout the *De monarchia,* and in other works where he treats political questions, make much use of biblical authority and the insights of Aristotelian moral philosophy, and he is quite concerned with specifying the relationships between political, ethical, and religious life.

The *De monarchia* is divided into three books, in which Dante attempts to prove the need for a universal empire, the justification for the possession of imperial authority on the

168. See, for example, Barbara Barclay Carter, "Dante's Political Conception," *Hibbert Journal, 35* (1937), 568–79; "Dante's Political Ideas," *Review of Politics, 5* (1943), 338–55; Francesco Ercole, *Il pensiero politico di Dante* (Milano, 1927–28); Arturo Graf, *Roma nella memoria e nelle immaginazioni del medio evo* (Torino, 1882–83), passim and especially *2,* 423–69; Hans Kelsen, *Die Staatslehre des Dante Alighieri* (Wien und Leipzig, 1905); Heinz Löwe, "Dante und das Kaisertum," *Historische Zeitschrift, 190* (1960), 517–52; Limentani, "Dante's Political Thought," *The Mind of Dante,* pp. 113–37, 517–52; John Joseph Roebiecki, *The Political Philosophy of Dante Alighieri* (Washington, 1921); Arrigo Solmi, *Il pensiero politico di Dante: Studi storici* (Firenze, 1922). Some scholars argue that Dante bases his political theory on purely human grounds and that he may thus be regarded as a Renaissance or modern thinker. See Ernst H. Kantorowicz, *The King's Two Bodies: A Study in Mediaeval Political Theology* (Princeton, 1957), pp. 451, 459–95; Prati, *La politica,* passim; Theodor Steinbüchel, *Grosse Gestalten des Abendlandes: Bild und Beispiel christlicher Verwirklichung* (Trier, 1955), p. 217.

169. See, for example, Johannes Jacob, *Die Bedeutung der Führer Dantes in der Divina Commedia: Virgil, Beatrix, St. Bernhard, in Bezug auf den idealen Zweck des Gedichtes und auf Grund der geistigen Lebensentwicklung des Dichters* (Leipzig, 1874); Fritz Kern, *Humana Civilitas: Staat, Kirche und Kultur. Eine Dante-Untersuchung* (Leipzig, 1913); P. E. Matheson, "Character and Citizenship in Dante," *Hibbert Journal, 5* (1907), 856–78; A. Meozzi, *L'utopia politica di Dante* (Milano, 1929); Edward Moore, *Studies in Dante: Second Series* (Oxford, 1899), p. 25; Passerin d'Entrèves, *Dante politico,* pp. 39–113; Luigi Pietrobono, "Dante e Roma," *GD, 33,* n. s., *3* (1930), 1–24; Augustin Renaudet, *Dante humaniste* (Paris, 1952), pp. 55–57, 479–555; Reto Roedel, "Individuo e comunità nella Divina Commedia," *Individuum und Gemeinschaft: Festschrift zur fünfzigjahrfeier der Handels-Hochschule St. Gallen* (St. Gallen, 1949), pp. 515–16; Nicolai Rubinstein, "The Beginnings of Political Thought in Florence: A Study in Mediaeval Historiography," *Journal of the Warburg and Courtauld Institutes, 5* (1942), 198–227; Helene Wieruszowski, "Der Reichsgedanke bei Dante," *DDJ, 14,* neue Folge, Band *5* (1932), 185–209.

part of the ancient Romans, and by extension the current Holy Roman Empire, and the invalidity of papal claims to temporal authority over the emperor. Indeed, the *De monarchia* may be regarded as part of the ongoing debate among medieval publicists on the respective powers of popes and emperors in the Christian commonwealth.[170] In dealing with these questions, Dante recapitulates the basic points that he sets forth in the *Convivio,* but expands the discussion considerably, having recourse to arguments drawn from scriptural authority, the authority of classical antiquity, reason (or his own deductions and definitions), and experience (or historical facts as he understands them). An ethical and religious, no less than a strictly political, motivation is evident throughout. This motivation underlies Dante's stated reason for writing about politics and his definition of the nature of his subject. He writes, he tells us, because the learned have a duty to serve the common weal.[171] His intention is to stimulate political reform; unlike mathematics, physics, and theology, he reminds the reader, politics is a matter subject to human control. Its aim is action, which falls under the jurisdiction of the virtue of prudence.[172]

Dante's basic justification for politics, as well as his arguments for a single universal empire, further underlines his association of civic life and ethics. His rationale for this association is the Aristotelian principle that political society is conducive to the good life, and that in a good society the good citizen and the good man are the same.[173] This being the case, Dante offers three main arguments in Book I of the *De monarchia* designed to identify a universal empire with the good society. Two of these are positive arguments; the third is partly positive and partly negative. He begins by agreeing with Aristotle that the end of man, both personal and social, is

170. Kantorowicz, *King's Two Bodies,* pp. 456–58.
171. *De mon.,* I, i.
172. Ibid., ii, 5–6; iii, 10.
173. Ibid., xii, 9–10.

the perfection of the intellect. The perfection of the intellect, then, is the end toward which political life is directed. As a basic precondition to his intellectual development, man needs peace, and the best means to achieve peace is one universal government.[174] Next Dante takes up the theme of unity, toward which, he thinks, agreeing with Aristotle on this point as well, all things tend. Man, he states, is made in the image of God. Mankind thus resembles God, and, since God is one, mankind should have one universal government and ruler. Dante thinks that unity is better than multiplicity on general principles, an idea which he regards as self-evident in the light of the convertibility of unity, as a metaphysical transcendental, with being and goodness.[175] Finally, he agrees with St. Augustine, noting that good order in the world is characterized by justice. He defines justice as rectitude (*rectitudo*), "or a rule which drives out obliquity." [176] In the abstract, he goes on, justice is a quality which admits of no degrees. But in concrete terms, justice is found mixed with other things contrary to it. In particular, it is found mixed with human sin and selfishness, as expressed by the vice of greed. Repeating his argument in the *Convivio,* Dante asserts that the only way to remove greed, the cause of wars and contentions, from political life on a permanent basis, is to have one universal ruler who possesses everything and who therefore lacks anything to covet. Once the possibility for greed is disposed of, greed itself will vanish, and, since it is the major obstacle to justice, justice will prevail. In this third argument Dante moves from a positive justification for a universal empire, the promotion of justice, to a negative justification, government as a remedy for sin, a point which he repeats in the third book of the *De monarchia.*[177]

174. Ibid., iii–v.
175. Ibid., vii–x, xiv–xv.
176. Ibid., xi, 3. Cf. *Convivio,* I, xii, 9, where he calls justice the most distinctively human virtue.
177. *De mon.,* I, xi, 3–20; xiii; III, iv, 14.

Dante's next problem is to demonstrate that universal dominion is rightly vested in the Roman Empire. He adds very little here that is not already present in the *Convivio* in his efforts to show that human reason, Divine authority, and history support his case. Starting from the proposition that the basis of political right (*ius*) is the will of God, which, like the intentions of men, can be detected only through visible signs,[178] he argues that the nobility or virtue of the Romans is attested by their own history [179] and by their self-sacrificing concern for the common good.[180] Their natural capacity for world rule is also proved by the justice and prudence of their laws.[181] God, furthermore, sanctioned the power of Rome by His miracles,[182] by permitting the Romans to conquer their enemies on the field of battle,[183] and, finally, by virtue of the fact that Christ chose to become incarnate during Roman imperial times and submitted Himself to Roman law.[184] Perhaps the most interesting point that Dante makes in the second book of the *De monarchia* is his association of the emperor with Christ and of his own argument with the sun, the symbol of Divinity:

> I . . . cry out in behalf of the glorious people and of Caesar in the words of him who cried out in behalf of the Prince of Heaven: "Why have the nations raged and the peoples devised vain things? The kings of the earth stood up and the princes met together against the Lord, and against his Christ" [Psalms 2:1–2]. But as love naturally does not permit derision to endure, and as the summer sun in his rising scatters the morning mists and bathes all in light, so I cease deriding and prefer to throw

178. Ibid., II, ii.
179. Ibid., iii.
180. Ibid., v.
181. Ibid., vi.
182. Ibid., iv.
183. Ibid., vii–x.
184. Ibid., I, xvi; II, xi–xii.

a correcting light upon the clouds of ignorance, to free from such clouds those raving kings and princes and to reveal a mankind free from the yoke of such rulers.[185]

Finally, Dante, in the tradition of medieval imperialists, addresses himself to combating the idea that the papacy should possess temporal power. Dante does not challenge the pope's spiritual authority, which, he holds, is vested in the papal office by Christ and is a correlative of the fact that man and society have spiritual ends.[186] He uses the sun-and-moon theory of Innocent III and the two-swords theory adumbrated by Gelasius I and Gregory VII and defined by St. Bernard as touchstones of the position that he wishes to refute, beginning with an attack on the papalists' technique of arguing their case from ecclesiastical tradition. Tradition flows from the Church, he asserts, and therefore it cannot be used to establish the Church's powers. Nor does he hesitate to resort to *ad hominem* arguments against various proponents of the papalist position, whom he excoriates as fanatical, greedy for power, and ignorant of anything but the decretals, which, though authoritative, should be subordinated to the Bible, the Church Fathers, and the decrees of general councils.[187] Next he deals with the sun-and-moon and the two-swords theories in particular. He has two major criticisms of them. Concerning the sun-and-moon theory, he says that it is illogical to deduce the nature of governments, which are accidental creations designed to deal with the circumstantial problems of men, from astronomical phenomena, which are permanent and essential parts of the creation[188]—a strange argument in the light of Dante's own interest in grounding governments in the natural and supernatural orders. Both the sun-and-moon theory and the two-swords theory, he adds, are fallacious because they

185. Ibid., II, i, 4–6, Schneider, pp. 24–25. Cf. *Convivio,* I, xiii, 2; III, xii, 6–8.
186. *De mon.,* III, i, viii.
187. Ibid., iii.
188. Ibid., iv.

are based on arbitrary, erroneous, or noncontextual interpretations of the Bible.[189]

Turning to what he regards as correct theory, Dante states that both papacy and empire have an authentic basis. The source of the pope's office, which is limited to spiritual matters, is Christ's will, as revealed by the Bible, and the life of Christ is the norm and pattern of ecclesiastical life.[190] The sources of the emperor's office, which is concerned with temporal matters and which does not derive from papal authority, are natural and supernatural. They flow from God's express mandate [191] and from human right,[192] the nature and needs of men, which, since they are aspects of the law of nature, may be assumed to be in conformity with the will of God.[193] The Divine and natural sanctions of the empire, independent of ecclesiastical authorization, are further proved by history; the Roman Empire, Dante notes, predates the Church, and thus cannot be dependent upon it.[194]

Dante draws several conclusions from these principles. Neither the papacy nor the empire can be the common denominator of the other.[195] No cession of temporal powers to popes by emperors is truly legitimate; and the usurpation of such powers by popes does not confer a right to them.[196] Rather, Dante insists, man has two ends, natural and supernatural. His own nature and the will of God ordain that there should be two institutions, the empire and the papacy, to guide men to these ends. These two institutions have distinct means appropriate to them. The empire employs philosophy, which operates in terms of man's moral and intellectual capacities, to lead man to the Earthly Paradise by means of reason. The

189. Ibid., iv–vi, ix.
190. Ibid., i, viii, xv.
191. Ibid., iv, xvi.
192. Ibid., x.
193. Ibid., ii.
194. Ibid., xiii.
195. Ibid., xii.
196. Ibid., x–xi.

Church employs religion, which operates in terms of man's theological capacities—faith, hope, and charity—to lead man to eternal bliss by means of revelation and grace.[197]

The *De monarchia* stresses the autonomy of imperial sanctions and functions from the papacy; at the same time Dante sees religious and political life as inextricably bound together. Reason, philosophy, and ethics are placed within the purview of politics; and politics, like language, is seen as springing from the needs of human nature as well as from the ordinance of God. The empire appears to be the more essential of the two institutions, since peace, which it alone can provide, is the prerequisite for the fulfillment of both the natural and the supernatural ends of man. Yet, politics is finally subordinated, as well as related, to religion, since life on earth is the means to the end of eternal beatitude in heaven.[198]

It is in terms of these priorities and functions that Dante views politics, ethics, religion, and literature, and his letters further cement the close ties which he establishes among them in his other works. Dante's letters bemoan the conditions of both Church and state. Christendom, he observes, is plagued with heresies; the cardinals have failed in their responsibility to guide the chariot of the Spouse of Christ and to enlighten the faithful. Rome is a widow, says Dante, adverting to the Babylonian Captivity. Rome has both religious and political significance for him. It is at once the rightful center of the Church and the source of Italian civil life.[199] Political life, too, is beset by abuses, all of which can be traced to lack of respect for imperial authority. Here, as in the *Convivio* and the *De monarchia*, he argues that only a single universal emperor can provide peace and justice, supporting his case with

197. Ibid., xvi.
198. Ibid.
199. *Epistola* VIII, Dante to the Italian Cardinals, May or June, 1314, Toynbee, pp. 127–42. Toynbee's dating and numbering of the letters has been followed throughout.

280

the Bible, reason, and history.[200] In the face of his ardent hope that the Emperor Henry VII would succeed in enforcing his claims to Italy and would effect the desired reforms, Dante's letters grow resonant with classical and biblical rhetoric. He describes or addresses Henry as the sun,[201] the bridegroom,[202] the lion of Judah, the new Moses,[203] the sign of God's will,[204] the elect of God,[205] the minister of God, the scion of Jesse, and the Lamb of God.[206] These Christological metaphors are combined with appeals to the classics. The descent of the emperor into Italy, says Dante, will initiate the return of the Saturian age prophesied by Vergil;[207] Henry is the imperial eagle,[208] the shepherd descended from Hector.[209] Florence, claims Dante, referring to a lengthy urban tradition, has particular cause to support the emperor, since the city, like the empire, is descended from Troy.[210] Yet, he fulminates, the Florentines shamefully reject their Roman traditions, sinfully opposing the will of God by turning their backs on the emperor.[211] Dante's association of politics with ethics and religion is so strong here that he virtually equates failure to support the emperor's claims in Italy with sin before

---

200. *Epistola* V, Dante to the princes and peoples of Italy, September or October, 1310, ¶ 7–10; *Epistola* VI, Dante to the Florentines, March 31, 1311, ¶ 1–2; *Epistola* VII, Dante to the Emperor Henry VII, April 17, 1311, ¶ 1, 3, 6; *Epistola* VII**, Dante to the Empress Margaret, Countess of Battifolle, April, 1311, Toynbee, pp. 55–58, 66–68, 89–90, 91–93, 96, 114.

201. *Epistola* V, ¶ 1; *Epistola* VII, ¶ 1, Toynbee, pp. 47–48, 89–90.

202. *Epistola* V, ¶ 1, 2, Toynbee, pp. 47–48, 49.

203. Ibid., ¶ 1, Toynbee, pp. 47–48.

204. Ibid., ¶ 8, Toynbee, pp. 55–56.

205. Ibid., ¶ 2; *Epistola* VI, ¶ 6, Toynbee, pp. 49, 76.

206. *Epistola* VII, ¶ 2, 8, Toynbee, pp. 90–91, 99.

207. Ibid., ¶ 1, Toynbee, pp. 89–90.

208. *Epistola* V, ¶ 4, Toynbee, p. 52.

209. Ibid., ¶ 5, Toynbee, p. 53.

210. Ibid., ¶ 4; *Epistola* VI, ¶ 2, 6, Toynbee, pp. 52, 68, 75. See Rubinstein, "Political Thought in Florence," *Journal of the Warburg and Courtauld Institutes, 5,* 198–218, for an excellent discussion of this tradition.

211. *Epistola* V, ¶ 4–6; *Epistola* VI, ¶ 2, 3–5, Toynbee, pp. 52–54, 68, 69–74.

God. Dante relates the classical and biblical aspects of the imperial office and the union of Florence with a Rome symbolizing both political and religious ideals to his blend of language, politics, and morality in a passage in which he compares the Florentines' rejection of the emperor with the arrogance of the builders of the tower of Babel: "Wherefore, then, being disabused of such an idle conceit, do you abandon the Holy Empire, and, like the men of Babel once more, seek to found new kingdoms, so that there shall be one polity of Florence, and another of Rome?" [212] Political and linguistic disintegration go hand in hand with sin, and they are all a deviation away from the ideal Rome. Rome, for Dante, stands for Florence, the empire, the Church, purified, working correctly, and revealed in their true glory, for moral regeneration and for linguistic and literary reform, for the classical and the Christian traditions. He carries over this complex of ideas to the *Divine Comedy,* and the component parts cannot be detached from each other without severely distorting it.[213]

Dante deals more expressly with literature in his letters as well. His tenth letter, written to his patron Can Grande della Scala, to whom he dedicated the *Paradiso,* in fact supplies us with his most fully developed statement on the subject of lit-

212. *Epistola* VI, ¶ 2, Toynbee, p. 68.

213. Thus, Vossler, *Mediaeval Culture, 1,* 352–53, sees the moral meaning as primary; Edward Armstrong, *Italian Studies* (London, 1934), pp. 12, 14, and A. M. Pellacani, *Dante vero: Nel poema della grazia l'apologia della ragione* (Padova, 1964), see the natural or human meaning as primary; Charles Allen Dinsmore, *Life of Dante Alighieri* (Boston, 1919), p. 233; Lenkeith, *Dante,* pp. 71–72; Hanns Lilje, *Dante als christlicher Denker* (Hamburg, 1955); Rocco Montano, *Suggerimenti per una lettura di Dante* (Napoli, 1956), p. 36, see the religious meaning as primary; E. G. Parodi, *Poesia e storia nella "Divina Commedia"* (Napoli, 1921), pp. 365–532; Paul Renucci, *Dante: Disciple et juge du monde gréco-latin* (Clermont-Ferrand, 1954), p. 412; Solmi, "Monarchia," *Nuova antologia, 70,* 321–31; Wicksteed, *Vita Nuova to Paradiso,* pp. xi–xii, see the political meaning as primary. A more unified picture is presented by Baldwin, *Medieval Rhetoric and Poetic,* p. 273; Barbi, *Life of Dante,* pp. 70–71; Charles Till Davis, *Dante and the Idea of Rome* (Oxford, 1957), the best work on this subject; Graf, *Roma,* passim; Kern, *Humana Civilitas;* Roedel, "Individuo e communità," *Individuum und Gemeinschaft,* pp. 515–18.

erary theory in its outline of how the *Divine Comedy* is to be understood.[214] He prefaces his remarks by asserting that the *Comedy* is a didactic work (*doctrinale opus*),[215] thereby affirming that poetry is capable of serving as a medium of instruction on the most exalted subjects. The truth of poetry, he observes, is dependent on its conformity to things as they are; [216] elsewhere in his letters he restates the principle that words, although they are accurate signs, fall short of the realities which they are designed to express.[217] Dante's explanation of the *Comedy* in the letter to Can Grande utilizes the rhetorical approach to poetry found in his previous works, but here, in his discussion of six basic characteristics of the work —its subject, author, form, aim, title, and the branch of philosophy to which it pertains—he expands this notion and removes some of his earlier theoretical inconsistencies.[218]

214. The subject of the authenticity of this letter has been debated extensively. A recent survey of the literature pro and con is supplied by Friedrich Schneider, "Der Brief an Can Grande," *DDJ, 34–35* (1957), 3–24. Schneider doubts the authenticity of the letter, and he is joined by C. G. Hardie, "The Epistle to Cangrande Again," *DDJ, 38* (1960), 51–74; Augusto Mancini, "Nuovi dubbi ed ipotesi sulla Epistola a Can Grande," *Atti della Reale Accademia d' Italia, Rendiconti della classe di scienzi morali e storiche,* serie settima, *4,* fasc. 9–12 (1943), 227–42; Luigi Pietrobono, "L'Epistola a Can Grande," *GD, 40, n. s., 10* (1937), 3–51; G. A. Scartazzini, *A Companion to Dante* (London, 1893), pp. 359, 442. Supporters of the authenticity of the letter include Edmund G. Gardner, *Dante* (New York, 1923), p. 128; Jacob, *Die Bedeutung der Führer Dantes,* p. 10; Francesco Mazzoni, "L'Epistola a Cangrande," *Accademia nazionale dei Lincei, Rendiconti della classe di scienzi morali, storiche e filologiche,* fasc. 3–4, serie 8, *10* (1955), 157–98; Philip McNair, "The Poetry of the 'Comedy,'" *The Mind of Dante,* ed. Limentani, p. 23; Edward Moore, *Studies in Dante: Third Series* (Oxford, 1903), pp. 296–343; Ovidio, *Studii,* pp. 448–85; Hiram Pflaum, "Il 'modus tractandi' della Divina Commedia," *GD, 39, n. s., 9* (1936), 153–78; Francesco Torraca, *Studi danteschi* (Napoli, 1912), pp. 249–304; Ernest Hatch Wilkins, *A History of Italian Literature* (Cambridge, Mass., 1954), p. 59.

215. *Epistola* X, Dante to Can Grande della Scala, ca. 1319, ¶ 6, Toynbee, p. 172. Toynbee considers the letter authentic, p. 163.

216. Ibid., ¶ 5, Toynbee, p. 172.

217. *Epistola* IV, Dante to Lord Moroello, Marquis of Malaspina, 1308–10, ll. 8–9, Toynbee, p. 37.

218. *Epistola* X, ¶ 6, Toynbee, p. 172.

Before doing this, however, he notes that the *Comedy* is polysemous. It contains four levels of meaning: the literal, allegorical, moral, and anagogical. The three latter levels, taken together, may be called allegorical in general. Dante illustrates this idea by analyzing the psalm *"In exitu Israel de Aegypto,"* following the standard fourfold method of scriptural exegesis.[219] It will be remembered that Dante also advocates this method in the *Convivio,* but his treatment of it in the letter to Can Grande represents a major theoretical departure. In the *Convivio,* Dante distinguishes between the allegory of theologians and the allegory of poets. He describes poetic allegory as a *bella menzogna,* a beautiful lie, masking the truth beneath it. The *Convivio* thus shows Dante tied to the theory of poetic fiction, which derogates from the truth of poetry by drawing a distinction between its true content and its fictive form. In the letter to Can Grande, however, Dante drops the bella menzogna attitude toward poetic form. He draws no distinction between the allegory of poets and the allegory of theologians, thereby assimilating to poetry the technique as well as the mission of theology. This point is essential to his conception of his role as the author of the *Comedy.* Dante arrogates to himself as a poet the tasks, methods, and powers of theology, and indicates his view that the *Comedy* can be understood in precisely the same way as Holy Scripture.

This thought has led to a good deal of debate among commentators. Some of them do not accept the idea that Dante really regarded himself as a theologian in the *Divine Comedy,* and thus view the work according to the critical principles of the *Convivio,* applying the bella menzogna idea to the *Comedy* or seeing no difference between the poetic theory in the *Convivio* and that in the letter to Can Grande.[220] Others perceive

219. Ibid., ¶ 7, Toynbee, p. 173–74. This point is confirmed by DeLubac, *Exégèse médiévale, 2,* part 2, 319–25.

220. See, for example, Sorrentino Andrea, "La coscienza poetica di Dante," *GD, 30* (1927), 182; De Bruyne, *L'Esthétique au moyen âge,* pp. 253–54; Francis Fergusson, *Dante's Drama of the Mind: A Modern Reading of the Purgatorio* (Princeton, 1953), pp. 3, 10, 26–27, 29, although he takes the op-

the differences between these two works and regard the letter to Can Grande, which makes possible a truly theological poetic, as an authentic guide to the understanding of the *Comedy*.[221] This latter group presents by far the more plausible case. Even if the letter to Can Grande should prove to be a forgery, it is, all agree, a contemporary document, and, what is equally important, the theory that it contains does explain the method of the *Comedy* in a far more complete, consistent, and convincing manner than the *Convivio* does.

Furthermore, the critical principles set forth in the letter to Can Grande find support in the ideas of some of Dante's contemporaries and in the earliest commentators on the *Divine*

posite view on p. 103; Allan H. Gilbert, *Dante and His Comedy* (New York, 1963), pp. 1–7, 12, 17, 28, 29–30, 42, 43; Charles Hall Grandgent, *The Power of Dante* (Boston, 1918), pp. 181–82; Richard Hamilton Green, "Dante's 'Allegory of the Poets' and the Mediaeval Theory of Poetic Fiction," *Comparative Literature, 9* (1957), 118–28; Engelbert Krebs, "Erlebnis und Allegorie in Dantes Commedia," *DDJ, 8* (1924), 11–25; *9* (1925), 98–108; P. Mandonnet, *Dante le théologien: Introduction à l'intelligence de la vie, des oeuvres et de l'art de Dante Alighieri* (Paris, 1935), pp. 182–83; Gustav E. Mueller, "Dante's Aesthetics," *The Personalist, 27* (1946), 386–98; Luigi Pietrobono, "L'allegorismo e Dante," *GD, 38,* n. s., *8* (1935), 86; Scartazzini, *Companion,* p. 441; Emanuele Testa, "Poetica e poesia in Dante," *Archivum Romanicum, 16* (1932), 211–53; Domenico Vittorini, *High Points in the History of Italian Literature* (New York, 1958), p. 26; Charles Williams, *The Figure of Beatrice: A Study in Dante* (New York, 1961), pp. 56–57.

221. See, for example, Barbi, *Life of Dante,* pp. 55–56; R. P. Blackmur, "Dante's Ten Terms for the Treatment of the Treatise," *Kenyon Review, 14* (1952), 291; Morton W. Bloomfield, "Symbolism in Medieval Literature," *Modern Philology, 56* (1958), 79; Curtius, "Medieval Basis of Western Thought," *Gesammelte Aufsätze,* p. 36; Giovanni Fallani, *Poesia e teologia nella Divina Commedia* (Milano, 1959), *1,* 5–21; Allan H. Gilbert, *Dante's Conception of Justice* (Durham, 1925), p. 67; Charles Hall Grandgent, *Dante* (New York, 1916), pp. 273–76; Mazzeo, *Medieval Cultural Tradition,* pp. 2–3; *Structure and Thought,* pp. 25–26, 33; Charles Grosvener Osgood, *Poetry as a Means of Grace* (Princeton, 1941), p. 31; Dorothy L. Sayers, *Introductory Papers on Dante* (New York, 1954), pp. xiv, 2, 7, 8–9, 11, 21–42, 102 ff., 107; Charles S. Singleton, *Commedia: Elements of Structure* (Cambridge, Mass., 1954), pp. viii, 1–2, 12, 14–16, 62, 84–98; "Dante and Myth," *Journal of the History of Ideas, 10* (1949), 489–502; *Journey to Beatrice* (Cambridge, Mass., 1958), p. 6; "The Irreducible Dove," *Comparative Literature, 9* (1957), 129–35; "The Other Journey," *Kenyon Review, 14* (1952), 189–206.

Comedy. Giovanni del Virgilio, a friend of Dante with whom he exchanged eclogues and correspondence, wrote an epitaph on him which aptly expresses the attitude toward poetry found in the letter to Can Grande:

> Dante, the theologian, skilled in every branch of knowledge that philosophy may cherish in her illustrious bosom, glory of the muses, author most acceptable to the vulgar, here lieth and smiteth either pole with his fame; who assigned their places to the defunct and their respective places to the twin swords, in laic and rhetoric fashion.[222]

The idea of the poet as theologian is also found in Mussato.[223] Benvenuto da Imola, one of the earliest commentators on the *Comedy,* sees Dante as a theologian whose style resembles that of Holy Scripture in that it presents an elevated subject in a readily accessible form.[224] Pietro Alighieri, Dante's son, who wrote a commentary on the *Divine Comedy* in 1340–41, adheres to the principles of the letter to Can Grande closely, calling his father a "glorious theologian, philosopher, and poet";[225] he uses the polysemous method as well in analyzing the work.

Later on in the fourteenth century, Boccaccio repeats and extends this idea, relating the contribution of Dante to his

222. Philip H. Wicksteed and Edmund G. Gardner, *Dante and Giovanni del Virgilio, Including a Critical Edition of the Text of Dante's 'Eclogae Latinae' and of the Poetic Remains of Giovanni del Virgilio* (Westminster, 1902), p. 175. The translation is Wicksteed and Gardner's. See also August Buck, "Dante im Urteil der Literaturästhetik des italienischen Humanismus," *DDJ, 28* (1949), 2–3; Ernst Robert Curtius, "Theologische Poetik im italienischen Trecento," *Zeitschrift für Romanische Philologie, 60* (1940), 1.

223. Curtius, "Theologische Poetik," pp. 3–15.

224. Louis B. Rossi, "Dante and the Poetic Tradition in the Commentary of Benvenuto da Imola," *Italica, 32* (1955), 215–21.

225. Pietro Alighieri, *Super Dantis ipsius genitoris Comoediam commentarium* (Florentiae, 1845), p. 3. See also John Paul Bowden, *An Analysis of Pietro Alighieri's Commentary on the Divine Comedy* (New York, 1951); Francesco Mazzoni, "Pietro Alighieri interprete di Dante," *Studi danteschi, 40* (1963), 279–360.

own humanistic conception of poetry. Boccaccio sees Dante as a poet, philosopher, and theologian, learned in all the arts, including that of divinity,[226] as a truly Christian poet, and as an innovator, in that no work on such a grand scale as the *Comedy* had been essayed in the vernacular by a layman before.[227] Dante wrote in the vernacular, according to Boccaccio, in order to teach and to delight his audience more effectively, out of the motive of service to those less learned than himself, as well as because it was the modern thing to do.[228] Dante's didacticism is adopted happily by Boccaccio, who develops it into the view that poetry is the supreme mode of knowledge, communication, and instruction. Poetry, he says, subsumes all the other arts, including theology; it is the most powerful way to move men's minds and hearts; and it is aided in its tasks by Divine inspiration.[229] While this theory goes farther than Dante's, it does not go very much farther. In his *Commento sopra il Dante,* a work deriving from the lectureship on Dante which Boccaccio held in Florence from 1373 to 1375, he applies the fourfold method to the *Comedy* in the manner of the letter to Can Grande.[230] All in all, Boccaccio strikes a note repeated by many Florentines of his period in praising Dante as the restorer of good poetry, the genius by whom the Muses returned to Italy.[231] Although some modern scholars may have had trouble with the point, Dante's contemporaries and immediate successors clearly had little difficulty in accepting the theological poetic of the letter to Can Grande and in applying it to the *Divine Comedy.*

Taking the letter to Can Grande at its word, then, let us re-

226. Giovanni Boccaccio, *Genealogie deorum gentilium libri,* XIV, 10, Romano, 2, 710; *Vita di Dante e difesa di poesia,* III, Muscetta, pp. 8–9.

227. *Vita di Dante,* XXVI, Muscetta, p. 46.

228. Ibid., Muscetta, p. 49.

229. Ibid., XXI–XXII, Muscetta, pp. 33–39; *Genealogie deorum,* XIV, 6–7, Romano, 2, 697–701.

230. Giovanni Boccaccio, *Il commento alla Divina Commedia e gli altri scritti intorno di Dante,* Lez. V, Guerri (Bari, 1918), *1,* 162–63. See also Edward Moore, *Dante and His Early Biographers* (London, 1890), pp. 4–5.

231. *Vita di Dante,* II, Muscetta, p. 7; Buck, "Dante," *DDJ, 28,* 4–7.

turn to Dante's analysis of the *Comedy's* subject, author, form, aim, title, and philosophical type. The subject, says Dante, is twofold, depending on whether one looks at the poem literally or allegorically. Literally speaking, the poem is about "the state of souls after death, pure and simple." Allegorically speaking, "the subject is man according as by his merits or demerits in the exercise of his free will he is deserving of reward or punishment by justice." [232] Both of these levels must be taken into account, since, according to the fourfold method, all senses of the text are present in it simultaneously. While the literal level is the foundation upon which the allegorical meanings are based, and must be established first, the allegorical levels of meaning do not subsume or obliterate the literal level.

This point is of major importance in understanding Dante's use of allegory in the *Divine Comedy*. It means, in the first place, that allegory is never extrinsic to the poem but is built into it. This is a notion which may need to be restated in the light of the recent debate on Dante between the followers of Benedetto Croce and his opponents. Croce and his followers maintain that all poetry is essentially lyrical, the expression of the inner emotions of the poet. They tend to regard didacticism and the allegories by means of which it operates in the *Divine Comedy* as obstructive, devoid of artistic merit. Whatever truly poetic qualities the poem contains, they argue, spring from a succession of lyric moments, all but hidden in the interstices of its allegorical superstructure. [233] Opponents

232. *Epistola* X, ¶ 8, Toynbee, p. 200.

233. A helpful summary of the pro- and anti-Crocean literature may be found in Egidio Guidubaldi, "Poesia e non-poesia negli ultimi quarant'anni di critica dantesca in Italia," *Civiltà cattolica, 110,* 4 (1959), 42–52. H. Hatzfeld, "Modern Literary Scholarship as Reflected in Dante Criticism," *Comparative Literature, 3* (1951), 289–309, is also useful. For Croce's position, see Benedetto Croce, *The Poetry of Dante* (New York, 1922), pp. 5–6, 11, 14–15, 19–20, 34–36, 91 ff., 296 ff. Croce has been more or less faithfully seconded by Francesco Biondolillo, *Poetica e poesia di Dante* (Messina, 1948); Getto, *Aspetti,* pp. 125–88; Allan H. Gilbert, "Doctrine and Romance in Dante's *Commedia*," *Renaissance Papers, 1960,* Published by the Southeastern Renaissance Conference, 1961,

of Croce's position and its recent variants have stressed, on the other hand, that allegory is an integral part of the *Comedy,* and that one must submit oneself to the aesthetic of the poem in order to understand it.[234]

This latter interpretation is supported by the scriptural attitude which Dante takes toward his own poem,[235] an attitude that he puts into practice within the *Comedy.* The symbolic point of view that he adopts toward his characters, like the fourfold method of biblical exegesis, may be described as typological.[236] Most of the figures whom Dante places in the

---

pp. 104–10; Gioacchino Natoli, "Il valore estetico del simbolo nell'arte di Dante," *Sophia, 23* (1955), 38–52; Francesco de Sanctis, *History of Italian Literature* (New York, 1959), *1,* 67–69, 160, 171, 176–77, 178–263; *Lezioni sulla Divina Commedia* (Bari, 1955), pp. 11–13, 14, 26, 33, 37–44; Theophil Spoerri, *Dante und die europäische Literatur* (Stuttgart, 1963); John Addington Symonds, *An Introduction to the Study of Dante* (London, 1906), pp. 103, 112; Tonelli, *Dante,* pp. 19, 20–21, 22–23, 28, 39–40.

234. See, for example, T. S. Eliot, *Dante* (London, 1930), 43; Mueller, "Dante's Aesthetics," *The Personalist, 27,* 392; Pietrobono, "L'allegorismo e Dante," *GD, 38,* n. s., *8,* 85–102; "Per l'allegoria di Dante," *GD, 25* (1922), 206–10; "Struttura allegorica e poesia nella Divina Commedia," *GD, 43,* n. s., *13* (1940), 9–45; Luigi Pirandello, "The Poetry of Dante," *Dante: A Collection of Critical Essays,* ed. John Freccero (Englewood Cliffs, N.J., 1965), pp. 14–22; Singleton, "Dante and Myth," *Journal of the History of Ideas, 10,* 489; Mark Van Doren, "The Divine Comedy," *Sewanee Review, 54* (1946), 349–95; Witte, *Essays on Dante,* p. 17.

235. Freccero, *Dante,* p. 3.

236. Quite a few scholars have noted the typological dimensions of Dante's symbolism. See Auerbach, *Dante,* pp. 86–90; "Figura," *Neue Dantestudien* (Istanbul, 1944), pp. 11–71; "Figurative Texts Illustrating Certain Passages of Dante's *Commedia,*" *Speculum, 21* (1946), 474–89; "Typological Symbolism in Medieval Literature," *Yale French Studies, 9* (1952), 3–10; Baldwin, *Medieval Rhetoric and Poetic,* p. 274; Michele Barbi, *Problemi fondamentali per un nuovo commento della Divina Commedia* (Firenze, 1956), pp. 118–19; Thomas G. Bergin, "On the *Personae* of the *Comedy,*" *Italica, 42* (1965), 1–7; Irma Brandeis, *The Ladder of Vision: A Study of Dante's Comedy* (London, 1960), pp. 17–18; Chydenius, *The Typological Problem,* p. 49 and passim; W. P. Ker, "Allegory and Myth," *Dante: Essays in Commemoration, 1321–1921,* ed. Antonio Cippico et al. (London, 1921), pp. 33–36; M.-J. Lagrange, "Le réalisme et le symbolisme de Dante," *Revue biblique, 46* (1937), 481–505; Mazzeo, *Medieval Cultural Tradition,* p. 7; Passerin d'Entrèves, *Dante politico,* p. 43; Sayers, *Introductory Papers on Dante,* pp. xiv, 7, 102–07; *Further Papers on Dante* (New York, 1957), pp. 56, 58–59; Charles S. Singleton, "In Exitu Israel

poem, with the exception of a number of classical monsters, had a real, historical existence. This real, earthly existence is the literal level; Dante's personnel, with the exception of those in Purgatory, are "frozen" eternally in the other world in precisely the moral condition in which they died. In the most obvious sense of the word, they represent themselves. At the same time, Dante's characters represent various ethical, political, intellectual, and religious types from which the reader can infer lessons for his own personal benefit and for the reform of Christian society. Since the poem depicts life after death, the characters in the *Comedy* also possess an anagogical dimension, pointing to the future, to the condition of the human soul and of Christian society at the end of time. Each character thus contains several levels of meaning, all of which are designed to instruct the reader. The historical existence of Dante's characters comes first; it is the foundation upon which their allegorical meanings are based. Virtues and vices do not exist in the abstract; they can only be found in the context of a concrete, human life.

Thus, allegory in the *Comedy* does not blot out historicity. The literal meaning points toward a profounder meaning; at the same time, the profounder meaning is present in, consistent with, and expressed through, the literal meaning. The higher and the lower do not stand over against each other. If one reads the *Comedy* rightly, there is no such thing as a character whose vivid humanity distracts one's eyes from his moral significance in the work, and there is no such thing as a character who is "purely symbolic." In accordance with the contemporary theory of biblical typology, the literal meaning may never be discarded as irrelevant or as merely ancillary to

de Aegypto," *Dante,* ed. Freccero, pp. 103, 112; "The Other Journey," *Kenyon Review, 14,* 189–206. On the other hand, for the view of allegory as sublimation or as "purely symbolic," see Irma Brandeis, "Metaphor in the Divine Comedy," *Hudson Review, 8* (1956), 557–75; Kenelm Foster, "The Mind in Love: Dante's Philosophy," *Dante,* ed. Freccero, p. 48; Eleanor F. Jourdain, *Le symbolisme dans la Divine Comédie de Dante* (Paris, 1904), p. 3; Mandonnet, *Dante,* pp. 29–65.

the allegorical meaning, even after the reader has grasped the symbolic reference. Dante's symbolism of personalities has a twofold thrust. There is a movement of sublimation, as the mind of the reader proceeds from the most concrete level of meaning to the most universal. At the same time, there is a movement of descent, in which the universal is realized in the concrete. The theoretical basis for this twofold process is the Incarnation,[237] which has corollaries for Dante in aesthetics as well as in ethics and epistemology. The Incarnation, for Dante no less than for Augustine, transforms the sensible world. As a result, concrete, material things, individual persons as moral ends, and earthly beauties as objects of authentic aesthetic experience become means by which God chooses to descend to man, in and through the conditions of human life. They are not merely rungs of a ladder by means of which man can transcend the world in order to get to God. The motive of Dantean typology is not to transcend human existence by using the world as a vehicle to God and then leaving it behind. Rather, its motive is to infuse the world and human existence with Divine wisdom, power, and love, to transform it from within. Only thus may the selfish and disintegrative tendencies of mankind be righted, and men achieve a relation of rectitude to other men and to God.

An important corollary of this idea is Dante's recognition of the cumulative nature of experience. He resists a simplistic presentation of individuals, including himself as a character in the *Comedy*. This can be seen by considering any number of characters in the poem, but it is particularly evident in the case of Dante's three guides in the *Comedy*, Vergil, Beatrice, and St. Bernard. There is a variety of reasons why these three personages are important to Dante. While efforts have

237. This point has been noted by Andrew Bongiorno, "The Divine Comedy," unpublished Humanities Lecture, Oberlin College, January 6, 1958, pp. 5–6 (my thanks to Professor Bongiorno for a copy of this lecture); Fletcher, *Dante,* p. 99; Freccero, *Dante,* p. 7; Montano, *Suggerimento,* pp. 20–21, 46; Singleton, *Commedia,* pp. 74–75; Williams, *The Figure of Beatrice,* pp. 9–11; Zingarelli, *La vita,* 2, 882.

been made to narrow their significance to one dimension, it is more accurate to say that each of them has several layers of meaning. These layers represent the stages of Dante's development or the various facets of ethics, politics, religion, literature, and public and private life which make up his central theme. It is worth keeping in mind, as Bergin has observed, that "temperamentally Dante was reluctant to admit any inconsistencies in his life; he had an almost obsessive drive for unity of pattern; superseded opinions or altered attitudes are never suppressed but always assimilated." [238]

This point is particularly true in the case of Beatrice. There is a progression in Dante's attitude toward Beatrice from the *Vita nuova* to the *Divine Comedy*.[239] Within the *Vita nuova*, Dante chronicles his shifting view of his lady as the purveyor of a purely secular type of ennoblement, according to the canons of the dolce stil nuovo, to the cause of the poet's religious conversion. While Beatrice drops from view in the *Convivio*, Dante chooses there to apostrophize philosophy in the image of a lady, which permits him to apply to her the stylistic conventions of his earlier lyrics while using them to denote a broader set of functions. In the *Comedy*, Beatrice is usually taken to represent grace, theology, the Church, Christ; [240] she is treated by Dante as a means of salvation in a clearly religious sense. Yet, for all this, she remains a real person.[241] All of the meanings that she has had for Dante during the course of his life are present in the Beatrice of the *Comedy*.[242]

238. Bergin, *Dante,* p. 98.

239. Gilbert, *Dante,* pp. 146–51.

240. As noted by Fletcher, *Dante,* pp. 139–40; Singleton, *Commedia,* pp. 51–59; *Journey to Beatrice,* pp. 86, 88; *Essay on the Vita Nuova,* pp. 4, 24, 56 (although he reads the Christ-Beatrice back into the *Vita nuova*); Bernard Stambler, "The Confrontation of Beatrice and Dante: *Purgatorio* XXX," *Italica, 42* (1965), 61–75.

241. Williams, *The Figure of Beatrice,* pp. 7–8. Cf. Gratia Eaton Baldwin, *The New Beatrice: Or the Virtue that Counsels* (New York, 1928), and Mandonnet, *Dante,* pp. 46–49, 56–65, who regard Beatrice as a purely transcendental figure or as the hypostasis of Dante's inner crises, respectively.

242. Auerbach, *Dante,* pp. 99–100.

The fusion of past and present is set forth by Dante in the emotion-charged scene where he first sets eyes upon Beatrice in the Earthly Paradise at the top of the mountain of Purgatory. Beatrice, like Dante's other guides, teaches, admonishes, and counsels him, illustrating through her conversation and behavior the attitude which she wants Dante to take to the sights and personages he encounters in the realms through which she leads him. But before she can do this, Dante must recognize the theological role she plays in the *Comedy,* which he does not do at once. In *Purgatorio* XXX and XXXI, Dante rehearses all his previous attitudes toward Beatrice and summarizes the change that he must undergo in order to perceive her current significance.

In the earlier portions of the *Comedy* Beatrice is described as an emissary from heaven, sent to assist Dante in the moral struggles which have led him into the dark wood of *Inferno* I.[243] Vergil occasionally invokes her mission in explaining Dante's presence in Hell and Purgatory to the souls or guardians of those realms; [244] he spurs on Dante's lagging spirit by reminding him that Beatrice is presiding over their journey, and that Dante can hope to see her at the top of the mountain of Purgatory.[245] The reader is thus prepared early in the work for a Beatrice whose function has become expressly religious. Dante contrasts this view of Beatrice, with which he has already supplied the reader, with the reaction to Beatrice that he experiences as a character in the poem. When Dante first sees the veiled lady clothed in red, white, and green, he recognizes her as the lady of the *Vita nuova:*

And my spirit, that now so long a time had passed,
　　since, trembling in her presence, it had been
　　broken down with awe,
Without having further knowledge by mine eyes through

243. *Inf.,* II, 52–142.
244. Ibid., XII, 88–90; *Purg.,* I, 52–54; VII, 24.
245. *Inf.,* X, 130–32; *Purg.,* VI, 43–48; IX, 52–57; XV, 76–78; XVIII, 73–75; XXVII, 34–42.

> hidden virtue which went out from her, felt the
> mighty power of ancient love
> Soon as on my sight the lofty virtue smote, which
> already had pierced me ere I was out of my boyhood,
> I turned to the left with the trust with which the
> little child runs to his mother when he is frightened
> or when he is afflicted,
> To say to Virgil: "Less than a drachm of blood is left
> in me that trembleth not; I recognize the tokens of
> an ancient flame." [246]

Vergil has, however, departed, and Dante weeps bitterly. Beatrice chides Dante, both for his seeking of a guide whom he no longer needs and for his response to her, a response indicating an unsatisfactory grasp of her current meaning. Standing "queenlike, in bearing yet stern," she addresses Dante by name—the only point in the *Comedy* where his name is mentioned—and underlines her words by repetition:

> Dante, for that Virgil goeth away, weep not yet, weep
> not yet, for thou must weep by other sword.

and

> Look at me well; verily I am, verily I am Beatrice.[247]

Straightaway the angels, "who ever accord their notes after the melodies of the eternal spheres," begin to sing, *In te, Domine, speravi,* and Dante is so moved that "the ice which had closed about my heart became breath and water." [248] Beatrice, however, tells the angels that she is inflicting suffering on Dante as a penance for having abandoned her. She notes that Dante has neglected his gifts of nature and grace, and that, after her death, he had failed to appreciate the deep-

---

246. *Purg.,* XXX, 34–48. This attitude is also reflected in XXVII, 37–42, where Dante alludes to Pyramus and Thisbe in referring to his attitude toward Beatrice.
247. Ibid., XXX, 55–57, 73.
248. Ibid., 92–93, 97–98.

ening inspiration which she gave him in life, until he had virtually lost himself. This, she explains, is why she sponsored his descent into Hell and his ascent of the mountain of Purgatory:

> Not only by the operation of the mighty spheres that
>   direct each seed to some end . . .
> But by the bounty of graces divine, which have for
>   their rain vapours so high that our eyes reach
>   not nigh them,
> This man was such in his new life potentially, that
>   every good talent would have made wondrous increase
>   in him.
> But so much the more rank and wild the ground becomes
>   with evil seed and untilled, the more it hath of
>   good strength of soil.
> Sometime I sustained him with my countenance; showing
>   my youthful eyes to him I led him with me turned to
>   the right goal.
> So soon as I was on the threshold of my second age, and
>   I changed life, he forsook me, and gave him
>   to others.
> When I was risen from flesh to spirit, and beauty
>   and virtue were increased within me, I was less
>   precious and less pleasing to him;
> And he did turn his steps by a way not true, pursuing
>   false visions of good, that pay back no promise
>   entire.
> Nor did it avail me to gain inspirations, with which
>   in dream and otherwise, I called him back; so
>   little he recked of them.
> So low sank he, that all means for his salvation were
>   already short, save showing him the lost people.
> For this I visited the portal of the dead, and to him
>   who has guided him up hither, weeping my prayers
>   were borne.

> God's high decree would be broken, if Lethe were passed,
> and such viands were tasted, without some scot of
> penitence that may shed tears.[249]

Beatrice then adjures Dante to confess his sins, asking him what drew him away from the desire for her which had once led him to love the good. Dante tells of his pursuit of false pleasures. Beatrice once more reminds him that, if her earthly state drew him to the good, so much more should her risen state have inspired him toward heavenly delights. To emphasize the point, she looks at the Griffon, the symbol of Christ, which Dante sees reflected in her eyes, from which, the angels note, "love once drew his shafts at thee." This sight makes Dante recognize the exalted state of Beatrice:

> . . . to me she seemed to surpass more her ancient
> self, than she surpassed the others here when she
> was with us.
> The nettle of repentance here so did sting me, that
> of all other things, that which turned me most to
> love of it became most hateful to me
> So much remorse gnawed at my heart that I fell van-
> quished, and what I then became, she knoweth who
> gave me the cause.[250]

The vision of the Griffon, reflected in Beatrice's eyes, in which Dante strives to quench his own eyes' "ten years' thirst," [251] momentarily blinds him. But, having grasped the present function of Beatrice, he is now ready to pass through Lethe and Eunoë, and to acquire, through Beatrice, the progressive strengthening of his sight which eventually enables him to look directly at Beatrice and then to move beyond her.

Dante's summary of the theme of the dolce stil nuovo lady whose meaning acquires transcendent proportions in the *Com-*

249. Ibid., 109–45.
250. Ibid., XXXI, 117, 83–90.
251. Ibid., XXXII, 2.

edy is matched by his frequent use of the dolce stil nuovo tropes of the lady's eyes and smile to denote the process of his religious enlightenment. It will be recalled that Dante retains these devices as he moves from the *Vita nuova* to the *Convivio,* and that he broadens their epistemological meaning in the latter work, the eyes and smile standing there for the lady's demonstrations and persuasions, respectively. In the *Comedy,* Dante exploits the demonstrative and persuasive functions of Beatrice's eyes and smile thoroughly, using them as metaphors of speech and as a means of describing Beatrice's mediation of wisdom and love to him. In addition, he integrates these tropes with his symbolism of light and darkness, which has frequently been noted in the *Comedy* as a metaphor of spiritual illumination or obfuscation, and which has been related to the symbol of God as light as manifested in medieval light metaphysics.[252] A full appreciation of the functions of Beatrice's eyes and smile in the *Comedy* can be gained only by viewing the sense of sight in the wider context of pleasant and unpleasant sensible environments as tokens of the spiritual atmospheres of the three realms, which embraces colors, sounds, smells, and the general physical comfort or discomfort experienced by Dante the traveler.

Dante makes clear the synaesthetic blending of the senses in his first statement about the atmosphere of Hell. He characterizes Hell as the realm "where the Sun is silent" [253] and where the souls manifest their grief through their eyes.[254] What colors there are in Hell are dark and depressing, with the exception of the Limbo of virtuous pagans, which is bright

252. Brandeis, *Ladder of Vision,* p. 115; Brizio Casciola, *L'Enimma dantesco* (Bergamo, 1950), p. 62; De Bruyne, *Études d'esthétique médiévale, 3,* 3–29; Gilbert, *Dante,* pp. 7–17, 22, 38; Ulrich Leo, *Sehen und Wirklichkeit bei Dante* (Frankfurt am Main, 1957), p. 84; Mazzeo, *Medieval Cultural Tradition,* pp. 23, 56–132, 170–71; *Structure and Thought,* pp. 1, 7–8, 10–14, 18; Singleton, *Commedia,* pp. 19, 22–23; *Journey to Beatrice,* pp. 15–34; Allen Tate, "The Symbolic Imagination: A Meditation on Dante's Three Mirrors," *Kenyon Review, 14* (1952), 272–77.

253. *Inf.,* I, 60.

254. Ibid., XVII, 46.

with an enamel-green lawn.[255] Dante notes the "dusky air"
of Hell [256] and its light from below as he descends into it.
Charon, the ferryman of the Styx, informs Dante and Vergil
that he is taking them into eternal darkness, and the topography of the river and its environs show a "livid marsh,"
"brown water," and a "dusky champaign." [257] As they go
farther into the "blind world" of Hell,[258] Dante comments
repeatedly on the dark and heavy air [259] and the fetid
odors [260] that they encounter. Specific areas of Hell are
given particularly unappetizing visual characteristics. The
avaricious and prodigal are depicted as so dark as to be
scarcely recognizable; having lived undiscerning lives, they
have become difficult to discern in death.[261] The marsh of
sloth, complete with "black mire," "dusky waves," and "water
darker than perse," bathes a "grey malignant shore." [262] The
wood of the suicides is uncharted; it is dusky, not green, and
is filled with distorted trees bearing gnarled branches on which
withered, poisonous thorns grow instead of fruit.[263] Male-
bolge is dark from end to end,[264] and the only colors which
Dante notes there are livid and iron-grey [265] and harsh, pun-
ishing flame.[266] At the very bottom of the pit of Hell, in Giu-
decca, where it is "less than night and less than day," Dante
comments on the "want of light," and the reader heaves a sigh
of relief with him as he at last leaves the Inferno to return to
the "bright world." [267]

255. Ibid., IV, 118.
256. Ibid., II, 1.
257. Ibid., III, 87, 98, 118, 130.
258. Ibid., IV, 13; XXVII, 25.
259. Ibid., VI, 11; IX, 82; XVI, 130; XXXI, 37.
260. Ibid., VI, 12; VII, 28; IX, 31; X, 136; XXIX, 50–51.
261. Ibid., VII, 52–54.
262. Ibid., 124, 104, 103, 108.
263. Ibid., XIII, 2–6.
264. Ibid., XXI, 6; XXIV, 71.
265. Ibid., XVIII, 2; XIX, 14.
266. Ibid., XIX, 25, 33; XXVI, 31, 38–42, 47–48, 52–54, 58, 64–65, 76, 79,
85–90; XXVIII, 1–2, 4–6, 13–15, 57–59, 63, 127, 130–32.
267. Ibid., XXXI, 10; XXXIV, 99, 134.

The move from Hell to Purgatory is at once marked by a distinct improvement in the sensible qualities of the atmosphere. The pleasing music of psalms and hymns is heard throughout this realm, and from time to time Dante mentions ambrosial fragrances.[268] As Dante approaches Purgatory, the morning star is rising; the sky reveals the "sweet hue of orient sapphire"; the heavens rejoice—a sight which, he observes, "to mine eyes restored delight." [269] In general, Dante finds it easy to see in Purgatory, except on the ledge of the wrathful, where smoke obscures his sight.[270] Angels appear occasionally in Purgatory. One of them is described as a light on the sea, a whiteness too bright to look at; [271] another is depicted as a beauteous creature, robed in white, with a face like the morning star.[272] Their clothing is not always white; in *Purgatorio* VIII, their raiment was "green, as tender leaves just born." [273]

Dante's physical surroundings in Purgatory are also bright and colorful. The colors may have specific symbolic meanings, as in the case of the white, black, and red steps of contrition, confession, and love, which Dante must ascend in order to enter Purgatory; [274] the white, green, and red garb of Beatrice, signifying faith, hope and charity; [275] and the purple foliage on the imperial tree, signifying royalty.[276] The Eagle which Dante sees in a dream has golden plumage,[277] and the trees which counsel abstinence and warn against gluttony have flourishing green leaves.[278] In other instances, however, brightness and color mainly designate the spiritual optimism

268. *Purg.*, VII, 80–81; XXIV, 150; XXVIII, 6–7; XXIX, 22, 36.
269. Ibid., I, 13, 16.
270. Ibid., XV, 142–XVII, 12.
271. Ibid., II, 17, 38–39; VIII, 34–35.
272. Ibid., XII, 88–90.
273. Ibid., VIII, 28–29.
274. Ibid., IX, 94–102.
275. Ibid., XXX, 31–33.
276. Ibid., XXXII, 58.
277. Ibid., IX, 20.
278. Ibid., XXIII, 69; XXIV, 103.

and confidence in God which pervade this realm. Even in the ante-Purgatory, Dante and Vergil can find a spot to spend the night decorated with brilliantly colored grass and flowers:

> Gold and fine silver, cramoisy and white, Indian
> wood bright and clear, fresh emerald at the
> moment it is split,
> Would each be surpassed in colour by the grass and
> by the flowers placed within that fold, as the
> less is surpassed by the greater.
> Not only had Nature painted there, but the sweetness
> of a thousand scents made there one, unknown and
> indefinable.[279]

The Earthly Paradise at the top of the mountain, manifesting the characteristics of the classical *locus amoenus,* is even more replete with pleasing sights. In *Purgatorio* XXVII, Dante finds himself in a grassy clearing in a lush and verdant forest, containing bright-hued and fragrant flowers, a stream, a sweet breeze, and singing birds.[280] Flowers are frequently mentioned in the Earthly Paradise, as are the colors gold, red, white, green, rose, and purple.[281] Significantly, the chariot symbolizing the corrupt Church is not given color.[282]

In Paradise, the variegated hues of Purgatory give way for the most part to pure light. Light is treated by Dante as a metaphysical principle, an epistemological principle, and an index of blessedness, and it grows increasingly brilliant as he advances farther and farther into heaven. He describes colors, where they occur, as the scintillations of jewels; thus he characterizes a cloud as a "diamond in the sun," the moon as the "eternal pearl,"[283] and the Virgin Mary as a "sapphire."[284]

279. Ibid., VII, 73–81.
280. Ibid., XXVIII, 1–2, 6–7, 14–18, 25–42, 55–56.
281. Ibid., 36, 41, 55–56; XXIX, 35, 65–66, 73–78, 84, 88, 93, 113–14, 122–31, 148; XXX, 23, 28, 31–33; XXXI, 16; XXXII, 58; XXXIII, 110.
282. Ibid., XXXII, 104–60.
283. *Par.,* II, 31–33, 34.
284. Ibid., XXIII, 101.

The blessed souls form a river of light in *Paradiso* XXX, and they are further depicted as blossoms, as topazes, and as rubies set in gold.[285] The angels hovering above the Empyrean Rose like bees are red, gold, and white.[286] However, it is not so much color as candlepower that characterizes the sights in Paradise. On arriving in heaven, Dante's first reaction is to notice that there is much more light here than elsewhere: "Meseemed that day was added unto day, as though he who hath the power, had adorned heaven with a second sun."[287] He invokes God as "O Love who rulest heaven, . . . who with thy light didst lift me up . . ." and he hears the harmony of the spheres, noting that "the newness of the sound and the great light kindled in me a longing for their cause."[288]

In Paradise, as elsewhere, sight and sound are joined. Dante hears many songs of unearthly beauty. The souls whom he meets above the Moon are described as lights, and they grow more brilliant and more beautiful the more perfectly they exemplify the love of God and man.[289] Both light and melody are anologized to joy.[290] The union of light, sound, and joy reveals Dante's acceptance of the Augustinian correlation of love and knowledge. He notes this correlation repeatedly throughout the *Comedy*[291] and underlines the point by reinterpreting his earlier lyric, "Luce intelletual, piena d'amore," in terms of heavenly vision in the Empyrean.[292] Dante's eyes are opened gradually as he moves through heaven, and at many points he is dazzled because his eyes are not yet strong

285. Ibid., XXX, 61–66, 76; IX, 69; XV, 85; XIX, 4; XXII, 29.

286. Ibid., XXXI, 13–14.

287. Ibid., I, 61–63.

288. Ibid., 74–75, 82–84.

289. Ibid., VIII, 46–48; IX, 13–15; X, 82–84; XI, 16–18; XII, 31–33; XIV, 37–42; XVIII, 25–27; XXI, 43–44.

290. Ibid., II, 28; V, 106–08, 133–39; XIV, 17–24; XXI, 64–66, 88–90.

291. *Inf.*, III, 1–9, 16–18; *Par.*, VII, 58–60; XI, 28–39; XIV, 37–42; XV, 73–75; XXVII, 88–90; XXVIII, 70–72; XXX, 40–42. Noted also by Steinbüchel, *Grosse Gestalten*, p. 218.

292. *Par.*, XXX, 40–42.

enough to perceive the objects before them. But at other points he notes that he is now able to see things that he previously could not see.[293] He must use various created lights, including Beatrice, as "mirrors" of the reflected glory of God; [294] but he must also learn to transcend them, as Beatrice observes in *Paradiso* XVIII: "Not only in my eyes is Paradise." [295] At the point when Beatrice is fast approaching the end of her tutelage of Dante, she directs him to "see now the height and breadth of the eternal worth, since it hath made itself so many mirrors wherein it breaketh." [296] Under the guidance of St. Bernard, Dante is once more instructed to develop his sight gradually in preparation for the vision of God,[297] which is finally depicted as three concentric circles of light.[298]

In the context of this symbolism of light and sound, related as it is to the interaction of love and knowledge, the eyes and smile of Beatrice retain, yet go far beyond, their dolce stil nuovo significance and are reinterpreted as tokens of her commission to guide Dante through the demonstrations of Divine wisdom and the persuasions of Christian charity. Beatrice's eyes and smile are sometimes treated separately. Dante describes her eyes as "the beauteous eyes whence love had made the noose to capture me." [299] They are sometimes turned upward, as a means of directing Dante's gaze to the things of heaven.[300] At other times, they are turned at Dante himself and convey Beatrice's instruction, forgiveness, and permission

293. *Purg.*, XXXII, 1–3; *Par.*, XIV, 76–84; XVIII, 13–21; XXI, 140–42; XXIII, 16–18, 46–48; XXX, 46–60.

294. *Par.*, XXI, 16–18.

295. Ibid., XVIII, 21. Note also in this connection Beatrice's joy when Dante's love of God eclipses her, X, 55–63.

296. Ibid., XXIX, 42–44.

297. Ibid., XXXI, 94–99; XXXII, 4–87, 109–50; XXXIII, 49–54.

298. Ibid., XXXIII, 115–33.

299. Ibid., XXVIII, 11–12.

300. *Purg.*, XXXI, 80–81; *Par.*, I, 46–47; II, 22; XVII, 114.

to speak, and generally manifest her joy and holiness.[301] Dante notes that she looks at him "to catch the eye and so possess the mind." [302] The smile, when referred to separately, is generally a manifestation of the love which persuades; the souls in *Paradiso* XXXI have smiling faces "suasive of love." [303] Usually Beatrice's smiles precede or are concurrent with her discourses; she smiles before or while speaking so that her words may move Dante's heart and mind.[304]

For Dante, Beatrice's eyes and smile are the chief characteristics of her beauty; [305] and beauty is a means of knowing and loving God. The union of love and knowledge and the Ciceronian ideals of delight, instruction, and persuasion are further reflected in the numerous passages where Dante blends Beatrice's eyes and smile or where he refers to one of them in terms of the other. Thus, Beatrice's eyes glow or sparkle as she smiles; [306] her eyes laugh and smile; [307] her smile is a light.[308] The integration of love and knowledge, vision and hearing, is further shown at the point when Beatrice removes all the scales from Dante's eyes after he has successfully described the nature of love to St. John.[309] Finally, to emphasize the idea still more, Dante states in the Heaven of the Fixed Stars, "Meseemed I was beholding the smile of the universe; wherefore my intoxication entered both by hearing and by sight." [310]

301. *Purg.*, XXX, 66; XXXI, 115–23; XXXIII, 16–21; *Par.*, I, 100–41; III, 124–30; IV, 139–42; V, 1–6; IX, 16–18; XVIII, 7–9; XXIII, 46–48; XXVI, 13–15.

302. *Par.*, XXVII, 92.

303. Ibid., XXXI, 50.

304. *Purg.*, XXXIII, 95; *Par.*, I, 95; II, 52; VII, 17; XVI, 13–16; XVII, 121–24; XXII, 10–11; XXV, 28; XXVII, 103–04.

305. *Par.*, XXI, 4–12; XXVIII, 11; XXX, 14–27.

306. Ibid., III, 24, 42; V, 125–26.

307. Ibid., X, 61–63; XV, 34.

308. Ibid., XVIII, 19.

309. Ibid., XXVI, 76–78.

310. Ibid., XXVII, 4–6. See also XV, 37.

The fact that Dante can present Beatrice's earlier meanings for him while expanding them in a new theological perspective indicates the many-layered significance that she possesses in the *Comedy*. An analogous variety of meanings is also visible in the case of Vergil and St. Bernard. St. Bernard represents mystical vision. He describes himself in *Paradiso* XXXI as a man who "in this world by contemplation tasted of that peace [of heaven]," [311] thus qualifying himself to guide Dante by stages through the Empyrean. Yet mystic vision based on a series of steps is not all that Bernard represents. If it were, there would be no particular reason for Dante to have chosen Bernard as his guide, rather than some other eminent mystic, and Dante places a number of them in Paradise, including Richard of St. Victor, "who, in contemplating, was more than man." [312] Bernard is particularly dear to Dante for two other reasons. He was a fervent proponent of the cult of the Virgin Mary, which he did much to popularize in the twelfth century. In his instructions to Dante in Heaven, he stresses devotion to the Virgin, observing that "the Queen of heaven for whom I am all burning with love, will grant us every grace, because I am her faithful Bernard." [313] He tells Dante to look upon Mary's face, "which is most likened unto Christ; for its brightness, and no other, hath power to fit thee to see Christ." [314] A sizable portion of the last canto of the *Paradiso* consists of Bernard's lengthy prayer to the Virgin, which immediately precedes Dante's vision of God. [315]

A less obvious but equally important reason why Dante selects Bernard as his guide is that Bernard combined the contemplative life of the mystic with the active life of the ecclesiastical statesman and reformer. Famed for his mellifluous ora-

311. Ibid., XXXI, 110–11. See Alexandre Masseron, *Dante et Saint Bernard* (Paris, 1953), for the fullest discussion of St. Bernard's role in the *Comedy*, and pp. 40–43 for St. Bernard as a mystic.

312. *Par.*, X, 133.

313. Ibid., XXXI, 100–02; Masseron, *Dante*, pp. 71–143.

314. *Par.*, XXXII, 85–87.

315. Ibid., XXXIII, 1–39.

tory, he preached the Second Crusade in 1144; he mediated the conflicts of the crowned heads of Europe; he combated heresy in the person of Peter Abelard. Bernard was also a strong proponent of reform. The most dynamic leader of the Cistercian movement, he founded the monastery of Clairvaux and was the moving spirit of this order in the twelfth century. In his *De consideratione* he denounced both the current worldliness of the papacy and its political aims.[316] He rejected the claims of the papacy to feudal suzerainty over the Norman kingdom of Naples and Sicily; he condemned the political ambitions of the popes in Italy and corresponded with various emperors, urging them to recover their claims in the peninsula. His devotion to the Virgin, his public-spirited oratory, and his specific political views correspond thoroughly with Dante's views on these subjects. The saint alludes to them in Paradise, contrasting by implication the leaders of a corrupt Christian society with "the great patricians of this most just and pious empire" [317] in the Empyrean, where Mary rules as Augusta. Thus, the personality and significance of St. Bernard possess several dimensions for Dante.

Of all the three guides in the *Comedy*, Vergil tutors Dante the longest, and he, like St. Bernard and Beatrice, has several meanings for the poet.[318] Vergil is usually taken to represent human reason unaided by grace. If one adheres exclusively to this interpretation of Vergil's significance, however, there would be no particular reason for Dante to have chosen him as a guide in preference to a philosopher exemplifying human wisdom, such as Aristotle, "the Master of those that know." [319] Vergil has a host of meanings besides that of human reason. He also represents the poet of empire, the reformer of the Roman vernacular of his day, the portrayer of a hero who takes an allegorical journey to the other world, a prophet of

316. Masseron, *Dante,* pp. 248–52.

317. *Par.,* XXXII, 116–17.

318. C. Galassi Paluzzi, "Perchè Dante scelse Virgilio a sua guida," *GD, 39,* n. s., *9* (1936), 287–307, discusses the literature on this question.

319. *Inf.,* IV, 131.

the coming of Christ, the bridge between pagan and Christian Rome, a seer, and a repository of literary craft and of poetic genius.[320] Throughout Hell and Purgatory, Vergil displays his knowledge of matters both philosophical and theological. Dante addresses him by a wide variety of titles, including poet, master, guide, sage, sea of all intelligence, lord, father, virtue supreme, teacher, escort, leader, comfort, light, and faithful comrade. Of all Vergil's functions, however, his role as poet is the one that Dante returns to most repeatedly and with the most evident interest.[321]

Students of the *Comedy* and the *Aeneid* are well aware of Dante's numerous borrowings from Vergil. More important for our purposes are the scenes where Dante permits himself and Vergil to advert specifically to Vergil's writings. They begin in *Inferno* I, when the two poets first meet. After encountering the Leopard, the Lion, and the She-wolf, Dante sees "one who seemed hoarse from long silence" [322] and asks who he is. Vergil acknowledges his place of birth, his Roman citizenship, the time when he lived, and his paganism. He describes his profession in the words "A poet I was; and sang of that just son of Anchises, who came from Troy after proud

320. See above, pp. 240–41. These views have been noted frequently. See Albert R. Bandini, "Virgil and Dante—and Statius," *Thought*, 5 (1930), 10; Bergin, *Dante*, p. 59; Domenico Comparetti, *Virgil in the Middle Ages* (London, 1908), passim and especially pp. 195–231; Davis, *Dante*, pp. 101–38; Dinsmore, *Life of Dante*, p. 229; Fletcher, *Dante*, pp. 175–76; Fortunato Laurenzi, *Ermetica ed ermeneutica dantesca* (Città di Castello, 1931), pp. 44–45, 52; Kenneth McKenzie, "Virgil & Dante," *The Tradition of Virgil: Three Papers on the History and Influence of the Poet* (Princeton, 1930), pp. 13–20; Moore, *Studies in Dante: First Series*, pp. 166–97; R. Palgen, "La légende virgilienne dans la *Divine Comédie*," *Romania*, 73 (1952), 332–90; Renucci, *Dante*, p. 340; Singleton, *Journey to Beatrice*, pp. 89–92; John Webster Spargo, *Virgil the Necromancer: Studies in Virgilian Legends* (Cambridge, Mass., 1934), p. 335; J. H. Whitfield, *Dante and Virgil* (Oxford, 1949), pp. 31, 68, 73, 93; Vladmiro Zabughin, *Vergilio nel rinascimento italiano da Dante a Torquato Tasso* (Bologna, 1923), *1*, 6, 7, 15–16.
321. Gilbert, *Dante*, pp. 42–44.
322. *Inf.*, I, 63.

Ilium was burnt." [323] Dante immediately recognizes Vergil, addresses him as "that fountain which pours abroad so rich a stream of speech," and praises Vergil as his poetic mentor:

> O glory, and light of other poets! May the long
> zeal avail me, and the great love, that made
> me search thy volume.
> Thou art my master and my author; thou alone art
> he from whom I took the good style that hath
> done me honour. [324]

Dante's recognition of Vergil's poetic superiority, bracketed with his allusions to his own literary eminence, is amplified in the Limbo of the virtuous pagans, where Dante meets the shades of Homer, Horace, Ovid, and Lucan. The poets are separated from the other virtuous pagans, Vergil explains, because the name of poet "gains favours in heaven which thus advances them." [325] The four shades exclaim, "Honour the great Poet!" as Vergil appears on the scene. This greeting Vergil takes as his due; "because each agrees with me in the name, . . . they do me honour: and therein they do well," he observes. [326] Dante is fully prepared to revere the classical poets and to extend the honor to himself:

> Thus I saw assembled the goodly school of that
> lord of highest song, who, like an eagle, soars
> above the rest.
> After they had talked a space together, they turned
> to me with a sign of salutation; and my Master
> smiled thereat.
> And greatly more they honoured me for they made me
> of their number, so that I was sixth amid such
> intelligences. [327]

323. Ibid., 73–75.
324. Ibid., 82–87.
325. Ibid., IV, 76–78.
326. Ibid., 80, 91–93.
327. Ibid., 94–102.

In the *Comedy*, Vergil acknowledges his authorship of the *Aeneid* and his literary accomplishments as a poet; he also at times refers to the contents of his epic in more detail. He describes the *Aeneid* as "my high Tragedy" [328] and invokes the shade of Ulysses in the name of the "High Verses" [329] which he wrote on earth. Speaking to Pier delle Vigne in the wood of the suicides, he tells him that Dante would not have broken a twig off Pier's tree-body had he (Dante) paid closer attention to the episode of Aeneas and Polydorus in *Aeneid* III.[330]

Other characters in the *Comedy* also testify to Vergil's poetic art. In the speech in which Beatrice enlists Vergil to guide Dante through Hell and Purgatory, she praises him in somewhat courtly language. Addressing Vergil as the "courteous Mantuan spirit," whose fame is immortal, she tells him that she has confidence in the power of his "noble speech, which honours thee, and them who have heard it," to help Dante out of the dark wood.[331] In Purgatory, the poet Sordello addresses Vergil as "O glory of the Latins, by whom our tongue showed forth all its power," [332] thereby manifesting Dante's bias in favor of continuity between the classical past and the medieval present. Still more effusive is Statius. Introducing himself as the poet who "sang of Thebes, and then of the great Achilles," he notes that "the sparks, which warmed me, from the divine flame whence more than a thousand have been kindled, were the seeds of my poetic fire: of the *Aeneid* I speak, which was a mother to me, and was to me a nurse in poesy." [333] He attributes to Vergil his Christian faith as well as his art:

> . . . thou first did send me towards Parnassus
> to drink in its caves, and then didst light
> me on to God.

328. Ibid., XX, 113.
329. Ibid., XXVI, 79–84.
330. Ibid., XIII, 46–49.
331. Ibid., II, 58–60, 67, 113–14.
332. *Purg.,* VII, 16–17.
333. Ibid., XXI, 92, 94–98.

> Thou didst like one who goes by night, and carries
>   the light behind him, and profits not himself,
>   but makes persons wise that follow him,
> When thou saidst: "The world is renewed, justice
>   returns and the first age of man, and a new
>   progeny descends from heaven."
> Through thee was I a poet, through thee a Christian. [334]

Vergil, in keeping with the medieval interpretation of his fourth *Eclogue*, thus functions as the prophet of Christ; in his brotherly reunion with his Mantuan compatriot, Sordello, he exemplifies good citizenship; [335] and, in his first speech to Dante, he refers to the evils besetting Italy and prophesies the appearance of its savior, the Greyhound.[336] It is precisely in Vergil's capacity as a great poet that Dante credits him with ethical, religious, and political insights. This does not mean, however, that he sees Vergil in one dimension. Dante himself was striving to convey his own ethical, religious, and political insights to his contemporaries by raising Italian to the level of a literary language and by writing a poetic masterpiece embodying these very ideas. As the author of the *Comedy* Dante sees himself as a second Vergil. Thus, by reading back into the historical Vergil his own conception of the role of the poet and his own views on current Italian and European problems, Dante can use Vergil's status as a poet as a sun from which his other meanings radiate.

The evidence could be multiplied to show that many other characters in the *Comedy* besides Dante's three guides possess typological significance. The fact that Dante fully intends the fourfold method of scriptural exegesis which he describes in the letter to Can Grande to be applied to the *Divine Comedy* is further revealed by the words that he puts into Beatrice's mouth as she explains Dante's trip to the other world to St. James in Paradise:

334. Ibid., XXII, 64–73.
335. Ibid., VI, 72–75; VII, 1–3.
336. *Inf.,* I, 91–129.

> Church militant hath not a child richer in hope,
>   as is written in the sun who o'errayeth all
>   our host;
> Therefore was it granted him to come from Egypt
>   to Jerusalem, to look on her, e'er the pre-
>   scribed limit of his soldiery.[337]

Dante's choice of the psalm "In exitu Israel de Aegypto" as a biblical text to analyze in order to explain the fourfold method in the letter to Can Grande is not fortuitous. Nor is his placement of the same psalm in the *Comedy*. It is the first psalm that he hears sung in Purgatory.[338] He inserts it into the poem at this juncture to indicate the time of year; the passage of the Israelites from Egypt and their celebration of the Passover are types of the Christian feast of Easter and the celebration of the Eucharist. But the bondage of the Israelites to the Egyptians is also a type of the bondage of the sinner to sin, a moral state which Dante has just symbolically abandoned by leaving Hell, and the wanderings of the Israelites in the desert after their departure from Egypt are a type of the temporal punishment for sin which Dante is symbolically about to undergo in Purgatory.

Dante's conception of the *Comedy* as a work of art capable of being treated critically in the same manner as the Bible is paralleled by his conception of himself, the poet, as a man who writes under the inspiration of God for didactic purposes.[339] Dante illustrates his idea of the poet as prophet in a number of ways in the *Comedy*. He frequently invokes God,

337. *Par.*, XXV, 52–57.

338. *Purg.*, II, 46.

339. This point has been noted frequently. See Andrea, "La coscienza poetica di Dante," *GD, 30,* 187; Erich Auerbach, "Dante's Addresses to the Reader," *Romance Philology,* 7 (1954), 268–78; Barbi, *Life of Dante,* p. 97; *Problemi,* p. 116; Frédéric Bergmann, *Dante: Sa vie et ses oeuvres* (Strasbourg, 1881), pp. 15–25; Curtius, *European Literature,* pp. 328, 359; Dinsmore, *Life of Dante,* p. 235; *The Teachings of Dante* (Boston, 1901), pp. 47–49; Foligno, "Dante," *Proceedings of the British Academy, 10,* 3–18; Gilbert, *Dante,* pp. 28–42; Hermann Gmelin, "Die Anrede an den Leser in Dantes Göttlicher Komödie,"

as well as the Muses, for inspiration,[340] describing himself as "one who, when Love inspires me take note, and go setting it forth after the fashion which he dictates within me." [341] Dante refers to his poem as "sacred," [342] a distinction it possesses in virtue of its sublime subject matter [343] and because "both heaven and earth . . . have set hand [to it]." [344] Dante issues numerous jeremiads throughout the *Comedy* directed against the corruption he sees in contemporary ethics, religion, and politics, and places in the mouths of various heavenly personages, from Cacciaguida [345] and Beatrice [346] to St. Peter Damien,[347] St. John,[348] and St. Peter,[349] warrants for his writing of a poem designed to instruct his fellow men. His frequent addresses to the reader, as Auerbach and Gmelin have noted, indicate that Dante takes his didactic role quite seriously,[350] as do his requests to souls in Hell and Purgatory to explain their state so that he can report it back to

DDJ, 29–30, neue Folge, Band 20–21 (1951), 130–40; Grandgent, *Power of Dante,* p. 233; A. G. Ferrers Howell *Dante: His Life and Work* (London, 1920), p. 83; Laurenzi, *Ermetica ed ermeneutica,* pp. 8, 44–52; Lenkeith, *Dante,* pp. 64, 71–72; Mazzeo, *Structure and Thought,* pp. 8, 36–37, 45; Moore, *Studies in Dante: Second Series,* pp. 1–78; Nardi, *Dante,* pp. 338, 340–41, 392; Pézard, *Dante,* pp. 253–61; Pietrobono, "Struttura allegorica e poesia," *GD, 43,* n. s., *13,* 12–45; Scandura, *L'Estetica,* pp. 79–80, 89–90; Vossler, *Mediaeval Culture, 2,* 103; Ernest Hatch Wilkins, "Dante as Apostle," *Symposium: Dante Six Hundred Years After* (Chicago, 1921), p. 43; *Dante: Poet and Apostle* (Chicago, 1921), pp. 19, 26, 42, 45–46, 55–56; *History of Italian Literature,* p. 61; Zingarelli, *La vita, 2,* 881.

340. *Inf.,* II, 7–9; *Purg.,* I, 7–12; XXIX, 40–42; *Par.,* I, 13–36; II, 8–9; XVIII, 82–87; XXII, 112–23; XXX, 97–99; XXXIII, 67–75.

341. *Purg.,* XXIV, 52–54.

342. *Par.,* XXIII, 62; XXV, 1.

343. Ibid., I, 27.

344. Ibid., XXV, 2.

345. Ibid., XVII, 124–42.

346. *Purg.,* XXXII, 103–05; XXXIII, 52–54.

347. *Par.,* XXI, 97–99.

348. Ibid., XXV, 129.

349. Ibid., XXVII, 64–66.

350. *Inf.,* IX, 61–63; XII, 49–51; XIV, 16–18; XVI, 118–20; XIX, 1–6; XX, 19–20; *Purg.,* VIII, 19–21; IX, 70–72; X, 104–11; XII, 70–72; XXIX, 97–102; *Par.,* II, 1–6; X, 7–9. See Auerbach, "Dante's Addresses to the Reader," *Ro-*

others after his pilgrimage to the other world is over and he returns to earth.[351]

Dante's view of himself in the *Comedy* as an inspired, prophetic teacher is explained in his letter to Can Grande under the rubrics of the aim of the *Comedy* and the branch of philosophy to which it pertains. "The aim of the whole and of the part," says Dante, "is to remove those living in this life from a state of misery, and to bring them to a state of happiness." [352] The branch of philosophy to which the poem pertains is ethics.[353] Ethics is a practical science; it is a means to an end, the end in this case being the eternal bliss of Dante's readers. Dante clearly believes that his work has this sort of public utility [354] and so relates his didacticism to a Ciceronian-Augustinian rhetoric, whose blend of instruction, persuasion, and delight is oriented to the common weal. Dante intends the *Comedy* to be useful and pleasant at the same time. The experience of aesthetic pleasure will draw the reader toward God.[355] Poetry is useful only if it is beautiful; the pleasing function of literature is not expendable for Dante, but integral to his rhetorical poetics. The instruction of the intellect by the poet must be matched by the movement of the will; as Baldwin has well put it, the *Divine Comedy* "arrives not at a demonstration, but at a catharsis." [356]

---

mance Philology, 7, 268–78; Gmelin, "Die Anrede an den Leser," *DDJ, 29–30,* neue Folge, 20–21, 130–40. Ernst Robert Curtius relates Dante's didactic conception of the *Comedy* to the symbol of the book in the poem, which represents doctrine, prophesy, and Divine revelation, in "Das Buch als Symbol in der Divina Commedia," *Festschrift zum sechszigsten Geburtstag von Paul Clemen* (Bonn, 1926), pp. 44–54. He supplies more details in his "Schrift- und Buchmetaphorik in der Weltliteratur," *Neue Beiträge deutscher Forschung: Wilhelm Worringer zum 60. Geburtstag,* herausgegeben von Erich Fidder (Königsberg, 1943), pp. 70–86, where he traces the sources of this idea in early Christian and medieval thought.

351. *Inf.,* XXIX, 103–08; XXXII, 133–39; *Purg.,* XXVI, 53–66.
352. *Epistola* X, ¶ 15, Toynbee, p. 202.
353. Ibid., ¶ 16, Toynbee, pp. 178–79.
354. Ibid., ¶ 32, Toynbee, p. 193.
355. Ibid., ¶ 33, Toynbee, p. 194.
356. Baldwin, *Medieval Rhetoric and Poetic,* p. 277.

This is a procedure that depends on God. In the letter to Can Grande, Dante reaffirms the inadequacy of language to express his vision of the other world; [357] he speaks of his need of God's assistance; [358] he describes poetry as "almost in the nature of a divine gift." [359] But the catharsis of the reader also depends on the poet's literary craft. Dante has much to say on this point in the letter to Can Grande. In the realm of literary tactics no less than in his moral orientation, Ciceronian-Augustinian rhetoric is Dante's touchstone. Thus, he advises, the exordium of the poem should make the audience "favorably disposed, attentive, and willing to learn." [360] With respect to the *Paradiso*, the moral profit which the reader can hope to acquire makes him favorably disposed to the work, the extraordinary nature of the subject matter catches his attention, and the fact that the objective of the poem, beatitude, is within the realm of possibility for the reader, makes him ready to learn.[361]

The orderly structure of the poem and its variegated literary texture will also appeal to the reader, and Dante discusses these aspects of the *Comedy* in the letter to Can Grande under the rubric of the form of the work, which he subdivides into the form of the treatise and the form of the treatment. The form of the treatise is threefold: the poem is divided into three cantiche, each of which is divided into thirty-three cantos with the exception of the *Inferno*, which contains an additional prefatory canto, and the rhyme scheme is terza rima. The form of the treatment is "poetic, fictive, descriptive, digressive, and figurative; and further it is definitive, analytical, probative, refutative, and exemplificative." [362] This statement leaves no doubt as to the epistemological force which Dante attributes to his poetry. It is also noteworthy

357. *Epistola* X, ¶ 28–29, Toynbee, pp. 189–93.
358. Ibid., ¶ 18, 31, Toynbee, pp. 179–80, 193.
359. Ibid., ¶ 18, Toynbee, p. 203.
360. Ibid., ¶ 19, Toynbee, p. 203.
361. Ibid., pp. 180–82.
362. Ibid., ¶ 9, Toynbee, p. 200.

that he distinguishes the poetic from the fictive, and that he assimilates philosophy to poetry here just as he has assimilated poetry to theology in his application of the fourfold method to the *Comedy*.

From a stylistic point of view, the letter to Can Grande also takes a major step in expanding Dante's notion of the genre and diction appropriate to a work on an exalted subject. Dante defines the author and title of the *Comedy* as "Incipit Comoedia Dantis Alagherii, Florentini natione, non moribus." [363] Outside of contrasting Dante, the "true Florentine," with his decadent and unappreciative compatriots, this title also leads Dante into a discussion of the nature of comedy and tragedy, which indicates an important shift in his conception of these genres. In the *De vulgari eloquentia,* Dante assigns to tragedy alone the prerogative of dealing with the most elevated subjects, and insists that it must use the illustrious vernacular and the canzone form, while elegy uses an abject style and comedy employs moderate or lowly diction.[364] The letter to Can Grande, and of course the *Divine Comedy* itself, however, indicate that Dante regards comedy as capable of dealing with an extremely exalted subject, human salvation. His distinction between tragedy and comedy in the letter to Can Grande is based on the idea that a tragedy begins happily and ends horribly, and that a comedy begins adversely and ends happily. He still maintains that tragic diction should be elevated and that comic diction should be humble, but, following Horace, adds that each genre may use the language of the other.[365] This attitude toward diction is manifested in the *Comedy,* where Dante employs a wide range of styles of diction, from the burlesque to the sublime. Examples could be drawn from the *Comedy* to illustrate all the vocabulary types which he enumerates in the *De vulgari eloquentia.* Dante's high subject no longer demands the most refined diction or the

363. Ibid., ¶ 10, Toynbee, p. 175.
364. See above, p. 272.
365. *Epistola* X, ¶ 10, Toynbee, pp. 175–77.

canzone form. The author of the *Comedy,* like the Christian orator of Augustine's *De doctrina christiana,* does not hesitate to be popular in order to reach the widest possible audience.

The literary theory of Dante's letter to Can Grande represents his full-blown theological poetics, the poetics which underlie and explain his *Divine Comedy.* In developing this theory, Dante adheres to some features of medieval poetics, particularly the rhetorical-didactic tradition. However, Dante elevates poetry above rhetoric while maintaining the unification of the two disciplines begun in classical times. He rejects the "falsity of poetry" tradition, and its modification in the form of the theory of poetic veils which must be removed in order to acquire the nugget of doctrine within. For Dante the style of poetry is integrally related to its truth. Regarding himself as an inspired poet-theologian, he uses a wide variety of techniques to delight, instruct, and move the reader toward the goal of beatitude. He considers his literary craftsmanship essential but is aware of the limits of language in conveying theological truths to the reader. His poetry celebrates a private vision put to the service of the community and reflecting the interdependence of the individual and the group. Dante's conception of himself as a poet reveals his thorough assimilation of Augustine's redefinition of Ciceronian rhetoric. It is expressed in the Italian vernacular; it reflects Dante's specific views on the ethical, religious, and political reforms which he thinks are needed by his age in order to promote a relationship of rectitude between man and God. This is the poetic theory which is exemplified in the *Divine Comedy.*

It is now our task to show that the verbal theory of knowledge formulated by Augustine and employed by the other thinkers with whom this study has been concerned is expressed by Dante in the theological poetics of the *Divine Comedy.* It may be well to recall to mind the salient aspects of the Augustinian theory of knowledge before examining the *Comedy* further for evidence of its existence in this work. In the first place, Augustine, blending classical sign theory and

315

biblical doctrines of religious knowledge, conceives of words as the basic symbolic intermediaries in the process of knowledge. This conception of words as the fundamental kind of epistemic signs, to which other kinds of signs can be reduced, springs from his preoccupation with religious knowledge, with the doctrine of Christ the Word as God's revelation to man, and with the biblical mandate to preach the Word. The doctrine of the Incarnation is a key idea for all the proponents of Augustine's verbal epistemology in the Middle Ages, whether, like Augustine and Anselm, they see its implications primarily in the redemption of human language and thought processes, or whether, as in Aquinas, its implications lie primarily in the realm of natural theology, in which Christ functions as the Logos of creation as well as the illuminator of the human mind. They all hold that human powers of speech and conceptualization are capable of signifying Divine truths accurately although incompletely. They also maintain that human words may turn the nonbeliever in the direction of God or help a believer to deepen his understanding of what he believes, but that the words of the speaker act in an instrumental rather than a heuristic manner in both of these cases. God, they assert, always remains in control of the accuracy of human signs which refer to Him; He thus controls what may be known about Him, dictating the moral as well as the intellectual conditions of this knowledge.

Dante reflects thoroughly the Augustinian combination of diffidence and enthusiasm with respect to the powers and limits of poetic language to signify the vision of the other world which his *Comedy* relates. Dante's firm conviction of his prophetic and didactic role as a poet, his repeated stress on the idea that he possesses heavenly warrant for what he writes,[366] and the progressive dissociation of his poetics from the doctrine of poetry as falsehood all show that he doubts neither the truth of poetry nor its unique aptitude for expressing Divine realities. He assimilates speech to poetry in his use of

366. See citations in footnotes 339, 341, 345–50.

the word *dire,* to speak, to mean, "to write poetry." [367] For Dante, the truth of poetry depends on its rectitude, its correspondence to realities as they are, as well as on a right moral attitude on the poet's part toward these realities. At the same time that Dante adverts to the powers of poetry, he fills the *Comedy* with statements pointing to its inadequacies.[368] Dante repeatedly notes that his mind cannot conceive nor his memory retain what he has experienced in Hell, Purgatory, and Paradise, and, with growing frequency, he confesses the poverty of his poetic art to express what he has seen in the other world.[369] This confession reaches its climax at the end of the *Paradiso,* where he acknowledges that Beatrice has become so ineffably beautiful that he must terminate his lifelong career of speaking about her.[370] And, ultimately, the vision of God in the last canto of the poem is so overwhelming that he feels forced to fall silent.[371] Dante's numerous appeals for supernatural assistance in relating his experiences to the reader underline the view that God endows the speaker with power to signify Divine truths which he would not ordinarily possess.[372] He recognizes the instrumental character of his poetry in the reader's instruction; the Divine gifts of faith and grace are needed to fill the gaps between language and

367. Gilbert, *Dante,* p. 42.

368. Ibid., pp. 42–60; Giovanni Chiapparini, "Dante e la poesia dell'ineffabile," *Rassegna nazionale,* 3ᵐᵒ serie, 22 (1934), 425–29; Dinsmore, *Life of Dante,* p. 236; Laurenzi, *Ermetica ed ermeneutica,* p. 3; Mazzeo, *Structure and Thought,* p. 39; Giovanni Pischedda, *L'Orrido e l'ineffabile nella tematica dantesca* (L'Aquila, 1958), pp. 87–89, 99; Tonelli, *Dante,* passim; Van Doren, "The Divine Comedy," *Sewanee Review, 14,* 370.

369. Dinsmore, *Life of Dante,* p. 236; Van Doren, "The Divine Comedy," *Sewanee Review, 14,* 270; *Inf.,* II, 10–36; IV, 145–47; IX, 34; XXVIII, 1–6; XXXII, 1–15; XXXIV, 22–24; *Purg.,* XII, 110–11; XXIX, 40–42; XXXI, 97–99, 139–45; *Par.,* I, 4–12, 70–72; VI, 61–63; X, 43–48; XIV, 103–05, 123; XV, 76–78; XVII, 92–93; XVIII, 7–12; XX, 11–12; XXI, 139–42; XXIII, 40–45, 49–63; XXIV, 22–27; XXVII, 73–75, 100–02; XXX, 19–36; XXXI, 136–38; XXXIII, 55–57, 106–08, 121–23, 142–45.

370. *Par.,* XXX, 19–36.

371. Ibid., XXXIII, 142–45.

372. See citations in footnote 340.

reality. Thus, he notes that only a believer can picture the heaven of the sun,[373] and observes, at the beginning of the *Paradiso*, that "to pass beyond humanity may not be told in words, wherefore let the example satisfy him for whom grace reserveth the experience." [374]

As a teacher, Dante instructs the reader through what he, as the author, describes, and through what he, as a character in the work, learns and experiences in the course of the *Comedy*. Discourse or conversation is the primary means that he uses to illustrate the right relations which he thinks should obtain among men and between man and God. Dante employs other media of communication, such as visual art, music, the sensory environment of the other world, dreams, the eyes and smile of Beatrice and others, as well as specific symbols. Like Augustine, he treats nonverbal signs as metaphors of speech, and thus interprets signification as such in a preeminently verbal manner.

There are several ways in which conversation functions in the *Comedy*. A large proportion of the poem is composed of Dante's conversations with his guides. Vergil, Beatrice, and St. Bernard continually explain the nature of the other world to Dante and give him permission to speak to the souls whom he meets. They set forth numerous philosophical and theological doctrines, forming Dante's will and enlightening his intellect through their instruction. Dante's guides do not aim merely at instruction. They aim also at persuasion and delight, which they achieve through the love and confidence which they inspire in Dante. Dante's progressive growth in love and knowledge is illustrated by the shifts in his use of dialogue in the *Comedy*. In Hell we find many more brief interchanges of questions and answers between Dante and his guide than we do in Purgatory or Paradise. Dante's questions in Hell are much more naïve than in the later portions of the poem. In the earlier cantos of the *Comedy* Dante sometimes depicts

373. *Par.*, X, 43–48.
374. Ibid., I, 70–72.

318

himself as embarrassed by the prospect that he may have asked a stupid question, and he is often upset and bewildered by Vergil's explanations.[375] All of this shows that Dante the traveler has much to learn at the outset of his journey. As the *Inferno* proceeds, however, Vergil speaks for longer and longer stretches of time, a tendency on the part of Vergil and Beatrice which increases in the *Purgatorio* and *Paradiso*. As Dante grows more enlightened and oriented toward God, he depends less and less on his guides to intercede on his behalf with the souls whom he wants to address, and, after finding his bearings within each of the realms of the other world, he requires fewer detailed explanations. As a token of the ending of his tutelage over Dante, Vergil tells him, "no more expect my word or my sign," at the top of the mountain of Purgatory.[376] Dante's guides often signify their recognition of his progress by registering their approval of the kinds of questions he has learned to ask and the attitude which he has learned to adopt toward the souls with whom he speaks.[377] They adjure him to speak briefly with the souls in Hell,[378] but to listen to, and to believe, the souls in Paradise.[379]

The souls in the other world also have much to say, and they illustrate their own moral states and the character of the realms in which they are located through their conversation, no less than through their appearance and the punishments and rewards they exemplify. Speech, for Dante, is a way of expressing oneself to others; it is therefore the means by which people interact in society. Each of the three realms of the other world is a society. Both vice and virtue have social consequences, and what the souls have to say reveals their attitude toward their fellow man as well as toward God. In Hell,

375. *Inf.*, III, 79–81; V, 70–72.
376. *Purg.*, XXVII, 139. On the length of Dante's guides' speeches, see Bergin, *Dante*, p. 265; Fletcher, *Dante*, pp. 91, 93–94, 98.
377. *Inf.*, VIII, 44–45; XIV, 133; XIX, 121–23; XXVI, 70–71; *Par.*, X, 61–63.
378. *Inf.*, III, 45, 51; X, 39; XVII, 40.
379. *Par.*, III, 31; V, 122–23.

the prevailing tendency on the part of the souls is to deny God, their own humanity, and other men. Verbal expression in Hell frequently takes the form of moans, whines, shrieks, curses, blasphemies, lamentations, and vituperations.[380] Speech in this realm is often perverted, and is represented as bestial, incomprehensible, or as otherwise distorted and inhuman. The gluttonous howl like dogs;[381] Vergil compares the voices of the avaricious and prodigal to barking.[382] The words of the false counselors must struggle through the flames which envelop their speakers;[383] "thus, having at their commencement no way or outlet from the fire, the dismal words were changed into its language."[384] Only after this process can the false counselors speak normally. Plutus speaks gibberish in the meaningless statement, "Pape Satan! Pape Satan aleppe,"[385] as does Nimrod, whom Dante holds responsible for the tower of Babel and the separation of tongues; he is incomprehensible to others and they to him.[386] The slothful "gurgle in their throats, for they cannot speak . . . in full words."[387] Curio's tongue is split so that he cannot speak at all;[388] the thieves' voices are "unsuitable for forming words."[389] Most horrible are the suicides changed to trees. Their words are empty air, like the wind in their branches, and when Pier delle Vigne speaks, "words and blood came forth together."[390]

---

380. *Inf.,* III, 22–24, 103–05; IV, 25–27; V, 25–27; VI, 76; IX, 121–23; XII, 102; XIII, 22; XIV, 27; XV, 42; XVI, 19–20; XVII, 122; XVIII, 103–04; XX, 7–8; XXIII, 58–60; XXIX, 43.

381. Ibid., VI, 19.

382. Ibid., VII, 43.

383. Ibid., XXVI, 85–90; XXVII, 7–15, 58–60, 130–32.

384. Ibid., XXVII, 13–15.

385. Ibid., VII, 1. Notwithstanding the later solutions that have been applied to this phrase, Dante the character in the poem treats it as incomprehensible.

386. Ibid., XXXI, 67, 70–75.

387. Ibid., VII, 125–26.

388. Ibid., XXVIII, 100–02.

389. Ibid., XXIV, 66.

390. Ibid., XIII, 43–44, 91–92, 138.

The guardians of the sinners and the sinners themselves are vicious and hostile; they do not welcome Dante and rarely have anything pleasant to say to him. The first soul whom Dante meets in Hell, after Vergil, is Charon, the boatman of the Styx, who greets Dante and Vergil with the words "woe to you, depraved spirits." [391] Minos, who assigns the souls to their places in Hell, addresses Dante harshly as "thou who comest to the abode of pain." [392] Plutus, as we have seen, speaks to Dante in gibberish; Phlegyas asks, "Now art thou arrived, fell spirit?" [393] The Centaurs are belligerent, attacking Dante with the words "To what torment come ye? . . . Tell from thence; if not, I draw the bow," [394] although the Centaur Nessus is the first monster in hell to act in a friendly manner to Dante. The souls are often hostile, too. Argenti asks resentfully, "Who art thou, that cometh before thy time?"; and his companions in Dis, angry that Dante should be permitted to travel through the other world before his death, are disdainful and curse him.[395] The usurer Rinaldo de' Scrovegni asks Dante, "What art thou doing in this pit? Get thee gone." [396] Venedico Caccianimico tries to hide from Dante, and when asked why he is in Hell, replies, "Unwillingly I tell it." Alessio Interminei shuns Dante with the words "Why art thou so eager in gazing at me?" [397] Vanni Fucci prophesies that the whites of Florence will suffer defeat purely out of malice toward Dante; "I have said this so that it may grieve thee," he observes,[398] concluding his speech with an obscenity.[399] In *Inferno* XXVIII, a soul rudely accuses Dante of being a sinner trying to escape his own punishment.[400]

391. *Inf.,* III, 84.
392. Ibid., V, 16.
393. Ibid., VIII, 18.
394. Ibid., XII, 61–63.
395. Ibid., VIII, 33, 84–93.
396. Ibid., XVII, 66–67.
397. Ibid., XVIII, 53, 118–19.
398. Ibid., XXIV, 151.
399. Ibid., XXV, 1–3.
400. Ibid., XXVIII, 43–45.

The hypocrites look Dante askance and discuss him invidiously among themselves before talking to him.[401] Bocca degli Abati is easily the most belligerent and uncommunicative soul whom Dante meets in Hell; he refuses to tell who he is or to speak with Dante at all, and instead picks a fight with him.[402]

With a few exceptions, the souls in Hell who do speak attempt to disavow responsibility for their sins and to blame others as equally bad or worse than themselves. While the blasphemer Capaneus revels in his sin: "What I was living, that am I dead," [403] Francesca da Rimini rejects her freedom of will, excusing her adultery by arguing that she and her lover Paolo had no choice but to sin:

> Love, which is quickly caught in gentle heart, took
>   him with the fair body of which I was bereft; and
>   the manner still afflicts me.
> Love, which to no loved one permits excuse for loving,
>   took me so strongly with delight in him, that, as
>   thou seest, even now it leaves me not.
> Love led us to one death.[404]

Pier delle Vigne, the suicide, excuses his injustice to himself by adverting to his justice to his master, the Emperor Frederick II.[405] The simoniac Pope Nicholas III contrasts his own lapses with the vices of Boniface VIII and Clement V.[406] The barrator Ciampolo accuses his fellow sinners, one of whom, Friar Gomita, he characterizes as "a sovereign barrator." [407] The souls grow more and more malicious and hostile toward each other the farther into Hell Dante goes, a condition symbolized by the fact that their torments result increasingly

401. *Inf.*, XXIII, 85–90.
402. Ibid., XXXII, 87–123.
403. Ibid., XIV, 51.
404. Ibid., V, 100–06.
405. Ibid., XIII, 58–78.
406. Ibid., XIX, 52–57, 66–87.
407. Ibid., XXII, 77–90.

from their punishment of each other. The hypocrite Malacoda deliberately gives Dante and Vergil false directions when asked the way.[408] When Dante asks rhetorically whether there is anyone as vain as the Sienese, the alchemist Capocchio responds by enumerating a list of sinners, and after commenting on his own virtuosity as a falsifier of nature, complains about the viciousness of another soul, Gianni Schicchi.[409] Adam of Brescia, wallowing in self-pity, says that he yearns to see the punishment of his partners in the crime of forgery; it is on them, not himself, that the blame for his sin rests. Then he picks a fight with another soul, and Dante leaves them hurling vituperations at each other.[410] Ugolino, whom Dante finds gnawing Archbishop Ruggieri of Pisa, curses his victim as a traitor and an evil-doer,[411] and Alberigo is so thoroughly obnoxious that Dante says, "To be rude to him was courtesy." [412]

After the maliciousness of the souls in Hell, the souls in Purgatory are noteworthy for their friendliness to Dante and to each other. The first group of souls whom Dante meets in this realm gather around him as if to hear a messenger bearing news of peace, and embrace him affectionately. The first words spoken by a soul in Purgatory express love; the poet Casella tells Dante, "Even as I loved thee in the mortal body so do I love thee freed," and when Dante asks him to sing, he responds graciously by offering one of Dante's poems.[413] This welcome is paralleled by Statius' greeting, "My brothers, God give you peace," and his quotation of a line from Vergil's fourth *Eclogue,* as well as Forese Donati's reception of Dante in the words "What grace is this to me?" [414] The souls in

408. Ibid., XXIII, 127–44.
409. Ibid., XXIX, 109–XXX, 33.
410. Ibid., XXX, 58–129.
411. Ibid., XXXIII, 13–78.
412. Ibid., 150.
413. *Purg.,* II, 70–114.
414. Ibid., XXI, 13; XXII, 70–72; XXIII, 43.

Purgatory give directions graciously. They freely acknowledge their sins and the goodness of God.[415] Exchanging courteous greetings with Dante, they speak to him readily and ask him only to pray for them.[416] Sordello tells Dante that it will give the souls joy to speak with him.[417] In contrast to the souls in Hell, the souls in Purgatory welcome their punishments.[418] They do not exalt themselves, but are modest about their own accomplishments. When Dante praises the painting of the illuminator Oderisi, he replies by praising in turn the work of Franco Bolognese and by noting the transience of earthly fame.[419] The avaricious explain their state by contrasting themselves with examples of voluntary poverty and generosity.[420] The poet Bonagiunta da Lucca questions Dante about the dolce stil nuovo, quoting a line from one of Dante's poems, and when Dante explains the methods of the new style, he accepts it as better than his own.[421] Dante warmly praises the dolce stil nuovo poet Guido Guinizelli, whom he calls "the father of me, and of others my betters," proclaiming that his works "will make the very ink precious." [422] Guido responds by pointing out the Provençal poet Arnaut Daniel, describing him as "a better craftsman of the mother tongue." [423] The souls in Purgatory express their good fellowship by their courtesy toward Dante and each other. Their good citizenship is reflected in their willingness to embrace compatriots even without knowing who they are, as in the case of the Mantuan Sordello and Vergil.[424] Moreover, they

415. See, for example, *Purg.*, III, 121–23; V, 52–57; XI, 58–72; XIII, 106–14; XIV, 81–85; XIX, 106–14; XXII, 27–54; XXIII, 61–75; XXVI, 83–91.
416. Ibid., III, 136–45; IV, 130–35; V, 130–36; XIII, 147; XXVI, 147.
417. Ibid., VIII, 43–45.
418. Ibid., XVIII, 103–05, 113–17; XIX, 115–26; XXIII, 61–72; XXVI, 139–48.
419. Ibid., XI, 79–117.
420. Ibid., XX, 9–33.
421. Ibid., XXIV, 45–62.
422. Ibid., XXVI, 97–98, 114.
423. Ibid., 117.
424. Ibid., VI, 74–75.

324

are capable of transcending Italian political conflcts in favor of a wider vision of citizenship; the Sienese Sapia, whose city was at war with Dante's Florence, greets Dante as "O brother mine, each one is a citizen of a true city." [425] Furthermore, the souls in Purgatory share a sense of religious community. They indicate the mutuality of their moral strivings by joining in common song. In virtually every canto of the *Purgatorio* there are hymns, psalms, and prayers drawn from the liturgy of the Church. They express a common worship of God; to the extent that they are drawn from the canonical hours, they indicate the time of day; and they reflect the moral character-istics of the various ledges of the mountain of Purgatory, as they move from songs of penitence through the Beatitudes to songs of joy. The sense of community is perhaps most strongly revealed in the *Gloria in excelsis Deo,* which all the souls sing to celebrate the completion of the penance of any one of their number.[426]

We find hymns and psalms sung in Paradise for similar rea-

---

425. Ibid., XIII, 94–95.

426. Hymns, psalms, prayers, Scriptural passages, liturgical texts, and allu-sions to them may be found in *Purgatorio* in II, 46 ("In exitu Israel de Aegypto"); V, 24 ("Miserere"); VII, 82 ("Salve, Regina"); VIII, 13 ("Te lucis ante"); IX, 140 ("Te Deum laudamus"); X, 1 ff. ("Paternoster"); XII, 110 ("Beati pauperes spiritu"); XIII, 29 ("Vinum non habent"); XV, 38 ("Beati misericordes"); XVI, 19 ("Agnus dei"); XVII, 68–69 ("Beati pacifici"); XIX, 49, 73 ("Beati qui lugent," "Adhaesit pavimento anima mea," "Neque nubent"); XX, 136 ("Gloria in excelsis Deo"); XXII, 6 ("Beati qui sitiunt"); XXIII, 11 ("Labia mea, Domine"); XXV, 121, 128 ("Summe Deus clementie," "Virum non cognosco"); XXVII, 8, 58 ("Beati mundo corde," "Venite, benedicti Patris mei"); XXVIII, 80 ("Delectasti"); XXIX, 3, 51, 85–87 ("Beati, quorum tecta sunt peccata," "Osanna," "Benedicta tue ne le figlie d'Adamo" [cf. "Benedicta tu in mulieribus"]); XXX, 11, 19, 83 ("Veni, sponsa de Libano," "Benedictus qui venis," "In te, Domine, speravi"); XXXI, 98 ("Asperges me"); XXXIII, 1, 10–12 ("Deus, venerunt gentes," "Modicum, et non videbitis me"). The functions of liturgical song in the *Comedy* have been noted by Baldwin, *Medieval Rhetoric and Poetic,* p. 273; Fallani, *Poesia e teologia, 2,* 15–28; Fletcher, *Dante,* pp. 140–41; and Singleton, *Commedia,* pp. 36–38. Surprisingly, Gilbert, *Dante,* p. 115, says that there is no evidence of formal worship in the *Comedy.*

sons,[427] and, in the main, conversation in this realm functions much as it does in Purgatory, on a more intense level. Long, courteous speeches packed with doctrine are the rule in Paradise, expressing the intellectual and moral power which the saints possess and which Dante is acquiring. The fluency and charity of the souls in Paradise is matched by their willingness to take the conversational initiative. Like Piccarda Donati, they are "eager to speak"[428] to Dante and often perceive what he wants to ask before he asks it.[429] Good fellowship is reflected throughout Paradise. The numerous souls in the Heaven of Jupiter express their sense of community by speaking as one.[430] All earthly rivalries are stilled in Paradise. Souls usually praise the virtues of others when they themselves are praised,[431] and live harmoniously with those with whom they have quarreled in life. This latter aspect of Paradise is best expressed in the Heaven of the Sun, where the Dominican St. Thomas Aquinas and the Franciscan St. Bonaventura exchange praises of the founders of each other's order. They do not merely magnify the founders of rival orders of friars; they are also capable of sharing their heaven peaceably with Siger of Brabant and Joachim of Flora, men whose ideas were anathema to Thomas and Bonaventura, respectively, during their lifetime.[432] Aquinas' graciousness to his former opponents is further shown when he explains the creation in terms of the doctrine of exemplarism, an idea far more characteristic of the teaching of Bonaventura than of his own.[433] Much has

427. *Par.*, III, 120–21 ("Ave Maria"); VII, 1–3 ("Osanna, sanctus Deus sabaoth"); VIII, 29 ("Osanna"); XVIII, 90–93 ("Diligite justitiam qui judicatis terram"); XXIV, 113 ("Dio laudamo" [cf. "Te Deum laudamus"]); XXV, 98 ("Sperent in te"); XXVI, 69 ("Santo, santo, santo" [cf. "Sanctus"]); XXVII, 1–2 ("Al Padre, al Figlio, a lo Spirito Santo, gloria" [cf. "Gloria patri"]); XXXII, 95 ("Ave Maria, gratia plena").

428. Ibid., III, 16, 42.

429. Ibid., IV, 16–18; VII, 19–24; X, 90–93; XIII, 46–48; XV, 70–72; XX, 88–90; XXVI, 103–05.

430. Ibid., XIX, 10–21.

431. Ibid., III, 109–20; XI, 28–139; XII, 31–145.

432. Ibid., X, 136–38; XII, 140–41.

433. Ibid., XIII, 52–81.

326

been written on the question of whether Dante was a Thomist,[434] an Averroist,[435] a Joachite,[436] and even a Scotist,[437] on the basis of the personnel of his Heaven of the Sun as well as on the basis of the philosophical doctrines which he is deemed to have expressed in the *Comedy*. It would seem more plausible, however, to see his assortment of philosophers and theologians in the Heaven of the Sun as a token of the idea that, in heaven, all earthly conflicts and enmities cease.

In Paradise Dante supplies further insight into the role of speech in drawing the individual toward God and in building a good society. The gracious and voluble reception which Dante is accorded by the saints reveals his notion of the functional interrelations between love and knowledge. The souls greet him so that they may converse, so that information may be exchanged. But this verbal interchange is not merely informative. It is also productive of joy; what the souls and Dante

434. Fletcher, *Dante*, p. 160; Mandonnet, *Dante le théologien*, pp. 10, 130–31, 137–41, 153–57, 255–61, 263–78; A. J. Waters, "The Poet-Theologian of the Middle Ages," *American Catholic Quarterly Review, 39* (1914), 152–59; Philip H. Wicksteed, *Dante & Aquinas* (London, 1913), passim, are among the many who regard the *Divine Comedy* as the *Summa theologiae* set to music. This view has been rebutted by Curtius, "Dante," *Romanische Forschungen, 57,* 171; *European Literature*, pp. 372, 595; Etienne Gilson, *Dante the Philosopher* (New York, 1949), p. 307; Daniel Sargent, "Dante and Thomism," *The Thomist, 5* (1943), 256–64; Sayers, *Further Papers on Dante*, pp. 38–43; H. L. Stewart, "Dante and the Schoolmen," *Journal of the History of Ideas, 10* (1949), 357–73.

435. Supporters of an Averroistic interpretation of Dante are Miguel Asín y Palacios, *Islam and the Divine Comedy* (New York, 1926), pp. 262–64; Bruno Nardi, *Dal "Convivio" alla "Commedia": Sei saggi danteschi* (Roma, 1960), pp. 37–74; "Dante e la filosofia," *Studi danteschi, 25* (1940), 5–42; "Intorno il tomismo di Dante e alla quistione di Sigieri," *GD, 22* (1914), 182–97; "L'Averroismo del 'primo amico' di Dante," *Studi danteschi, 25* (1940), 43–79; "L'Averroismo di Sigieri e Dante," *Studi danteschi, 22* (1938), 83–113.

436. R. E. Kaske, "Dante's 'DXV' and 'Veltro,'" *Traditio, 17* (1961), 185–254; Gertrude Leigh, *New Light on the Youth of Dante* (London, 1929), passim; *The Passing of Beatrice: A Study of the Heterodoxy of Dante* (London, 1932), passim, support a Joachite interpretation. Davis, *Dante*, pp. 205–54, reviews the literature on this question and concludes that Dante was not a Joachite.

437. Gertrude Leigh, "Links between Dante and Duns Scotus," *Church Quarterly Review, 96* (1923), 306–31.

learn from each other increases their mutual love.[438] Love, in turn, is expressed verbally. Cacciaguida, who, according to Dante, reflects a perfect balance between love and knowledge, speaks "in clear words, and with precise discourse." [439] Speech, for Dante as for Augustine, is a form of prayer, a confession of faith, hope, and charity.[440] Furthermore, discourse communicates both wisdom and power.[441] In the *Paradiso* Dante reaffirms the link between speech and moral action which he establishes in his earlier works by placing a discussion of nobility, which recapitulates his ideas on this subject in the *Convivio*, in the Heaven of Venus. The third heaven signifies love and rhetoric, Dante tells us in the *Convivio*, whose second tractate is given over to an analysis of the canzone "Voi che 'ntendendo il terzo ciel movete," and whose fourth tractate goes into the problem of nobility and other aspects of public morality. This association of ideas is carried over into the *Paradiso*, where Charles Martel, the chief speaker in the Heaven of Venus, quotes Dante's canzone and goes on to discuss nobility and civic virtue.[442] In the *Comedy*, no less than in his earlier works, Dante connects eloquence to wisdom and virtue, and therefore relates the state of language to the state of Christian society. Thus, near the end of his heavenly journey, after he has been tested on faith, hope, and charity, Dante encounters Adam, who explains the origin of speech and the *ur-Sprache* of Eden. In Dante's last conversation with a soul before he ascends to the Empyrean, he takes occasion in this way to reaffirm the connection between language and ethics, by having Adam allude to the division of tongues springing from the presumption of Babel.[443]

Dante uses discourse in the literal sense, both spoken and

---

438. *Par.,* V, 105, 119–20; VIII, 46–48; XXI, 64–66.

439. Ibid., XVII, 34–35.

440. Ibid., XIV, 88–90; XXIV, 106–54; XXV, 67–139; XXVI, 13–66; XXXIII, 1–39.

441. Ibid., III, 1–3; XXIX, 73–75; XXX, 55–57.

442. Ibid., VIII, 32–148.

443. Ibid., XXVI, 91–142.

written,[444] to reveal the moral and intellectual status of the souls whom he meets and to show how he, as a character in the *Comedy*, advances in love and knowledge. He also uses a number of nonverbal signs for these purposes, and, like Augustine, he tends to treat them in verbal terms. Music, as we have seen, is found frequently in Purgatory and Paradise. Its impact derives as much from its lyrics, drawn from the Bible and from liturgical texts, as from its melody. Dante treats the eyes and smile of Beatrice, prominent instruments in his enlightenment and motivation, as figures of speech, retaining his *Convivio* interpretation of these devices as the demonstrations and persuasions of the lady. It is true that, on one level, seeing in the *Comedy* may be contrasted with speaking, as vision may be contrasted with knowledge of God by faith, through a glass darkly. This view is substantiated by Dante's increasing tendency in the poem to confess his linguistic ineptitude as his eyes grow progressively stronger, until the vision of God at the end of the *Paradiso* inspires the reaction of silence on the part of the poet. On the other hand, or on another level, it is also possible to regard the senses, particularly sight, as figurative of or correlative with sound, and hence as reducible to linguistic signs. Dante indicates his intention of treating vision in sonic, linguistic terms at the outset of the *Inferno,* which he describes as a realm "where the Sun is silent." [445] He continues this treatment up through the *Paradiso,* where the order and beauty of the heavens are manifested in the harmony of the celestial spheres.[446] While Dante frequently describes the created intermediaries of knowledge as a series of mirrors reflecting the Divine light,[447] in his final vision when he sees

444. In addition to the spoken word, Dante uses the written word, as in the message over the gate of Hell, the inscription on Pope Anastasius' tomb identifying the occupant, and the phrase "Diligite justitiam qui judicatis terram" spelled out by the souls in the Heaven of Jupiter. *Inf.,* III, 1–9; XI, 8–9; *Par.,* XVIII, 90, 93.

445. *Inf.,* I, 60.

446. *Par.,* I, 76–78.

447. Ibid., XXIX, 142–44.

the universe as it exists in God, he has recourse to a verbal symbol, the book of nature, "bound by love in one volume." [448]

Dreams and visual art are other nonverbal devices which Dante treats verbally in explaining the process of his instruction in the other world. The personages whom he meets in dreams do not merely present themselves to be seen, but speak or sing.[449] In *Purgatorio* X and XII, Dante tells the reader of the sculptures he sees on the wall and pavement as he walks up the mountain. This sculpture is didactic, as it contains figures illustrating types of humility and pride. Dante judges the sculpture excellent and marvelous because of the skill and craftsmanship that went into it and because the figures correspond so graphically to the persons they are designed to signify:

> What master were he of brush or of graver, who
>   drew the shades and the lineaments, which
>   there would make every subtle wit stare?
> Dead seemed the dead, and the living, living.
>   He saw not better than I who saw the reality
>   of all that I trod upon while I was going
>   bent down.[450]

Dante specifies the realism of the sculpture by interpreting it in verbal terms; he describes it as a "story set in rock," stating that the figures are so vivid that one can almost hear them speaking.[451] Expressing his inversion of Horace's dictum, *ut pictura poesis,* he calls the sculpture "visible speech." [452] Dante also stresses the connections between morality and knowledge in this passage by placing the sculptures counseling

448. Ibid., XXXIII, 86. See Ernst Robert Curtius, "Das Buch als Symbol in der Divina Commedia," *Festschrift zum sechzigsten Geburtstag von Paul Clemen* (Bonn, 1926), pp. 44–54; "Schrift- und Buchmetaphorik in der Welt-literatur," *Neue Beiträge deutscher Forschung: Wilhelm Worringer zum 60. Geburtstag* (Königsberg, 1943), pp. 70–86.

449. *Purg.*, XVII, 34–39; XIX, 7–33; XXVII, 97–108.

450. Ibid., XII, 64–69.

451. Ibid., X, 52, 39–45, 58–60, 82–93.

452. Ibid., 95.

humility on the wall and those illustrating pride on the pavement; the humble are exalted while the proud are cast down. The viewer who has seen the images of humility and has absorbed their message proceeds with downcast head; it is only in this position that he is able to see the images of pride and to learn from them as well.

Dante also employs a number of symbols as key words. By repeating them in several different contexts and by linking them to several different concepts and persons, he achieves an economical association in the reader's mind among these concepts and persons. The *Comedy* expresses Dante's unification of social, political, religious, personal, and literary concerns,[453] and the repetition of these key symbolic terms is one of the ways in which he reveals this unification. Let us content ourselves with three examples. The richest symbol which Dante uses in this manner is the eagle. The eagle symbolizes the empire, the just ruler, and the supremely social virtue of justice, as well as the rapacity and injustice of a depraved Church and empire.[454] At the same time the eagle, the only creature that can look directly at the sun, signifies Beatrice.[455] The eagle which, in Dante's dream, carries him to the steps of the gate of Purgatory, where he experiences penitence, can be taken to represent grace or the Holy Spirit, which inspires contrition in the soul of the sinner,[456] while St. John, the evangelist of charity, is described in Paradise as "Christ's eagle," [457] tying John's Dantean significance with

453. Noted by Baldwin, *Medieval Rhetoric and Poetic,* pp. 273, 279; Freccero, *Dante,* pp. 2–3; Gilbert, *Dante's Conception of Justice,* passim; Wilkins, *Dante,* p. 37.

454. *Purg.,* X, 79–81; *Par.,* VI, 1–9; XVIII, 70–136; *Purg.,* XXXII, 112–17, 124–41.

455. *Par.,* I, 48.

456. *Purg.,* IX, 19–49. In this connection, see Exodus 19:4: "Ye have seen what I did unto the Egyptians and how I bore you on eagle's wings and brought you unto myself." On the exodus theme in the *Comedy,* see Singleton, "In Exitu Israel de Aegypto," *Dante,* ed. Freccero, pp. 102–21, and especially 117, 120–21. I am indebted to Professor Andrew Bongiorno for this reference.

457. *Par.,* XXVI, 53.

331

his traditional Apocalyptic symbolism as the eagle in the tet-
ragrammaton. The craft of poetry also participates in this
symbol. As Dante avers after joining the classical poets in the
Limbo of the virtuous pagans, the lord of highest song, vari-
ously identified as Homer or Vergil, transcends the others like
the eagle.[458]

Dante uses the symbol of the sun in a similar fashion. The
sun traditionally symbolizes God,[459] the "planet that leads
men straight on every road," [460] the Christ Whom Vergil was
born too late to know.[461] The reflection of the Christ-Griffon
in Beatrice's eyes is like the sun in a mirror.[462] But the sun
also symbolizes Beatrice herself.[463] It is Apollo, the sun god,
the leader of the Muses, whom Dante invokes for poetic
aid,[464] and, in the *Convivio* and the *De monarchia,* he describes his own writing as the sun dispersing the surrounding
darkness.[465] The sun signifies Divine illumination,[466] but it
also signifies political and ecclesiastical power and their proper
relationships. Adverting to a prominent theme of his *De monarchia,* Dante places in the mouth of Marco Lombardo a
speech observing that the Church and the empire are ideally
equal, independent, and Divinely sanctioned, like two suns.[467]
A third highly connotative symbol is the tree. The image
of the tree in itself conjures up associations of the tree of the
knowledge of good and evil in the garden of Eden and the
cross of the Crucifixion. Dante uses two speaking trees in Purgatory to express the virtue of moderation, as opposed to
avarice and prodigality.[468] He describes the French mon-

458. *Inf.,* IV, 94–96.
459. *Par.,* I, 47.
460. *Inf.,* I, 17–18.
461. *Purg.,* VII, 25–27.
462. Ibid., XXXI, 121–23.
463. Ibid., XXXII, 1–12 ; *Par.,* III, 1–6.
464. *Par.,* I, 13–15.
465. *Convivio,* I, xiii, 12 ; *De mon.,* II, i, 4–6.
466. *Par.,* I, 61–63.
467. *Purg.,* XVI, 106–14.
468. Ibid., XXII, 130–54 ; XXIV, 100–26.

archy, the current threat disturbing the right political and ecclesiastical order of Europe, as an "evil tree." [469] In the Earthly Paradise, Beatrice shows Dante a barren tree, despoiled of its foliage, representing the empire. Then she shows him the same tree blossoming again with leaves and flowers of imperial purple, inviting him to sit with her at its roots, saying, "Here shalt thou be a short time a forester, and with me everlastingly shalt be a citizen of that Rome whereof Christ is Roman." [470] The tree also signifies the laurel, emblem of poetic distinction. In his invocation to Apollo, Dante affirms, "Thou shalt see me come to thy chosen tree and crown me, then, with the leaves of which the matter and thou shalt make me worthy." [471] Finally, Dante uses the symbol of the tree to express his own moral regeneration after passing through Eunoë at the top of Purgatory: "I came back from the most holy waves, born again, even as new trees renewed with new foliage, pure and ready to mount to the stars." [472] Thus Dante binds together his own personal morality, his poetry, Beatrice, his ideal of the Christian society, and God, by applying the same literary symbols to all of them.

Dante's aesthetic of poetic rectitude leads him to strive to make his words and images correspond to their significata. If they did not, his poetry would not possess rectitude. It would lack truth, and hence would be incapable of instructing the reader in the truth. At the same time, the Incarnational point of view which Dante shares with other proponents of Augustinian sign theory, as well as his typological approach to symbolism, lead him to strive to express spiritual realities in tangible, material, earthly terms, in the terms of daily life. These two objectives interact to produce one of the most distinctive and most frequently noted features of Dante's style. His language, vocabulary, diction, and syntax, the phonetic devices

469. Ibid., XX, 43–44.
470. Ibid., XXXII, 100–03, 37–60, 86–99.
471. *Par.*, I, 25–27.
472. *Purg.*, XXXIII, 142–45.

and sonic effects that he uses, are highly concrete, mimetic, and precise. The *Comedy*'s linguistic structure and its variety of linguistic styles always clearly reflect the significative and didactic functions which Dante applies to language.[473]

Let one major example suffice to underline this point. One of Dante's chief means of communicating doctrine to the reader is through persons.[474] Persons, in turn, are delineated through their conversation. What Dante's characters say and the way in which they say it express their own, unique, historical personalities, no less than the moral states they represent in the poem.[475] This fact has both ethical and epistemological importance. Dante wishes to stress the idea that vices and virtues do not exist in the abstract, but only in the context of actual human lives. The human context, therefore, acquires crucial significance. Suicide, for instance, cannot be understood simply as an abstract category of sin, which invariably draws the same response from God. There are several characters in the *Comedy* who are guilty of suicide, but they are not all treated in the same way. Dante places Dido and Cleopatra in the circle of lust in Hell, since they killed themselves in despair over the termination of their passionate, adulterous love affairs, in both cases, it might be noted, at the expense of their political obligations as ruling queens. Pier delle Vigne, the

473. Auerbach, *Dante,* pp. 49, 97–98, 160–73; Barbi, *Life of Dante,* pp. 72, 83; Luigi Cellucci, "La poetica di Dante e la sua poesia," *Cultura neolatina, 10,* fasc. 1 (1950), 89; Gilbert, *Dante,* pp. 62, 64–66; Grandgent, *Power of Dante,* pp. 224–25; Laurenzi, *Ermetica ed ermeneutica,* p. 10; Malagoli, *Linguaggio e poesia,* passim and especially pp. 7–26; Mazzeo, *Medieval Cultural Tradition,* p. 9; *Structure and Thought,* pp. 46–47; Singleton, *Journey to Beatrice,* p. 7; Williams, *Figure of Beatrice,* p. 199; Zingarelli, *La vita, 2,* 773–74.

474. Bergin, "On the *Personae* of the *Comedy,*" *Italica, 42,* 1–7.

475. As shown by Erich Auerbach's exemplary analysis of the speeches of Farinata and Cavalcanti in *Mimesis: The Representation of Reality in Western Literature* (Garden City, N.Y., 1957), pp. 151–76; and Renato Poggioli's "Paolo and Francesca," *Dante,* ed. Freccero, pp. 61–77. Many other characters in the *Comedy* are susceptible of this kind of analysis, and await their Auerbachs and Poggiolis. It goes without saying that Dante, like other medieval thinkers, regards most of the characters in classical fiction as historical personages.

minister of Frederick II, is also in Hell, in the circle of violence. Dante subdivides this circle into four categories: violence against others, violence against oneself, violence against
God, and violence against nature and art. He classifies Pier as
violent against himself. This classification is based not merely
on the fact that Pier took his own life. It is also based on the
reasons for his behavior. As Pier explains it, he killed himself
in despair at false accusations of disloyalty to Frederick,
which led to his imprisonment and blinding on the orders of
the prince. Pier maintains that he remained faithful and just
to Frederick throughout. But, Dante emphasizes, it is impossible to be just to others if one is unjust to himself. Dante
contrasts Pier's self-destruction in the face of unjust treatment by his prince with the case of Romeo of Villeneuve,
chamberlain to Raymond Berengar IV of Provence. On losing
his office after years of faithful service, Romeo became a wan-
dering beggar and holy man.[476] There is another suicide in
the *Comedy,* Cato of Utica. Far from being punished in Hell
for having taken his own life, Cato represents the infused cardinal virtues and guards the gate of Purgatory. An opponent
of Caesar, Cato committed suicide so as not to have to live
under the empire after the battle of Thapsus in 46 B.C. Dante
regards Cato's suicide as a supreme sacrifice for the sake of
liberty. As such, it is a virtue, not a vice, and hence the position of eminence that he gives to Cato in the *Comedy.*

It is clear from this example that the location of the suicides in the other world depends on the reasons why they
killed themselves and involves a concrete knowledge of their
lives and personalities on the part of the reader. A concrete
projection of his characters thus becomes an important task of
the writer, because, as Dante notes through the words of Beatrice, the didactic function of the poem depends on the ability
of the reader to recognize the persons who are being rewarded
or punished for their actions on earth.[477] It is therefore es-

476. *Par.,* VI, 127–42.
477. *Par.,* XVII, 124–42.

sential for Dante to choose characters who are historical personages well known to his audience and to put speeches into their mouths capable of expressing their personalities with realism and precision.

Dante's imagery and figures of speech, too, are highly concrete and realistic. His similes and metaphors always play a clarifying role and are never merely coloristic or ornamental.[478] As Bergin has so aptly put it, "For Dante the beginning was the word"; Dante's imagery, no less than his diction, reveals "a richness of objective correlatives." [479] Dante uses a comparatively small number of figures of speech drawn from allusions to literature.[480] He also draws few of his similes from the vegetable world.[481] Many images, however, are taken from the behavior or appearance of animals,[482] from climatic conditions and specific landscapes,[483] from common

478. Auerbach, *Dante,* pp. 19–21, 154–55; Barbi, *Life of Dante,* p. 83; Bergin, *Dante,* pp. 252, 279–86; "Hell: Topography and Demography," *Essays on Dante,* ed. Mark Musa (Bloomington, Ind., 1964), pp. 77–78; Eliot, *Dante,* p. 24; Gilbert, *Dante,* pp. 84–100; Ker, *Essays,* p. 49; Pischedda, *L'Orrido e l'ineffabile,* pp. 100 ff.; Sayers, *Introductory Papers on Dante,* pp. 8–9, 121–42; *Further Papers on Dante,* p. 55; Scandura, *L'estetica di Dante, Petrarca e Boccaccio,* pp. 109 ff.; Vittorini, *High Points,* pp. 10–11.

479. Bergin, *Dante,* pp. 279, 286.

480. *Inf.,* XXVII, 7–15; XXX, 1–27; XXXI, 4–6; *Purg.,* XXVII, 37–42; XXIX, 4–7; *Par.,* I, 68; II, 16–18; XVII, 46–48; XXXIII, 66.

481. *Inf.,* II, 127–32; III, 112–17; XXV, 58–60; *Purg.,* XXXII, 52–60; XXXIII, 142–45; *Par.,* IV, 130–31; XXII, 52–57; XXVI, 85–90.

482. *Inf.,* II, 44–48; III, 115–17; V, 40–49, 82–87; VI, 28–33; VII, 82–84; VIII, 49–51; IX, 76–81; XII, 22–25; XIII, 109–14, 124–26; XVI, 1–3; XVII, 16–24, 48–50, 127–35; XXII, 19–30, 127–32; XXV, 130–32; XXVI, 28–33; XXX, 25–27; XXXII, 30–36, 50–51; XXXIV, 46–51; *Purg.,* II, 124–33; IX, 13–18; XII, 1–3; XIII, 67–72, 122–23; XIX, 64–67; XXIV, 64–69; XXV, 10–15; XXVI, 34–39, 43–48, 133–35; XXVII, 76–87; XXXII, 128–35; *Par.,* IV, 1–6, 127–28; V, 82–84, 100–05; VIII, 52–54; XVIII, 73–78; XIX, 34–39, 91–96; XX, 73–78; XXI, 34–45; XXIII, 1–12; XXV, 19–24; XXVI, 97–102; XXXI, 7–12.

483. *Inf.,* V, 28–30; VII, 13–15; IX, 64–72, 112–17; XII, 4–10; XIII, 7–9; XIV, 28–30, 79–81; XV, 4–12; XVI, 94–105; XX, 61–93; XXIV, 1–18; XXXII, 22–30; XXXIV, 4–7; *Purg.,* III, 49–51; IV, 25–27; V, 37–42, 94–129; X, 7–9; XII, 100–08; XIV, 16–21, 130–35; XVII, 1–12; XXIV, 145–50; XXVIII, 7–21; XXX, 85–99; XXXIII, 109–11; *Par.,* VIII, 58–78; IX, 25–31; XI, 43–54; XVI, 82–84; XX, 19–21; XXI, 106–11; XXII, 99; XXIII, 40–45; XXVII, 28–30, 67–72; XXVIII, 79–87; XXX, 46–51; XXXI, 118–32.

human activities, reactions, attitudes, and experiences,[484] from familiar objects undergoing common chemical and physical processes,[485] and from a host of miscellaneous everyday things.[486] The keynote in Dante's figurative comparisons is always on the commonplace and the familiar. Dante aims at expressing the strange and wondrous things which he experiences in the other world of the spirit in the terms of this world so that they will be immediately and utterly recognizable to his audience. His motive is didactic, and the underlying rationale of his imagery is Incarnational typology.

It can be seen from this inspection of Dante's poetics, as exemplified in the *Divine Comedy,* that Dante is in full possession of Augustine's linguistic epistemology and that he applies this theory to his poem while shifting Augustine's emphasis in some respects. Dante develops his own poetic theory gradually, drawing upon some aspects of the classical and medieval tradition of literary criticism and rejecting others. He explains his own theory fully only in his letter to Can Grande, and he illustrates it fully only in the *Divine Comedy.*

484. *Inf.,* I, 22–27, 55–58; II, 37–42; VIII, 22–24; XV, 16–21, 120–24; XVI, 22–27, 130–36; XVII, 85–88; XVIII, 22–33; XIX, 49–50; XX, 7–9; XXI, 7–18; XXIII, 1–3, 37–42; XXIX, 46–51; XXX, 52–57, 91–92, 136–41; XXXI, 34–39; XXXII, 32–33, 127–29; XXXIV, 44–45; *Purg.,* II, 10–12; IV, 19–24, 103–05; VI, 1–12; IX, 16–18, 41–42, 64–67; XII, 127–29; XIII, 58–66; XV, 3; XVI, 10–14, 85–94; XVII, 40–45; XXIII, 1–3, 16–21; XXIV, 70–74, 94–97, 106–08; XXV, 4–7; XXVI, 67–70; XXVII, 44–45; XXVIII, 52–57; XXX, 58–63, 79–81; XXXI, 64–67; XXXII, 19–24, 67–68; XXXIII, 130–34; *Par.,* I, 51, 101–02; II, 127–29, 133–38; IV, 1–3; X, 79–81; XVIII, 58–69; XXII, 1–6; XXIII, 121–26; XXIV, 46–51, 148–51, 148–54; XXV, 102–08, 133–39; XXX, 82–96, 138–41; XXXI, 43–48; XXXII, 139–41; XXXIII, 58–61, 106–08; 133–36.

485. *Inf.,* VIII, 13–18; XIV, 37–39; XVII, 135–36; XIX, 28–30; XXIII, 46–49; XXV, 57–66; XXVI, 38–39, 85–87; XXXIV, 10–12; *Purg.,* XV, 16–24; XVII, 31–33; XXIV, 136–39; XXV, 17–18, 91–99; XXX, 85–90; XXXI, 15–21, 96; XXXIII, 79–81; *Par.,* I, 40–42, 58–60; II, 22–24, 31–36, 89–90; V, 91–94; VIII, 16–21; IX, 112–14; XIV, 1–9, 52–57; XV, 22–24; XVI, 28–32; XVII, 121–23; XVIII, 70–72; XIX, 4–6, 19–21; XX, 22–27, 79–81; XXI, 28–29; XXIV, 13–16; XXVIII, 4–12, 88–93; XXIX, 25–30; XXX, 109–14.

486. *Inf.,* XVII, 19–20, 100–05; XVIII, 10–13; XIX, 16–18; XXVIII, 22–27; XXIX, 73–84; XXXI, 58–59, 136–45; XXXII, 49–50; XXXIV, 46–48; *Purg.,* I, 2; IV, 91–93; X, 130–39; XVII, 77–78; XXIV, 1–3; XXXII, 116–17; *Par.,* II, 1–15; V, 37–39; X, 139–48; XIV, 118–23; XX, 142–48; XXIII, 67–69.

Dante, like the other proponents of medieval verbal epistemology treated in this study, conceives of the signs which
mediate knowledge in fundamentally linguistic and sensible
terms, whether these verbal signs be conceived literally or figuratively. He holds that poetic language signifies God truly,
and, in fact, that poetry is the discipline best suited to this
purpose but that its power to represent Divine realities always
remains partial. The significata of his poem are the norm of
the rectitude of the terms in which he expresses them, a principle that requires the use of evocative images and a variety of
specific stylistic devices. For Dante, the plausibility of representing spiritual truths in highly concrete, material, and temporal terms is a corollary of the latent Aristotelianism in the
Augustinian sign theory, the doctrine of the Incarnation, and
the typological method of allegory transposed from Scripture
to Christian poetry.

On the subjective level, Dante's poem is designed to teach,
to delight, and to persuade the reader, to orient him toward
virtue. It assumes the functions of Christian rhetoric as defined by Augustine. Yet, in specifying the nature and aims of
rhetorical Christian poetry, Dante introduces an emphasis
characteristically his own. The rectitude toward which Dante's reader is to be stimulated is an amalgam of personal ethics, religion, and civic virtue, modeled on the Dantean pattern
of a regenerated Christian commonwealth, which will restore
the cultural and political centrality of Italy to the Holy Roman Empire and to the Church and which will bring back the
ancient nonpartisan virtues of the Florentines, in addition to
integrating Christian Europe, depressing the political currency
of France, and eliminating greed and war. Didactic poetry
written according to rules in a unified Italian vernacular is to
be the means of moving the reader toward these goals. Within
the didactic poem there is a variety of stylistic strategies
through which the author hopes to teach, delight, and persuade his audience, ranging from the content of the poem,
which he thinks will evoke general interest, to a host of spe-

338

cific characters and images designed to make the message immediate to the reader.

Pleasure, for Dante, is never a subordinate aim in rhetorical poetry. The reader cannot appropriate the intellectual content of the *Comedy* except by appropriating it aesthetically. Dante stresses this point by making the chief character in the *Comedy* himself, an initially bewildered pilgrim through Hell, Purgatory, and Heaven who learns through conversation, observation, experience, and human love. By casting himself as a character with whom the reader can identify, Dante the author creates the possibility of the reader's vicariously experiencing what Dante the character experiences. The ultimate objective of Dante the author, outside of winning fame, is to reproduce in the reader a conversion similar to the series of catharses and illuminations which Dante the traveler undergoes. Dante stands for the reader at the same time that he stands above the reader and instructs him; the reader of the *Comedy,* like the reader of Augustine's *Confessiones,* shares the spiritual state of the author, if not his knowledge, talent, or sanctity. The traveler, and by extension, the reader, grows in knowledge as he grows in love and as his aesthetic senses are strengthened. Dante illustrates this idea in his use of the theme of light, in his stress on visual and aural perception, and by the important role that he assigns to the emotional relationships between Dante the character and his guides. In this way he underlines the notion that love and beauty are ways of knowing. Joy, for Dante, is not the consequence of knowledge, but its concomitant.

Both as author and character, Dante frequently expresses his need for God's grace. The mediation of grace, through other human beings, is the crucial factor in the traveler's progressive enlightenment, and, by extension, the enlightenment of the reader. God is revealed in man, for Dante, not in the vestiges of the Trinity impressed in the human soul, but in the total human personality and in the context of complete human relationships, both personal and social. For these me-

339

dia to function as channels of love and knowledge, however, God must deliberately choose to act through them on specific occasions. Thus Dante reveals his adherence to the Augustinian notion that signs play an instrumental, not a heuristic role in conveying knowledge to the subject.

In assessing whether Dante posits both commemorative and indicative functions for his *Comedy,* in determining whether he wrote the poem for an audience composed of both believers and nonbelievers, the student of Dante faces an interesting paradox. Dante's heavy reliance on traditional Christian doctrines, characters, and images, his equally heavy reliance on characters and figurative allusions familiar only to his contemporaries, and his great stress on linguistic reform manifested in his use of the Tuscan dialect in the *Comedy,* indicate that he conceives of himself as addressing a specific audience existing in a specific time and place. This audience is composed of Italians who are at least nominal Christian believers. The function of the poem vis-à-vis this audience is hence commemorative. Dante aims at bringing to the minds of his contemporaries truths, both Divine and human, which they already hold, but which they have pushed aside and ceased to use as guides to life. He wants to help this kind of reader deepen his appreciation of these truths. Singleton is therefore quite correct in describing the epistemological character of the *Comedy* in the terms of *fides quaerens intellectum.*[487] This Anselmian principle, like the moral and epistemological norm of rectitude, indeed provides us with a fitting framework in which to view the poem. However, unlike Anselm, Dante does not pay much attention, even in theory, to the presumptive needs of a nonbelieving audience or to the reader who, unlike an early fourteenth-century Italian, would not be able to recognize all of his scenic descriptions, figurative allusions, or characters. Yet the history of the reception of the *Comedy* indicates that Dante's masterpiece has found a wide audience

487. Singleton, "Dante and Myth," *Journal of the History of Ideas, 10,* 484–87.

among readers who do not share his theological, philosophical, or political views. This fact amply testifies to the inadvertent indicative power of the *Comedy*, although it has also produced some interpretative distortions of the work, in which Dante's *bello stile* and the aesthetic pleasure to be derived from the *Comedy* have been occasionally divorced from the poem's doctrinal content and from the poet's didactic poetics. In any event, Dante, of the four thinkers discussed in this study, is certainly the one who devotes the least amount of attention to the problem of communicating religious knowledge to the nonbeliever, and he makes the fewest ostensible attempts to speak comprehensibly to him. Yet such is the power of Dante's art that he has probably communicated to the nonbeliever, as well as to the believer, more effectively through the centuries than Augustine, Anselm, or Aquinas.

Conclusion

This study of the theory of signs in religious knowledge in the thought of St. Augustine, St. Anselm, St. Thomas Aquinas, and Dante Alighieri has shown that there are powerful links binding the four together as well as many points of difference among them. Their basic similarities derive from the fact that they possess a common core of Christian ideas on the ways in which man may know God by faith, *per speculum in aenigmate*. All four of them believe that religious knowledge is always mediated through Christ the Word in this life. All four combine this belief with a verbal species of sign theory derived from classical antiquity by way of the trivium. This classical sign theory provides them with their mental tools and with the Aristotelian certainty that sense data conduce authentically to a knowledge of prior and non-sensible realities. The differences among the four thinkers are dictated largely by the fact that each inherits, and in some cases helps to crystallize, a stress on one or the other of the disciplines of the trivium.

Thus Augustine conceives of human modes of knowing God as literal or figurative statements about Him. The specific shape of these statements is determined by their objective reference, the need to represent an object of knowledge that is intrinsically mysterious, and by their function in Christian rhetoric of instructing and persuading an audience. Anselm seeks an accurate grammatical denomination of God, a name of God that takes into account the knower's need for an intellectual and moral attitude appropriate to Him. Rectitude is the idea which describes the name of God that satisfies these requirements. He bases the arguments which he uses to support the view that his name of God possesses rectitude upon the usages of eleventh-century grammar. Aquinas approaches

342

the problem of knowing God by the avenue of scholastic logic, with its principles of demonstration and dialectic, its syllogistic structure, and its empirical foundations. This orientation leads him to work out an epistemology of the hidden God through the knowledge of the natural world. Dante adverts once again to rhetoric, but he re-expresses Augustinian rhetoric in the form of Christian poetics. In this poetic theory, the poet's creation of a didactic work of art is his means of expressing the Word; and the reader's aesthetic appreciation of the poem is the means of his moral and intellectual instruction, persuasion, and delight. The differences in the ways by which these four thinkers approach the same problem reflect the varying milieux in which they labored and to which they spoke. They also reflect their variations in professional emphasis and personal style.

Yet, Augustine, Anselm, Aquinas, and Dante all adhere to the same doctrine of words as signs in the knowledge of God. In the theory of signification they all employ, being is prior to knowing. This presupposition is consistent both with the metaphysical bias of the classical philosophy from which they derived the theory and with their concentration on God as the object of knowledge and the intellectual light par excellence. They warrant their search for signs and analogues of God in nature, history, and human psychology with scriptural assertions proclaiming that the creation bears witness to God, and that it is a way of knowing Him. At the same time, their reading of the Bible encourages them to place limits on the significative and communicative powers of signs. Their frequent avowal of literary and conceptual ineptitude in the face of the mystery of God underlines their belief that God always transcends anything that men can think or say about Him. Their stress on the extrinsic effectiveness of signs in the acquisition and transmission of religious knowledge flows from their belief that the normative knowledge of God is a knowledge by faith. Faith, they hold, is a gift of God. God gives it to men on His own initiative, irrespective of human efforts. Their interest in

343

the moral as well as the intellectual character of knowledge reflects their conviction that faith has both moral and intellectual consequences. Faith, they affirm, is not a static mental relationship between God and man but a dynamic condition, in which the believer moves toward the vision of God, a beatitude which perfects the whole man and which transforms all of his human relationships.

These Christian precepts combine with classical doctrines on the functions and values of signs in the cognitive process to form the verbal sign theory basic to medieval symbolic thought. In this theory, signs represent things truly but partially. They are never identical with their objects, and their accuracy is always judged by reference to these objects. Signs never produce knowledge in the subject in the first instance. The subjective function of signs in helping to communicate knowledge depends on the knower's previous relationship to the object. If he is already a believer, he can recognize the sign as a sign of God and can judge how Godlike it is; the sign in turn can deepen his awareness of God. If he is not a believer, the sign can merely indicate the direction in which he should turn in order to orient himself toward God. Signs are instrumental in the subject's acquisition of belief or of a deeper insight into it only when God wills this to occur in the case of a particular subject at a particular time. For the thinkers here studied, the primary objects of knowledge are God, and, to a lesser extent, man and the universe seen in a God-related perspective. The principal signs of God, in a literal sense, are the verbal testimonies of teachers of the Word, whether they be scriptural writers, preachers, theologians, or poets. In a figurative sense, the principal sign of God is the creation, and above all the human soul, in which the vestiges of the Trinity have been impressed.

Augustine frames this theory for the Western Middle Ages in its first and most explicit form. He is also the best example of its expression in the mode of rhetoric. Both of these facts are direct consequences of his conversion from pagan rhetoric to Christian eloquence, an event which forced him to reshuffle

344

his previous views on verbal signs in order to explain how they worked in a Christian epistemology. One may also attribute Augustine's stress on the bond between the Incarnation and the Christian use of words in the knowledge of God to the nature of his intellectual voyage to Christianity and the dangerous, yet tempting, obstacles which he encountered on his way. The Incarnation, to be sure, is central in any Christian theology. In Augustine's thought it is not merely prominent; it also plays a distinctive role. On the level of metaphysics, the Incarnation serves as a compass by means of which he charts his course around the shoals of Manicheism and Neoplatonism. On the level of rhetoric, the immediate implication that Augustine perceives in the Word made flesh is the redemption of human speech. Since he is a rhetorician after his conversion as well as before it, he therefore interprets the theologian's role as a participation in the Incarnational task of expressing the Word to the world.

For Anselm, the Incarnational dimensions of theological statements are implicit rather than explicit. On the whole, despite his extensive borrowings from Augustine, his approach to theology is quite different from that of the Bishop of Hippo. While Anselm, like Augustine, can be thought of as a pastoral theologian, he has far fewer problems of communication than Augustine. He is not a bishop faced regularly with the task of addressing a heterogeneous congregation in his cathedral. Nor is he an apologist faced with combating a diverse series of heresies. Instead, Anselm's task is to edify a small group of Benedictine monks, who can be regarded as fairly homogeneous in terms of their education, their intellectual methods, and their vocation. He strives not to extract a theory of signs from the amplitude of classical culture but to translate a spiritually oriented form of meditation on God into a grammatical style of theological speculation. Working with a very limited number of classical sources in an environment not especially fraught with spiritual turmoil, he develops a way of speaking about God which provides for its audience the heightened tang of old wine poured from new bottles. His accomplishment is more a consequence of circumstantial developments in the discipline of grammar than a portent of the future, since the peculiar form of Aristotelianized grammar and the predominantly monastic style of exegesis that he incorporates into his theological method were rapidly to be replaced after his death.

In some ways, Aquinas resembles Augustine more than Anselm, despite the gap in time which separates him from the Bishop of Hippo. He, too, is in possession of a fairly wide range of classical materials, although he channels them through logic as inexorably as Augustine appropriates his own sources in rhetorical terms. Aquinas, like Augustine, is faced with the problem of intellectual diversity and apologetic dispute. His works, both in their structure and in the arrangement of their contents, are occasion pieces, despite their ostensibly systematic character; his emphasis is often dictated as much by the nature and extent of the objections that he has set himself to answer as by the intrinsic importance of a given subject to his teachings. However, despite the fact that Thomas has to address a variety of points of view, unlike Augustine, he can speak to them all in the same intellectual language, the language of the thirteenth-century university. He expects his opponents to engage him in debate at the academic level and in the technical terminology of the professional scholastic theologian. Thomas' adherence to Aristotelian epistemology dictates an approach to religious signification which makes the natural world its point of departure and which concentrates on the question of how knowledge enters the human mind. There are points at which this method appears to set Thomas off from Augustine and Anselm, neither of whom is interested in analyzing the process of conceptualization in detail, and both of whom manifest only the most transitory concern with nature as a source of signs of God. While he reflects the contemporary thirteenth-century emphasis on cosmology, Thomas does not always manage to fuse it with complete success to the conventional stress on the mind of man as the most fruitful source of signs of God. His empir-

346

icism, deep-rooted though it is, in no way prescinds from his acknowledgment that it is God Who guarantees the truth of what men may think about Him through His signs. The important place Christology holds in Augustine's expression of the theory of verbal signs takes a form in Thomas' thought corresponding to the Dominican's emphasis on nature. For Aquinas, God's self-revelation through signs resides preeminently in Christ as the logos of the creation. The restoration of man to God takes place through the redemption of nature and of man's knowledge of it.

The fact that the Augustinian theory of signs can be, and was, applied to religious literature as well as to technical theology is amply demonstrated by Dante. With the zeal of a reformer and the aesthetic convictions of a supreme artist, Dante formulates a theory of literature, put into practice in his *Divine Comedy,* which provides a rationale for a layman to teach the truth about God, man, and Christian society through a work of poetry. Dante develops this theory gradually. In the process of doing so, he draws upon the various strands of medieval poetics, some of which he rejects and some of which he accepts and reorients. In particular, he receives from his medieval and classical predecessors a conflation of rhetoric and poetics, in which rhetoric absorbs poetry. As Dante appropriates this tradition, however, he changes it in two ways. He understands rhetoric in a Christian sense, according to the Augustinian model, and conceives of it in a political and social context. Also, he stands the conflation of poetics and rhetoric on its head by assimilating rhetoric to poetry. Thus, for Dante, poetic language acquires all the epistemological and moral powers and limitations which Augustine attributes to rhetoric, and which Anselm and Aquinas, following Augustine, attribute to grammar and logic, and for exactly the same reasons. Dante's verbal signs encompass the full repertoire of poetic technique, from syntax and vocabulary to similes and symbols. His objective is to express Divine truths perceived in a fictional other-worldly vision in language that possesses rectitude. Rectitude implies accuracy and humility

347

vis-à-vis his subject matter and a delightful and convincing mode of expression vis-à-vis his audience. This in turn entails a concrete, precise, and realistic style. Dante's interest in expressing spiritual realities in highly sensible and tangible terms reflects his certainty that sensible signs can convey authentic information about non-sensible significata. Language is itself a sensible sign; but above and beyond this, Dante's poetic style focuses on aurally pleasing sonic effects and vivid visual images. This focus reveals the Christological dimensions of Dante's theory; a work on a transcendent theme expressed concretely and tangibly is the poetic corollary of the Incarnation. Dante selects man above all other creatures as the principal source of signs of God. But, unlike Augustine, Anselm, or Aquinas, he does not stress the vestiges of the Trinity in the human soul. Man, for Dante, participates in the mission of Christ; he signifies and mediates God to his fellow men through a just and peaceful social life in the Divinely sanctioned human institutions, the Church and the empire, through idealized human love, and through inspired Christian poetry.

Each of these four thinkers employs a characteristic mode of expression; yet none of them is completely at liberty to choose his own theological language. Before the fact, Augustine, Anselm, Aquinas, and Dante are committed to the classical disciplines of thought and expression which have been engrained in their minds by their education and which provide them with their intellectual tools. But to the extent that Augustine, Anselm, Aquinas, and Dante are conscious of current options, they make their choices with an eye to the fitness of given classical or medieval epistemological doctrines to the task of expressing the knowledge of God, and of expressing it to the times which they each address. All of them are sensitive to the theologian's simultaneous responsibility to be true and to be meaningful; and all of them are bold in their acceptance of the innovations of their day and in their willingness to convert them to Christian purposes.

348

Bibliography

WORKS OF REFERENCE

Bourke, Vernon J., *Thomistic Bibliography, 1920–1940,* Supplement to *The Modern Schoolman, 21,* St. Louis, The Modern Schoolman, 1945.

Deferrari, Roy J., *A Latin-English Dictionary of St. Thomas Aquinas,* Boston, St. Paul Editions, 1960.

DuCange, C., *Glossarium mediae et infimae latinitatis, 1,* Graz, Akademische Druck- u. Verlagsanstalt, 1954.

Forcellini, Aegidius, *Totius latinitatis lexicon, 1,* Prati, Aldini Edenti, 1858.

Mandonnet, P., and J. Destrez, *Bibliographie thomiste,* 2ᵐᵉ éd. rev. M.-D. Chenu, Bibliothèque thomiste, *1,* Paris, Librairie Philosophique J. Vrin, 1960.

Thesaurus linguae latinae, editus auctoritate et consilio quinque Academiarum Germanicarum Berolinensis Goetingensis Lipsiensis Monacensis Vindobonensis, *1,* Lipsiae, B. G. Teubner, 1900.

Wyser, Paul, *Thomas von Aquin,* Bibliographische Einführungen in das Studium der Philosophie, herausgegeben von I. M. Bochenski, *13–14,* Bern, A. Francke, 1950.

PRIMARY SOURCES

Abbo of Fleury, *Quaestiones grammaticales, Patrologia latina cursus completus, 139,* ed. J. P. Migne, Paris, 1853.

Alcuin, *Grammatica, Patrologia latina cursus completus, 101,* ed. J. P. Migne, Paris, 1851.

Alighieri, Dante, *Epistolae,* ed. and trans. Paget Toynbee, Oxford, The Clarendon Press, 1920.

———— *Opere,* a cura di Fredi Chiapelli, Milano, Ugo Mursia Editore, 1965.

Alighieri, Pietro, *Super Dantis ipsius genitoris Comoediam commentarium,* ed. Vincentio Nannucci & G. J. Bar. Vernon, Florentiae, Apud Guilielmum Piatti, 1845.

Anselm of Besate, *Rhetorimachia*, ed. Karl Manitius, *Monumenta Germaniae Historica, Quellen zur Geistesgeschichte des Mittelalters*, Band 2, Heft 2, Weimar, Hermann Böhlaus Nachfolger, 1958.

Aristotle, *Categoriae vel praedicamenta*, ed. Laurentius Minio-Paluello, *Aristoteles latinus, 1*, 1–5, Union Académique Internationale, Corpus Philosophorum Medii Aevi, Bruges-Paris, Desclée de Brouwer, 1961.

—— *Rhetoric*, trans. W. Rhys Roberts, New York, The Modern Library, 1924.

—— *The Works of Aristotle, 1*, ed. W. D. Ross, Oxford, The Clarendon Press, 1928.

Boccaccio, Giovanni, *Il commento alla Divina Commedia e gli altri scritti intorno di Dante*, ed. Domenico Guerri, 3 vols. Scrittori d'Italia, Bari, Gius. Laterza & Figli, 1918.

—— *Genealogie deorum gentilium libri*, ed. Vincenzo Romano, 2 vols. Scrittori d'Italia, Bari, Gius. Laterza & Figli, 1951.

—— *Vita di Dante e difesa di poesia*, ed. Carlo Muscetta, Roma, Edizioni dell'Ateneo, 1963.

Boethius, Anicius Manlius Severinus, *Commentaria in Porphyrium; Commentaria in Aristotelem, Patrologia latina cursus completus, 64*, ed. J. P. Migne, Paris, 1847.

Cicero, *Academica*, trans. and ed. H. Rackham, Loeb Classical Library, London, William Heinemann Ltd., 1933.

—— *De divinatione*, trans. and ed. William Armistead Falconer, Loeb Classical Library, London, William Heinemann, 1923.

—— *De inventione; De optimo genere oratorum; Topica*, trans. and ed. H. M. Hubbell, Loeb Classical Library, Cambridge, Mass., Harvard University Press, 1949.

—— *Orator*, trans. and ed. H. M. Hubbell, Loeb Classical Library, Cambridge, Mass., Harvard University Press, 1942.

—— *De oratore*, trans. and ed. E. W. Sutton and H. Rackham, 2 vols. Loeb Classical Library, Cambridge, Mass., Harvard University Press, 1942.

—— *De partitione oratoria*, trans. and ed. H. Rackham, Loeb Classical Library, Cambridge, Mass., Harvard University Press, 1943.

—— *Rhetorica ad Herennium*, trans. and ed. Harry Caplan, Loeb Classical Library, Cambridge, Mass., Harvard University Press, 1954.

Disputatio catholicorum patrum adversus dogmata Petri Abaelardi,
    Patrologia latina cursus completus, 180, ed. J. P. Migne, Paris,
    1855.

Donatus, *Ars grammatica,* ed. Heinrich Keil, *Grammatici latini,* ed.
    Heinrich Keil, *4,* Leipzig, B. G. Teubner, 1864.

Eadmer, *The Life of St. Anselm, Archbishop of Canterbury,* ed. and
    trans. R. W. Southern, Nelson's Medieval Texts, London,
    Thomas Nelson and Sons, Ltd., 1962.

Gunzo, *Epistola ad Augienses,* ed. Karl Manitius, *Monumenta Ger-
    maniae Historica, Quellen zur Geistesgeschichte des Mittel-
    alters,* Band 2, Heft 1, Weimar, Hermann Böhlaus Nachfolger,
    1958.

Lanfranc, *Liber de corpore et sanguine Domini, Patrologia latina
    cursus completus, 150,* ed. J. P. Migne, Paris, 1854.

Latini, Brunetto, *Li Livres dou Trésor,* ed. P. Chabaille, Collection
    de documents inédits sur l'histoire de France, publiées par les
    soins du Ministre de l'Instruction publique, 1ʳᵉ série, Paris,
    Imprimerie Impériale, 1863.

Mansi, Joannes Dominicus, ed., *Sacrorum conciliorum, nova, et
    amplissima collectio,* ed. Phil. Labbeus and Gabr. Cossartius,
    and Nicolaus Coleti, 31 vols. first series, Florentiae, Expensis
    Antonii Zatta Veneti, 1759–98.

Ordericus Vitalis, *Historiae ecclesiasticae, 2,* ed. Augustus LePrevost,
    Société de l'histoire de France, Paris, Julius Renouard et So-
    cios, 1840.

Plato, *The Dialogues,* trans. B. Jowett, 4th ed. 4 vols. Oxford, The
    Clarendon Press, 1953.

Priscianus, *Institutionum grammaticarum libri XVIII,* ed. Martin
    Herz, *Grammatici latini,* ed. Heinrich Keil, *2–3,* Leipzig, B. G.
    Teubner, 1865–69.

Quintilian, *Institutiones oratoriae,* trans. and ed. H. E. Butler, 4 vols.
    Loeb Classical Library, London, William Heinemann, 1933–36.

Rabanus Maurus, *De clericorum institutione, Patrologia latina cur-
    sus completus, 107,* ed. J. P. Migne, Paris, 1851.

Remigius of Auxerre, *In Artem Donati minorem commentum,* ed. W.
    Fox, Bibliotheca scriptorum graecorum et romanorum Teub-
    neriana, Lipsiae, B. G. Teubner, 1902.

St. Anselm, *Opera omnia,* ed. Franciscus Salesius Schmitt, 6 vols.
    Edinburgh, Thomas Nelson and Sons, 1940–61.

St. Augustine, *De civitate dei,* ed. Bernardus Dombart and Alphonsus Kalb, *Corpus christianorum*, series latina, *48*, Turnholti, Typographi Brepols Editoris Pontifici, 1955.

———— *Confessiones*, ed. Pius Knöll, *Corpus scriptorum ecclesiasticorum latinorum, 33*, Vindobonae, F. Tempsky, 1896.

———— *Contra academicos*, ed. Pius Knöll, *Corpus scriptorum ecclesiasticorum latinorum, 63*, Vindobonae, Hölder-Pichler-Tempsky A. G., 1922.

———— *De doctrina christiana; De vera religione*, ed. Iosephus Martin and K. -D. Daur, *Corpus christianorum*, series latina, *32*, Turnholti, Typographi Brepols Editoris Pontifici, 1962.

———— *Enarrationes in Psalmos*, ed. D. Eligius Dekkers and Ioannes Fraipont, *Corpus christianorum*, series latina, *38–40*, Turnholti, Typographi Brepols Editoris Pontifici, 1956.

———— *Enchiridion de fide, spe et charitate; De catechizandis rudibus, Patrologia latina cursus completus, 40*, ed. J. P. Migne, Paris, 1845.

———— *In Epistolam Ioannis ad Parthos tractatus X, Patrologia latina cursus completus, 25*, ed. J. P. Migne, Paris, 1845.

———— *Epistula*, ed. Al. Goldbacher, *Corpus scriptorum ecclesiasticorum latinorum, 34*, Vindobonae, Tempsky, 1895–1923.

———— *De fide et symbolo . . . ; De mendacio contra mendacium*, ed. Iosephus Zycha, *Corpus scriptorum ecclesiasticorum latinorum, 40*, Vindobonae, F. Tempsky, 1900.

———— *In Ioannis Evangelium tractatus CXXIV*, ed. D. Radbodus Willems, *Corpus christianorum*, series latina, *36*, Turnholti, Typographi Brepols Editoris Pontifici, 1954.

———— *De libero arbitrio*, ed. Guilelmus M. Green, *Corpus scriptorum ecclesiasticorum latinorum, 74*, Vindobonae, Hoelder-Pichler-Tempsky, 1956.

———— *De magistro*, ed. Guenther Weigel, *Corpus scriptorum ecclesiasticorum latinorum, 77*, Vindobonae, Hoelder-Pichler-Tempsky, 1961.

———— *Retractationum*, ed. Pius Knöll, *Corpus scriptorum ecclesiasticorum latinorum, 36*, Vindobonae, F. Tempsky, 1902.

———— *Sermones de Scripturis, Patrologia latina cursus completus, 38*, ed. J. P. Migne, Paris, 1845.

———— *Soliliquiorum, Patrologia latina cursus completus, 32*, ed. J. P. Migne, Paris, 1845.

———— *De spiritu et littera*, ed. Carolus F. Urba and Iosephus Zycha,

Corpus scriptorum ecclesiasticorum latinorum, 60, Vindobonae, F. Tempsky, 1913.

———— *De trinitate, Patrologia latina cursus completus, 42,* ed. J. P. Migne, Paris, 1845.

———— *De utilitate credendi,* ed. Iosephus Zycha, *Corpus scriptorum ecclesiasticorum latinorum, 25,* Vindobonae, F. Tempsky, 1891.

St. Thomas Aquinas, *In duodecim libros Metaphysicorum Aristoteles expositio,* ed. M. R. Cathala, rev. R. Spiazzi, Turin, Marietti, 1950.

———— *De ente et essentia,* ed. Charles Boyer, Rome, Gregorian University Press, 1933.

———— *Expositio super librum Boethii de trinitate,* ed. Bruno Decker, Studien und Texte zur Geistesgeschichte des Mittelalters, herausgegeben von Joseph Koch, Leiden, E. J. Brill, 1955.

———— *In librum beati Dionysii de Divinis nominibus expositio,* ed. Ceslai Pera, Turin, Marietti, 1950.

———— *Opera Omnia iussu impensaque Leonis XIII P. M. edita,* 16 vols. Romae, Typographia Polyglotta, 1882–1948.

———— *Opuscula omnia,* ed. P. Mandonnet, 5 vols. Paris, P. Lethiellieux, 1927.

———— *Quaestiones disputatae,* editio VIII revisa, ed. Raymundi Spiazzi, cura et studio P. Bazzi, M. Calcaterra, T. S. Centi, E. Odetto, and P. M. Pession, 2 vols. Taurini-Romae, Marietti, 1949.

———— *Scriptum super libros Sententiarum magistri Petri Lombardi Episcopi Parisiensis,* ed. P. Mandonnet and M. F. Moos, 4 vols. Paris, P. Lethiellieux, 1929–47.

Schmitt, Franciscus Salesius, ed., *Ein neues unvollendetes Werk des Hl. Anselm von Canterbury, Beiträge zur Geschichte der Philosophie und Theologie des Mittelalters,* herausgegeben von Martin Grabmann, Band *33,* Heft 3, Münster, i.W., Aschendorffschen Verlagsbuchhandlung, 1936.

William of St. Thierry, *Disputatio adversus Petrum Abaelardum ad Gaufridum Carnotensem et Bernardum, Patrologia latina cursus completus, 180,* ed. J. P. Migne, Paris, 1855.

TRANSLATIONS OF PRIMARY SOURCES
QUOTED IN THE TEXT

Alighieri, Dante, *Convivio,* trans. William Walrond Jackson, Oxford, The Clarendon Press, 1909.

—— *The Divine Comedy,* trans. J. A. Carlyle, Thomas Okey, P. H. Wicksteed, intro. by C. H. Grandgent, New York, The Modern Library, 1950.

—— *The Latin Works,* trans. Philip H. Wicksteed and A. G. Ferrers Howell, Temple Classics, London, J. M. Dent and Co., 1904.

—— *De monarchia,* trans. Herbert W. Schneider, 2d ed. New York, Liberal Arts Press, 1957.

McKeon, Richard, ed. and trans., *Selections from Medieval Philosophers, 1,* New York, Charles Scribner's Sons, 1929.

St. Anselm, *Basic Writings,* trans. S. N. Deane, intro. by Charles Hartshorne, La Salle, Ill., Open Court Publishing Co., 1962.

St. Augustine, *The Greatness of the Soul; The Teacher,* trans. Joseph M. Colleran, Ancient Christian Writers, *9,* Westminster, Md., The Newman Press, 1950.

SECONDARY SOURCES

Abelson, Paul, *The Seven Liberal Arts: A Study in Mediaeval Culture,* New York, 1906.

Adler, Mortimer J., "The Demonstration of God's Existence," *The Maritain Volume of the Thomist, The Thomist, 5* (1943), New York, Sheed and Ward, 1943, 188–218.

Alexander, Paul J., *The Patriarch Nicephorus of Constantinople: Ecclesiastical Policy and Image Worship in the Byzantine Empire,* Oxford, The Clarendon Press, 1958.

Alfaric, Prosper, *L'Evolution intellectuelle de Saint Augustin, 1,* Paris, Émile Nourry, 1918.

Allen, R. E., "The Ontological Argument," *The Philosophical Review, 70* (1961), 56–66.

Alston, William P., "The Ontological Argument Revisited," *The Philosophical Review, 69* (1960), 452–74.

Anderson, James F., et al., "Some Basic Propositions concerning Metaphysical Analogy," *Review of Metaphysics, 5* (1952), 465–72.

Andrea, Sorrentino, "La coscienza poetica di Dante," *Giornale dantesco, 30* (1927), 181–90.

Antonelli, M. T., "Il significato del Proslogion di Anselmo d'Aosta," *Rivista Rosminiana, 45* (1951), 260–68; *46* (1952), 35–43.

Antweiler, Anton, "Anselmus von Canterbury, Monologion und Proslogion," *Scholastik: Vierteljahresschrift für Theologie und Philosophie, 8* (1933), 551–60.

Apel, Karl Otto, *Die Idee der Sprache in der Tradition des Humanismus von Dante bis Vico,* Archiv für Begriffsgeschichte: Bausteine zu einem historischen Wörterbuch der Philosophie, Band *8,* Bonn, H. Bouvier u. Co. Verlag, 1963.

Armstrong, Edward, *Italian Studies,* ed. Cecilia M. Ady, London, Macmillan and Co., Ltd., 1934.

Asín y Palacios, Miguel, *Islam and the Divine Comedy,* trans. and abridged Harold Sunderland, New York, E. P. Dutton and Co., 1926.

Atkins, J. W. H., *Literary Criticism in Antiquity: A Sketch of Its Development, 2,* New York, Peter Smith, 1952.

Auber, C., *Histoire et théorie du symbolisme religieux avant et depuis le christianisme,* 4 vols. Paris, Librairie de Féchoz et Letouzey, 1884.

Auerbach, Erich, *Dante: Poet of the Secular World,* trans. Ralph Manheim, Chicago, University of Chicago Press, 1961.

——— "Dante's Addresses to the Reader," *Romance Philology, 7* (1954), 268–78.

——— "Figura," *Neue Dantestudien,* Istanbuler Schriften, *5,* Istanbul, 1944.

——— "Figurative Texts Illustrating Certain Passages of Dante's *Commedia," Speculum, 21* (1946), 474–89.

——— *Mimesis: The Representation of Reality in Western Literature,* trans. Willard Trask, Garden City, N.Y., Doubleday Anchor Books, 1957.

——— "Typological Symbolism in Medieval Literature," *Yale French Studies, 9* (1952), 3–10.

Baldwin, Charles Sears, *Ancient Rhetoric and Poetic Interpreted from Representative Works,* New York, The Macmillan Co., 1924.

——— *Medieval Rhetoric and Poetic (to 1400) Interpreted from Representative Works,* New York, The Macmillan Co., 1928.

———— "St. Augustine and the Rhetoric of Cicero," *Proceedings of the Classical Association, 22* (1925), 24–46.

Baldwin, Gratia Eaton, *The New Beatrice: Or the Virtue that Counsels,* New York, Columbia University Press, 1928.

Ballard, Edward G., "An Augustinian Doctrine of Signs," *The New Scholasticism, 23* (1949), 207–11.

Balthasar, Nicholas, *L'Abstraction métaphysique et l'analogie des êtres dans l'être,* Louvain, Em. Warny, 1935.

Bandini, Albert R., "Virgil and Dante—and Statius," *Thought, 5* (1930), 209–23.

Barbi, Michele, *Life of Dante,* trans. and ed. Paul G. Ruggiers, Berkeley and Los Angeles, University of California Press, 1954.

———— *Problemi fondamentali per un nuovo commento della Divina Commedia,* Firenze, G. C. Sansoni, 1956.

Bardy, Gustave, *Saint Augustin: L'homme et l'oeuvre,* 7ᵐᵉ éd. Paris, Desclée de Brouwer, 1948.

Barry, M. Inviolata, *St. Augustine the Orator: A Study of the Rhetorical Qualities of St. Augustine's Sermones ad Populum,* Catholic University of America Patristic Studies, 6, Washington, The Catholic University of America, 1924.

Barth, Karl, *Anselm: Fides quaerens intellectum. Anselm's Proof of the Existence of God in the Context of His Theological Scheme,* trans. Ian W. Robertson, Richmond, Va., John Knox Press, 1960.

Battenhouse, Roy W., ed., *A Companion to the Study of St. Augustine,* New York, Oxford University Press, 1955.

Bayart, J., "The Concept of Mystery according to St. Anselm of Canterbury," *Recherches de théologie ancienne et médiévale, 9* (1937), 125–66.

Behm, Johannes, "Das Bildwort vom Spiegel I. Korinther 13, 12," *Reinhold-Seeberg-Festschrift, 1,* herausgegeben von Wilhelm Koepp, Leipzig, A. Diechertsche Verlagsbuchhandlung D. Werner Scholl, 1929, 315–42.

Bergenthal, Ferdinand, "Ist der 'ontologische Gottesbeweis' Anselms von Canterbury ein Trugschluss?," *Philosophisches Jahrbuch, 59,* Heft 2 (1949), 155–68.

Bergin, Thomas G., *Dante,* New York, Orion Press, 1965.

———— "On the *Personae* of the *Comedy*," *Italica, 42* (1965), 1–7.

Bergmann, Frédéric, *Dante: Sa vie et ses oeuvres,* Strasbourg, C. F. Schmidt, 1881.

Berlinger, Rudolph, *Augustins dialogische Metaphysik,* Frankfurt am Main, Vittorio Klostermann, 1962.

Bertoni, Giulio, "La lingua di Dante," *Nuova antologia, 68,* fasc. 1462 (1933), 481–90.

Bethurum, Dorothy, ed., *Critical Approaches to Medieval Literature: Selected Papers from the English Institute, 1958–59,* New York, Columbia University Press, 1960.

Betzendörfer, Walter, "Glauben und Wissen bei Anselm von Canterbury," *Zeitschrift für Kirchengeschichte, 48,* neue Folge, 11 (1929), 354–70.

Beumer, Johannes, "Thomas von Aquin zum Wesen der Theologie," *Scholastik: Vierteljahresschrift für Theologie und Philosophie, 30* (1955), 196–214.

Bilancioni, Guglielmo, *Il suono e la voce nell'opera di Dante,* Pisa, Mariotti e Pacini, 1927.

Biondolillo, Francesco, *Poetica e poesia di Dante,* Biblioteca di cultura contemporanea, *19,* Messina, Casa Editrice G. d'Anna, 1948.

Blackmur, R. P., "Dante's Ten Terms for the Treatment of the Treatise," *Kenyon Review, 14* (1952), 286–300.

Blanche, F. A., "L'Analogie," *Revue de philosophie, 23* (1923), 248–70.

——— "La notion d'analogie dans la philosophie de S. Thomas d'Aquin," *Revue des sciences philosophiques et théologiques, 10* (1921), 169–93.

——— "Une théorie de l'analogie," *Revue de philosophie,* n. s., *3* (1932), 37–78.

Bloomfield, Morton W., "Symbolism in Medieval Literature," *Modern Philology, 56* (1958), 73–81.

Bochenski, I. M., "On Analogy," *The Thomist, 11* (1948), 424–47.

Boehner, Philotheus, *Medieval Logic: An Outline of Its Development from 1250–c.1400,* Manchester, Manchester University Press, 1952.

Bonhoeffer, Thomas, *Die Gotteslehre des Thomas von Aquin als Sprachproblem,* Beiträge zur historischen Theologie, herausgegeben von Gerhard Ebeling, *32,* Tübingen, J. C. B. Mohr, 1961.

357

Bonnefoy, Jean F., *La Nature de la théologie selon Saint Thomas d'Aquin,* Paris, Librairie Philosophique J. Vrin, 1939.

—— "La théologie comme science et l'explication de la Foi selon saint Thomas d'Aquin," *Ephemerides Theologicae Lovanienses, 14* (1937), 412–46, 600–31; *15* (1938), 491–516.

Bonner, Gerald, *St. Augustine of Hippo: Life and Controversies,* Philadelphia, Westminster Press, 1963.

Bourke, Vernon J., *Augustine's Quest of Wisdom: Life and Philosophy of the Bishop of Hippo,* Milwaukee, Bruce Publishing Co., 1945.

Bowden, John Paul, *An Analysis of Pietro Alighieri's Commentary on the Divine Comedy,* New York, 1951.

Boyer, Charles, *Essais sur la doctrine de Saint Augustin,* Paris, Gabriel Beauchesne et ses fils, 1932.

—— *L'Idée de Vérité dans la philosophie de saint Augustin,* Paris, Gabriel Beauchesne, 1920.

—— "La preuve de Dieu augustinienne," *Archives de philosophie, 7,* cahier 2 (1930), 105–41.

Bradley, Ritamary, "Backgrounds of the Title *Speculum* in Mediaeval Literature," *Speculum, 29* (1954), 100–15.

—— "The Mirror of Truth according to St. Thomas," *The Modern Schoolman, 31* (1954), 307–17.

Brandeis, Irma, *The Ladder of Vision: A Study of Dante's Comedy,* London, Chatto & Windus, 1960.

—— "Metaphor in the Divine Comedy," *Hudson Review, 8* (1956), 557–75.

Brown, Patterson, "St. Thomas' Doctrine of Necessary Being," *The Philosophical Review, 73* (1964), 76–90.

Bruyne, Edgar de, *L'Esthétique du moyen âge,* Essais philosophiques, *3,* Louvain, Éditions de l'Institut Supérieur de Philosophie, 1947.

—— *Études d'esthétique médiévale,* 3 vols. Brugge, De Tempel, 1946.

Bryar, William, *St. Thomas and the Existence of God: Three Interpretations,* Chicago, Henry Regnery Co., 1951.

Buck, August, "Dante im Urteil der Literaturästhetik des italienischen Humanismus," *Deutsches Dante-Jahrbuch, 28* (1949), 1–15.

Burke, Kenneth, *The Rhetoric of Religion: Studies in Logology,* Boston, Beacon Press, 1961.

Burnaby, John, *Amor Dei: A Study of the Religion of St. Augustine,* London, Hodder and Stoughton, 1938.

Burrell, David, "Aquinas on Naming God," *Theological Studies, 24* (1963), 183–212.

———— "A Note on Analogy," *The New Scholasticism, 36* (1962), 225–32.

———— "Religious Language and the Logic of Analogy: Apropos of McInerny's Book and Ross' Review," *International Philosophical Quarterly, 2* (1962), 643–58.

Butler, Cuthbert, *Western Mysticism: The Teaching of SS. Augustine, Gregory and Bernard on Contemplation and the Contemplative Life. Neglected Chapters in the History of Religion,* London, Constable & Co. Ltd., 1922.

Byles, M. Esdaile, "The Analogy of Being," *The New Scholasticism, 16* (1942), 331–64.

Caplan, Harry, "Classical Rhetoric and the Mediaeval Theory of Preaching," *Historical Studies of Rhetoric and Rhetoricians,* ed. Raymond F. Howes, Ithaca, N.Y., Cornell University Press, 1961, pp. 71–89.

Cappuyns, D. M., "L'Argument de S. Anselme," *Recherches de théologie ancienne et médiévale, 6* (1934), 313–30.

Carré, Meyrick H., *Realists and Nominalists,* Oxford, Oxford University Press, 1946.

Carter, Barbara Barclay, "Dante's Political Conception," *Hibbert Journal, 35* (1937), 568–79.

———— "Dante's Political Ideas," *Review of Politics, 5* (1943), 338–55.

Casciola, Brizio, *L'Enimma dantesco,* Bergamo, Istituto Italiano d'Arti Grafiche, 1950.

Casotti, Mario, "Il 'De magistro' di S. Agostino e il metodo intuitivo," *S. Agostino: Pubblicazione commemorativa del XV centenario della sua morte, Rivista di filosofia neoscolastica,* supplemento speciale al volume *23* (1931), 57–74.

Caturelli, Alberto, *La doctrina agustiniana sobre el maestro y su desarrollo en Santo Tomás de Aquino,* Universidad de Córdoba (Argentina), Facultad de Filosofía, Córdoba, Instituto de Metafísica, 1954.

Cayré, Fulbert, *La Contemplation augustinienne: Principes de la spiritualité de saint Augustin*, Paris, André Blot, 1927.

—— *Initiation à la philosophie de saint Augustin*, Bibliothèque Augustinienne, Études de Philosophie, *1*, Paris, Desclée de Brouwer, 1947.

Cellucci, Luigi, "La poetica di Dante e la sua poesia," *Cultura neolatina, 10*, fasc. 1 (1950), 77–97.

Charlesworth, M. J., "St. Anselm's Argument," *Sophia: A Journal for Discussion of Philosophical Theology, 1* (1962), 25–36.

Chenu, M.-D., "Un essai de Méthode théologique au XIIᵉ siècle," *Revue des sciences philosophiques et théologiques, 24* (1935), 258–67.

—— "Grammaire et théologie aux XIIᵉ et XIIIᵉ siècles," *Archives d'histoire doctrinale et littéraire du moyen âge, 10* (1935), 5–28.

—— *Introduction à l'étude de Saint Thomas d'Aquin*, 2ᵐᵉ éd. Université de Montréal Publications de l'Institut d'Études Médiévales, *11*, Montréal-Paris, Institut d'Études Médiévales-Librairie Philosophique J. Vrin, 1954.

—— "Les 'Philosophes' dans la Philosophie chrétienne médiévale," *Revue des sciences philosophiques et théologiques, 26* (1937), 27–40.

—— "La psychologie de la foi dans la théologie du XIIIᵉ siècle," *Études d'histoire littéraire et doctrinale du XIIIᵉ siècle*, Publications de l'Institut d'Études Médiévales d'Ottawa, *2*, Librairie Philosophique J. Vrin, 1932, 163–91.

—— *La Théologie au douzième siècle*, Études de philosophie médiévale, *45*, Paris, Librarie Philosphique J. Vrin, 1957.

—— "La théologie comme science au XIIIᵉ siècle," *Archives d'histoire doctrinale et littéraire du moyen âge, 2* (1927), 31–71.

—— *La théologie comme science au XIIIᵉ siècle*, 3ᵐᵉ éd. Bibliothèque thomiste, *33*, Paris, Librairie Philosophique J. Vrin, 1957.

Chiapparini, Giovanni, "Dante e la poesia dell'ineffabile," *Rassegna nazionale*, 3ᵐᵒ serie, *20* (1934), 425–29.

Chydenius, Johan, *The Theory of Medieval Symbolism*, Societas Scientiarum Fennica, Commentationes Humanarum Litterarum, *27, 2*, Helsingfors, Centraltryckeriet, 1960.

—— *The Typological Problem in Dante: A Study in the History*

360

of Medieval Ideas, Societas Scientiarum Fennica, Commentationes Humanarum Litterarum, *25,* 1, Helsingfors, Centraltryckeriet, 1958.

Cicchetti, Armando, *L'Agostinismo nel pensiero di Anselmo d'Aosta,* Roma, Editoriale "Arte e Storia," 1951.

Cippico, Antonio, et al., eds., *Dante: Essays in Commemoration, 1321–1921,* London, University of London Press, 1921.

Clark, Donald Lemen, *Rhetoric in Graeco-Roman Education,* New York, Columbia University Press, 1957.

Clarke, M. L., *Rhetoric at Rome: A Historical Survey,* London, Cohen & West Ltd., 1953.

Clayton, Joseph, *Saint Anselm: A Critical Biography,* Milwaukee, Bruce Publishing Co., 1933.

Cochrane, Charles Norris, *Christianity and Classical Culture: A Study of Thought and Action from Augustus to Augustine,* New York, Oxford University Press, 1957.

Combès, Gustave, *Saint Augustin et la culture classique,* Paris, Librairie Plon, 1927.

Comeau, Marie, *La Rhétorique de Saint Augustin d'après les Tractatus in Ioannem,* Paris, Boivin & Cie, Éditeurs, 1930.

———— *Saint Augustin: Exégète du quatrième évangile,* Paris, Gabriel Beauchesne, 1930.

Comparetti, Domenico, *Vergil in the Middle Ages,* trans. E. F. M. Beneke, London, Swan Sonnenschein & Co., 1908.

Conklin, Henry Ernest, "The Aesthetic of Dante," *Rice Institute Pamphlet, 8,* no. 2 (1921), 118–38.

Connolly, Thomas Kevin, "The Basis of the Third Proof for the Existence of God," *The Thomist, 17* (1954), 280–349.

Contri, Siro, *Il problema della verità in S. Tommaso d'Aquino,* Torino, Società Editrice Internazionale, 1925.

Copleston, F. C., *Aquinas,* Baltimore, Penguin Books, 1955.

———— *A History of Philosophy, 1–2,* new and rev. ed. Westminster, Md., The Newman Press, 1957–59.

Cottiaux, Jean, "La Conception de la théologie chez Abélard," *Revue d'histoire ecclésiastique, 28* (1932), 247–95, 533–51, 788–828.

Courcelle, Pierre, *Les Confessions de Saint Augustin dans la tradition littéraire: Antécédents et posterité,* Paris, Études Augustiniennes, 1963.

361

—— *Recherches sur les Confessions de Saint Augustin,* Paris, E. De Boccard, 1950.

Creaven, J. A., "Aspects of analogy," *Philosophical Studies, 8* (1958), 71–88.

Croce, Benedetto, *The Poetry of Dante,* trans. Douglas Ainslie, New York, Henry Holt and Co., 1922.

Crowe, M. B., "St. Thomas against the Gentiles," *Irish Theological Quarterly, 29* (1962), 93–120.

Curtius, Ernst Robert, "Das Buch als Symbol in der Divina Commedia," *Festschrift zum sechzigsten Geburtstag von Paul Clemen,* Bonn, Fried. Cohen, 1926, pp. 44–54.

—— "Dante und das lateinische Mittelalter," *Romanische Forschungen, 57,* Heft 2–3 (1943), 153–85.

—— *European Literature and the Latin Middle Ages,* trans. Willard Trask, Bollingen Series, *36,* New York, Pantheon Books, 1953.

—— "The Medieval Basis of Western Thought," *Gesammelte Aufsätze zur romanischen Philologie,* Bern und München, Franke Verlag, 1960, pp. 28–39.

—— "Neue Dantestudien," *Gesammelte Aufsätze zur romanischen Philologie,* Bern und München, Franke Verlag, 1960, pp. 305–45.

—— "Schrift- und Buchmetaphorik in der Weltliteratur," *Neue Beiträge deutscher Forschung: Wilhelm Worringer zum 60. Geburtstag,* herausgegeben von Erich Fidder, Königsberg, Kanter-Verlag, 1943, pp. 60–100.

—— "Theologische Poetik im italienischen Trecento," *Zeitschrift für romanische Philologie, 60* (1940), 1–15.

—— "Zur Geschichte des Wortes Philosophie im Mittelalter," *Romanische Forschungen, 57,* Heft 2–3 (1943), 290–309.

Dallari, Gino, "Sul concetto della nobiltà nella terza canzone del 'Convivio' Dantesco," Reale Istituto Lombardo di scienze e lettere, *Rendiconti,* serie 2, *61* (1928), 572–80.

Dal Pra, Mario, "Gaunilone e il problema logico del linguaggio," *Rivista critica di storia della filosofia, 9* (1954), 456–84.

—— "Il problema del fondamento del significato nella controversia fra Anselmo e Gaunilone," *Rivista critica di storia della filosofia, 9* (1954), 132–55.

362

———— "Studi sul problema logico del linguaggio nella filosofia medioevale: I. 'Cogitatio vocum' e 'cogitatio rerum' nel pensiero di Anselmo," *Rivista critica di storia della filosofia, 9* (1954), 309–43.

D'Alton, J. F., *Roman Literary Theory and Criticism: A Study in Tendencies,* London, Longmans, Green and Co., 1931.

Damon, Phillip, "The Two Modes of Allegory in Dante's *Convivio*," *Philosophical Quarterly, 40* (1961), 144–49.

Daniélou, Jean, *From Shadows to Reality: Studies in the Biblical Typology of the Fathers,* trans. Wulstan Hibberd, London, Burns & Oates, 1960.

———— *God and the Ways of Knowing,* trans. Walter Roberts, New York, Greenwich Editions, 1957.

Daniels, P. Augustinus, *Quellenbeiträge und Untersuchungen zur Geschichte der Gottesbeweise im dreizehnten Jahrhundert mit besonderer Berucksichtingung des Arguments im Proslogion des Hl. Anselm, Beiträge zur Geschichte der Philosophie des Mittelalters,* herausgegeben von Clemens Bauemker, Band *8,* Heft 1–2, Münster i. W., Aschendorffschen Buchhandlung, 1909.

D'Arcy, M. C., *Thomas Aquinas,* London, Ernest Benn Ltd., 1930.

———— et al., *St. Augustine,* New York, Meridian Books, 1957.

Davies, A. E., "The Problem of Truth and Existence as Treated by Anselm," *Proceedings of the Aristotelian Society,* n. s., *20* (1920), 167–90.

Davis, Charles Till, *Dante and the Idea of Rome,* Oxford, The Clarendon Press, 1957.

Dedek, John F., "*Quasi experimentalis cognitio:* A Historical Approach to the Meaning of St. Thomas," *Theological Studies, 22* (1961), 357–90.

De Lacy, Estelle Allen, "Meaning and Methodology in Hellenistic Philosophy," *The Philosophical Review, 47* (1938), 390–409.

De Lacy, Phillip H., "The Epicurean Analysis of Language," *American Journal of Philology, 40* (1939), 85–92.

———— and Estelle Allen De Lacy, *Philodemus: On Methods of Inference. A Study in Ancient Empiricism,* Philological Monographs Published by the American Philological Association, *10,* Philadelphia, American Philolgical Association, 1941.

De Lubac, Henri, *Augustinisme et théologie moderne,* Théologie: Études publiées sous la direction de la faculté de théologie S. J. de Lyon-Fourvière, *63,* Paris, Aubier, 1965.

—— *Exégèse médiévale: Les quatre sens de l'Ecriture,* 4 vols. in 2, Théologie: Études publiées sous la direction de la faculté de théologie S. J. de Lyon-Fourvière, *41, 59,* Paris, Aubier, 1959–64.

—— *Le mystère du surnaturel,* Théologie: Études publiées sous la direction de la faculté de théologie S. J. de Lyon-Fourvière, *64,* Paris, Aubier, 1965.

—— " 'Typologie' et 'Allegorisme,' " *Recherches de science religieuse, 34* (1947), 180–226.

Demus, Otto, *Byzantine Mosaic Decoration: Aspects of Monumental Art in Byzantium,* London, Kegan Paul Trench Trubner & Co. Ltd., 1948.

Diggs, Bernard J., "St. Augustine against the Academicians," *Traditio, 7* (1949–51), 73–93.

Dinsmore, Charles Allen, *Life of Dante Alighieri,* Boston, Houghton Mifflin Co., 1919.

—— *The Teachings of Dante,* Boston, Houghton Mifflin Co., 1901.

Domet de Vorges, le Comte, *Saint Anselme,* Les grandes philosophes, Paris, Félix Alcan, 1901.

Dondaine, H. F., *Le Corpus dionysien de l'Université de Paris au XIIIᵉ siècle,* Roma, Edizioni de Storia e Letteratura, 1953.

Donovan, Mary Annice, *The Henological Argument for the Existence of God in the Works of St. Thomas Aquinas,* Notre Dame, Ind., 1946.

Douglas, David C., *William the Conquerer: The Norman Impact upon England,* Berkeley and Los Angeles, University of California Press, 1964.

Dragonetti, Roger, *Aux frontières du langage poétique: Études sur Dante, Mallarmé, Valéry,* Romanica Gandensa, *9,* Rijksuniversiteit te Gent, Faculteit der Wijsbegeerte en Letteren, 1961.

Dunbar, H. Flanders, *Symbolism in Medieval Thought and Its Consummation in the Divine Comedy,* New Haven, Yale University Press, 1929.

Dunne, John S., "St. Thomas' Theology of Participation," *Theological Studies, 18* (1957), 487–512.

364

Durantel, J., *Le Retour à Dieu par l'intelligence et la volunté dans la Philosophie de S. Thomas,* Paris, Félix Alcan, 1918.

Elders, Léon, "Justification des 'cinq voies,'" *Revue thomiste, 61* (1961), 207–25.

Eliot, T. S., *Dante,* The Poets on the Poets, no. 2, London, Faber & Faber, 1930.

Endres, Jos. Ant., *Forschungen zur Geschichte der frühmittelalterlichen Philosophie, Beiträge zur Geschichte der Philosophie des Mittelalters,* herausgegeben von Clemens Bauemker, Band *17,* Heft *2–3,* Münster i. W., Aschendorffsche Verlagsbuchhandlung, 1915.

Ercole, Francesco, *Il pensiero politico di Dante,* 2 vols. Milano, Edizioni "Alpes," 1927–28.

Eskridge, James Burnette, *The Influence of Cicero upon Augustine in the Development of His Oratorical Theory for the Training of the Ecclesiastical Orator,* Menasha, Wisc., The Collegiate Press, 1912.

Ewert, A., "Dante's Theory of Language," *Modern Language Review, 35* (1940), 355–66.

Fallani, Giovanni, *Poesia e teologia nella Divina Commedia,* 2 vols. Milano, Marzorati, 1959–61.

Faral, Edmond, *Les Arts poétiques du XIIᵉ et du XIIIᵉ siècle: Recherches et documents sur la technique littéraire du moyen âge,* Bibliothèque de l'École des Hautes Études, fasc. *238,* Paris, Librairie Ancienne Honoré Champion-Édouard Champion, 1924.

Fehr, J., "Offenbarung und Analogie: Ihr Verhältnis in dialektischen und thomistischen Theologie," *Divus Thomas, 15* (1937), 291–307.

Féret, H.-M., *"Sacramentum. Res.* dans la langue théologique de saint Augustin," *Revue des sciences philosophiques et théologiques, 29* (1940), 218–43.

Fergusson, Francis, *Dante's Drama of the Mind: A Modern Reading of the Purgatorio,* Princeton, Princeton University Press, 1953.

Filliatre, Charles, *La philosophie de Saint Anselme: Ses principes, sa nature, son influence,* Paris, Librairie Félix Alcan, 1920.

Finaert, Joseph, *L'Évolution littéraire de saint Augustin,* Collection d'Études latines publiée par la Société des Études latines sous la direction de J. Marouzeau, Série scientifique, *17*, Paris, Société d'Édition "Les Belles Lettres," 1939.

────── *Saint Augustin rhéteur*, Collection d'Études latines publiée par la Société des Études latines sous la direction de J. Marouzeau, Série scientifique, *18*, Paris, Société d'Édition "Les Belles Lettres," 1939.

Finili, Antoninus, "Is There a Philosophical Approach to God?," *Dominican Studies, 4* (1951), 80–101.

Fischer, Joseph, *Die Erkenntnislehre Anselms von Canterbury, Beiträge zur Geschichte der Philosophie des Mittelalters*, herausgegeben von Clemens Bauemker, Band *10*, Heft 3, Münster i. W., Aschendorffsche Verlagsbuchhandlung, 1911.

Flanigan, Thomas Marguerite, "The Use of Analogy in the *Summa contra gentiles*," *The Modern Schoolman, 35* (1957), 21–37.

Fletcher, Jefferson B., "The Allegory of the *Vita Nuova*," *Modern Philology, 11* (1913), 19–37.

────── *Dante*, New York, Henry Holt and Co., 1916.

────── "The Philosophy of Love of Guido Cavalcanti," *Annual Report of the Dante Society, Cambridge, Mass., 22* (1904), 9–35.

────── "The 'True Meaning' of Dante's *Vita Nuova*," *Romanic Review, 11* (1920), 95–148.

Foligno, Cesare, "Dante: The Poet," *Proceedings of the British Academy, 10* (1921), 3–18.

Freccero, John, ed., *Dante: A Collection of Critical Essays*, Twentieth Century Views, ed. Maynard Mack, Englewood Cliffs, N.J., Prentice-Hall, Inc., 1965.

Frutos Cortés, Eugenio, et al., *San Agustín: Estudios y coloquios*, Actos de los coloquios convocados por la Institución "Fernando el Católico" para conmemorar el XVI centenario de San Agustín, Zaragoza, Institución "Fernando el Católico," 1960.

Funaioli, Gino, "Dante e il mondo antico," *Medioevo e Rinascimento: Studi in onore di Bruno Nardi, 1*, Firenze, G. C. Sansoni, 1955, 321–38.

Gardeil, A., *Le donné révélé et la théologie*, 2ᵐᵉ éd. Juvisy, Les Éditions du Cerf, 1932.

────── "Le donné théologique," *Revue thomiste, 17* (1909), 385–405.

Gardner, Edmund G., *Dante*, New York, E. P. Dutton & Co., 1923.

────── *Dante and the Mystics: A Study of the Mystical Aspects of the Divina Commedia and Its Relations with Some of Its Mediaeval Sources,* London, J. M. Dent & Sons Ltd., 1913.

Garrigou-Lagrange, Reginald,"La foi éclairée par les dons," *La Vie Spirituelle, 64* (1946), 657–66.

Garvey, Mary Patricia, *Saint Augustine: Christian or Neoplatonist?,* Milwaukee, Marquette University Press, 1939.

Geiger, L. -B., *La Participation dans la philosophie de S. Thomas d'Aquin,* Bibliothèque thomiste, *23,* Paris, Librairie Philosophique J. Vrin, 1942.

Geny, P., "A propos des preuves thomistes de l'existence de Dieu," *Revue de philosophie, 24* (1924), 575–601.

Germain, Pierre, "La théologie de saint Thomas d'Aquin, science de la foi," *Revue de l'Université d'Ottawa,* section spéciale, *28* (1958), 156*–84*.

Getto, Giovanni, *Aspetti della poesia di Dante,* Biblioteca del Leonardo, *37,* Firenze, G. C. Sansoni, 1947.

Ghellinck, J. de, *L'Essor de la littérature latine au XIIe siècle,* 2 vols. Museum Lessianum, Section Historique, *4–5,* Bruxelles, L'Édition Universelle, 1946.

——— *Le mouvement théologique du XIIe siècle,* 2me éd. Museum Lessianum, Section historique, *10,* Bruges, "De Tempel," 1948.

Gilbert, Allan H., *Dante and His Comedy,* New York, New York University Press, 1963.

——— *Dante's Conception of Justice,* Durham, N.C., Duke University Press, 1925.

——— "Doctrine and Romance in Dante's *Commedia,*" *Renaissance Papers, 1960,* Published by the Southeastern Renaissance Conference, 1961, pp. 104–10.

Gilby, Thomas, *Barbara Celarent: A Description of Scholastic Dialectic,* London, Longmans Green and Co., 1949.

Gilson, Etienne, *The Christian Philosophy of Saint Augustine,* trans. L. E. M. Lynch, New York, Random House, 1960.

——— *The Christian Philosophy of St. Thomas Aquinas,* trans. L. K. Shook, New York, Random House, 1956.

——— *Dante the Philosopher,* trans. David Moore, New York, Sheed and Ward, 1949.

——— *A History of Christian Philosophy in the Middle Ages,* New York, Random House, 1955.

——— *Philosophie et Incarnation selon Saint Augustin,* Conférence

Albert le Grand, 1947, Montréal, Institut d'Études Médiévales, 1947.

—— *The Philosophy of St. Thomas Aquinas*, 2d ed. trans. Edward Bullough, ed. G. A. Elrington, St. Louis, B. Herder, 1941.

—— "Sens et nature de l'argument de Saint Anselme," *Archives d'histoire doctrinale et littéraire du moyen âge, 9* (1934), 5–51.

Giussani, Carlo, "La questione del linguaggio secondo Platone e secondo Epicuro," *Memorie del Reale Istituto Lombardo di scienze e lettere, classe di lettere, scienze storiche e morale, 20,* 11 della serie 3, Milano, Tipografia Bernardoni di C. Rebeschini e C., 1899, 103–41.

Glatstein, Irwin Lee, "Semantics, too, Has a Past," *The Quarterly Journal of Speech, 32* (1946), 48–51.

Glover, Terrot Reaveley, *Life and Letters in the Fourth Century,* Cambridge, The University Press, 1901.

Glunz, H. H., *Die Literaturästhetik des europäischen Mittelalters,* Das Abendland: Forschungen zur Geschichte des europäischen Geisteslebens, herausgegeben von Herbert Schöffler, *2,* Bochum-Langendreer, Verlag von Heinrich Pöppinghaus o. H. -G., 1937.

Gmelin, Hermann, "Die Anrede an den Leser in Dantes Göttlicher Komödie," *Deutsches Dante-Jahrbuch, 29–30,* neue Folge, 20–21 (1951), 130–40.

Grabmann, Martin, "Il concetto di scienza secondo S. Tommaso d'Aquino e le relazioni della Fede e della teologia con la filosofia e le scienze profane," *Rivista di filosofia neoscolastica, 26* (1934), 127–55.

—— *Die Geschichte der scholastischen Methode*, 2 vols. Darmstadt, Wissenschaftliche Buchgesellschaft e. V., 1956.

—— "Die geschichtliche Entwicklung der mitteralterlichen Sprachphilosophie und Sprachlogik," *Mélanges Joseph de Ghellinck, 2,* Museum Lessianum, section historique, *14,* Gembloux, J. Duclutot, 1951, 421–34.

—— *The Interior Life of St. Thomas Aquinas,* trans. Nicholas Ashenbrenner, Milwaukee, Bruce Publishing Co., 1951.

—— *Mittelalterliches Geistesleben: Abhandlungen zur Geschichte der Scholastik und Mystik, 1,* München, Max Hueber Verlag, 1926.

———— "Scientific Cognition of Truth: Its Characteristic Genius in the Doctrine of St. Thomas Aquinas," *The New Scholasticism,* *13* (1939), 1–30.

———— *Die theologische Erkenntnis- und Einleitungslehre des hl. Thomas von Aquin auf seiner Schrift "In Boethium de Trinitate" im Zusammenhang der Scholastik des 13. und beginnenden 14. Jahrhunderts dargestellt,* Thomistische Studien, Schriftenreihe des *Divus Thomas, 4,* Freiburg in der Schweitz, Paulusverlag, 1948.

———— *Thomas Aquinas: His Personality and Thought,* trans. Virgil Michel, New York, Longmans, Green and Co., 1928.

———— and Joseph Mausbach, eds., *Aurelius Augustinus: Die Festschrift der Görres-Gesellschaft zum 1500. Todestag des heiligen Augustinus,* Köln, Verlag J. P. Bachem, 1930.

Graf, Arturo, *Roma nella memoria e nelle immaginazioni del medio evo,* 2 vols. Torino, Ermanno Loescher, 1882–83.

Grandgent, Charles Hall, *Dante,* New York, Duffield & Co., 1916.

———— *The Power of Dante,* Boston, Marshall Jones Co., 1918.

Grandgeorge, L., *Saint Augustin et le néo-Platonisme,* Paris, E. Leroux, 1898.

Grant, Mary A., and George Converse Fiske, "Cicero's *Orator* and Horace's *Ars Poetica,*" *Harvard Studies in Classical Philology,* *35* (1924), 1–74.

Grasso, Vincenzo, *Il De Consolatione Philosophiae di Boezio in Dante, Petrarca, Chaucer: Contributo allo studio delle loro fonti,* Catania, Vincente Muglia, 1923.

Grave, S. A., "The Ontological Argument of St. Anselm," *Philosophy, 27* (1952), 30–38.

Green, Richard Hamilton, "Dante's 'Allegory of Poets' and the Mediaeval Theory of Poetic Fiction," *Comparative Literature, 9* (1957), 118–28.

Grene, Marjorie, *A Portrait of Aristotle,* Chicago, University of Chicago Press, 1963.

Guardini, Romano, *The Conversion of Augustine,* trans. Elinor Briefs, Westminster, Md., The Newman Press, 1960.

———— *Vision und Dichtung: Der Charakter von Dantes göttlicher Komödie,* Tübingen und Stuttgart, Rainer Wunderlich Verlag, 1946.

369

Guidubaldi, Egidio, "Poesia e non-poesia negli ultimi quarant'anni di critica dantesca in Italia," *Civiltà cattolica, 110,* no. 4 (1959), 42–52.

Hardie, C. G., "The Epistle to Cangrande Again," *Deutsches Dante-Jahrbuch, 38* (1960), 51–74.

Harrison, Frank R., III, "Some Brief Remarks concerning the Quinque Viae of Saint Thomas," *Franciscan Studies, 21* (1961), 80–93.

Hart, Charles A., "Participation and the Thomistic Five Ways," *The New Scholasticism, 26* (1952), 266–82.

—— *The Thomistic Concept of Mental Faculty,* Washington, The Catholic University of America, 1930.

Hartford, R. R., "Fides quaerens intellectum," *Hermathena: A Series of Papers on Literature, Science, and Philosophy by Members of Trinity College, Dublin, 74* (1949), 1–8.

Hartman, Robert S., "Prolegomena to a Meta-Anselmian Axiomatic," *Review of Metaphysics, 14* (1961), 637–75.

Hartshorne, Charles, *The Logic of Perfection and Other Essays in Neoclassical Metaphysics,* La Salle, Ill., Open Court Publishing Co., 1962.

—— "The Logic of the Ontological Argument," *The Journal of Philosophy, 58* (1961), 471–73.

—— *Man's Vision of God, and the Logic of Theism,* Chicago, Willet, Clark & Co., 1941.

Hatzfeld, H., "Modern Literary Scholarship as Reflected in Dante Criticism," *Comparative Literature, 3* (1951), 289–309.

Henle, Paul, "Uses of the Ontological Argument," *The Philosophical Review, 70* (1961), 102–09.

Henle, R. J., *Saint Thomas and Platonism: A Study of the 'Plato' and 'Platonici' Texts in the Writings of Saint Thomas,* The Hague, Martinus Nijhoff, 1956.

Henry, C., "Histoire des preuves de l'existence de Dieu au Moyen âge, jusqu'à la fin de l'apogée de la scholastique," *Revue thomiste, 19* (1911), 1–24, 141–58.

Henry, Desmond Paul, *The De Grammatico of St. Anselm: The Theory of Paronymy,* University of Notre Dame Publications in Mediaeval Studies, *18,* Notre Dame, Ind., University of Notre Dame Press, 1964.

————— "The Proslogion Proofs," *The Philosophical Quarterly, 5* (1955), 147–51.

————— "Saint Anselm's 'De grammatico,' " *The Philosophical Quarterly, 10* (1960), 115–26.

————— "Why 'Grammaticus'?," *Archivum Latinitatis Medii Aevi, 28*, fasc. 2–3 (1958), 165–80.

Hessen, Johannes, *Augustins Metaphysik der Erkenntnis*, Berlin und Bonn, Ferd. Dümmlers Verlag, 1931.

————— *Die Philosophie des heilegen Augustinus*, Görres-Bibliothek, *55*, Freising, Glock und Lutz, 1948.

Heyer, George S., Jr., *"Rectitudo* in the Theology of St. Anselm," Yale University Ph.D. dissertation, 1963.

Hoenen, Peter, *Reality and Judgment according to St. Thomas*, trans. Henry F. Tiblier, appendix by Charles Boyer, Chicago, Henry Regnery Co., 1952.

Hoffmann, Ernst, *Platonismus und christlicher Philosophie*, Gesammelte Abhandlungen und Vorträge zur Geschichte der Philosophie, herausgegeben unter Mitwirkung der Heidelberger Akademia der Wissenschaft von Hans-Georg Gadamer, Walter Rüegg, Paul Wilpert, Zürich und Stuttgart, Artemis-Verlag, 1960.

Hoffmans, P. Hadelin, "Roger Bacon. L'Intuition mystique et la science," *Revue néoscolastique, 16* (1909), 370–97.

Horváth, Alexander M., "Der wissenschaftliche Charakter der Apologetik," *Divus Thomas, 25* (1947), 29–52, 177–91, 395–408.

Howell, A. G. Ferrers, *Dante: His Life and Work*, rev. ed. London, T. C. & E. C. Jack, Ltd., 1920.

Hufnagel, Alfons, *Intuition und Erkenntnis nach Thomas von Aquin*, Veröffentlichungen des katholischen Institutes für Philosophie, Albertus-Magnus-Akademie zu Köln, *2*, Heft 5–6, Münster in Westphalen, Aschendorffschen Verlagsbuchhandlung, 1932.

Hunt, Richard William, "The Introduction to the 'Artes' in the Twelfth Century," *Studia Mediaevalia in honorem admodum Reverendi Patris Raymundi Josephi Martin*, Bruges, De Tempel, 1948, pp. 85–112.

————— "Studies on Priscian in the Eleventh and Twelfth Century," *Mediaeval and Renaissance Studies, 1* (1941–43), 194–231.

Jacob, Johannes, *Die Bedeutung der Führer Dantes in der Divina Commedia: Virgil, Beatrix, St. Bernhard, in Bezug auf den idealen Zweck des Gedichtes und auf Grund der geistigen Lebensentwicklung des Dichters*, Leipzig, J. C. Hinrichs'sche Buchhandlung, 1874.

Jacquin, A. -M., "Les 'rationes necessariae' de Saint Anselme," *Mélanges Mandonnet: Études d'histoire littéraire et doctrinale du moyen âge, 2*, Bibliothèque thomiste, *14*, Paris, Librarie Philosophique J. Vrin, 1930, 67–78.

Jansen, Bernhard, "Geist und Form der Philosophie des H. Augustinus," *Miscellanea Augustiniana: Gedenkboek samengesteld uit Verhandelingen over S. Augustinus bij de Viering van Zijn Zalig overlijden vóór 15 Eeuwen CDXXX–MCMXXX*, Rotterdam, P. P. Augustinjnen der Nederlandsche Provincie, 1930, pp. 275–305.

Jansen, François, "Saint Augustin et la Rhétorique," *Nouvelle revue théologique, 57* (1930), 282–97.

Jolivet, Régis, "La Doctrine augustinienne de l'Illumination," *Revue de philosophie*, n. s., *1*, XVe centenaire de la mort de saint Augustin (1930), 383–502.

Jourdain, Eleanor F., *Le symbolisme dans la Divine Comédie de Dante*, Paris, Alphonse Picard & Fils, 1904.

Jourdan, Eduard, "Dante et l'idée de 'virtù,'" *Mélanges sur Dante: Publiés par la Nouvelle revue d'Italie à l'occasion du sixième centenaire de la mort du poète*, éd. Maurice Mignon, Rome, Nouvelle Revue d'Italie, 1924, pp. 79–92.

Kantorowicz, Ernst H., *The King's Two Bodies: A Study in Mediaeval Political Theology*, Princeton, Princeton University Press, 1957.

Kaske, R. E., "Dante's 'DXV' and 'Veltro,' " *Traditio, 17* (1961), 185–254.

Kelsen, Hans, *Die Staatslehre des Dante Alighieri*, Wiener Staatswissenschaftliche Studien, *6*, Heft 3, Wien und Leipzig, Franz Deutiche, 1905.

Ker, W. P., *Essays on Medieval Literature*, London, Macmillan and Co., 1905.

Kern, Fritz, *Humana Civilitas: Staat, Kirche und Kultur. Eine Dante-Untersuchung*, Mittelalterliche Studien, herausgegeben von Fritz Kern, *1*, Heft 1, Leipzig, K. F. Koehler, 1913.

Kimmerle, Helmut, *Die Gottesbeweis Anselms von Canterbury: Ihre Voraussetzungen und ihre Bedeutung für die philosophische Theologie,* Berlin, Ernst-Reuter-Gesellschaft, 1961.

Klubertanz, George P., "The Problem of the Analogy of Being," *Review of Metaphysics, 10* (1957), 553–79.

—— *St. Thomas Aquinas on Analogy: A Textual Analysis and Systematic Synthesis,* Jesuit Studies, Chicago, Loyola University Press, 1960.

Knowles, David, *The Evolution of Medieval Thought,* London, Longmans, Green and Co. Ltd., 1962.

—— *The Historical Context of the Philosophical Works of St. Thomas Aquinas,* London, Blackfriars, 1958.

Kolping, Adolf, *Anselms Proslogion-Beweis der Existenz Gottes im Zusammenhang seines spekulativen Programms Fides quaerens intellectum,* Bonn, Hch. Ludwig, 1938.

Koyré, Alexandre, *L'Idée de Dieu dans la philosophie de St. Anselme,* Paris, Éditions Ernest Leroux, 1923.

Krebs, Engelbert, "Erlebnis und Allegorie in Dantes Commedia," *Deutsches Dante-Jahrbuch, 8* (1924), 11–25; *9* (1925), 98–103.

Krogmann, Willy, "Die Mannigfaltigkeit der Sprache in der Sicht Dantes," *Die Metaphysik im Mittelalter: Ihr Ursprung und ihre Bedeutung, Vorträge des II. internationalen Kongresses für mittelalterliche Philosophie, Köln, 31. August-6. September 1961,* Miscellanea Mediaevalia: Veroffentlichungen des Thomas-Instituts an der Universität Köln, herausgegeben von Paul Wilpert, *2,* Berlin, Walter de Gruyter & Co., 1963, 136–43.

Kroner, Richard, *Speculation and Revelation in the Age of Christian Philosophy,* Philadelphia, Westminster Press, 1959.

Kuhn, "Glauben und Wissen nach St. Thomas," *Theologische Quartalschrift, 42,* 2 (1860), 273–340.

Kuypers, K., *Der Zeichen- und Wortbegriff im Denken Augustins,* Amsterdam, N. V. Swets & Zeitlinger Boekhandel & Uitgeversmaatschappij, 1934.

Labourdette, M. -M., "La Vie théologale selon S. Thomas," *Revue thomiste, 60* (1960), 364–80.

Lachance, L., "Saint Thomas dans l'histoire de la logique," *Études d'histoire littéraire et doctrinale du XIIIe siècle,* Publications de l'Institut d'Études Médiévales d'Ottawa, *1*, Paris, Librairie Philosophique J. Vrin, 1932, 61–103.

Ladner, Gerhart B., *The Idea of Reform: Its Impact on Christian Thought and Action in the Age of the Fathers,* Cambridge, Mass., Harvard University Press, 1959.

Lafont, Ghislain, *Structures et méthode dans la Somme théologique de Saint Thomas d'Aquin,* Paris, Desclée de Brouwer, 1961.

Lagrange, M. -J., "Le réalisme et le symbolisme de Dante," *Revue biblique, 46* (1937), 481–505.

Laistner, M. L. W., "The Christian Attitude toward Pagan Literature," *History,* n. s., *20* (1935), 49–54.

——— *Thought and Letters in Western Europe A.D. 500 to 900,* 2d ed. London, Methuen and Co. Ltd., 1957.

Landry, B., "L'analogie de proportion chez saint Thomas d'Aquin," *Revue néoscolastique de philosophie, 24* (1922), 257–80.

——— "L'analogie de proportionnalité chez saint Thomas d'Aquin," *Revue néoscolastique de philosophie, 24* (1922), 454–64.

——— *La Notion d'analogie chez saint Bonaventure et saint Thomas d'Aquin,* Louvain, Institut Supérieur de Philosophie, 1922.

Lang, Hugo, *Die Lehre des hl. Thomas von Aquin von der Gewissheit des übernatürlichen Glaubens,* Augsburg, Benno Filser, 1929.

Laurenzi, Fortunato, *Ermetica ed ermeneutica dantesca,* Collezione di opusculi danteschi inediti o rari, *137–39,* Città di Castello, S. Lapi, 1931.

Leclercq, Jean, *The Love of Learning and the Desire for God: A Study of Monastic Culture,* trans. Catherine Misrahi, New York, New American Library, 1962.

——— "Le magistère du prédicateur au XIIIᵉ siècle," *Archives d'historie doctrinale et littéraire du moyen âge, 21* (1946), 105–47.

——— "Prédication et rhétorique au temps de Saint Augustin," *Revue bénédictine, 57* (1947), 117–31.

Leder, Hermann, *Untersuchungen über Augustins Erkenntnistheorie in ihren Beziehungen zur antiken Skepsis, zu Plotin und zu Descartes,* Marburg, N. G. Elwert'sche Verlagsbuchhandlung, 1901.

Leeuwen, Antoine van, "L'analogie de l'être: Genèse et contenu du concept d'analogie," *Revue néoscolastique de philosophie, 39* (1936), 293–320.

Llamas, P. J., "San Agustín y la multiplicidad de sentidos literales en la Escritura," *Religión y cultura, 15* (1931), 238–74.

Lonergan, Bernard, "The Concept of *Verbum* in the Writings of St. Thomas Aquinas," *Theological Studies, 7* (1946), 349–92; *8* (1947), 35–79, 404–44; *10* (1949), 3–40, 359–93.

Löwe, Heinz, "Dante und das Kaisertum," *Historische Zeitschrift, 190* (1960), 517–52.

Lyttkens, Hampus, *The Analogy between God and the World: An Investigation of Its Background and Interpretation of Its Use by Thomas of Aquino,* Uppsala, Almqvist & Wiksells Boktryckeri AB, 1952.

Maier, Franz Georg, *Augustin und das antike Rom,* Tübinger Beiträge zur Altertumswissenschaft, Heft *39,* Stuttgart und Köln, W. Kohlhammer Verlag, 1955.

Malagoli, Luigi, *Linguaggio e poesia nella Divina Commedia,* Genoa, Briano, 1949.

Malcolm, Norman, "Anselm's Ontological Argument," *The Philosophical Review, 69* (1960), 41–62.

Mancini, Augusto, "Nuovi dubbi ed ipotesi sulla Epistola a Can Grande," *Atti della Reale Accademia d'Italia, Rendiconti della classe di scienze morali e storiche,* serie settima, *4,* fasc. 9–12 (1943), 227–42.

Mandonnet, P., *Dante le théologien: Introduction à l'intelligence de la vie, des oeuvres et de l'art de Dante Alighieri,* Bibliothèque d'histoire, Paris, Desclée de Brouwer, 1935.

Manitius, Max, *Geschichte der lateinischen Literatur des Mittelalters,* 3 vols. Handbuch der Altertumswissenschaft, begründet von Iwan von Müller, fortgesetzt von Robert von Pöhlmann, herausgegeben von Walter Otto, *9,* München, C. H. Beck'sche Verlagsbuchhandlung, 1911–31.

Manthey, Franz, *Die Sprachphilosophie des hl. Thomas von Aquin und ihre Anwendung auf Probleme der Theologie,* Paderborn, Verlag Ferdinand Schöningh, 1937.

Maquart, Xavier, "La Causalité du signe: Réflexions sur la valeur philosophique d'une explication théologique," *Revue thomiste, 32,* n. s., *10* (1947), 40–60.

Marías Aguilera, Julián, *San Anselmo y el insensato y otros estudios de filosofía,* 2d ed. Madrid, Revista de Occidente, 1954.

SECONDARY SOURCES

Leigh, Gertrude, "Links between Dante and Duns Scotu
Quarterly Review, 96 (1923), 306–31.
———— New Light on the Youth of Dante, London, Fab
1929.
———— The Passing of Beatrice: A Study of the Het
Dante, London, Faber & Faber, 1932.

Leisegang, Hans, "La connaissance de Dieu au miroir de
la nature," Revue d'histoire et de philosophie rel
(1937), 145–71.

Lemaître, Charles, "Quarta Via: La preuve de l'existen
par les degrés des êtres," Nouvelle revue théo
(1927), 321–39, 436–68.

Lenkeith, Nancy, Dante and the Legend of Rome, Me
Renaissance Studies, ed. Richard Hunt and Ra}
bansky, supplement 2, London, The Warburg
1952.

Leo, Ulrich, Sehen und Wirklichkeit bei Dante, Analecta
Beihefte zu den Romanischen Forschungen, herausg
Fritz Schalk, 4, Frankfurt am Main, Vittorio K
1957.

Levasti, Arrigo, Sant'Anselmo: Vita e pensiero, Bari, Giu{
Figli Editore, 1929.

Liebeschütz, Hans, "Kosmologische Motive in der Bildu
Frühscholastik," Vorträge der Bibliothek Warburg
24), 83–148.

Lilje, Hanns, Dante als christlicher Denker, Hambu1
Verlag, 1955.

Limentani, U., ed., The Mind of Dante, Cambridge, The
Press, 1965.

Lindbeck, George, "Participation and Existence in the
tion of St. Thomas Aquinas," Franciscan Studies,
1–22, 107–25.

Linehan, James Coleman, The Rational Nature of Man w
lar Reference to the Effects of Immorality on Inte
cording to Saint Thomas Aquinas, Catholic U1
America Philosophical Studies, 37, Washington, T
University of America, 1937.

Little, Arthur, The Platonic Heritage of Thomism, Dut
Eagle Books Ltd., 1949.

Maritain, Jacques, *The Angelic Doctor: The Life and Thought of Saint Thomas Aquinas,* trans. J. F. Scanlan, New York, Dial Press, 1931.

——— *Distinguish to Unite, or the Degrees of Knowledge,* 4th ed. trans. Gerald B. Phelan, New York, Charles Scribner's Sons, 1959.

Markus, R. A., "A Note on the Meaning of *Via,*" *Dominican Studies,* 7 (1954), 239–45.

——— "St. Augustine on Signs," *Phronesis, 2* (1957), 60–83.

Marrou, Henri-Irénée, *Saint Augustin et la fin de la culture antique,* Bibliothèque des écoles françaises d'Athènes et de Rome, *145,* Paris, E. de Boccard, 1938.

——— *Saint Augustin et la fin de la culture antique: "Retractatio,"* Bibliothèque des écoles françaises d'Athènes et de Rome, *145* bis, Paris, E. de Boccard, 1949.

Martin, Edward James, *A History of the Iconoclastic Controversy,* London, Society for Promoting Christian Knowledge, n.d.

Masiello, Ralph J., "The Analogy of Proportion according to the Metaphysics of St. Thomas," *The Modern Schoolman, 35* (1958), 91–106.

Masseron, Alexandre, *Dante et Saint Bernard,* Paris, Éditions Albin Michel, 1953.

Masure, E., *Le Signe: Le passage du visible à l'invisible,* Paris, Bloud & Gay, 1953.

Matheson, P. E., "Character and Citizenship in Dante," *Hibbert Journal, 5* (1907), 856–78.

Mathew, Gervase, *Byzantine Aesthetics,* New York, Viking Press, 1963.

Maurer, Armand, "St. Thomas and the Analogy of Genus," *The New Scholasticism, 29* (1955), 127–44.

May, Rollo, ed., *Symbolism in Religion and Literature,* New York, George Braziller, 1960.

Mazzeo, Joseph Anthony, *Medieval Cultural Tradition in Dante's 'Comedy,'* Ithaca, N.Y., Cornell University Press, 1960.

——— "St. Augustine's Rhetoric of Silence," *Journal of the History of Ideas, 23* (1962), 175–96.

——— *Structure and Thought in the 'Paradiso,'* Ithaca, N.Y., Cornell University Press, 1958.

Mazzoni, Francesco, "L'Epistola a Cangrande," *Accademia nazionale dei Lincei, Rendiconti della classe di scienze morali, storiche e filologiche,* fasc. 3–4, serie 8, vol. *10* (1955), 157–98.

—— "Pietro Alighieri interprete di Dante," *Studi danteschi, 40* (1963), 279–360.

McInerny, Ralph, "The Logic of Analogy," *The New Scholasticism, 31* (1957), 149–71.

—— *The Logic of Analogy: An Interpretation of St. Thomas,* The Hague, Martinus Nijhoff, 1961.

McKenzie, Kenneth, "Virgil & Dante," *The Tradition of Virgil: Three Papers on the History and Influence of the Poet,* Princeton, Princeton University Press, 1930, pp. 11–21.

McKeon, Richard, "Medicine and Philosophy in the Eleventh and Twelfth Centuries: The Problem of Elements," *The Thomist, 24* (1961), 211–56.

—— "Poetry and Philosophy in the Twelfth Century: The Renaissance of Rhetoric," *Modern Philology, 43* (1946), 217–34.

—— "Renaissance and Method in Philosophy," *Studies in the History of Ideas, 3,* New York, Columbia University Press, 1935, 37–114.

—— "Rhetoric in the Middle Ages," *Speculum, 17* (1942), 1–32.

—— "Thomas Aquinas' Doctrine of Knowledge and Its Historical Setting," *Speculum, 3* (1928), 425–44.

McLean, George, "Symbol and Analogy: Tillich and Thomas," *Revue de l'Université d'Ottawa,* section spéciale, *28* (1958), 193*– 233*.

Meissner, William W., "Some Aspects of the *Verbum* in the Texts of St. Thomas Aquinas," *The Modern Schoolman, 36* (1958), 1– 30.

—— "Some Notes on a Figure in St. Thomas," *The New Scholasticism, 31* (1957), 68–84.

Meozzi, A., *L'utopia politica di Dante,* Milano, Edizioni Athena, 1929.

Meyer, Hans, *The Philosophy of St. Thomas Aquinas,* trans. Frederic Eckhoff, St. Louis, B. Herder Book Co., 1948.

Miller, Robert G., "The Ontological Argument in St. Anselm and Descartes," *The Modern Schoolman, 32* (1955), 341–49.

Minio-Paluello, Lorenzo, "The Genuine Text of Boethius' Translation of Aristotle's *Categories*," *Mediaeval and Renaissance Studies, 1* (1941–43), 151–77.

—— "The Text of the *Categoriae*: The Latin Tradition," *The Classical Quarterly, 39* (1945), 63–74.

——"Les traductions et les commentaires aristotéliciens de Boèce," *Studia Patristica, 2*, Papers presented to the Second International Conference on Patristic Studies held at Christ Church, Oxford, 1955, part II, ed. Kurt Aland and F. L. Cross, Berlin, Akademie-Verlag, 1957, 358–65.

Montagnes, Bernard, *La Doctrine de l'analogie de l'être d'après saint Thomas d'Aquin*, Philosophes médiévaux, *6*, Louvain, Publications Universitaires, 1963.

Montano, Rocco, *Suggerimenti per una lettura di Dante*, Napoli, Conte, 1956.

Moody, Ernest A., *Truth and Consequence in Medieval Logic*, Amsterdam, North-Holland Publishing Co., 1953.

Moore, Edward, *Dante and His Early Biographers*, London, Rivingtons, 1890.

—— *Studies in Dante: First Series*, Oxford, The Clarendon Press, 1896.

—— *Studies in Dante: Second Series*, Oxford, The Clarendon Press, 1899.

—— *Studies in Dante: Third Series*, Oxford, The Clarendon Press, 1903.

Moré-Pontgibaud, Ch. de, "Sur l'Analogie des noms divins," *Recherches de science religieuse, 19* (1929), 481–512; *20* (1930), 193–223.

Motte, A. R., "Théodicée et Théologie chez S. Thomas d'Aquin," *Revue des sciences philosophiques et théologiques, 26* (1937), 5–26.

Mueller, Gustav E., "Dante's Aesthetics," *The Personalist, 27* (1946), 386–98.

Mullane, Donald T., *Aristotelianism in St. Thomas*, Washington, The Catholic University of America, 1929.

Murari, Rocco, *Dante e Boezio: Contributo allo studio delle fonti dantesche*, Bologna, Nicola Zanichelli, 1905.

Musa, Mark, ed., *Essays on Dante*, Bloomington, Indiana University Press, 1964.

379

Nardi, Bruno, "L'Averroismo del 'primo amico' di Dante," *Studi danteschi, 25* (1940), 43–79.

———— "L'Averroismo di Sigieri e Dante," *Studi danteschi, 22* (1938), 83–113.

———— *Dal "Convivio" alla "Commedia"*: *Sei saggi danteschi,* Istituto storico italiano per il medio evo, studi storici, *35–39,* Roma, nella Sede dell'Istituto, Palazzo Borromini, 1960.

———— *Dante e la cultura medievale,* 2d ed. Biblioteca di cultura moderna, no. *368,* Bari, Gius. Laterza & Figli, 1949.

———— "Dante e la filosofia," *Studi danteschi, 25* (1940), 5–42.

———— "Due capitoli di filosofia dantesca: I. La conoscenza humana; II. Il linguaggio," *Giornale storico della letteratura italiana,* miscellanea dantesca, supplemento *19–21,* Torino, Giovanni Chiantore, 1921, 205–64.

———— *La filosofia di Dante,* Milano, Carlo Marzorati 1952.

———— "Intorno al tomismo di Dante e alla quistione di Sigieri," *Giornale dantesco, 22* (1914), 182–97.

———— *Nel mondo di Dante,* Roma, Edizioni di "Storia e Letteratura," 1944.

———— "Nomina sunt consequentia rerum," *Giornale storico della letteratura italiana, 93* (1929), 101–05.

———— *Studi di filosofia medievale,* Storia e Letteratura: Raccolta di studi e testi, *78,* Roma, Edizioni di Storia e Letteratura, 1960.

Natoli, Gioacchino, "Il valore estetico del simbolo nell'arte di Dante," *Sophia, 23* (1955), 38–52.

Nehring, Alfons, "A Note on Functional Linguistics in the Middle Ages," *Traditio, 9* (1953), 430–34.

Nemetz, Anthony A., "Logic and the Division of the Sciences in Aristotle and St. Thomas Aquinas," *The Modern Schoolman, 33* (1956), 91–109.

Neumann, Siegfried, *Gegenstand und Methode der theoretischen Wissenschaften nach Thomas von Aquin aufgrund der Expositio super librum Boethii de Trinitate,* Münster in Westfalen, Max Kramer, 1963.

Norden, Eduard, *Die Antike Kunstprosa vom VI. Jahrhundert v. Chr. bis in die Zeit der Renaissance, 2,* Leipzig, B. G. Teubner, 1898.

Nugent, James B., *The Fundamental Theistic Argument in the Meta-*

physical Doctrine of Saint Thomas Aquinas, The Catholic University of America, Philosophical Studies, *192,* Abstract 42, Washington, The Catholic University of America, 1961.

O'Brien, Ignatius, "Analogy and Our Knowledge of God," *Philosophical Studies, 6* (1956), 91–104.

O'Donoghue, Dermot, "An Analysis of the *Tertia Via* of St. Thomas," *Irish Theological Quarterly, 20* (1953), 129–51.

O'Keefe, Dermot L., *Theology and Contemplation according to St. Thomas Aquinas,* Romae, Officium Libri Catholici, 1952.

O'Neil, C. J., ed., *An Etienne Gilson Tribute,* Milwaukee, Bruce Publishing Co., 1959.

O'Neill, M. S., "Some Remarks on the Analogy of God and Creatures in St. Thomas Aquinas," *Mediaeval Studies, 23* (1961), 206–15.

Ong, Walter J., "Wit and Mystery: A Revaluation in Mediaeval Latin Hymnody," *Speculum, 22* (1947), 310–41.

Osgood, Charles Grosvener, *Poetry as a Means of Grace,* Princeton, Princeton University Press, 1941.

Ouspensky, Léonide, *L'Icone: Vision du monde spirituel. Quelques mots sur son sens dogmatique,* Mélanges de l'Institut Orthodoxe Française de Paris, Paris, Sétor, 1948.

—— and Vladimir Lossky, *The Meaning of Icons,* trans. G. E. H. Palmer and E. Kadloubovsky, ed. Titus Burckhardt, Olten, Switzerland, Urs Graf-Verlag, 1952.

Ovidio, Francesco d', *Dante e la filosofia del linguaggio,* Napoli, Tipografia della Regia Università, 1892.

—— *Studii sulla Divina Commedia,* Milan-Palermo, Remo Sandron, 1901.

Owens, Joseph, "Analogy as a Thomistic Approach to Being," *Mediaeval Studies, 24* (1962), 303–22.

—— "The Conclusion of the *Prima Via,*" *The Modern Schoolman, 30* (1952–53), 33–53, 109–21, 203–16.

Palgen, R., "La légende virgilienne dans la *Divine Comédie,*" *Romania, 73* (1952), 332–90.

Paluzzi, C. Galassi, "Perchè Dante scelse Virgilio a sua guida," *Giornale dantesco, 39,* n. s., *9* (1936), 287–307.

Parker, H., "The Seven Liberal Arts," *English Historical Review, 5* (1890), 417–61.

Parodi, E. G., *Poesia e storia nella "Divina Commedia,"* Nuova Biblioteca di Letteratura, Storia ed Arte, *9*, Napoli, Francesco Perrella, 1921.

Passerin d'Entrèves, Alessandro, *Dante politico e altri saggi*, Torino, Giulio Einaudi, 1955.

Patch, Howard Rollin, *The Tradition of Boethius: A Study of His Importance in Medieval Culture*, New York, Oxford University Press, 1935.

Paulus, Jean, "Le caractère métaphysique des preuves thomistes de l'existence de Dieu," *Archives d'histoire doctrinale et littéraire du moyen âge, 9* (1934), 143–53.

Pegis, Anton C., *The Middle Ages and Philosophy: Some Reflections on the Ambivalence of Modern Scholasticism*, Chicago, Henry Regnery Co., 1963.

———— "St. Anselm and the Argument of the Proslogion," *Mediaeval Studies, 28* (1966), 228–67.

———— *St. Thomas and Philosophy*, Aquinas Lecture, 1964, Milwaukee, Marquette University Press, 1964.

———— *Saint Thomas and the Greeks*, Aquinas Lecture, 1939, Milwaukee, Marquette University Press, 1943.

Pellacani, A. M., *Dante vero: Nel poema della grazia l'apologia della ragione*, Il pensiero critico, collana di studi letterari e storici, diretta da Carmelo Ottaviano, prima serie, *7*, Padova, CEDAM, 1964.

Penido, M. J. L., *Le Rôle de l'analogie en théologie dogmatique*, Bibliothèque thomiste, *15*, section théologique, 2, Paris, Librairie Philosophique J. Vrin, 1931.

Perino, Renato, *La dottrina Trinitaria di S. Anselmo nel quadro del suo metodo teologico e del suo concetto di Dio*, Studia Anselmiana philosophica theologica edita a professoribus Instituti Pontificii S. Anselmi de Urbe, *29*, Romae, Herder, 1952.

Persson, Per Erik, "Le plan de la Somme théologique et la rapport 'Ratio-Revelatio,' " *Revue philosophique de Louvain, 56* (1958), 545–72.

Petrocchi, Giorgio, *Il "De Vulgari Eloquentia" di Dante*, Facoltà di lettere e filosofia, Università di Messina, Messina, La Editrice Universitaria, 1961.

Pézard, André, *Le "Convivio" de Dante*, Annales de l'Université de Lyon, 3me série, *9*, Paris, Société d'Édition Les Belles Lettres, 1940.

Riet, Georges van, "Y a-t-il chez saint Thomas une philosophie de la religion?," *Revue philosophique de Louvain, 61* (1963), 44–81.

Rivière, Jean, "Saint Anselme logicien," *Revue des sciences religieuses, 17* (1937), 306–15.

Robert, Brother S., "Rhetoric and Dialectic according to the First Latin Commentary on the Rhetoric of Aristotle," *The New Scholasticism, 31* (1957), 484–98.

Robert, Jean-Dominique, "Eléments d'une définition analogique de la connaissance chez S. Thomas," *Revue philosophique de Louvain, 55* (1957), 443–69.

Robertis, Domenico de, *Il libro della "Vita Nuova,"* Quaderni degli "Studi danteschi," *1*, Firenze, G. C. Sansoni, 1961.

Roberts, W. Rhys, *Greek Rhetoric and Literary Criticism,* New York, Longmans, Green and Co., 1928.

Roebiecki, John Joseph, *The Political Philosophy of Dante Alighieri,* Washington, The Catholic University of America, 1921.

Roedel, Reto, "Individuo e communità nella Divina Commedia," *Individuum und Gemeinschaft: Festschrift zur fünfzigjahrfeier der Handels-Hochschule St. Gallen,* St. Galler wirtschaftswissenschaftliche Forschungen, *7,* St. Gallen, Verlag der Fehr'schen Buchhandlung, 1949, 515–60.

Rolfes, E., "Zu dem Gottesbeweise des hl. Thomas aus den Stufen der Vollkommenheit," *Philosophisches Jahrbuch der Görres-Gesellschaft, 26* (1913), 146–59.

Rosa, P. Enrico, *S. Anselmo di Aosta, Arcivescovo Cantuariense e dottore della Chiesa,* Firenze, Libreria Editrice Fiorentina, 1909.

Ross, James F., "Analogy as a Rule of Meaning for Religious Language," *International Philosophical Quarterly, 1* (1961), 468–502.

Rossi, Louis B., "Dante and the Poetic Tradition in the Commentary of Benvenuto da Imola," *Italica, 32* (1955), 215–21.

Rostagni, Augusto, "Risonanze dell'estetica di Filodemo in Cicerone," *Atene e Roma,* n. s., *3* (1922), 28–44.

Rotta, Paolo, *La filosofia del linguaggio nella Patristica e nella Scolastica,* Torino, Fratelli Bocca Editori, 1909.

Rousselot, Pierre, *L'Intellectualisme de Saint Thomas,* Paris, Félix Alcan, 1908.

Rubinstein, Nicolai, "The Beginnings of Political Thought in Florence: A Study in Mediaeval Historiography," *Journal of the Warburg and Courtauld Institutes, 5* (1942), 198–227.

Rule, Martin, *The Life and Times of St. Anselm, Archbishop of Canterbury and Primate of the Britains,* 2 vols. London, Kegan Paul, Trench, & Co., 1883.

Ryan, John K., "The Problem of Truth," *Essays in Thomism,* ed. Robert E. Brennan, New York, Sheed & Ward, 1942, pp. 65–79.

Salamucha, Jan, "The Proof 'Ex Motu' for the Existence of God: Logical Analysis of St. Thomas' Arguments," *The New Scholasticism, 32* (1958), 334–72.

Samuel, Otto, *Über die Beweisbarkeit der Existenz Gottes: Konsequenzen des anselmischen Beweisverfahrens,* Forschungen zur Geschichte und Lehre des Protestantismus, herausgegeben von Paul Althaus, Karl Barth und Karl Heim, Achte Reihe, *3,* München, Chr. Kaiser Verlag, 1936.

Sánchez-Ruiz, José Maria, *Las pruebas de la existencia de Dios en el Tomismo,* Turin, Pontificio Ateneo Salesiano, 1957.

Sanctis, Francesco de, *History of Italian Literature, 1,* trans. Joan Redfern, New York, Basic Books, 1959.

—— *Lezioni sulla Divina Commedia,* ed. Michele Manfredi, Scrittori d'Italia, Opere de Francesco de Sanctis, *11,* Bari, Gius. Laterza & Figli, 1955.

Santeler, Josef, *Der Platonismus in der Erkenntnislehre des heiligen Thomas von Aquin,* Philosophie und Grenzwissenschaften. Schriftenreihe herausgegeben vom Innsbrucker Institut für scholastische Philosophie, Band *7,* Heft 2–4, Leipzig, Felizian Rauch, 1939.

Sargent, Daniel, "Dante and Thomism," *The Thomist, 5* (1943), 256–64.

Sayers, Dorothy L., *Further Papers on Dante,* New York, Harper & Brothers, 1957.

—— *Introductory Papers on Dante,* New York, Harper & Brothers, 1954.

Scandura, Sebastiano, *L'Estetica di Dante, Petrarca e Boccaccio,* Acireale, Tipografia Edit. XX Secolo, 1928.

Scartazzini, G. A., *A Companion to Dante,* trans. Arthur John Butler, London, Macmillan and Co., 1893.

Schindler, Alfred, *Wort und Analogie in Augustins Trinitätslehre,*

Hermeneutische Untersuchungen zur Theologie, 4, Tübingen, J. C. B. Mohr, 1965.

Schneider, Friedrich, "Der Brief an Can Grande," Deutsches Dante-Jahrbuch, 34–35 (1957), 3–24.

Schneider, Wilhelm, Die Quaestiones Disputatae de Veritate des Thomas von Aquin in ihrer philosophiegeschichtlichen Beziehung zu Augustinus, Beiträge zur Geschichte der Philosophie und Theologie des Mittelalters, herausgegeben von Martin Grabmann, Band 27, Heft 3, Münster in Westfalen, Aschendorffschen Verlagsbuchhandlung, 1930.

Schumacher, Matthew, The Knowableness of God: Its Relation to the Theory of Knowledge in St. Thomas, Notre Dame, Ind., Notre Dame University Press, 1905.

Schwartz, Herbert Thomas, "Analogy in St. Thomas and Cajetan," The New Scholasticism, 28 (1954), 127–44.

Sciacca, M. F., Saint Augustin et le néoplatonism: La possibilité d'une philosophie chrétienne, Chaire Cardinal Mercier, 1954, Louvain, Publications Universitaires de Louvain, 1956.

Scott, J. A., "Dante's 'Sweet New Style' and the Vita Nuova," Italica, 42 (1965), 98–107.

Seiferth, Wolfgang, "Zur Kunstlehre Dantes," Archiv für Kulturgeschichte, 17 (1927) 194–225.

Sertillanges, A.-D., S. Thomas d'Aquin, 2 vols. Paris, Félix Alcan, 1910.

Shaw, James E., Guido Cavalcanti's Theory of Love: The Canzoni d'Amore and Other Related Problems, University of Toronto Romance Series, 1, Toronto, University of Toronto Press, 1949.

——— The Lady "Philosophy" in the Convivio, Cambridge, Mass., Dante Society of Cambridge, Mass., 1938.

Sillem, Edward, Ways of Thinking about God: Thomas Aquinas and Some Recent Problems, London, Darton, Longman & Todd, 1961.

Singleton, Charles S., Commedia: Elements of Structure, Dante Studies, 1, Cambridge, Mass., Harvard University Press, 1954.

——— "Dante and Myth," Journal of the History of Ideas, 10 (1949), 482–502.

——— An Essay on the Vita Nuova, Published for the Dante Society, Cambridge, Mass., Harvard University Press, 1949.

———— "The Irreducible Dove," *Comparative Literature, 9* (1957), 129–35.

———— *Journey to Beatrice,* Dante Studies, 2, Cambridge, Mass., Harvard University Press, 1958.

———— "The Other Journey," *Kenyon Review, 14* (1952), 189–216.

Skysgaard, K. E., "La connaissance humaine d'après Saint Thomas d'Aquin," *Classica et Medievalia, 2,* 1 (1939), 86–120.

Smalley, Beryl, *The Study of the Bible in the Middle Ages,* Oxford, The Clarendon Press, 1941.

Smart, Hugh R., "Anselm's Ontological Argument: Rationalistic or Apologetic?," *Review of Metaphysics, 3* (1949), 161–66.

Solmi, Arrigo, "La 'Monarchia' di Dante," *Nuova antologia, 70,* fasc. 1513 (1935), 321–31.

———— *Il pensiero politico di Dante: Studi storici,* Firenze, La Voce, 1922.

Southern, R. W., "Lanfranc of Bec and Berengar of Tours," *Studies in Medieval History presented to Frederick Maurice Powicke,* ed. R. W. Hunt, W. A. Pantin, and R. W. Southern, Oxford, The Clarendon Press, 1948, pp. 27–48.

———— *Saint Anselm and His Biographer: A Study of Monastic Life and Thought 1059–c.1130,* Cambridge, The University Press, 1963.

———— "St. Anselm and His English Pupils," *Mediaeval and Renaissance Studies, 1* (1941–43), 3–34.

Spargo, John Webster, *Virgil the Necromancer: Studies in Virgilian Legends,* Harvard Studies in Comparative Literature, *10,* Cambridge, Mass., Harvard University Press, 1934.

Spedalieri, Fr., "Anselmus an Gaunilo? Seu de recta argumenti sancti Doctoris interpretatione," *Gregorianum, 28* (1947), 54–77.

———— "De intrinseca argumenti S. Anselmi vi et natura," *Gregorianum, 29* (1948), 204–12.

Spicilegium Beccense, 1, Congrès Internationale du IXe centenaire de l'arrivée d'Anselme au Bec, Le Bec-Hellouin, Notre-Dame du Bec et Paris, J. Vrin, 1959.

Spoerri, Theophil, *Dante und die europäische Literatur,* Sprache und Literatur, *6,* Stuttgart, W. Kohlhammer Verlag, 1963.

Stambler, Bernard, "The Confrontation of Beatrice and Dante: *Purgatorio* XXX," *Italica, 42* (1965), 61–93.

Steenberghen, Fernand van, *Aristote en occident: Les origines de l'aristotélisme parisien,* Louvain, Éditions de l'Institut Su-periéur de Philosophie, 1946.

——— "Le problème de l'existence de Dieu dans le 'Scriptum super Sententiis' de saint Thomas," *Studia Mediaevalia in honorem admodum Reverendi Patris Raymundi Josephi Martin,* Bruges, De Tempel, 1948, pp. 331–49.

Steinbüchel, Theodor, *Grosse Gestalten des Abendlandes: Bild und Beispiel christlicher Verwirklichung,* ed. Alfred Schüler, 2d ed. Trier, Paulinus-Verlag, 1955.

Stewart, H. L., "Dante and the Schoolmen," *Journal of the History of Ideas, 10* (1949), 357–73.

Stolz, Anselm, *Anselm von Canterbury,* München, Verlag Kösel-Pustet, 1937.

——— " 'Vere esse' im Proslogion des Hl. Anselm," *Scholastik: Vierteljahresschrift für Theologie und Philosophie, 9* (1934), 400–06.

——— "Zur Theologie Anselms im Proslogion," *Catholica, 2* (1933), 1–24.

Sundby, Thor, *Della vita e delle opere di Brunetto Latini,* Firenze, Succesori Le Monnier, 1884.

Suraci, Antonio, *Il pensiero e l'opere educativa di Sant'Anselmo di Aosta (1033–1109),* Torino, Società Editrice Internazionale, 1953.

Sweeney, Leo, "Analogy and Being," *The Modern Schoolman, 39* (1962), 253–62.

Symonds, John Addington, *An Introduction to the Study of Dante,* 4th ed. London, Adam and Charles Black, 1906.

Talbot, Edward F., *Knowledge and Object,* Washington, The Catholic University of America, 1932.

Tate, Allen, "The Symbolic Imagination: A Meditation on Dante's Three Mirrors," *Kenyon Review, 14* (1952), 256–77.

Testa, Emanuele, "Poetica e poesia in Dante," *Archivum Romanicum, 16* (1932), 211–53.

Testard, Maurice, *Saint Augustin et Cicéron: Cicéron dans la formation et dans l'oeuvre de Saint Augustin,* 2 vols. Paris, Études Augustiniennes, 1958.

Thurot, Charles, "Notices et extraits de divers manuscrits latins pour servir à l'histoire des doctrines grammaticales au moyen âge,"

Notices et extraits des manuscrits de la Bibliothèque Impériale et autres Bibliothèques, 22, 2me partie, Paris, Imprimerie Impériale, 1868.

Tonelli, Luigi, *Dante e la poesia dell'ineffabile,* Firenze, G. Barbèra, 1934.

Torraca, Francesco, *Studi danteschi,* Nuova Biblioteca di letteratura, storia ed arte, *7,* Napoli, Francesco Perrella, 1912.

Toynbee, Paget, "The Bearing of the *Cursus* on the Text of Dante's De vulgari eloquentia," *Proceedings of the British Academy, 11* (1923), 1–19.

Ueberweg, Friedrich, *Grundriss der Geschichte der Philosophie, 2,* 11th ed. herausgegeben von Bernhard Geyer, Berlin, E. S. Mittler & Sohn, 1928.

Urban, Wilbur Marshall, *Language and Reality: The Philosophy of Language and the Principles of Symbolism,* London, George Allen & Unwin Ltd., 1939.

Valentini, Giuseppina, "Ricerche intorno al 'De Magistro' di S. Agostino," *Sophia, 4* (1936), 83–89.

Vallis, Maurice, "Dante et l'apologie de l'Empire," *Mercure de France, 287* (1938), 586–91.

Van Ackeren, Gerald F., *Sacra Doctrina: The Subject of the First Question of the Summa Theologica of St. Thomas Aquinas,* Romae, Officium Libri Catholici, 1952.

Van Doren, Mark, "The Divine Comedy," *Sewanee Review, 54* (1946), 349–95.

Vanni Rovighi, Sofia, *S. Anselmo e la filosofia del secolo XI,* Storia della filosofia italiana, diretta da M. F. Sciacca, *1,* Milano, Fratelli Bocca, 1949.

Vergnes, Jules, "Les sources de l'argument de Saint Anselme," *Revue des sciences religieuses, 4* (1924), 576–79.

Vignaux, Paul, *Philosophy in the Middle Ages: An Introduction,* trans. E. C. Hall, New York, Meridian Books, Inc., 1959.

———— "Structure et sens du *Monologion,*" *Revue des sciences philosophiques et théologiques, 31* (1947), 192–212.

Vijver, A. van de, "Les étapes du développement philosophique du Haut Moyen-Age," *Revue Belge de philologie et d'histoire, 8* (1929), 425–52.

Vincent, E. R., "The Crisis in the *Vita Nuova,*" *Centenary Essays* on *Dante by Members of the Oxford Dante Society*, Oxford, The Clarendon Press, 1965, pp. 132–42.

Vittorini, Domenico, *High Points in the History of Italian Literature*, New York, David McKay Co., Inc., 1958.

Vossler, Karl, *Mediaeval Culture: An Introduction to Dante and His Times*, 2 vols. trans. William Cranston Lawton, New York, Harcourt, Brace and Co., 1929.

Walker, C. R., "St. Anselm: A Revaluation," *Scottish Journal of Theology, 5* (1952), 362–73.

Warnach, Viktor, "Das äussere Sprechen und seine Funktionen nach der Lehre des hl. Thomas von Aquin," *Divus Thomas, 16* (1938), 393–419.

———— "Erkennen und Sprechen bei Thomas von Aquin: Ein Deutungsversuch seiner Lehre auf ihrem geistesgeschichtlichen Hintergrund," *Divus Thomas, 15* (1937), 189–218, 263–90; *16* (1938), 161–96.

Waters, A. J., "The Poet-Theologian of the Middle Ages," *American Catholic Quarterly Review, 39* (1914), 152–59.

Wébert, J., "L'image dans l'oeuvre de saint Thomas," *Revue thomiste, 31*, n. s., 9 (1926), 427–45.

Weddington, A. van, *Essai critique sur la philosophie de S. Anselme de Cantorbéry, Mémoires couronnés,* publiés par l'Académie royale des sciences, des lettres, et des beaux-arts de Belgique, *25,* Bruxelles, F. Hayez, 1875.

Weigel, Gustave, and Arthur G. Madden, *Religion and the Knowledge of God*, Englewood Cliffs, N.J., Prentice-Hall, 1961.

Weiss, R., "Links between the 'Convivio' and the 'De Vulgari Eloquentia,'" *Modern Language Review, 37* (1942), 156–68.

Wendschuh, Georg, *Verhältnis des Glaubens zum Wissen bei Anselm von Canterbury: Ein Beitrag zu Anselms Erkenntnistheorie,* Weida i. Thür., Thomas & Hubert, 1909.

White, Victor, *Holy Teaching: The Idea of Theology according to St. Thomas Aquinas*, Aquinas Society of London, Aquinas Paper, *33,* London, Blackfriars, 1958.

———— "The Prolegomena to the Five Ways," *Dominican Studies, 5* (1952), 134–58.

Whitfield, J. H., *Dante and Virgil*, Oxford, Basil Blackwell, 1949.

Wicksteed, Philip H., *Dante & Aquinas*, London, J. M. Dent & Sons Ltd., 1913.

———— *From Vita Nuova to Paradiso: Two Essays on the Vital Relations between Dante's Successive Works*, Publications of the University of Manchester, *151*, Manchester, Manchester University Press, 1922.

———— and Edmund G. Gardner, *Dante and Giovanni del Virgilio, Including a Critical Edition of the Text of Dante's 'Eclogae Latinae' and of the Poetic Remains of Giovanni del Virgilio*, Westminster, Archibald Constable & Co., 1902.

Wieruszowski, Helene, "*Ars Dictaminis* in the Time of Dante," *Medievalia et Humanistica, 1* (1943), 95–108.

———— "Der Reichsgedanke bei Dante," *Deutsches Dante-Jahrbuch, 14*, neue Folge, 5 (1932), 185–209.

Wilhelm, James J., *The Cruelest Month: Spring, Nature, and Love in Classical and Medieval Lyrics*, New Haven and London, Yale University Press, 1965.

Wilkins, Ernest Hatch, "Dante as Apostle," *Symposium: Dante Six Hundred Years After*, Chicago, Chicago Literary Club, 1921, pp. 41–47.

———— *Dante: Poet and Apostle*, Chicago, University of Chicago Press, 1921.

———— *A History of Italian Literature*, Cambridge, Mass., Harvard University Press, 1954.

Williams, Charles, *The Figure of Beatrice: A Study in Dante*, New York, Noonday Press, 1961.

Williams, C. J. F., "Existence and the Meaning of the Word 'God,' " *Downside Review, 77* (1958–59), 53–71.

Wilmart, André, "Le premier ouvrage de saint Anselme contre le trithéisme de Roscelin," *Recherches de théologie ancienne et médiévale, 3* (1931), 20–30.

Wilpert, Paul, *Das Problem der Wahrheitssicherung bei Thomas von Aquin: Ein Beitrag zur Geschichte der Evidenzproblems, Beiträge zur Geschichte der Philosophie und Theologie des Mittelalters*, herausgegeben von Martin Grabmann, *30*, Heft 3, Münster in Westfalen, Aschendorffeschen Verlagsbuchhandlung, 1931.

Winance, Eleuthère, "L'Essence divine et la connaissance humaine dans le Commentaire sur les Sentences de Saint Thomas," *Revue philosophique de Louvain, 55* (1957), 171–215.

Witte, Karl, *Essays on Dante*, selected, trans., and ed. C. Mabel

Lawrence and Philip H. Wicksteed, London, Duckworth and Co., 1910.

Wolz, Henry G., "The Empirical Basis of Anselm's Arguments," *The Philosophical Review, 60* (1951), 341–61.

Wulf, Maurice de, "Augustinisme et aristotélisme au XIIIᵉ siècle," *Revue néoscolastique, 8* (1901), 151–66.

—— *History of Mediaeval Philosophy*, 2 vols. trans. Ernest C. Messenger, 3d ed. London, Longmans, Green and Co., 1935–38.

—— *The System of Thomas Aquinas*, New York, Dover Publications, 1959.

Wyser, Paul, "Die wissenschaftstheoretischen Quaest. V. u. VI. in Boethium de Trinitate des hl. Thomas von Aquin," *Divus Thomas, 25* (1947), 437–85; *26* (1948), 74–98.

Zabughin, Vladmiro, *Vergilio nel rinascimento italiano da Dante a Torquato Tasso, 1,* Bologna, Nicola Zanichelli, 1923.

Zingarelli, Nicola, *La vita, i tempi e le opere di Dante,* 2 vols. Storia letteraria d'Italia, *3,* Milano, Francesco Vallardi, 1931.

Index

Abati, Bocca degli, 322

Abbo of Fleury, 96-97

Abelard, Peter: Trinitarian doctrine as criticized by St. Bernard, 121 n., 305; as a dialectician, 159, 162

Academic skepticism: in Cicero, 16-17; in St. Augustine, 37, 40 n.

Accursius, 242 n.

Adam: in *Convivio,* 260; in *De vulgari eloquentia,* 264; in *Divine Comedy,* 328

Adam of Brescia, 323

Adam of St. Victor, 239

Adeodatus, 54

Aenigma, vii, ix, 7, 17, 19-20, 50, 72-73, 79, 80, 104, 137-38, 146, 201, 208, 329, 332, 342

Alain de Lille, 233

Alberigo, 323

Albert the Great, St., 168-69, 204, 236

Albertus Magnus. *See* Albert the Great, St.

Alcuin, 100, 231

Alexander of Hales, 204

Alexander of Villedieu, 232

Alighieri, Dante, x, xi, xiii-xiv, xv-xvi, xvii, xviii, 7, 224-341, 342, 343-44, 347-48; poetic practice in *Divine Comedy,* 224, 225, 226, 238, 240, 245, 247, 270, 273, 282-341, 347; symbolism of the senses, 296-303; the poet as prophet in, 310-11, 315, 316; Augustinian sign theory in, 315-41; literary language and style in, 333-34, 336-37, 338-39

poetic theory of, 224-73, 282-89, 291, 310-15, 316, 333, 335, 337-38, 341, 343: its medieval antecedents, 224-25, 226-28, 230-39, 250; its classical antecedents, 227-31, 232,

233, 234, 235, 236, 269, 272; influence of Brunetto Latini on, 241-44, 263-64; influence of *dolce stil nuovo* and troubadour poetics on, 244-47, 249, 255; in *Vita nuova,* 246-51, 254-55, 267, 270, 292, 297: idea of rectitude in, 248; eyes and smile of lady in, 248-49, 251, 297; in *Convivio,* 251-62, 267, 270, 275, 276, 277, 278 n., 280, 284-85, 292, 297, 328, 329, 332: eyes and smile of lady in, 254, 297; distinction between biblical typology and poetic allegory in, 255-56, 284-85; political and ethical theory in, 257-61, 262; in *De vulgari eloquentia,* 262-73, 314: nature and origin of language, 261-64; on justification of the vernacular and establishment of a unified Italian language, 264-67; functions and techniques of literature in the illustrious vernacular, 267-72; poetry of rectitude, 269-72; in letter to Can Grande della Scala, 282-85, 286-89, 309-15, 337; rectitude in, 283, 291, 317, 333, 338, 340; identification of biblical typology with poetic allegory in, 284-85, 286-89, 309-10; seconded by early Dante commentaries, 285-86

political theory of, 257-61, 262, 273-82, 332: in *De monarchia,* 257, 273-80, 332; in *Convivio,* 257-61, 262; in political letters, 273, 280-82; justice as rectitude, 276

allegorical treatment of characters in, 289-96, 302, 304-09, 334-36: Beatrice, 291, 292-96, 302, 304, 305, 309; St. Bernard, 291, 304-05, 309; Vergil, 291, 304, 305-09

399